THE CASE FOR CATHOLICISM

TRENT HORN

# The Case for Catholicism

Answers to Classic and Contemporary
Protestant Objections

IGNATIUS PRESS    SAN FRANCISCO

Church Father citations, unless otherwise noted, are taken from *Ante-Nicene and Nicene and Post-Nicene Fathers*, 10 vols. Edited by Alexander Roberts, James Donaldson, and A. Cleveland Coxe. Buffalo, NY: Christian Literature Publishing, 1885. Revised and edited for New Advent by Kevin Knight, http://www.newadvent.org/fathers/02101.htm.

Portions of chapters 5 and 6 have been adapted from "Defending the Papacy", *Catholic Answers Magazine*, September–October 2015.

Portions of chapter 7 have been adapted from "God Chooses to Use Human Intermediaries", *Catholic Answers Magazine*, March–April 2016.

Portions of chapter 12 were used in the Trent Horn vs. James White debate "Can Christians Lose Their Salvation?" Georgia International Convention Center, January 18, 2017.

Cover photograph:
Statue of Saint Peter at the Vatican
© www.123rf.com/alessandro0770

Cover design by Enrique J. Aguilar

© 2017 by Ignatius Press, San Francisco
All rights reserved
ISBN 978-1-62164-144-5 (PB)
ISBN 978-1-68149-789-1 (eBook)
Library of Congress Control Number 2017945108
Printed in the United States of America ∞

For Thomas

# CONTENTS

# PREFACE

The motivation for writing this book came from the desire to publish a comprehensive defense of the Catholic faith in light of the five-hundredth anniversary of the Protestant Reformation.

Since the sixteenth century, Catholic authors like Saint Francis de Sales and John Henry Cardinal Newman have written eloquent defenses of Catholicism. But after the Second Vatican Council many Catholics saw apologetics as being antithetical to the council's emphasis on ecumenism in the modern world. Fortunately, in the late twentieth century lay Catholics such as Karl Keating, Patrick Madrid, and Scott Hahn helped ignite a "renaissance" in Catholic apologetics. According to C. John McCloskey and Russell Shaw in their book *Good News, Bad News: Evangelization, Conversion and the Crisis of Faith*:

> In the decades since the Second Vatican Council, there has been a shift in apologetics away from simply defending the faith to spreading it. Without losing its grounding in sound arguments, apologetics has become more centered on Christ as he is present in Scripture. During the last two decades in the United States there has been a veritable explosion in this new apologetics, reflected in magazines, videos, Web sites, conferences, and the splendid ongoing work of the Eternal Word Television Network.[1]

As the five-hundredth anniversary of the Protestant Reformation drew near I realized that the field of Catholic apologetics was lacking a comprehensive, up-to-date, single-volume defense of the faith.

The most famous previous entry in this genre was Karl Keating's *Catholicism and Fundamentalism*,[2] which was instrumental in my own

---

[1] C. John McCloskey and Russell Shaw, *Good News, Bad News: Evangelization, Conversion and the Crisis of Faith* (San Francisco: Ignatius Press, 2007), 67.

[2] Karl Keating, *Catholicism and Fundamentalism: The Attack on "Romanism" by "Bible Christians"* (San Francisco: Ignatius Press, 1988).

conversion as well as the conversion of many others. While that book ably addressed challenges to the faith from Protestant fundamentalists, in the thirty years since its publication, new, more sophisticated Protestant apologetics emerged. This present work will address those arguments as well as objections found in those works that have their roots in the older Protestant Reformers—in particular, works by Martin Luther and John Calvin.

One of the limitations of this book, however, is that each of the topics it addresses could be expanded into a book-length treatment. Indeed, several Catholic apologists have addressed these topics in single-book treatments, and their research and conclusions have been included in this current work. My goal in this book is to present the best arguments that previous Catholic apologists have made and also to complement those arguments with my own original research. Some of that research includes the findings of Protestant scholarship that *supports* arguments made in favor of the Catholic faith.

Finally, I want to acknowledge the individuals and groups who made this book possible. First, I am indebted to the work of Catholic apologists who have gone before me. These include saints and scholars throughout Church history as well as modern apologists such as Karl Keating, Patrick Madrid, Tim Staples, Jimmy Akin, Steve Ray, Gary Michuta, Scott Hahn, and many others. I am grateful for the work of the Catholic Answers apostolate both in the counsel I have received from my colleagues there and in the role they played in forming me as an apologist. I am especially grateful for Jimmy Akin's review of this manuscript and the suggestions he made that strengthened its arguments.

Second, I am thankful for the editorial work of Ignatius Press and their guidance in the final stages of writing this book. Finally, I am thankful to God, who through his grace brought me into his family through baptism in the Catholic Church; I pray that all people can know the joy of following Christ and his Church like I have known over these past fifteen years.

Part I

By Whose Authority?

I

# *Sola Scriptura*

Four years after he published his ninety-five theses, Martin Luther stood before an imperial assembly (or diet) in the German city of Worms. Charged with the crime of heresy, Luther was ordered to recant his claims that the pope lacked the authority to grant indulgences along with his other arguments against the authority of the Catholic Church. But rather than recant, Luther uttered this famous declaration that served as a rallying cry for the Protestant Reformation:

> Unless I am convinced by the testimony of the Scriptures or by clear reason (for I do not trust either in the pope or in councils alone, since it is well known that they have often erred and contradicted themselves), I am bound by the Scriptures I have quoted and my conscience is captive to the Word of God. I cannot and I will not retract anything, since it is neither safe nor right to go against conscience. I cannot do otherwise, here I stand, may God help me, Amen.[1]

The central issue of contention between Catholics and Protestants has always been the issue of authority. The formal principle of the Protestant Reformation was *sola scriptura*, or the belief that the Bible is the ultimate authority regarding the Christian faith. Even today, when Catholics share their faith with Protestants, they are usually met with the question, but where is that in the Bible? The question reflects the assumption that the Bible is a Christian's sole source of authority and everything he believes must be explicitly found in its pages.

[1] Martin Luther, *Luther's Works*, 32, ed. Jaroslav Pelikan and Helmut T. Lehmann, 55 vols. (Philadelphia: Fortress Press, 1961), 111. Unless otherwise indicated, all citations from *Luther's Works* are from this edition.

Therefore, before we make a case for the authority of the Catholic Church, we must examine the authority Protestants have appealed to in support of their doctrines for the past five hundred years—the Bible alone.

## Sola Scriptura Defined

Some Protestant apologists say *sola scriptura* means that Scripture is the believer's "sole, infallible rule of faith", but this definition is too ambiguous. Is it sufficient for a doctrine merely not to contradict Scripture, or must it be found explicitly or implicitly within Scripture? Defenders of *sola scriptura* seem to opt for the latter, which is evident in the Protestant apologists Norm Geisler and Ralph MacKenzie's declaration that "the Bible—nothing more, nothing less, and nothing else—is all that is necessary for faith and practice."[2]

In a recent defense of *sola scriptura*, the Reformed theologian Matthew Barrett wrote, "Sola scriptura means that only Scripture, because it is God's inspired Word, is our inerrant, sufficient, and final authority for the church.... All things necessary for salvation and for living the Christian life in obedience to God and for his glory are given to us in the Scriptures."[3]

One corollary of *sola scriptura* is the belief that no other authority, like the Church, is necessary for arriving at a correct interpretation of Scripture. Rather, every individual believer is capable of perceiving at least the essential doctrines of the faith through his own personal reading of the Bible. Some Protestants put it this way: "The main things are the plain things, and the plain things are the main things." Luther went so far as to claim that "they who deny the all-clearness

[2] Norman L. Geisler and Ralph E. MacKenzie, *Roman Catholics and Evangelicals: Agreements and Differences* (Grand Rapids, MI: Baker Books, 1995), 178.

[3] Matthew Barrett, *God's Word Alone: The Authority of Scripture* (Grand Rapids, MI: Zondervan, 2016), 334. This parallels the 1646 Westminster Confession of Faith, which said that "the whole counsel of God concerning all things necessary for His own glory, man's salvation, faith and life, is either expressly set down in Scripture, or by good and necessary consequence may be deduced from Scripture: unto which nothing at any time is to be added, whether by new revelations of the Spirit, or traditions of men." Westminster Confession of Faith 1.6, Center for Reformed Theology and Apologetics, copyright © 1996–2016, http://www.reformed.org /documents/wcf_with_proofs/. All subsequent quotations from the Westminster Confession of Faith are from this source.

and all-plainness of the scriptures, leave us nothing else but dark-ness."[4] But this perspicuity of Scripture, as some Protestants call it, is demonstrably false.

Protestants disagree over "main things" like baptismal regeneration, predestination, the presence of Christ in the Eucharist, or whether salvation can be lost. The Bible itself teaches that some passages of Scripture are "hard to understand, which the ignorant and unsta-ble twist to their own destruction" (2 Pet 3:16). Notice that Peter warns his readers about misinterpretations that bring about a per-son's destruction, which only makes sense if they involve the "main things" of the Christian faith rather than tangential, theological issues.

When presented with this objection many Protestants claim that the perspicuity of Scripture only means that Scripture "is capable of being understood rightly, not that all believers will understand it rightly".[5] But this undercuts the claim that Scripture is clear not just to scholars but to ordinary believers as well. Calvinist Robert Godfrey says, "All things *necessary* for salvation and concerning faith and life are taught in the Bible with enough clarity that the ordinary believer can find them there and understand."[6] According to the Westminster Confession of Faith,

> Those things which are necessary to be known, believed, and observed for salvation are so clearly propounded, and opened in some place of Scripture or other, *that not only the learned, but the unlearned* [emphasis added], in a due use of the ordinary means, may attain unto a sufficient understanding of them. (1.7)

---

[4] Martin Luther, *The Bondage of the Will*, trans. J.I. Packer and O.R. Johnston (Pea-body, MA: Hendrickson Publishers, 2008), 82. According to the Protestant historian Alister McGrath, "Luther demanded that all Christians should be able to read the Bible for them-selves. The agenda here was both political and theological. Lay access to the Bible was about power as much as it was about encouraging personal spirituality. Pressure for the Bible to be placed in the hands of the ordinary person was an implicit demand for the emancipation of the laity from clerical domination." Alister McGrath, *Reformation Thought: An Introduction*, 4th ed. (West Sussex: Wiley Blackwell, 2012), 111.

[5] Wayne Grudem, "The Perspicuity of Scripture: Tyndale Fellowship Conference; The John Wenham Lecture, July 8, 2009" (lecture, Cambridge, UK, July 8, 2009), http://www.waynegrudem.com/wp-content/uploads/2012/04/Perspicuity-of-Scripture-for-Themelios-Word-97-3.pdf.

[6] W. Robert Godfrey, "What Do We Mean by Sola Scriptura?", in *Sola Scriptura: The Protestant Position on the Bible* (Lake Mary, FL: Ligonier Ministries, 2009), 2.

In contrast to Scripture being clearly understandable, consider the time when the evangelist Philip came across a eunuch reading the prophet Isaiah. He asked him, "Do you understand what you are reading?" to which the eunuch answered, "How can I, unless some one guides me?" (Acts 8:30–31). Given that Protestants hold contradictory positions on mutually exclusive issues (such as whether baptism takes away sin), this shows that many who defend *sola scriptura* do *not* understand what they are reading. It's no wonder that 2 Peter 1:20–21 tells us that "no prophecy of Scripture is a matter of one's own interpretation, because no prophecy ever came by the impulse of man, but men moved by the Holy Spirit spoke from God."

## *Sola Scriptura* or *Solo Scriptura?*

Some Protestant apologists respond to this criticism by saying it only applies to a distortion of their doctrine they call "*solo*" *scriptura* (unlike *sola*, "solo" comes from English rather than Latin, so *solo scripture* would be more accurate). They say Scripture becomes "twisted" only when a person reads it outside the context of Christian tradition. According to Keith Mathison, it follows from practicing *solo scriptura* that "tradition is not allowed in any sense; the ecumenical creeds are virtually dismissed; and the Church is denied any real authority."[7] The difference between *sola scriptura* and *solo scriptura* could be understood with the following illustration.

Adherents of *solo scriptura* are like people who attempt to cross the wilderness using nothing but a map to guide them. They don't seek any advice but simply trust that their map-reading skills will be sufficient to guide them on their journey. They approach the Bible like the nineteenth-century preacher Alexander Campbell, who said he "endeavored to read the scriptures as though no one had read them before me".[8] Defenders of *sola scriptura* say it's no surprise that people who read Scripture in isolation from other believers wander into heresy.

Adherents of *sola scriptura*, on the other hand, take into account what others have learned from previously crossing this same wilderness.

---

[7] Keith Mathison, *The Shape of Sola Scriptura* (Moscow, ID: Canon Press, 2001), 238.
[8] Cited in Mark Knoll, *The Scandal of the Evangelical Mind* (Grand Rapids, MI: Wm. B. Eerdmans, 1995), 98.

They still only use the map to guide them, but they make sure their reading of that map doesn't lead them into hazards other travelers have warned them about. For example, they seek guidance from the teachings of the first ecumenical councils and, consequently, reject interpretations of Scripture that deny the deity of Christ.

But adherents of *solo scriptura* and *sola scriptura* both hold as their ultimate authority the individual's interpretation of Scripture. Protestants like Mathison may cite from early ecumenical councils, but they only do so to support their previous interpretation of Scripture. So, for example, they may cite Pope Leo's defense of traditional Christology at Chalcedon, but they ignore his invocation of papal authority in his other letters.[9] Or consider the Protestant philosopher William Lane Craig, who believes that Christ has only one will. This heresy, called Monothelitism, was condemned at the Third Council of Constantinople (A.D. 680–681), a fact Craig fully understands. Yet his reply to critics shows the practical equivalence between *solo scriptura* and *sola scriptura*. He writes:

> No earnest Christian wants to be considered a heretic. But we Protestants recognize Scripture alone as our ultimate rule of faith (the Reformation principle of *sola scriptura*). Therefore, we bring even the statements of Ecumenical Councils before the bar of Scripture.[10]

*Solo scriptura* and *sola scriptura* represent a distinction in emphasis without a difference in substance. Under the latter view Christian tradition is given more *consideration*, but it isn't given more *authority*. This is evident in things like the 1978 Chicago Statement on Inerrancy, a popular statement among conservative Evangelicals, which says, "We deny that Church creeds, councils, or declarations have authority greater than scripture or equal to the authority of the Bible."[11] Both groups deny that tradition has any ability to overrule an individual

---

[9] "But the bishops' assents, which are opposed to the regulations of the holy canons composed at Nicæa in conjunction with your faithful Grace, we do not recognize, and by the blessed Apostle Peter's authority we absolutely dis-annul in comprehensive terms." Pope Leo the Great, *Letter* 105.3.

[10] William Lane Craig, "Monotheletism", Q&A, no. 75, ReasonableFaith.com, September 21, 2008, http://www.reasonablefaith.org/monotheletism.

[11] Chicago Statement on Inerrancy, Article II, http://www.alliancenet.org/the-chicago-statement-on-biblical-inerrancy.

Christian who believes his interpretation of Scripture is correct, no matter what long-standing doctrine of the faith it may reject.

Finally, if it were true that all Christian doctrine is explicitly found in Scripture, then one would expect the doctrine of *sola scriptura* to be found there as well. This could be in the form of a Bible passage that teaches *sola scriptura* or even a logical argument derived from multiple passages that, when taken together, teach the same doctrine. For example, even though the Bible never uses the word "Trinity", it does teach that doctrine because the Bible affirms that there is one God and that the Father, the Son, and the Holy Spirit are each divine Persons who are distinct from one another.

Of course, if *sola scriptura* were as implicit in Scripture as the doctrine of the Trinity, then why didn't the early Christians affirm it? The answer is that *sola scriptura* is not found in the Scriptures and, consequently, the early Church did not teach that doctrine. This will become clear as we examine the evidence Protestant apologists try to assemble from these biblical and patristic sources.

## The Gospels and the Book of Acts

The Gospels never record Jesus instructing the disciples to consider written records to be the Church's sole infallible rule of faith. Perhaps this is why some Protestant apologists cite Jesus' actions instead of his teachings in their defense of *sola scriptura*. For example, Geisler and MacKenzie say, "Jesus and the apostles constantly appealed to the Bible as the final court of appeal."[12] Apologist Ron Rhodes similarly cites Jesus' three replies during his temptation in the wilderness, all of which contain citations from the Old Testament, as evidence for *sola scriptura*.[13] But it is a fallacy to argue that because Jesus recognized Scripture as *a* rule of faith it follows that Scripture is the Church's *only* rule of faith.

When Jesus answered Satan in the desert, he quoted Deuteronomy 8:3, saying, "Man shall not live by bread alone, but by every word

---

[12] Geisler and MacKenzie, *Roman Catholics and Evangelicals*, 185.

[13] "Following Jesus' lead, Scripture alone must be our supreme and final authority." Ron Rhodes, *Reasoning from the Scriptures with Catholics* (Eugene, OR: Harvest House Publishing, 2000), 58.

that proceeds from the mouth of God" (Mt 4:4). Jesus did not limit God's word to the written word alone. Prior to his Ascension into heaven, Jesus never even commanded the apostles to write anything down. He also did not command them to collect any new writings to serve as the Church's ultimate authority.

The book of Acts also does not record the apostles collecting any new sacred writings that would later serve as the Church's sole rule of faith. While Acts 4:12 says there is salvation in no one else but Christ, Acts never says there is no revelation in anything else but Scripture. In fact, the only passage in this book that is cited in defense of *sola scriptura* is Acts 17:11.

The previous ten verses in the chapter describe how Paul and Silas caused a stir in a Thessalonian synagogue, which resulted in the Christians of the city sending them to nearby Berea for their own safety. According to verse 11, "Now these [Berean] Jews were more noble than those in Thessalonica, for they received the word with all eagerness, examining the Scriptures daily to see if these things were so."[14] According to Barrett,

> What is assumed in the Berean response to Paul? First, their actions assume that Scripture is the final authority. The validity and veracity of Paul's message is tested against the Scriptures. Second, their actions assume that Scripture is enough; it is enough to verify or disprove Paul's message.[15]

But Acts 17:1–11 does not contain a formal teaching or treatise on Scripture. It is a narrative that describes certain Jews accepting and rejecting Paul's message. As such, it provides an insufficient framework to build a foundation for the formal principle of the Protestant Reformation. At most, this episode shows that Christian doctrine should not contradict Scripture, not that all doctrine is explicitly found within Scripture.

After all, the Old Testament does not explicitly say the Messiah would rise from the dead three days after being crucified. The Bereans

---

[14] According to systematic theologian Clark Pinnock, "Our guides are the noble Bereans who searched the Scriptures daily to see if these things were so" (Acts 17:11). Clark Pinnock, *Biblical Revelation* (Eugene, OR: Wipf and Stock, 1998), 96.

[15] Barrett, *God's Word Alone*, 341.

had to trust Paul's preaching of the new truths of the Christian faith, a proclamation the believing Thessalonians received, "not as the word of men but as what it really is, the word of God" (1 Thess 2:13). Even Mathison says, "There is nothing in this passage which warrants a radically individualized concept of solo scriptura apart from the apostolic rule of faith."[16]

The argument also hinges on Luke's assertion that the Bereans were "more noble" than the Thessalonians. Protestant apologists claim their superior nobility came from the fact that they examined the Scriptures "to see if these things [in Paul's teachings] were so". But Luke never says the Thessalonians did *not* examine the Scriptures and were thus ignoble. He only says some of the Thessalonians were persuaded by Paul's scriptural arguments whereas others incited a riot.

According to Evangelical scholar David Peterson, "The term used here referred originally to noble birth, but came to be applied more generally to high minded behavior."[17] This includes qualities associated with members of the upper class such as "openness, tolerance, and generosity".[18] Peterson concurs with exegete C. K. Barrett that "Luke means that the Berean Jews allowed no prejudice to prevent them from giving Paul a fair hearing."[19] This can be demonstrated by noting the general pattern in both stories.

Acts 17:1–9 describes how Paul and Silas went to Thessalonica and argued for three weeks in the synagogue that Jesus was the Messiah, which resulted in the conversion of some Jews and Gentiles. Unfortunately, the unconvinced Jews started a riot, forcing Paul and Silas to flee. Acts 17:10–12 then describes how Paul and Silas went to Berea and argued over several days that Jesus was the Messiah. This resulted in the conversion of some Jews and Gentiles. However, unlike the Thessalonians, the Berean Jews did not start a riot.[20]

---

[16] Mathison, *Shape of Sola Scriptura*, 162.

[17] David Peterson, *The Acts of the Apostles* (Grand Rapids, MI: Wm. B. Eerdmans, 2009), 484.

[18] William J. Larkin, "Acts", in *The Gospel of Luke, Acts*, by Allison A. Trites and William J. Larkin, ed. Philip Wesley Comfort, Cornerstone Biblical Commentary, vol. 12 (Carol Stream, IL: Tyndale House Publishers, 2006), 540.

[19] Peterson, *Acts of the Apostles*, 484.

[20] Peterson notes that "the conversions in Berea were similar in character to those in Thessalonica. The real difference between the situations was that the unconverted in Berea did not persecute the missionaries and seek to silence them". Ibid., 484.

The Bereans' nobility may also be due to their zealous passion for the truth, which is evident in the fact that they met in the synagogue during the week for religious discussions instead of only on the Sabbath. Indeed, their nobility may be due not to the fact that they examined the Scriptures, but that they did so *every day*. In any case, since Luke tells us that the word of God was preached in Berea (Acts 17:13), we can conclude that the word of God is not confined to the written word alone. This and everything else we have discussed shows that Acts 17:11 does not support the Protestant doctrine of *sola scriptura*.

## Apostolic Writings

The letters and revelation of the apostle John are often considered one of the last parts of the New Testament to be written. But nowhere in John's writings does he instruct his readers only to consider what he and the other New Testament authors wrote as their sole source of doctrine. Instead, we read about how John "would rather not use paper and ink" (2 Jn 12; cf. 3 Jn 13) but wanted to speak to his audience "face to face" (3 Jn 14).

Even still, some apologists cite Revelation 22:18–19 as evidence for *sola scriptura* because John says, "Every one who hears the words of the prophecy of this book: if any one adds to them, God will add to him the plagues described in this book." This kind of reasoning can be found in the 1561 Confession of Faith (commonly known as the Belgic Confession, the Reformed Belgic statement of faith), which says: "For since it is forbidden to add to or subtract from the Word of God, this plainly demonstrates that the teaching is perfect and complete in all respects."[21] Kenneth Samples likewise says the idea that Sacred Tradition is equal in authority to Scripture "violate[s] the commands of Scripture itself (Rev. 22:18–19, Deut 4:2, Prov. 30:5–6)".[22]

First, Revelation 22:18–19 says not to add to or take away from "the prophecy of this book"; the Greek word for "book" is *biblion*, which could mean "small book" or "scroll". The Bible was neither of

---

[21] Confession of Faith, article 7, cited in Kenneth Samples, *A World of Difference: Putting Christian Truth-Claims to the Worldview Test* (Grand Rapids, MI: Baker Books, 2007), 16.

[22] Samples, *World of Difference*, 118.

these. In the first century the Bible was a *collection* or *library* of books. It was not published as a single volume until centuries later. The natural meaning of the phrase thus indicates a single book of prophecy: Revelation itself. That means if this verse proved *sola scriptura*, it would also prove *sola Revelation* since John's warning refers only to this book of Scripture.[23]

Second, even if John's warning in Revelation applied to the whole of Scripture and not just the book of Revelation, that would not prove *sola scriptura*. Revelation 22:18–19 only proves that no one has the authority to alter the words of Scripture, not that all Christian doctrine is explicitly found in Scripture. This can even be seen in Samples' use of citations from the Old Testament.

Imagine a second-century Jew telling Samples that the New Testament illicitly adds to God's word and violates Deuteronomy 4:2 ("You shall not add to the word which I command you, nor take from it") and Proverbs 30:5–6 ("Every word of God proves true.... Do not add to his words"). Samples would probably respond by saying the New Testament does not add any words to the books of the Old Testament. Instead, the New Testament constitutes authentic revelation from God that complements what is found in the Old Testament. But if that's true, then Catholics can argue by analogy that God's word found in Sacred Tradition does not add anything to the books of the Bible. Instead, it complements the revelation found in God's written word.

Among the other apostolic writings there are two passages in Saint Paul's letters that are often cited in defense of *sola scriptura*. The first passage, 1 Corinthians 4:6, can be dealt with briefly because it is an incredibly obscure verse to rest any doctrine upon, especially one as foundational as *sola scriptura*. It says, "I have applied all this to myself and Apollos for your benefit, brethren, that you may learn by us not to go beyond what is written, that none of you may be puffed up in favor of one against another."

Rhodes claims this verse means that "scripture sets parameters beyond which we are not free to go."[24] Other Protestant apologists simply quote Paul's exhortation and assume Paul is referring to *sola*

<hr>

[23] I owe this observation to Jimmy Akin.
[24] Rhodes, *Reasoning from the Scriptures*, 63.

*scriptura* when he says we should not "go beyond what is written".[25] But New Testament scholarship has revealed not only that this verse does not plainly refer to *sola scriptura*; it is difficult to discern as to what it refers.

In his study of this verse, biblical scholar Ronald Tyler considers the possibility that Paul is making an allusion to how school children are taught to trace over letters when they learn to write.[26] Just as school children should not go beyond the lines drawn for them in the words they learn, new Christians should not go beyond the example Paul set for them. In favor of this interpretation is the fact that later in the chapter Paul speaks of being a "father" (4:15) to his "children" (4:14) and implores his children to "be imitators" of him (4:16).

Of course, this is just one interpretation among many, including the possibility that the entire verse was an erroneous scribal interpolation. According to Bradley Bitner in his study of First Corinthians, "In many ways, the history of scholarship on this verse resembles a demolition zone littered with the debris of collapsed and tottering hypotheses."[27] He especially notes that "the phrase [*to me huper ha gegraptai*, "not beyond what is written"] is surely the stone over which most interpreters have stumbled and the one that has crushed the most hypotheses in the history of scholarship."[28]

This shows that 1 Corinthians 4:6 cannot support a doctrine so foundational to the Protestant worldview as *sola scriptura*. In his commentary on First Corinthians, Anthony Thiselton offers seven possible interpretations of the phrase, none of which correspond to the modern doctrine of *sola scriptura*.[29] Tim Savage says this verse "probably refers to the five scriptural quotations which Paul has already cited

---

[25] "Paul warns the Corinthians: 'Do not go beyond what is written' (4:6)." Matthew Barrett, *God's Word Alone*, 326. "The Bible constantly warns us 'not to go beyond what is written' (1 Cor. 4:6)." Geisler and MacKenzie, *Roman Catholics and Evangelicals*, 187. "Scriptural warnings such as 'do not go beyond what is written' (1 Cor. 4:6) ..." Samples, *World of Difference*, 121.

[26] "Paul refers to a pedagogical education conception which his hearers would recognize from their early education." Ronald L. Tyler, "First Corinthians 4:6 and Hellenistic Pedagogy", *Catholic Biblical Quarterly* 60 (January 1998): 101.

[27] Bradley J. Bitner, *Paul's Political Strategy in 1 Corinthians 1–4: Constitution and Covenant* (New York: Cambridge University Press, 2015), 289.

[28] Ibid., 294.

[29] Anthony C. Thiselton, *The First Epistle to the Corinthians* (Grand Rapids, MI: Wm. B. Eerdmans, 2013), 354.

in 1 Corinthians 1–3", a view John Calvin also held.[30] In fact, none of the Protestant Reformers used this passage in their defenses of *sola scriptura*, and modern defenses of *sola scriptura* tend to ignore it.[31]

It's no surprise then that many Protestants prefer to rest their case on Paul's description of Scripture in 2 Timothy 3:16–17.

## "All Scripture Is Inspired ..."

In 2 Timothy 3:16–17, Paul is exhorting Timothy to beware of evil men who will persecute and deceive Christians. He reminds Timothy that "all Scripture is inspired by God and profitable for teaching, for reproof, for correction, and for training in righteousness, that the man of God may be complete, equipped for every good work." Samples claims, "This passage contains the essence of sola scriptura,"[32] but a thorough examination of "all Scripture is inspired" shows otherwise.

First, there is a legitimate translation issue concerning the phrase "all Scripture" (Greek, *pasa graphe*). The non-Catholic scholar J. N. D. Kelly notes that "there is no definite article [here] in the Greek and where pas ('all' or 'every') is used with a noun in the singular without the article it usually means 'every' rather than 'whole' or 'all'.... The balance of argument seems in favor of Every Scripture."[33] Other commenters reach a similar conclusion but see no problem using the translation "all" instead of "every".

According to Thomas Lea and Hayne Griffin, "If we affirm that each part of Scripture is inspired, we come eventually to assert that its entire context is inspired."[34] If Scripture's inspiration means it is the word of God and so it is useful for teaching, then saying *all* Scripture is inspired is equivalent to saying *every* individual Scripture is inspired. Each book of the Bible, as well as the Bible as a whole, equips the man of God with divine revelation that can help him teach and do good works.

---

[30] Timothy B. Savage, *Power through Weakness: Paul's Understanding of the Christian Ministry in 2 Corinthians* (New York: Cambridge University Press, 1996), 59.

[31] Patrick Madrid, "Going Beyond", *Catholic Answers Magazine*, May 28, 2016, https://www.catholic.com/magazine/print-edition/going-beyond.

[32] Samples, *World of Difference*, 121.

[33] J. N. D. Kelly, *Pastoral Epistles* (New York: Bloomsbury Academic, 2001), 202.

[34] Thomas D. Lea and Hayne P. Griffin, *1, 2 Timothy, Titus: An Exegetical and Theological Exposition of Holy Scripture* (Nashville, TN: B&H Publishing Group, 1992), 235.

The problem for Protestant apologists, however, is their claim that Scripture's inspiration means it is a believer's sole source of doctrine and authority. In that case, saying "*every* Scripture is inspired" is not the same as saying "*all* Scripture is inspired." The former statement would mean that individual books of the Bible, such as the Gospel of John or the book of Genesis, contain all necessary divine revelation and each is sufficient to be the believer's sole source of authority.

Second, Protestant apologists erroneously read a foundation of *sola scriptura* into Paul's description of Scripture as being "inspired" (Greek, *theopneustos*). According to Adam Murrell, "Unless tradition is also *theopnuestos* it cannot be equal to the rest of the Word of God. For there can only be one ultimate authority and that is why the evangelical's supreme authority is, without question or reservation, the God-breathed Scriptures and nothing more".[35]

*Theopneustos* is a *hapax legomenon*, or a word that occurs only once in the Bible (it's also very uncommon in other ancient Greek literature). It is derived from the Greek words for "God" (*theos*) and "breathe" or "breath" (*pneo*). However, to say the definition of *theopneustos* is "God-breathed" merely because that is the meaning of the word's component parts commits the etymological or "root" fallacy.[36] For example, the English word "nice" comes from the Latin word *nescire*, which means "not known", but this does not mean a nice person is also an ignorant person or an unknown person. In order to understand the meaning of the word "nice", we must examine how it is used in communication between people. Since *theopnuestos* is used infrequently, this makes it difficult to determine the word's meaning.

The Evangelical author Kern Trembath says it is an "assumption that that we know what the word [*theopnuestos*] means, but we do not, in spite of the staggering amount of attention it has received over several generations".[37] This doesn't mean the word is completely

---

[35] Adam Murrell, *Essential Church History: And the Doctrinal Significance of the Past* (Eugene, OR: Wipf and Stock, 2009), 109.

[36] D. A. Carson, *Exegetical Fallacies* (Grand Rapids, MI: Baker Academic, 1996), 28.

[37] Kern Robert Trembath, *Evangelical Theories of Biblical Inspiration: A Review and Proposal* (New York: Oxford University Press, 2007), 6. Craig Allert likewise says, "To claim that we know the meaning of the term theopnuestos, regardless of whether it is to be understood in the active or passive sense, is saying more than the Bible actually does." Craig D. Allert, *A High View of Scripture? The Authority of the Bible and the Formation of the New Testament Canon* (Grand Rapids, MI: Baker Academic, 2007), 154.

unknown, only that its precise meaning is debatable.[38] The Baptist
scholar Lee Martin McDonald points out that "in the early church
the common word for 'inspiration' (*theopneustos*; see 2 Tim. 3:16) was
used not only in reference to the Scriptures (Old Testament or New
Testament) but also of individuals who spoke or wrote the truth of
God."[39] These and other reasons show that it is an exegetical over-
reach to say only that which is *theopnuestos* can be an inerrant source
of divine revelation.

As we will see in the next chapter, the Catholic Church holds that
Tradition is part of the word of God, and so—if God breathes all his
words—then Tradition is inspired in the sense that it is God's word.
Like Scripture, it is backed by divine authority but, unlike Scripture, the
expressions of Tradition are not inspired like the words of Scripture
(i.e., the writings of the Church Fathers are not divinely inspired).
Their truth and authority, however, remain the same, and God can
ensure that this teaching is conveyed accurately and authoritatively,
even if he's not inspiring the exact wording that is used to convey it.
The Protestant apologist carries the burden of proving that something
lacks divine authority, including the word of God preserved in unwritten form (2 Thess 2:15), just because it is not described as *theopneustos*.

Besides, as the Evangelical scholar Craig Allert notes, "The stress
of this passage is not on *theopneustos*; instead it is on the usefulness of
scripture."[40] Paul does not say Scripture is *necessary* or *sufficient* for
teaching, reproof, training, or correction in righteousness. Instead,
Paul only describes Scripture as being useful or "profitable" (Greek,
*ophelimos*) for those tasks.

At this point, Protestant apologists usually move to verse 17 and
claim that it teaches the doctrine of *sola scriptura* because it says Scripture makes a man of God "complete" (Greek, *artios*) and "equipped"

---

[38] "In the NT [*theopneustos*] occurs only in 2 Tm. 3:16. The word here is used attributively
to describe [*graphe*] more closely as 'holy.' The emphasis, however, is on [*ophelimos*].... It is
thus evident that the author is differentiating the writings ordained by God's authority from
other, secular works." *Theological Dictionary of the New Testament*, ed. Gerhard Kittel et al.,
vol. 6 (Grand Rapids, MI: Eerdmans, 1964), 453.

[39] Lee Martin McDonald, *The Biblical Canon: Its Origin, Transmission, and Authority* (Grand
Rapids, MI: Baker Academic, 2007), 418. One example McDonald provides is that of Gregory of Nyssa describing Basil's commentary on the creation story as being inspired in *Apolo-
gia hexaemeron*.

[40] Allert, *High View of Scripture?*, 156.

(Greek, *exartismenos*) for "every good work" (Greek, *pan ergo aga-thon*). According to Protestant apologist Eric Svendsen, "If the man of God is fully equipped by the Scriptures to teach correct doctrine and lifestyle, and to combat heretical counterparts, then the Scriptures need not be supplemented by oral tradition."[41]

In other words, *sola scriptura* is true because 2 Timothy 3:17 says Scripture is enough to equip the man of God for *every* good work. If the man of God only needs Scripture in order to accomplish his good works, this must mean that all the doctrine he must believe is found completely and only in those same Scriptures. But Scripture also speaks of other things that prepare us for "every good work" and even "perfect" believers that are not sole sources of doctrine or authority.

In 2 Timothy 2:21 Paul says that if Timothy keeps himself from bad influences, "he will be a vessel for noble use, consecrated and useful to the master of the house, ready for any good work." The Greek phrase "every good work" (*pan ergon agathon*) is identical to what is used in 2 Timothy 3:17, but no Protestant would claim that a Christian only needs to stay away from bad influences in order to live the Christian life. James 1:4 uses stronger language to describe how endurance makes one "perfect" (*teleioi*) and "complete" (*holokleroi*) rather than "equips" believers, but of course our faith does not rest on the virtue of patience alone.[42]

In 2 Corinthians 9:8 Paul says that God gives an abundance of blessings "for every good work". Jesus likewise said, "Apart from me you can do nothing" (Jn 15:5). The man of God needs prayer, grace,

[41] Eric Svendsen, *Evangelical Answers: A Critique of Current Roman Catholic Apologists* (Atlanta: New Testament Restoration Foundation, 1999), 106.

[42] Svendsen objects, saying, "The Greek word used here is different than that found in [2] Tim 3:17 ([*teleos*] is used, not [*artios*])" (ibid., 138), but this is actually worse for the Protestant apologist because *teleos* communicates a stronger sense of completeness than *artios* (which the New American Standard Bible renders in 2 Timothy 3:17 as "adequate"). Svendsen then comments that James 1:4 only says that patience perfects the man of God in relation to "the 'testing of your faith' whereas Scripture makes the man of God 'fully equipped' to 'teach, rebuke, correct, and train'" (ibid., 139). But a person's faith can certainly be tested by someone who challenges it and requires correction or proper teaching in response. Therefore, this does not change the fact that Protestant arguments for *sola scriptura* based on 2 Timothy 3:16–17 can also be applied, in the style of *argumentum ad absurdum*, to James 1:4 and show that if patience is not a sole rule of faith despite its ability to perfect us in the face of trials, then Scripture is not a sole rule of faith despite its ability to equip us to teach and correct others.

and holiness to perform "every good work", so Paul could not be speaking of Scripture alone as being sufficient for that task. Moreover, as we will show in chapter 4, Scripture doesn't equip the man of God for the "good work" of knowing what is and is not Scripture. Therefore, 2 Timothy 3:17 does not prove that all Christian doctrine is found in Scripture alone, so it fails to support the Protestant doctrine of *sola scriptura*.

## The Church Fathers

According to Matthew Barrett, "Innovation is often the first indication of heresy. This is why the Reformers sought to tie their exegesis all the way back to the patristic tradition."[43] Contemporary Protestant apologists attempt to do the same when they claim that several prominent early Church Fathers taught the doctrine of *sola scriptura*. However, when one examines the writings of the Church Fathers, it is important to understand the difference between the material and formal sufficiency of Scripture.

Material sufficiency refers to Scripture containing all of divine revelation, or at least everything necessary for salvation, in either explicit or implicit form. In this sense, Scripture is sufficient for theology because it provides all the necessary materials for that cause. This would be like saying a lumberyard is materially sufficient for the goal of living in a house. The materials are present for that task, but a skilled builder is still necessary in order to achieve the goal of living in a house.

Formal sufficiency, on the other hand, refers to Scripture containing the material of divine revelation in a clearly understandable form. This would be akin to a suburban housing development being "formally sufficient" for the purpose of living in a house. One could simply walk in and buy a home apart from any special knowledge about how to build those houses. The Protestant position on scriptural sufficiency would imply that just as a builder isn't necessary to live in a completed home, the Church is not necessary for interpreting or understanding Scripture. The Westminster Confession bluntly said, "The infallible rule of interpretation of Scripture is the Scripture itself" (1.9).

---

[43] Barrett, *God's Word Alone*, 314.

While some Protestant apologists claim that the Church Fathers held to the formal view of sufficiency, the Evangelical author Timothy Ward says that "in general the Fathers assert the material sufficiency of scripture but deny its formal sufficiency."[44] Consider Saint Athanasius, who said, "The sacred and inspired Scriptures are sufficient to declare the truth." On its own, this statement may seem to show that Athanasius believed that Scripture was all a believer needed (or formal sufficiency). But let's examine the words in their proper context:

> For although the sacred and inspired Scriptures are sufficient to declare the truth—while there are other works of our blessed teachers compiled for this purpose, if he meet with which *a man will gain some knowledge of the interpretation of the Scriptures* [emphasis added], and be able to learn what he wishes to know—still, as we have not at present in our hands the compositions of our teachers, *we must communicate in writing to you what we learned from them—the faith, namely, of Christ the Savior* [emphasis added].[45]

For Athanasius, the Scriptures do contain the truth of the gospel, but one must also seek out the correct interpretation of that truth from those who teach the faith. That's why in his letter to the bishops of Africa Athanasius instructs them to "let the Faith confessed by the Fathers at Nicæa alone hold good among you." He also reminds his readers, "As I handed the traditions to you, so ye hold them fast" [1 Cor 11:2].[46] When we examine other Fathers that are cited in defense of *sola scriptura*, we see similar conflations between their *earnest veneration* of Scripture and the Protestant idea of the *formal sufficiency* of Scripture.

For example, Saint Basil of Caesarea is often quoted as saying to heretics, "Let God-inspired scripture decide between us."[47] This is taken to mean that Scripture is the only standard by which a Christian should determine what is and is not correct doctrine. But that is not the point Basil is making.

---

[44] Timothy Ward, *Word and Supplement: Speech Acts, Biblical Texts, and the Sufficiency of Scripture* (New York: Oxford University Press, 2002), 25.

[45] St. Athanasius, *Contra Gentes* 1.

[46] St. Athanasius, *Ad Afros Epistola Synodica* 10.

[47] St. Basil of Caesarea, *Letter* 189.3.

In this context, Basil's opponents accused him of heresy because of his orthodox Trinitarian theology that disagreed with their traditions (or custom) and understanding of Scripture. Against their custom, Basil said it was permissible for him to "put forward on my side the custom which obtains here". However, since his opponents did not accept his orthodox traditions, Basil had to use Scripture as a place of common ground in order to engage them. This is similar to how Catholic apologists might use Scripture alone when debating non-Catholics who reject the authority of Christian tradition.

In fact, Basil did not believe that all doctrine is found in the Bible alone, since he relied on Tradition in order to combat critics who claimed that his doxology ("Glory to the Father, with the Son, together with the Holy Spirit") was unbiblical and thus invalid. Basil points out to them that Christians believe many things that are not found in the Bible, including the sign of the cross and the baptismal promise to renounce Satan. He then says, "Some [Catholic beliefs and practices] we possess derived from written teaching; others we have received delivered to us in a mystery by the tradition of the apostles; and both of these in relation to true religion have the same force."[48]

What about Cyril of Jerusalem? He said, "Even to me, who tell you these things, give not absolute credence, unless you receive the proof of the things which I announce from the Divine Scriptures."[49] Cyril was instructing catechumens, or those who were new to the faith, how to avoid falling into heresy. He taught that if they clung to Scripture, heretics who peddled "clever arguments" would not deceive them. But Cyril also taught that the Church

> is called Catholic then because it extends over all the world, from one end of the earth to the other; and because it teaches universally and completely one and all the doctrines which ought to come to men's knowledge, concerning things both visible and invisible, heavenly and earthly; and because it brings into subjection to godliness the whole race of mankind.[50]

---

[48] St. Basil of Caesarea, *De Spiritu Sancto* 27.
[49] St. Cyril of Jerusalem, *Catechetical Lecture* 4.17.
[50] Ibid., 18.23.

Finally, let's examine Saint Augustine, whom Protestant apologists quote as saying, "What more can I teach you, than what we read in the Apostle? For holy Scripture sets a rule to our teaching."[51] In commenting on this passage William Whitaker writes, "Augustine says that the rule of doctrine is fixed in scripture: therefore, if we teach anything that is not laid down in scripture, whether of our own invention or otherwise, it is foreign from the rule of doctrine."[52] But Augustine is talking about the fullness of revelation that is found in Scripture and its usefulness as a result. This is similar to another work where he says, "The things that are plainly laid down in Scripture are to be found [in] all matters that concern faith and the manner of life—to wit, hope and love."[53]

This did not mean that Augustine rejected anything not explicitly found in Scripture. For example, in regard to infant baptism Augustine wrote, "There are many things which are observed by the whole Church, and therefore are fairly held to have been enjoined by the apostles, which yet are not mentioned in their writings."[54] Ward points out that these and other statements by the Fathers that speak of Scripture's sufficiency do not

> tell the whole theological story. Throughout the patristic period no programmatic distinction was made between Scripture and church with regard either to teaching or authority. The church was ascribed the right of determining the correct interpretation of Scripture, although not explicitly as an authority over against scripture.[55]

Augustine even said, "For my part, I should not believe the gospel except as moved by the authority of the Catholic Church."[56] Church history professor Mark Ellingsen, a Protestant, says of Augustine,

---

[51] St. Augustine, *Of the Good of Widowhood* 2.

[52] William Whitaker, *A Disputation on Holy Scripture: Against the Papists* (Cambridge: University Press, 1849), 698.

[53] St. Augustine, *On Christian Doctrine* 2.9.

[54] St. Augustine, *On Baptism, Against the Donatists* 5.23.

[55] Ward, *Word and Supplement*, 24.

[56] St. Augustine, *Against the Fundamental Epistle of Manichaeus* 5. In this section Augustine is replying to the Manicheans, whose leader has written an epistle claiming to have authority as an apostle of Jesus Christ. Augustine replies by saying he believed in the canonical gospel only because of the testimony of the Catholic Church and so, by that same testimony, he rejects the letter and claims of Manichaeus.

When decisions were to be made about ecclesiastical matters, he appealed to both the Bible and tradition, allowing them to function especially in cases where scripture laid down no definite rule.... Indeed, against the Manichee heretics, Augustine contended that the reason for believing is not found in the Scriptures alone, but is grounded in the Catholic tradition.[57]

Indeed, after Luther declared that he would base his theology on "Scripture alone", the Catholic scholar Johann Eck (who previously debated Luther at Leipzig) replied, "Martin, there is no one of the heresies which have torn the bosom of the church, which has not derived its origin from the various interpretation of the Scripture. The Bible itself is the arsenal whence each innovator has drawn his deceptive arguments."[58] That is why in the fifth century Saint Vincent of Lérins wrote, Therefore, "it is very necessary, on account of so great intricacies of such various error, that the rule for the right understanding of the prophets and apostles should be framed in accordance with the standard of Ecclesiastical and Catholic interpretation."[59]

[57] Mark Ellingsen, *The Richness of Augustine: His Contextual and Pastoral Theology* (Louisville, KY: Westminster John Know Press, 2005), 27.
[58] Martin Luther, *The Life of Luther*, trans. William Hazlitt (London: David Bogue, 1904), 93.
[59] St. Vincent of Lérins, *Commonitory* 2.5.

# 2

# Sacred Tradition

According to the historian Carter Lindberg, "Whereas the German Reformation was sparked by Luther's academic theological disputation over the sacrament of penance and indulgences, the Swiss Reformation went public with the so-called 'Affair of Sausages' ".[1] Specifically, in 1522 the Zurich city council arrested a printer for breaking the Lenten fast by serving sausages to some of his workers. In response, a Catholic priest named Ulrich (or Huldrych) Zwingli defended the printer and preached a sermon in defense of an individual's right to fast or not to fast.

Zwingli grounded his defense on the fact that the Bible does not prohibit eating meat during specific times of the year such as Lent. He asked, "Show me on the authority of the Scriptures that one cannot fast with meat."[2] While Protestants like Luther retained many Catholic traditions that they felt did not contradict Scripture, Zwingli was more critical of them.

A few months after the Affair of Sausages, Zwingli petitioned the local bishop to allow priests to marry (at the time he was living with a widow named Anna Reinhart). As the Reformation continued, a common theme in anti-Catholic literature (which has persisted to the present day) was that Catholics believed in unbiblical "traditions of men" whereas Protestants believed in the biblical principle of *sola scriptura*.

We've seen that the Bible and the early Church did not support the Protestant doctrine of *sola scriptura*. Now we will examine the

[1] Carter Lindberg, *The European Reformations*, 2nd ed. (West Sussex, UK: Blackwell, 2010), 161.

[2] Ulrich Zwingli, *The Latin Works and the Correspondence of Hulderich Zwingli: Together with Selections from His German Works 1510–1522*; trans. Henry Preble, Walter Lichtenstein, and Lawrence A. McLough; ed. Samuel Jackson (Eugene, OR: Wipf and Stock, 2010), 88.

biblical and historical evidence that shows God's revelation was not confined to Sacred Scripture but can also be found in what Catholics call Sacred Tradition.

## The Catholic View of Tradition

At its most basic level, "tradition" refers to what is "handed on" (which is the meaning of the Latin word *tradere*). This means, for example, that Sacred Scripture is a part of the tradition that has been handed on to the Church from the apostles. The Second Vatican Council taught in its Dogmatic Constitution on Divine Revelation *Dei Verbum* that "the apostolic preaching, which is expressed in a special way in the inspired books, was to be preserved by an unending succession of preachers until the end of time."[3]

In order to distinguish it from Scripture, the communication of this preaching through oral or unwritten means is called Sacred Tradition (or sometimes just Tradition). Quoting *Dei Verbum*, the *Catechism of the Catholic Church* (*CCC*) reiterates that through this means of revelation the Church " 'perpetuates and transmits to every generation all that she herself is, all that she believes' (*DV* 8 §1). 'The sayings of the holy Fathers are a witness to the life-giving presence of this Tradition, showing how its riches are poured out in the practice and life of the Church, in her belief and her prayer' (*DV* 8 §3)" (*CCC* 78).

Before we continue we must draw a distinction between "Tradition" and "tradition". The latter kind of tradition (with a lowercase "t") includes such things as pious customs that developed over time (like certain kinds of prayers) or ecclesial laws and instructions that regulate how believers live and practice the faith (like many of the particular rules for celebrating liturgies). They come from the authority Christ gave the Church, and so they can be altered or in some cases dispensed with entirely.

Tradition (with a capital "T"), on the other hand, includes the Deposit of Faith given to the apostles that has been transmitted to the

[3] Second Vatican Council, Dogmatic Constitution on Divine Revelation *Dei Verbum* (November 18, 1965), no. 8, http://www.vatican.va/archive/hist_councils/ii_vatican_council /documents/vat-ii_const_19651118_dei-verbum_en.html (hereafter cited as *DV*).

Church apart from Scripture. Some prominent examples of Sacred Tradition include the validity of infant baptism, essential elements for administering the sacraments of baptism and the Eucharist, and the permissibility of praying for the dead.[4] Both Sacred Scripture and Sacred Tradition are the word of God, and so they cannot be changed or erased; but they are not each the word of God in the exact same sense.

In the case of Sacred Scripture, God inspired the form through which his word would be communicated so that the authors of Scripture would be "true authors, [who] consigned to writing everything and only those things which He wanted".[5] God is equally the author of the Sacred Traditions that have been received in the Church apart from the written word. However, God did not inspire the precise form or words through which Sacred Tradition would be expressed. This means Sacred Tradition is not inspired in the same way Sacred Scripture is inspired, but it is as inerrant and authoritative as Scripture.

According to the Second Vatican Council, "There exists a close connection and communication between sacred tradition and Sacred Scripture. For both of them, flowing from the same divine well-spring, in a certain way merge into a unity and tend toward the same end."[6] The council explicitly taught that divine revelation is not found in Scripture alone, but it did not elaborate on the relationship between the divine revelation found in Scripture and the divine revelation found in Tradition. Two popular views on the subject include the *partim-partim* view and the *totum-totum* view.

The first view derives its name from the original draft of the Council of Trent's fourth session. It said, "This truth [of the gospel] is contained partly [*partim*] in written books, partly [*partim*] in unwritten traditions."[7] This could mean there are some truths about the faith found only in Scripture and other truths that are found only in Tradition. However, this passage was not included in the final decree but

---

[4] Yves Congar, *The Meaning of Tradition* (San Francisco: Ignatius Press, 2004), 37.

[5] *DV* 11.

[6] *DV* 9.

[7] Jaroslav Pelikan, *The Christian Tradition: A History of the Development of Doctrine*, vol. 5, *Christian Doctrine and Modern Culture (since 1700)* (Chicago: University of Chicago Press, 1971), 261.

was replaced with this instead: "Truth and discipline [which in this context refer to divine revelation] are contained in the written books, and the unwritten traditions."[8] This leaves open the possibility that everything that is contained in the unwritten traditions is, explicitly or implicitly, contained in the written books.

The alternative to the *partim-partim* view could be called the *totum-totum* view. It holds that everything found in Sacred Scripture is also found in Sacred Tradition (and vice versa).[9] One of its most prominent modern defenders is the late Dominican theologian Yves Congar, who said:

> "Written" and "unwritten" indicate not so much two material domains as two modes or states of knowledge, two ways in which the Church triumphs over time and its passing and remains still purely and fully *apostolic* [emphasis in original]. This explains why the idea of the sufficiency of Scripture has never and will never invalidate the necessity of tradition.[10]

Defenders of the *totum-totum* view usually say that Scripture contains all truths that are necessary for salvation while tradition contains the orthodox way of understanding Scripture. Congar claimed, "There is not a single point of belief that the Church holds by tradition alone, without any reference to scripture; just as there is not a single dogma that is derived from Scripture alone, without being explained by tradition."[11] While Congar does state his view very strongly, we must remember that this is one possible view of tradition and that the *partim-partim* view may also be correct.

Our examination of Sacred Tradition will include beliefs related to the cessation and recognition of divine revelation that may be entirely absent from Scripture and exist only as sacred, unwritten

---

[8] The Council of Trent, the Fourth Session, Decree concerning the Canonical Scriptures (April 8, 1546), from *The Canons and Decrees of the Sacred and Oecumenical Council of Trent*, trans. J. Waterworth (London: Dolman, 1848), 17–21, https://history.hanover.edu/texts/trent/cto4.html.

[9] Congar attributes this term to Henry Cardinal Newman, who is believed to have said, "Totum in Scriptura, totum in Traditione" ["All is in scripture, all in tradition"]. Yves Congar, *Tradition and Traditions* (New York: Macmillan, 1967), 413.

[10] Ibid., 414.

[11] Congar, *Meaning of Tradition*, 39–40.

tradition. But no matter which view best explains the concept of Sacred Tradition, our aim is to show that the Deposit of Faith is not completely contained formally in Scripture. The written word of God is a form of the living Tradition, both of which ultimately proceed from Christ and the apostles and were given to the Church to possess until Christ's Second Coming.

## Tradition in the New Testament

In the prologue to his Gospel, Luke describes his writing of "an orderly account" (1:3) of the events surrounding Jesus using sources that were "delivered [Greek, *paredosan*] to us by those who from the beginning were eyewitnesses and ministers of the word" (1:2). The root of the Greek verb *paredosan* is *paradidomi*, which means "to convey something in which one has a relatively strong personal interest, hand over, give (over), deliver, entrust".[12] The sources that were "handed over" to Luke may have been written documents, but more often than not they would have been oral communication, or what we call "tradition".

In fact, the Greek word for tradition is *paradosis*, which means "the content of instruction that has been handed down, tradition" (the Latin word *traditio* also means "handing over" or "handing on"). When Saint Paul spoke about the Lord's Supper, he began by saying, "For I received [Greek, *parelabon*] from the Lord what I also delivered to you [*paredoka*]" (1 Cor 11:23). In his commentary on First Corinthians, the non-Catholic scholar Anthony Thiselton says Paul was communicating an

> *apostolic tradition* concerning *the Lord's Supper* that Paul *received from the Lord* and *handed on* to the church. The words translated *received* and *handed on* found together in this way (Greek *paralambano* ... *paradidomi*) denote the transmission of a living *tradition*. Hence the phrase from the Lord refers to the origins of this tradition as coming from Christ himself through the earliest apostles [emphasis in original].[13]

---

[12] William F. Arndt, Frederick W. Danker, and Walter Bauer, *A Greek-English Lexicon of the New Testament and Other Early Christian Literature*, 3rd ed. (Chicago: University of Chicago Press, 2000), 761.

[13] Anthony C. Thiselton, *1 Corinthians* (Grand Rapids, MI: Wm. B. Eerdmans, 2011), 183.

Some Protestants admit that the truths found in the New Testament first existed in oral form but claim those truths were all eventually consigned to a written form that is now located in Sacred Scripture.[14] But as Congar notes, "Neither Jesus, who wrote nothing, nor St. Paul ever said: 'You will believe only what is written in the Gospels or in my letters,' but we do find 'You will believe what has been transmitted and taught to you.'"[15]

For example, Saint Paul commended the Corinthians when he said, "You remember me in everything and maintain the traditions even as I have delivered them to you" (1 Cor 11:2). Paul instructed Timothy, "What you have heard from me before many witnesses entrust to faithful men who will be able to teach others also" (2 Tim 2:2). Notice that Paul doesn't tell Timothy to entrust simply Paul's *writings* to others who will be able to teach the faith but what Timothy had *heard* from Paul himself.

Perhaps the clearest reference to the apostles communicating doctrine through Sacred Tradition is 2 Thessalonians 2:15: "So then, brethren, stand firm and hold to the traditions which you were taught by us, either by word of mouth or by letter." In his prior letter to the Thessalonians, Paul referred to the time when his hearers "received the word of God which you heard from us" and how they "accepted it not as the word of men but as what it really is, the word of God" (1 Thess 2:13). Now he instructs this same community to "stand firm and hold to the traditions which you were taught by us, either by word of mouth or by letter." In his defense of *sola scriptura*, Matthew Barrett states,

> At first the faith was delivered orally, but then it was put in writing. As Paul indicates in 2 Thessalonians 2:15, the traditions he passed on were not only through our spoken word but, by our letter (ESV). This written tradition was meant by God to be permanent, and the churches were to receive it as authoritative (e.g. Col 4:16).[16]

Many Protestants respond to 2 Thessalonians 2:15 by saying there is no difference between what the apostles preached orally and what

---

[14] Eric Svendsen, *Evangelical Answers: A Critique of Current Roman Catholic Apologists* (Atlanta: New Testament Restoration Foundation, 1999), 114.

[15] Congar, *Meaning of Tradition*, 34.

[16] Matthew Barrett, *God's Word Alone: The Authority of Scripture* (Grand Rapids, MI: Zondervan, 2016), 188.

is now found in the Bible. One commentary says, "Inspired tradition, in Paul's sense, is not a supplementary oral tradition completing our written Word, but it is identical with the Written Word *now* complete [emphasis in original]."[17] The Reformed apologist James R. White says, "The traditions Paul speaks of are not traditions about Mary or papal Infallibility.... No, [Paul] is exhorting them to stand firm *in the Gospel* [emphasis in original]."[18] But these arguments amount to nothing more than speculation.

How does White know, for example, that "the Gospel" Paul was referring to did not contain truths like "Mary gave birth to God" or "the Church will never be led into error"? Paul gives thanks for God choosing the Thessalonians through the gospel he and others preached (2 Thess 2:14), but Paul does not say in the next verse to stand firm and hold to the *gospel* either by word of mouth or by letter. He says to "stand firm and hold to the *traditions* which you were taught by us, either by word of mouth or by letter." Despite the assumptions that Protestant apologists make, the New Testament does not say these two are identical or that only one of these ways of communicating apostolic truth would be normative for the future Church. An example that Paul's written and oral teachings were not identical can even be found in 2 Thessalonians.

Earlier in the second chapter of this letter Paul speaks of "the man of lawlessness" (2 Thess 2:3) who, before Christ's coming, "takes his seat in the temple of God, proclaiming himself to be God" (2 Thess 2:4). In the next two verses Paul reminds his listeners, "Do you not remember that when I was still with you I told you this? And you know what is restraining him now so that he may be revealed in his time."

The Thessalonians may know what is restraining "the man of law-lessness", but we don't because Paul doesn't tell us in any of his writings. The Reformed scholars G. K. Beale and Benjamin Gladd propose several possible explanations of the identity of "the restrainer", including God, angels, empires, the Jewish nation, and even Satan.[19] But as biblical scholar Thomas Schreiner admits,

---

[17] Ron Rhodes, *Reasoning from the Scriptures with Catholics* (Eugene, OR: Harvest House Publishing, 2000), 79.

[18] James R. White, *The Roman Catholic Controversy* (Minneapolis: Bethany House, 1996), 96–97.

[19] G. K. Beale and Benjamin Gladd, *Hidden but Now Revealed: A Biblical Theology of Mystery* (Downers Grove, IL: InterVarsity Press, 2014), 118.

Only the Thessalonians and Paul know the identity of the restrainer since it was part of their oral communication (2 Thess. 2:5), and thus Paul feels no need to be specific. He never informs us about the identity of the restrainer since he had already communicated the matter orally to the Thessalonians.[20]

Since the apostles taught and instructed Christians for decades, most of their oral teaching has not been received into Sacred Tradition (just as the other letters some of the apostles wrote have not been received into Sacred Scripture).[21] The identity of the restrainer in 2 Thessalonians 2:7 is one of these teachings that was not passed on to future generations and so it is not a part of Sacred Tradition. What this example does show, however, is that the apostles didn't simply repeat the content of their letters when they spoke in public.[22] They shared other important truths of the faith, some of which were passed on through the centuries as Sacred Traditions that became normative for the Body of Christ. But before we examine the historical evidence for this Tradition, we must answer the most common biblical argument against it.

## "Traditions of Men"

Some Protestants reject Catholic tradition at the outset because some passages in Scripture criticize tradition. Lynette Marie Ordaz writes, "Catholics need to search their hearts and ask themselves where they put their faith and trust: In the Bible, the inspired Word of God, or Roman Catholic traditions of men. There is a difference as they often contradict each other."[23]

Catholics agree that if a tradition contradicts Scripture, then that tradition does come from men rather than from God and shouldn't be followed. But the existence of heretical traditions does not invalidate

---

[20] Thomas Schreiner, *Paul, Apostle of God's Glory in Christ: A Pauline Theology* (Downers Grove: InterVarsity Press, 2001), 464.

[21] In 1 Corinthians 5:9 Paul describes a previous letter he sent that has not been preserved to the present day: "I wrote to you in my letter not to associate with immoral men."

[22] "[Paul's] preaching and teaching were simply the declaration and interpretation of the inspired Word of God." William Webster, *The Church of Rome at the Bar of History* (Carlisle, PA: Banner of Truth Trust, 1995), 16.

[23] Lynette Marie Ordaz, *The Real Mary: Comparing the Mother of Jesus to the Mary of Roman Catholicism* (Bloomington, IN: AuthorHouse, 2007), 27.

genuine, apostolic traditions any more than the existence of forged apostolic writings (2 Thess 2:2) invalidates genuine apostolic writings. As we will see in chapter 4, Sacred Tradition helps the Church know which writings are truly orthodox and apostolic and which are not.

The other common passage cited against Sacred Tradition is found in Mark 7 (as well as its parallel in Matthew 15). It records when Jesus told the Pharisees, "You leave the commandment of God, and hold fast the tradition of men.... You have a fine way of rejecting the commandment of God, in order to keep your tradition!" (Mk 7:8–9; cf. Mt 15:2–3). Protestant apologists are usually aware that Catholics don't believe their Sacred Traditions are purely "man-made", but they contend this episode proves we should measure everything, including allegedly Sacred Traditions, against the rule of Scripture alone.[24] Before we critique those arguments, however, it will be helpful to explain the context of Jesus' condemnation of this particular tradition of the scribes and Pharisees.

In this passage the Pharisees criticized Jesus because his disciples did not follow the Jewish tradition of washing hands before they ate (this was done for the sake of ritual purity, not just for sanitary purposes). Jesus, in response, pointed to a tradition of the Pharisees that contradicted the word of God. He told them:

> For Moses said, "Honor your father and your mother"; and, "He who speaks evil of father or mother, let him surely die"; but you say, "If a man tells his father or his mother, What you would have gained from me is Corban" (that is, given to God)—then you no longer permit him to do anything for his father or mother, thus making void the word of God through your tradition which you hand on. (Mk 7:10–13; cf. Mt 15:4–6)

According to Gerhard Kittel's *Theological Dictionary of the New Testament*, "corban" (also rendered in the English alphabet as *korban* and *qurban*) is a Hebrew "loan-word" that, in the Old Testament, meant "what is offered".[25] This offering to God could take the form of food, possessions, or even individuals and families (in the sense of being

---

[24] White, *Roman Catholic Controversy*, 68.

[25] K. H. Rengstorf, "korban", in *Theological Dictionary of the New Testament: Abridged in One Volume*, ed. Gerhard Kittel and Gerhard Friedrich, trans. Geoffrey W. Bromiley (Grand Rapids, MI: Wm. B. Eerdmans, 1985), 459.

devoted to serving God). The word later came to refer to offerings made in the form of donations to the Temple (the treasury box in the Temple was called a *korbanas*).

The dispute with Jesus involves the practice of men vowing to give their assets to the Temple so that they would not have to use them to support their aging parents. E. P. Sanders, who has conducted an extensive study of first-century Judaism, says this particular practice "would be based on spite or malice; the man did not profit by declaring his goods *korban*, he just kept his parents from using them."[26]

So how does this episode prove the Protestant doctrine of *sola scriptura*?

Usually apologists will say this proves that Scripture is our ultimate authority and anything, even a tradition that claims to be of divine origin, must be tested by what we know to be our only infallible rule of faith. Adam Murrell offers a common argument:

> Jesus is not here condemning all tradition, but neither do proponents of *sola Scriptura*. In fact, we love tradition. However, all we ask for is that believers emulate Jesus by holding up any and all traditions and examining them in light of the Word, comparing them to that which is *theopneustos*.[27]

Catholics agree that we should not follow any tradition that contradicts Scripture. In this passage Jesus said that the Pharisees nullified or made void the written word of God through their application of the *korban* tradition. But Jesus didn't teach that Scripture must *corroborate* tradition; he only taught that tradition couldn't *contradict* Scripture.

Neither did Jesus teach that Scripture always has a higher authority than tradition just because traditions that falsely claim to be of divine origin are exposed with Scripture. The early Church relied on apostolic tradition to distinguish Gospels that have a divine origin from those like the Gospel of Thomas that do not, but this wouldn't show that Scripture has *less* authority than tradition just because Scripture is judged by tradition.

---

[26] E. P. Sanders, *Jewish Law from Jesus to the Mishnah: Five Studies* (Minneapolis: Fortress Press, 2016), 77.

[27] Adam Murrell, *Essential Church History: And the Doctrinal Significance of the Past* (Eugene, OR: Wipf and Stock, 2009), 109.

The Protestant apologist William Webster goes so far as to claim that "what Jesus is saying is that tradition is not inspired and therefore not inherently authoritative."[28] But in this passage Jesus never says anything about the nature of "tradition", much less that it is not inspired. Rather, he chides the Pharisees for holding to the "tradition of men" (Mk 7:8) or "your tradition" (Mk 7:13) and rebukes them for contradicting Scripture. Just because one false tradition contradicts Scripture, it doesn't follow that all tradition is not as authoritative as Scripture.

If Jesus had taught that Scripture had a higher authority than tradition, this would mean Jesus' own words, which existed as an oral tradition after his Ascension, would have had less authority than Scripture. Whenever the first Christians said that the Lord Jesus "declared all foods clean" (Mk 7:19), the Jews could have used Jesus' own words against them by saying Jesus' oral tradition was less authoritative than the Old Testament's written kosher laws. The words Jesus spoke during his earthly ministry that we have received through Scripture, as well as the words he spoke to the apostles that they transmitted to the Church through Sacred Tradition, both represent the word of God and are equal in authority.

Another mistake some Protestants make when interpreting this passage is the assumption that the scribes were following an unknown extrabiblical tradition when they should have relied on the testimony of Scripture alone. But the Hebrew word *korban* (or *qurban*, to give a more precise transliteration) is used dozens of times in the Old Testament in reference to offerings made to God. Declaring that something had been given to God and so was unavailable for personal use, either by oneself or one's family, is thoroughly biblical. The tradition Jesus was criticizing involved the Jewish leaders' *interpretation* of biblical rules related to vows and offerings.[29]

They believed that if a man vowed a gift to God through a donation to the Temple, then he could not go back on that vow. To do

---

[28] Webster, *Church of Rome at the Bar of History*, 17.

[29] "Early rabbinic literature also provides evidence about the usage of korban and refers to disputes between the schools of Hillel and Shammai about the question [*sic*] what vows are binding (m. *Ma'as.S* 4:10; m. *Ned.* 1:2–4, 2:2.5, 3:2.5, 9:7, 11:5; m. *Naz.* 2:1–3)." Albert L. A. Hogeterp, *Paul and God's Temple: A Historical Interpretation of Cultic Imagery in the Corinthian Correspondence* (Leuven, Belgium: Peeters Publishers, 2006), 167–68.

so would contradict Numbers 30:2, which says, "When a man vows a vow to the LORD, or swears an oath to bind himself by a pledge, he shall not break his word; he shall do according to all that proceeds out of his mouth" (in the time of Jesus *korban* meant "vow" more than "offering", but the two concepts are related).[30] Even if a man's vow of giving to the Temple caused his parents hardship, the verse seems clear: the vow can't be broken.

Jesus, however, argued that such a vow was invalid from the start because the man could not donate something to the Temple that God's law required him to use to support his parents. In short, the statute in the book of Numbers not to break vows to the Lord is superseded by the commandment in the book of Exodus to "honor your father and your mother" (20:12).

The "*korban* dispute" was, therefore, not a case of Jesus correcting the Pharisees' extrabiblical traditions with the Protestant principle of *sola scriptura*. Instead, the Pharisees had embraced a tradition of interpreting Scripture that was of human rather than divine origin. Jesus then responded with the correct understanding of God's word. The Catholic Church sees Sacred Tradition as playing a similar role in that it guides the Church in her understanding of the written word of God, a truth we will see in the early Christians' testimony about tradition. J. N. D. Kelly described their view this way:

> If scripture was abundantly sufficient in principle, tradition was recognized as the surest clue to its interpretation, for in tradition the church retained, as a legacy from the apostles which was embedded in all the organs of her institutional life, an unerring grasp of the real purport and meaning of the revelation to which scripture and tradition alike bore witness.[31]

## Tradition in the Church Fathers

As we saw in our discussion of *sola scriptura*, the early Church did not believe the doctrines of the faith were found in the written

---

[30] Rengstorf, "korban", in Kittel and Friedrich, *Theological Dictionary of the New Testament*, 459.

[31] J. N. D. Kelly, *Early Christian Doctrines*, 5th ed. (New York: Bloomsbury Academic, 2000), 48.

word alone. For example, Clement of Rome exhorted his readers to "approach the glorious and venerable rule of our tradition (Greek, *paradosis*)" rather than a solely biblical rule of faith.[32] In the second century Origen said, "The teaching of the Church, transmitted in orderly succession from the apostles, and remaining in the Churches to the present day, is still preserved, that alone is to be accepted as truth which differs in no respect from ecclesiastical and [apostolic] tradition."[33]

Some of the Fathers defended the use of Sacred Tradition with the same New Testament verses we have just examined. For example, citations of 2 Thessalonians 2:15 in defense of authoritative apostolic teaching given to the Church through Tradition can be found in the writings of Saint Cyril of Jerusalem and Saint John Chrysostom.[34] In the previous chapter we learned how Saint Basil's doxology was challenged because it was not found in Scripture. Basil said in reply to his critics:

> If the greater number of our mysteries are admitted into our constitution without written authority, then, in company with the many others, let us receive this one. For I hold it apostolic to abide also by the unwritten traditions. "I praise you," it is said, that you remember me in all things, and keep the ordinances as I delivered them to you [1 Cor 11:2]; and "Hold fast the traditions which you have been taught whether by word, or our Epistle" [2 Thess 2:15].[35]

Two centuries earlier Saint Irenaeus practiced this same reverence toward tradition, saying, "For, although the languages of the

[32] St. Clement of Rome, *1 Clement* 7, in *The Apostolic Fathers*, trans. Kirsopp Lake, vol. 1 (London: W. Heinemann, 1912).

[33] Origen, *De Principiis*, preface, 2.

[34] St. Cyril of Jerusalem said, "Just as the mustard seed in one small grain contains many branches, so also this Faith has embraced in few words all the knowledge of godliness in the Old and New Testaments. Take heed then, brethren, and hold fast the traditions which you now receive, and write them on the table of your heart." *Catechetical Lecture* 5. St. John Chrysostom likewise said, "Not by letters alone did Paul instruct his disciple in his duty, but before by words also which he shows, both in many other passages, as where he says, whether by word or our Epistle 2 Thessalonians 2:15, and especially here. Let us not therefore suppose that anything relating to doctrine was spoken imperfectly. For many things he delivered to him without writing." *Homilies on Second Timothy* 3.1.

[35] St. Basil of Caesarea, *On the Holy Spirit* 29.71.

world are dissimilar, yet the import of the tradition is one and the same."[36] However, Webster claims that "to Irenaeus, tradition is simply another term for the oral proclamation of the truth of Scripture in preaching, teaching or creedal statements. It is not an independent source of revelation but a verbal presentation of the one authoritative revelation of God—the Holy Scriptures."[37]

It's true that the content of Scripture was handed down in the Church and thus formed part of Tradition. But it doesn't follow that Tradition is merely the rearticulation of what Christians learned from Scripture. Irenaeus explains how Tradition includes not just a passing on of the truths found in Scripture, but also a passing on of *truths about truths found in Scripture*:

> Suppose there arise a dispute relative to some important question among us, should we not have recourse to the most ancient Churches with which the apostles held constant intercourse, and learn from them what is certain and clear in regard to the present question? For how should it be if the apostles themselves had not left us writings? Would it not be necessary, [in that case,] to follow the course of the tradition which they handed down to those to whom they did commit the Churches?[38]

According to non-Catholic Church historian Jaroslav Pelikan's study of Irenaeus, "So palpable was this apostolic tradition that even if the apostles had not left behind the Scriptures to serve as normative evidence of their doctrine, the church would still be in a position to follow 'the structure of the tradition which they handed on to those to whom they committed the churches'."[39]

## Objections to Sacred Tradition

Geisler and MacKenzie advance several objections to Sacred Tradition including the claim that "oral traditions are notoriously unreliable.

---

[36] St. Irenaeus, *Against Heresies* 1.10.2.

[37] Webster, *Church of Rome at the Bar of History*, 25.

[38] St. Irenaeus, *Against Heresies* 3.4.1.

[39] Jaroslav Pelikan, *The Christian Tradition: A History of the Development of Doctrine*, vol. 1, *The Emergence of the Catholic Tradition (100–600)* (Chicago: University of Chicago Press, 1971), 116.

They are the stuff of which legends and myths are made."[40] However, in another context describing the Old Testament, Geisler says,
"Oral tradition was very important in the Jewish culture and served
as one of the main ways to transfer information, among many other
things."[41] Similarly, in a work defending the reliability of the Gospels, Geisler says, "First-century people in Palestine, by necessity,
developed strong memories in order to remember and pass on information.... In such an oral culture, facts about Jesus may have been
put into a memorable form."[42]

If Geisler and MacKenzie believe that the Holy Spirit providentially
protected oral traditions that existed for centuries before the apostles
and their successors were born, as well as traditions that existed before the apostles wrote the New Testament, then they should believe
that the same Spirit could be protecting traditions that existed after
the time of the apostles.

The authors then claim, "It is utterly presumptuous to assert that
what a fallible human being writes is clearer than what the infallible
Word of God declares!"[43] But clarity and fallibility (or inerrancy)
are not related. A fallible human being can utter clear, theological
truths like "God exists." Conversely, the infallible Scriptures contain
statements that are difficult to understand (2 Pet 3:16), which is why
fallible human beings routinely write commentaries on the infallible
word of God.

This objection also assumes that fallible human beings did not write
Sacred Scripture and that Sacred Tradition is not the word of God.
But in an article for *Evangelical Quarterly* Geisler said of the Bible's
composition, "Some men freely chose to co-operate with the Spirit,
so that he could guide them in an errorless way. Or it may have been

[40] Norman L. Geisler and Ralph E. MacKenzie, *Roman Catholics and Evangelicals: Agreements and Differences* (Grand Rapids, MI: Baker Books, 1995), 194. John Armstrong likewise
says, "Oral transmission is far more subject to change, deviation, and corruption than written communication." John Armstrong, "The Authority of Scripture", in *Sola Scriptura! The
Protestant Position on the Bible*, ed. Don Kistler (Morgan, PA: Sola Deo Gloria Publications,
1995), 108.

[41] Joseph M. Holden and Norman Geisler, *The Popular Handbook of Archaeology and the Bible*
(Eugene, OR: Harvest House Publishers, 2013), 51.

[42] Norman L. Geisler and Frank Turek, *I Don't Have Enough Faith to Be an Atheist* (Wheaton, IL: Crossway, 2004), 245.

[43] Geisler and MacKenzie, *Roman Catholics and Evangelicals*, 190.

that the Holy Spirit simply chose to use those men and occasions which he infallibly knew would not produce error."[44]

So if God could providentially use fallible human beings to *write* the word of God without error, why couldn't he providentially use fallible human beings to *transmit* the word of God in a nonwritten form?

Next, Geisler and MacKenzie claim that there are contradictory oral traditions that make it impossible to trust tradition. It's true that some of the Church Fathers disagreed with one another, but that is not the same as saying there are "contradictory oral traditions". As we saw earlier, the *Catechism* speaks of the sayings of the Fathers as "a witness" to the life-giving presence of this Tradition (*CCC* 78). It does not say the writings of the Fathers are *identical* to Sacred Tradition. The Fathers of the Church were fallible and their writings are not inspired, but the Sacred Tradition that is present in these writings is inerrant and a part of divine revelation. A similar analogy can be drawn from Sacred Scripture.

Skeptics often say the Bible contains contradictory passages, and even many Protestants disagree with one another about the meaning of various Bible passages. But this only shows that certain *interpretations* of the Bible lead to contradictions, not that the Bible contains contradictions or error. In the same way, *expressions* of the Church's Sacred Tradition (including those found in some early Christian writings) may be in error, but the Sacred Traditions they do correctly describe are just as inerrant and authoritative as the written word of God.

At this point some Protestants will object that our analogy breaks down because the written word of God exists in the form of Sacred Scripture. Even if there are conflicting interpretations about it, at least we can agree on the makeup of the text we are trying to interpret.[45] The same, they say, is not true of Sacred Tradition. If past Christians can be wrong about Sacred Tradition, then how does the Church

---

[44] Norman L. Geisler, "Inerrancy and Free Will: A Reply to the Brothers Basinger", *Evangelical Quarterly* 57 (1985): 352. Cited in William Lane Craig, "Middle Knowledge & Biblical Inspiration", in *Oxford Readings in Philosophical Theology*, vol. 2, *Providence, Scripture, and Resurrection*, ed. Michael C. Rea (New York: Oxford University Press, 2009), 179–80.

[45] While there is wide agreement on the nature of the biblical text, there are still hundreds of variants in the Greek manuscripts that scholars disagree about, so it is not accurate to say there is complete agreement about the entire biblical text without question.

know which practices and beliefs they attest to are a part of Sacred Tradition and which are not? Does the Church merely "cherry-pick" from the Fathers in order to support her own doctrines by calling those select citations "Sacred Tradition"?

Unlike Sacred Scripture, Sacred Tradition is not expressed in a fixed, material reality (like words on parchment). Instead, it is a living, dynamic reality that exists in the form of the Church's lived teaching and practice (or orthodoxy and orthopraxy). Sacred Tradition is the way Christ's Church understands and lives out the faith, so it is not a concrete entity that one can simply locate like Scripture.

It is, however, an essential prerequisite to all the concrete realties that make up the faith, including Scripture and the creeds formed at ecumenical councils (i.e., these things are themselves products of Sacred Tradition). Since it is a reality that is lived out before it is passed on to successive generations of believers, the Church's understanding of Sacred Tradition grows and develops over time (just as her understanding of Sacred Scripture grows over time).

Some of the things the Church understands to be a part of Sacred Tradition come from the unanimous teaching of the Fathers (e.g., the Trinity, baptismal regeneration) or at least a substantial number of them (the perpetual virginity of Mary, opposition to millenarianism), so this is not a case of the Church merely "cherry-picking" a few patristic witnesses. Indeed, the idea that the Church simply proposes a doctrine ex nihilo and then scrambles to find patristic citations so that it can be located in "Sacred Tradition" does not represent the historical reality of how doctrine develops.

Rather, what happens is that the magisterial teaching authority of the Church recognizes something that has long been believed by the faithful (and probably been speculated about by theologians) but was never formally defined. When a heresy or dispute about this teaching arises, the Church decides whether it is prudent to intervene and declare that something is permissible to believe (but not required), propose it as a doctrine for belief on behalf of the Church, or require belief by infallibly defining it to have been divinely revealed.

A good example of such a development in doctrine would be the Monothelite heresy of the sixth and seventh centuries, which denied that Christ had both a truly human will and a truly divine will. Scripture does not explicitly discuss this matter, and the early Fathers did not explicitly address it in their christological writings. But Christ promised that the gates of hell would not prevail against the Church (Mt 16:18), so in the seventh century the Church examined the issue and rendered an infallible judgment against Monothelitism, labeling it a christological heresy at the Third Council of Constantinople (A.D. 680–681). This became a formal part of Sacred Tradition that even Protestant Christians recognize since most reject Monothelitism and recognize it as a heresy.

The Protestant apologist Chris Castaldo actually provides a helpful analogy related to the development of doctrine. He points out that when Protestants study the Old Testament they see allusions to Christ that later grow into explicit references in the New Testament like the protoevangelium in Genesis 3:15 or the messianic prophecies in Isaiah 53. He then writes,

> As Protestants look to the New Testament for clarity and definition of the seminal ideas that grow out of the Old Testament, Catholics rely on the teaching and practices of Church history for authoritative definition of ideas that they find in the Bible. Over time, century by century, the church recognizes that these ideas grow and develop, taking shape into specific formulations of doctrine.[46]

Ultimately, discussions with Protestants about Sacred Tradition or other sources of divine revelation seem to boil down to a search for the "ultimate authority". They might ask, "Who is the ultimate authority that determines Sacred Tradition? Who is the ultimate authority that determines the meaning of Sacred Scripture?" The simple answer is "God", but, of course, what they mean is what *human* authority tells us what God has revealed.

We have seen so far that Christ did not give us one ultimate authority in Scripture, nor did he give us this authority in Sacred Tradition alone. Neither is the Church some kind of tyrannical "ultimate authority". Instead, God has given believers his word both written and unwritten, as well as a Church that still possesses the teaching

---

[46] Christopher A. Castaldo, *Talking with Catholics about the Gospel: A Guide for Evangelicals* (Grand Rapids, MI: Zondervan, 2015), 89. Castaldo says he does not defend this practice but merely wants to explain it. He thinks that the arguments for *sola scriptura* are enough to refute Catholic claims about Sacred Tradition.

authority to listen to that word and teach its contents. In cases of doubt, it is the Church's role as the pillar and foundation of truth (1 Tim 3:15) to identify which items, among disputed traditions and writings, genuinely express the word of God. According to the Second Vatican Council:

> The task of authentically interpreting the word of God, whether written or handed on, has been entrusted exclusively to the living teaching office of the Church, whose authority is exercised in the name of Jesus Christ. This teaching office is not above the word of God, but serves it, teaching only what has been handed on, listening to it devoutly, guarding it scrupulously and explaining it faithfully in accord with a divine commission and with the help of the Holy Spirit, it draws from this one deposit of faith everything which it presents for belief as divinely revealed.[47]

## Catholic and Protestant Traditions

Even though Protestant apologists champion *sola scriptura* and reject the idea of sacred or authoritative tradition not explicitly found in Scripture, they can't live by this principle. Most of them, including scholars who have studied Scripture, believe in truths about the Christian faith that come from Tradition rather than Scripture. For example, most Protestants believe that general revelation ceased after the death of the last apostolic man. This means there will be no more additions to the Bible or public revelations such as the Book of Mormon, which portrays itself as "another testament of Jesus Christ".

Catholics also believe this, but not on the basis of what Scripture alone says.[48] For Protestants who derive their doctrines from Scripture alone, the closure of public revelation becomes a difficult doctrine to prove. Some have argued that this truth is described in Jude 3, which speaks of "the faith which was once for all delivered to the saints", but this verse on its own cannot support the claim that public revelation has ceased. Many scholars think Jude was a source for Second Peter, which means Second Peter would not be a part of

[47] *DV* 10.
[48] See *DV* 4.

divine revelation, since it was written after the faith was "once for all delivered to the saints".[49]

Even if Jude were the last book of the Bible to be written, that wouldn't prove public revelation ceased with the death of the last apostle. Protestant apologist John MacArthur says that the Greek word translated "delivered" in this verse "refers to an act completed in the past with no continuing element".[50] He also says the phrase "once for all" (Greek, *hapax*) means "nothing needs to be added to the faith that has been delivered 'once for all'." This would mean that the "faith" had been delivered before Jude was written, which means Jude and its teaching about the cessation of public revelation would not have been a part of that original Deposit of Faith. MacArthur even says this verse, "penned by Jude before the NT was complete, nevertheless looked forward to the completion of the entire canon".[51]

This shows that using Jude 3 to prove public revelation has ceased doesn't work because it confuses "giving the faith" to the saints with public revelation. Jesus gave "the faith" once and for all to the apostles, but the public revelation of the faith continued for decades after his interactions with them during the writing of the New Testament. There isn't any explicit biblical evidence that this revelation ceased after the death of the last apostle (or that it didn't continue for centuries rather than decades). There is also no evidence that there were no more living apostles who could give such revelations.

While membership among the Twelve was restricted to those who had accompanied Jesus during his ministry (Acts 1:21–22), this was not a prerequisite for being an apostle. Paul was an apostle (Gal 1:1; 1 Cor 9:1) along with Barnabas (Acts 14:14) even though the Bible never records either man meeting Jesus before his death in Jerusalem. In addition, there is no record of the resurrected Jesus appearing to Barnabas, which many Protestants say is a requirement for being an apostle. Even if this were a requirement, the Bible never says Jesus

---

[49] "Most scholars now believe that 2 Peter depends on Jude, questioning whether Jude would have written his letter otherwise, since he restated much of 2 Peter." Thomas Schreiner, *1, 2 Peter, Jude: An Exegetical and Theological Exposition of Holy Scripture* (Nashville, TN: B&H Publishing Group, 2003), 417–18.

[50] John MacArthur, "Does God Still Give Revelation?", *The Master's Seminar Journal* 14, no. 2 (Fall 2003): 231.

[51] Ibid., 230.

would stop appearing to people and commissioning them to be apostles. The absence of any living apostles would therefore be a truth of the faith that is known through tradition rather than Scripture.

Finally, perhaps the most obvious example of an authoritative, nonbiblical tradition that even Protestants recognize would be the canon of Scripture itself. Geisler and MacKenzie claim, "There is no evidence that all the revelation God gave [the apostles] to express was not inscripturated in the twenty-seven books of the New Testament."[52] But Geisler and MacKenzie are assuming that all the revelation God gave the apostles to express was inscripturated in the *twenty-seven books* of the New Testament. In trying to force Catholics to disprove *sola scriptura* (instead of proving there is no divine revelation outside Scripture), Geisler and MacKenzie assume a belief about the New Testament (i.e., that it has a certain number of books) that is not found in any of those books.

In other words, Geisler and MacKenzie's objection contains its own refutation because it relies on an extrabiblical Sacred Tradition. We will now examine this tradition, or the canon of Scripture, and show that it cannot be affirmed with certainty apart from the judgment of the Church.

---

[52] Geisler and MacKenzie, *Roman Catholics and Evangelicals*, 189.

# 3

# The Old Testament Canon

In 1566 a Jewish convert to Catholicism named Sixtus of Siena created a three-tiered classification system for the books of the Old Testament. At the top is the *protocanon*, the thirty-nine books of the Old Testament that Catholics and Protestants agree are the inspired word of God. At the bottom are the *apocrypha*, works that both Catholics and Protestants have not regarded as the inspired word of God, such as the book of Enoch.[1]

But between the protocanon and the apocrypha are a group of books Catholics believe to be inspired but Protestants do not. Sixtus calls these the *deuterocanonical* books, or the "second canon", though some Protestants number these books among the apocrypha. Included are seven books that were written between the years 200 B.C. and 50 B.C.: Tobit, Judith, Wisdom, Sirach, Baruch, and 1 and 2 Maccabees; also included are additions to the books of Daniel and Esther.

How one views these books is usually revealed in one of two questions the person asks about them. Those who ask, "Why are Catholic Bibles bigger than Protestant Bibles?" usually imply that Catholics must justify adding these books to the Bible. But the question can be turned around. One can also ask, "Why are Protestant Bibles smaller than Catholic Bibles?" That's because the larger Old Testament canon was the norm in Christian circles prior to the Reformation.

In order to defend a shorter Old Testament canon, Protestants must propose criteria that they say disqualifies the deuterocanonical books from the Bible but not the protocanonical books. These criteria include *external attestation*, or sources outside the Bible that

[1] Some Eastern Christians, including the Syrian and Ethiopian Orthodox churches, consider some of the apocryphal works to be canonical; examples include 1 Enoch and 2 Baruch.

argue against the inspired nature of these writings, and *internal composition*, or elements within these works that argue against their inspired nature. Likewise, Catholics who defend the sacred nature of these books appeal to sources inside and outside of the Bible that argue *for* the inspired nature of these writings. Let's begin with the criteria of internal composition and see if the deuterocanonical books themselves support or disqualify themselves from being considered Sacred Scripture.

## Arguments from Internal Composition

One element of internal composition that supports the inspiration of the deuterocanonical books is the absence of any discussion of a closed Hebrew canon. The current canon of the Hebrew Bible is divided into a threefold structure: "the Law" (which includes the first five books of the Bible called the Pentateuch), "the prophets", and "the writings", or in Hebrew, the *ketuvim*. Did the authors of the deuterocanonical books believe that the Hebrew canon was closed and therefore their works were not inspired contributions to the Bible?

The prologue to the book of Sirach is only aware of "the law and the prophets and the others that followed them" or "the law itself, the prophecies, and the rest of the books". Second Maccabees describes Judas the Maccabee encouraging his troops only with words "from the law and the prophets" (15:9). In fact, none of the authors of the deuterocanonical books refer to a formal list of "writings", or *ketuvim*, within a closed Hebrew canon that did not include their own works. According to Old Testament scholar Otto Kaiser, the deuterocanonical books "presuppose the validity of the Law and the Prophets and also utilize the Ketubim or 'Writings' collection which was, at the time, still in the process of formation and not yet closed."[2]

Some Protestants say the deuterocanonicals are not Scripture because they never *explicitly* claim to be inspired. However, many books of the Bible never claim to be inspired, and many nonbiblical

---

[2] Otto Kaiser, *Old Testament Apocrypha: An Introduction* (Peabody, MA: Hendrickson Publishers, 2004), 2.

works (e.g., the Book of Mormon) do claim to be inspired. Therefore, a mere claim to inspiration does not prove that fact, nor does the
absence of a claim to inspiration prove a work is not inspired. But do
the deuterocanonical books *deny* they are inspired?

Protestant apologist James McCarthy says the claim that these
books are inspired must be rejected because "the author of 2 Maccabees says that his work is the abridgement of another man's work
(2 Macc. 2:23). He concludes the book by saying, 'If it is well written and to the point, that is what I wanted; if it is poorly done and
mediocre, that is the best I could do' (2 Macc. 15:38, NAB)."[3] But
by McCarthy's standard the Gospel of Luke would not be inspired,
because it admits to being an adaptation of earlier sources (Lk 1:1–3).
First Corinthians would likewise be uninspired, because Paul says
he can't remember whom he baptized (1:15). These passages only
demonstrate the humility of the Bible's human authors—not any lack
of divine inspiration in their writings.

Geisler and MacKenzie say the deuterocanonicals are not inspired
because they lack miraculous "feats of nature" or "predictive prophecy" that are found in the protocanonical books of Scripture.[4] But
this criterion fails because if it were a sufficient condition for being
canonical, then it would include noncanonical works that abound in
the supernatural, like Homer and Herodotus. If it were a necessary
condition, then it would exclude mundane protocanonical books
such as Lamentations that lack both miracles and predictive prophecy.

Moreover, some of the deuterocanonical books do record miracles
(Tob 8:2–3), and others contain predictive prophecy. For example,
many Protestant scholars say Wisdom 2:12–20 is either a genuine
messianic prophecy or that Matthew used this passage as a template
when he described Jesus' Crucifixion.[5] The *Fortress Bible Commentary*
says that when it comes to the book of Baruch, "a number of church
fathers (including Irenaeus, Clement, Origen, Tertullian, Ambrose,
and Hilary) understood 3:37 (3:38 in the Greek), and Wisdom

---

[3] James McCarthy, *The Gospel according to Rome* (Eugene, OR: Harvest House Publishers,
1995), 338.
[4] Norman L. Geisler and Ralph E. MacKenzie, *Roman Catholics and Evangelicals: Agreements
and Differences* (Grand Rapids, MI: Baker Books, 1995), 167.
[5] Craig Keener, *The Gospel of Matthew: A Socio-Rhetorical Commentary* (Grand Rapids, MI:
Wm. B. Eerdmans, 2009), 682.

appearing on earth, by analogy with John 1:14, to refer to the incarnation of the Preexistent Christ."[6]

## Alleged Errors

Evangelical scholar Josh McDowell says the deuterocanonical books "abound in historical and geographical inaccuracies and anachronisms. They teach doctrines which are false and foster practices which are at variance with inspired Scripture."[7] But when Protestant apologists are shown similar difficulties in the protocanonical books of Scripture, they do not deny the inspiration of those books. Instead, they claim that these books only contain *apparent* errors rather than *actual* errors. According to Geisler:

> What is thus far unexplained is not therefore unexplainable. [The Christian scholar] does not assume that discrepancies are contradictions. And, when he encounters something for which he has no explanation, he simply continues to do research, believing that one will eventually be found.[8]

If the Protestant apologist is allowed to describe difficulties in the books of his Bible as being the result of "unexplained, apparent errors" that are waiting to be resolved, then Catholic apologists are justified in using the same approach for difficulties in the deuterocanonical books of Scripture. As Catholic apologist Gary Michuta puts it, "The question of inspiration must be answered before the question of inerrancy, since the doctrine of inerrancy flows from the doctrine of inspiration."[9]

Moreover, the alleged errors in the deuterocanonical books, such as Judith identifying Nebuchadnezzar as the king of Assyria instead

---

[6] Karina Martin Hogan, "Baruch", in *Fortress Commentary on the Bible: The Old Testament and Apocrypha*, ed. Gale A. Yee, Hugh R. Page, and Matthew J. M. Coomber (Minneapolis: Fortress Press, 2014), 1030.

[7] Josh McDowell, *The New Evidence That Demands a Verdict* (Nashville, TN: Thomas Nelson, 1999), 29.

[8] Norman L. Geisler and Thomas Howe, *The Big Book of Bible Difficulties* (Grand Rapids, MI: Baker Books, 1999), 15.

[9] Gary Michuta, *The Case for the Deuterocanon: Evidence and Arguments* (Livonia, MI: Nikaria Press, 2015), 349.

of as the king of Babylon (Jud 1:1), or Tobit being described as having lived for more than 150 years (Tob 14:11), can be explained. Specifically, these statements are only errors if the author was asserting a literal description of history, but even Protestant scholars agree that the authors of Judith and Tobit were not writing in the genre of literal history.

When it comes to the book of Tobit, Martin Luther called it a "pious comedy",[10] Bruce Metzger called it an "adventure story",[11] and J. C. Dancy called it a "folk tale".[12] Kaiser called it a "didactic narrative" based on "fairy tale and biblical motifs".[13] Kaiser goes on to say, however, that in spite of its motifs, Tobit "is no fairy tale. Based on its content, it may more readily be characterized as a wisdom moral tale with didactic tendencies, although this does not sufficiently describe its literary form."[14] Pope John Paul II said that "the Books of Tobit, Judith, and Esther, although dealing with the history of the Chosen People, have the character of allegorical and moral narrative rather than history properly so called."[15]

Concerning Judith, Luther said it was fictional due to its titular character Judith (a name that literally means "Lady Jew") being a symbol for the Jewish people.[16] In his commentary on the book, Carey Moore says the author's apparent gaffe about Nebuchadnezzar is "no slip of the pen". His excellent understanding of history in the fifth chapter means the obvious anachronisms in the first chapter must have an intentional, nonliteral purpose. Moore even says that if the author of Judith read his work aloud, "he would have given his listeners a slight smile or a sly wink".[17] Kaiser agrees and says,

---

[10] J. C. Dancy, *The Shorter Books of the Apocrypha* (Cambridge: Cambridge University Press, 1972), 1.

[11] Bruce Metzger, *An Introduction to the Apocrypha* (New York: Oxford University Press, 1957), 31.

[12] Dancy, *Shorter Books of the Apocrypha*, 1.

[13] Kaiser, *Old Testament Apocrypha*, 30.

[14] Ibid., 30–31.

[15] John Paul II, General Audience (May 8, 1985), in "The Light of Revelation in the Old Testament: Catechesis by Pope John Paul II on God the Father", Totus2us, accessed July 7, 2017, http://www.totus2us.com/teaching/jpii-catechesis-on-god-father-creator/the-light-of-revelation-in-the-old-testament/.

[16] Metzger, *Introduction to the Apocrypha*, 51.

[17] Carey Moore, *Judith* (New York: Doubleday, 1985), 79.

"Judith 1:1 already shows anyone who knows the history of Israel and of the ancient Near East that Judith is fiction."[18]

James White calls this approach to the alleged errors in books like Judith an "imaginative" solution, which implies that it is ad hoc and unsound, but he does not interact with any evidence for the nonliteral nature of these texts.[19] Scholars of Hellenistic Jewish literature, on the other hand, are well aware of how ancient authors used anachronism in order to underscore the didactic nature of their historical fiction.

For example, language scholar Sara Johnson says the inaccuracies in Judith aren't a playful disregard for historical accuracy, but rather a "tour de force of deliberate historical fiction".[20] She writes, "Historical absurdities did not apparently bother the original authors or audiences of these fictions, but they certainly do disturb modern editors and readers."[21] The fact that many alleged anachronisms occur in the very first lines of these books signals to the reader that what he is about to read should not be taken literally.

Claims that the deuterocanonical books contradict theological truths in the protocanonical books also fall flat. One example is the claim that the teaching that honoring one's father and almsgiving can atone for sin (Sir 3:3; Tob 4:11) contradicts the New Testament's teaching that only Christ can atone for our sins. But the book of Proverbs teaches that "by loyalty and faithfulness [or what many Protestants would call 'works'] iniquity is atoned for" (16:6). First Peter says that "love covers a multitude of sin" (4:8), and Acts records an angel saying to the Gentile Cornelius, "Your prayers and your alms have ascended as a memorial before God" (10:4).

Other claims of theological contradiction are circular, such as the claim that Second Maccabees is not inspired because it records the "unbiblical practice" of praying for the dead. But Protestants only say the practice is "unbiblical" because they do not regard Second Maccabees as part of the Bible. If Second Maccabees is inspired,

[18] Kaiser, *Old Testament Apocrypha*, 41.

[19] James R. White, *Scripture Alone: Exploring the Bible's Accuracy, Authority and Authenticity* (Bloomington, MN: Bethany House, 2004), 113.

[20] Sara Johnson, *Historical Fictions and Hellenistic Jewish Identity: Third Maccabees in Its Cultural Context* (Los Angeles: University of California Press, 2004), 25.

[21] Ibid., 24.

however, then praying for the dead *is* a biblical practice even if it is only described in one book of the Bible. To make a comparison, the Gospel of Matthew is the only book in the Bible that records a Trinitarian baptismal command (28:19), but that doesn't make such a command "unbiblical".

Finally, some Protestant apologists say the deuterocanonical books are not inspired because they are inferior in style to the protocanonical books of Scripture. Raymond Surburg writes, "When a comparison is instituted of the style of the Apocrypha with the style of the Biblical Hebrew Old Testament writings, there is a considerable inferiority, shown by the stiffness, lack of originality and artificiality of expression characterizing the apocryphal books."[22]

But this is a wholly subjective criterion that, if taken seriously, would put Shakespeare in the Bible and take books like Numbers or Philemon out of it. This argument also ignores the work of Protestant writers like Bruce Metzger or Martin Luther whom we cited earlier who affirm the literary quality of some deuterocanonical books even though they deny that those books are inspired Scripture.

Now, let's turn to the criteria of external attestation and see if it is true, as some Protestant apologists allege, that "there is virtually an unbroken line of support from ancient to modern times for rejecting the [deuterocanonical books] as part of the canon."[23]

## Jewish Evidence (200 B.C.–A.D. 150)

The composition of the deuterocanonical books ended at around the beginning of the first century before Christ. One example of external attestation from this time period is the Dead Sea Scrolls, which are a collection of nearly one thousand writings composed between the years 400 B.C. and A.D. 100.

---

[22] Raymond Surburg, *Christian News*, November 24, 1980, p. 7. The seventeenth-century Reformed theologian Francis Turretin makes a similar argument: "The style does not equal the majesty and simplicity of the divine style, but is redolent of the evil and weakness of human learning, with folly, flattery, conceit, affectation, pseudoerudition and false eloquence, all of which occur frequently (non raro), there is in [these books] so much that is not only inconsequential and frivolous, but also false, superstitious, and contradictory, that it is very plain that [these books] were of human, not divine, composition." *The Doctrine of Scripture* 9.4.

[23] Geisler and MacKenzie, *Roman Catholics and Evangelicals*, 167.

Not every deuterocanonical book of Scripture is found among the scrolls, but not every protocanonical book is found there either (specifically, Esther is missing). Geisler and MacKenzie admit that fragments of Sirach, Tobit, and Baruch have been found at Qumran and other Dead Sea scroll archaeological sites, but they say the absence of commentaries on these texts as well as their not being penned with special parchment or script "indicates that the Qumran community did not view the apocryphal books as canonical".[24] But Geisler and MacKenzie's arguments are both irrelevant and factually inaccurate.

They are irrelevant because there are no commentaries at Qumran for most of the protocanonical books of the Old Testament. They are inaccurate because deuterocanonical books like Sirach were penned in a special sticho-graphical style that is unique to writings the Qumran community considered to be Scripture. According to Dead Sea scholar Emanuel Tov, "There is a special layout for poetical units that is almost exclusive to biblical texts (including Ben Sira), and is not found in any of the non-biblical poetical compositions from the Judean desert."[25]

It is also true, as Geisler and MacKenzie claim, that the Jewish philosopher Philo (20 B.C.–A.D. 40) does not cite the deuterocanonical books in his writings. This is not surprising given that of the nearly two thousand biblical citations in his work, only fifty come from outside the Pentateuch.[26] According to the *Cambridge History of the Bible*, Philo also did not quote from "Ezekiel, Song of Songs, Ruth, Lamentations, Ecclesiastes, Esther, and Daniel".[27]

Two other important Jewish witnesses to the Hebrew canon of the Bible in the first century are the historian Josephus and rabbinical commentaries from the first and second century after Christ.

---

[24] Ibid., 165.

[25] Emanuel Tov, *Textual Criticism of the Hebrew Bible* (Minneapolis: Fortress Press, 2012), 202. Cited in Michuta, *Case for the Deuterocanon*, 102–3.

[26] Ralph Brucker, "Observations on the Wirkungsgesschichte of the Septuagint Psalms in Ancient Judaism and Early Christianity", in *Septuagint Research: Issues and Challenges in the Study of the Greek Jewish Scriptures*, ed. Wolfgang Kraus and R. Glenn Wooden (Atlanta: Society of Biblical Literature, 2004), 358. Brucker also cites F. H. Coulson, "Philo's Quotations from the Old Testament", JTS 41 (1940): 238, as saying that for "about 2000 citations, fifty [are] not from the Pentateuch."

[27] G. W. Anderson, "Canonical and Non-Canonical", *The Cambridge History of the Bible: From the Beginnings to Jerome*, vol. 1, ed. P. R. Ackroyd and C. F. Evans (Cambridge: Cambridge University Press, 1970), 148.

Concerning Josephus, some Protestants cite his mention of twenty-two books of sacred history that terminate in the reign of Artaxeres of Persia (465–424 B.C.) as evidence that the Hebrew canon was closed before the deuterocanonical books were written. They first claim that these twenty-two books only account for the thirty-nine books of the Protestant Old Testament. Then they claim that this testimony proves there were no prophets in Israel during the time when the deuterocanonicals were composed, which means they can't be inspired Scripture. Turretin said of Josephus, "The writings of his people after the time of Artaxeres are not of equal trustworthiness and authority with the earlier ones, as not being in the true succession of the prophets."[28]

But Josephus only says *the exact line of succession* among the prophets had ceased by the death of Artaxeres, not that the divine gift of prophecy itself was no more.[29] Josephus describes several prophets during the intertestamental period such as John Hyrcanus and Manaemus the Essene as well as Jesus, son of Ananus, before the First Jewish-Roman War (A.D. 66–73).[30] The New Testament says Jesus was considered a prophet (Mt 21:11; Lk 7:16), and Jesus explicitly says that John the Baptist was a prophet (Mt 11:9–10), which would not make sense if Jews believed the gift of prophecy had ceased centuries earlier at the death of Artaxeres of Persia.

Scholars also recognize that Josephus used exaggerated language when he extolled the virtues of Judaism over its pagan competitors. His mention of the number of books in the Hebrew canon is found in his polemic against the Egyptian writer Apion, where he also boasts that "from their very birth" all Jews know and esteem the books of the Bible. Josephus speaks of how "no one has ventured to add, or to remove, or to alter a syllable"[31] of the Hebrew Scriptures, even

---

[28] Turretin, *Doctrine of Scripture* 9.3.

[29] In response some critics cite 1 Maccabees 9:27, which says, "There was great distress in Israel, such as had not been since the time that prophets ceased to appear among them." But the author of Maccabees does not say that there would never be any future prophets, nor does he tells us when the prophets ceased to appear among the people. Since prophetic activity was not continual but intermittent in the Old Testament, it would not be surprising to see this kind of revelation in the intertestamental period as well.

[30] See Josephus, *Antiquities of the Jews* 13.8; 15.10.5; and *War of the Jews* 6.5.3.

[31] Josephus, *Against Apion* I. Cited in Lee Martin McDonald, *The Origin of the Bible: A Guide for the Perplexed* (London: T&T Clark, 2011), 66.

though modern scholarship has shown there were multiple Hebrew manuscript traditions at this time.

In his study of Josephus and the Hebrew canon, Jonathan Campbell points out that the roughly contemporaneous text of 4 Ezra assumes the existence of ninety-four Jewish Scriptures (which is probably a combination of the symbolic numbers twenty-four and seventy). Josephus' list of the Hebrew canon also includes the symbolic number twenty-two, which is the number of letters in the Hebrew alphabet. Campbell states that when it comes to claims about a universal Hebrew canon that has never been altered, "Josephus' rhetoric has run ahead of reality.... [It undermines] the theory that there was a single canon by the late first century C.E."[32]

That the Jews were not entirely unified on the issue of the canon is evident in rabbinical writings from the early second century after Christ. The Talmudic tract *Sanhedrin 100B* refers to rabbis "withdrawing" Sirach, or declaring it to be no longer inspired and thus withdrawn from synagogue reading. Rabbi Akiba Ben Joseph condemned Jews who continued to read from Hebrew books written after Sirach. He said, "The Gospels and heretical books do not defile the hands. The books of Ben Sira and all other books written from then on do not defile the hands."[33] In other words, these books are not holy like the Torah, and so they do not make the reader "impure" in comparison when they are held in one's hand.

Rabbi Akiba's second-century declaration in particular shows that enough Jews were reading these books that a leading rabbi at the time had to declare that for him and those of his school of thought they were not Scripture. This means that there was no single, closed Hebrew canon during the time of Christ, and some Jews considered the deuterocanonical books to be Scripture.

## Christian Evidence (A.D. 50–A.D. 100)

The most obvious example of divergence of thought among first-century Jews on the canon is that the Sadducees only regarded

[32] Jonathan G. Campbell, "Josephus' Twenty-Two Book Canon and the Qumran Scrolls", in *The Scrolls and Biblical Traditions: Proceedings of the Seventh Meeting of the Ioqs in Helsinki*, edited by George Brooke et al. (Leiden: Brill, 2012), 41, 43.

[33] Akiba Ben Joseph, *Tosefta Yadayim* 2.13. Cited in Michuta, *Case for the Deuterocanon*, 55.

the Pentateuch as being authoritative. For example, the Sadducees denied the existence of a future resurrection (Mk 12:18; Acts 23:8) even though the prophets explicitly speak of the resurrection of the dead (Dan 12:2).[34] Lee Martin McDonald says of the Sadducees, "Given what we read about them in the New Testament and the early Church fathers, this leads us to conclude that their Scriptures were different from those adopted by the Pharisees or the Essenes."[35]

Scholars agree that the New Testament primarily cites from the Septuagint, and the first-century Septuagint contained the deutero-canonical books. Timothy Michael Law, who serves as the co-editor of the *Oxford Handbook on the Septuagint*, says these books "were included in the Septuagint" and that "it would also be mistaken to imagine that they have never been read as divine scripture."[36]

In response to this evidence Ron Rhodes claims that none of the Septuagint manuscripts prior to the fourth century after Christ contain the deuterocanonical books. But all the manuscripts prior to this time are fragmentary, and so they lack many books in the protocanon as well. Rhodes even seems to realize this and says, "If a first-century manuscript were found with the Apocrypha in the Septuagint, that still does not mean the Apocrypha belong in the canon." Rhodes makes this claim based on the fact that "there is not a single quote from the Apocrypha in [the apostles']

---

[34] Roger Beckwith counters this argument by saying, "It could equally well be argued that since the Sadducees rejected belief in angels (which appear in Gen. 19:1,15; 28:12; 32:1 etc.) the Pentateuch cannot have been in their canon either." Roger Beckwith, *The Old Testament Canon of the New Testament Church: And Its Background in Early Judaism* (Eugene, OR: Wipf and Stock, 1985), 87–88. However, it may be the case that the Sadducees only denied that divine revelation came by spirits or angels, not the existence of those beings themselves. Citing earlier research on the Sadducees and angels by Bernard Bamberger and Solomon Zeitlin, Kristian Bendoraitis writes, "Bamberger cites rabbinic evidence that is adverse toward the cult of angels, not to angels themselves. According to Zeitlin, the function of an angel had ceased at the advent of prophecy. In this way, the Sadducees would disregard what Paul was saying since it was revealed to him by a spirit or angel (Acts 23:9)." It's also possible that this was a reference to states of being that exist before the resurrection for human beings, such as being a disembodied spirit, and not to a denial of angels themselves. Kristian Bendoraitis, *"Behold, the Angels Came and Served Him": A Compositional Analysis of Angels in Matthew* (London: Bloomsbury T&T Clark, 2015), 149.

[35] Lee Martin McDonald, *The Biblical Canon: Its Origin, Transmission, and Authority* (Grand Rapids, MI: Baker Academic, 2007), 142.

[36] Timothy Michael Law, *When God Spoke Greek* (New York: Oxford University Press, 2013), 59–60.

writings."[37] McCarthy likewise claims, "Though the New Testament quotes virtually every book of the Old Testament, there is not a single quotation from the Apocrypha."[38]

First, it would be odd if Jesus and the apostles quoted from a translation of the Scriptures that contained seven uninspired writings. Since they never warned their listeners to avoid these writings, we can infer they considered the Septuagint to be Scripture.[39] Second, as Metzger observes, "nowhere in the New Testament is there a direct quotation from the canonical books of Joshua, Judges, Chronicles, Ezra, Nehemiah, Esther, Ecclesiastes, the Song of Solomon, Obadiah, Zephaniah, and Nahum; and the New Testament allusions to them are few in number."[40]

Third, there are significant allusions in the New Testament to the deuterocanonical books. According to Methodist scholar David A. deSilva, "New Testament authors weave phrases and recreate lines of arguments from Apocryha books into their new texts. They also allude to events and stories contained in these texts. The word 'paraphrase' very frequently provides adequate description of the relationship."[41]

When Protestant apologists confront the New Testament allusions to the deuterocanonicals, they often point out that other nonbiblical works such as the book of Enoch or the Greek poet Menander are also alluded to or even directly quoted in the New Testament (e.g., Jud 14; 1 Cor 15:33, respectively). Mere allusions to the deuterocanonical books, they say, are insufficient to prove that the authors of the New Testament considered these books to be inspired.

Of course, this makes the requirement that the deuterocanonical books be quoted in the New Testament a classic case of "heads

[37] Ron Rhodes, *Reasoning from the Scriptures with Catholics* (Eugene, OR: Harvest House Publishing, 2000), 39.

[38] McCarthy, *Gospel according to Rome*, 338.

[39] Some apologists also claim Jesus' reference to "the blood of Abel" and "the blood of Zechariah" (Lk 11:50) is describing a prophet from the first book of the Bible (Genesis) and the last book (2 Chronicles) of what is now the current Hebrew canon. But the assumptions this argument requires, like the identity of the Zechariah being mentioned or the position of 2 Chronicles among the Old Testament scrolls in Jesus' time, are far too tenuous to allow any conclusions to be drawn from a reference Jesus made that was not about the canon of Scripture but the hypocrisy of the Pharisees.

[40] Metzger, *Introduction to the Apocrypha*, 171.

[41] David A. deSilva, *Introducing the Apocrypha: Message, Context, and Significance* (Grand Rapids, MI: Baker Academic, 2004), 22.

I win, tails you lose." The absence of deuterocanonical quotations proves that the apostles did not consider them to be inspired, but even if they were present, any such quotations would prove nothing since the apostles also quote other uninspired works. What can't be dismissed, however, is that the authors of the New Testament allude to the deuterocanonical books in order to describe events in salvation history or to affirm divine prophecy, which they don't do with their citations of pagan literature.

In Matthew 27:43 the chief priests say of the crucified Jesus, "He trusts in God; let God deliver him now, if he desires him; for he said, 'I am the Son of God.'" The passage parallels Psalm 22:8 ("let him rescue him, for he delights in him!"), but that verse does not mention the Son of God. However, the 1611 King James Bible cross-references this passage with Wisdom 2:18: "For if the righteous man is God's son, he will help him, and will deliver him from the hand of his adversaries."

Hebrews 11:35 describes a group of people in the Old Testament period who "were tortured, refusing to accept release, that they may rise again to a better life." The only record of this is found in 2 Maccabees 7, which describes brothers who accept torture at the hands of the Seleucids instead of eating pork and violating Jewish law. Since the context of Hebrews 11 includes "the men of old [who] received divine approval" (v. 2), it follows that the books describing the Maccabean martyrs were part of the Old Testament that was used by the author of the Letter to the Hebrews.[42]

Other Protestant apologists claim that because "the Jews [were] entrusted with the oracles of God", as Paul says in Romans 3:2, this means Christians should imitate modern Jews and reject the deuterocanonical books of Scripture.[43] Geisler and MacKenzie claim, "Since the New Testament explicitly states that Israel was entrusted with the oracles of God and was the recipient of the covenants and the Law (Rom. 3:2), the Jews should be considered the custodians of the limits of their own canon. And they have always rejected the Apocrypha."[44] But even today, not all Jews are in agreement on the canon of Scripture since Ethiopic Jews accept the deuterocanonical

---

[42] Michuta, *Case for the Deuterocanon*, 13.
[43] Turretin, *Doctrine of Scripture* 9.3. See also White, *Scripture Alone*, 113.
[44] Geisler and MacKenzie, *Roman Catholics and Evangelicals*, 169.

books.[45] The situation was even more diverse in the first century, when different groups of Jews—Sadducees, Pharisees, Essenes, and others—accepted different books as sacred and canonical.

The only group that survived and prospered in the wake of the Jewish-Roman wars was the Pharisees, and they became influential in modern, rabbinic Judaism, while the other schools of thought passed from the scene. But even the rabbis continued to debate the precise boundaries of their canon for centuries afterward. Consequently, it does not make sense to look at a single surviving Jewish school of thought, however influential, and treat it as if it represented the opinion of all Jews in the first century or to make it normative for Christians.

Further, Romans 3:2 says nothing about the authority of the Jewish people to determine the canon of Scripture. Paul is merely saying that even though both Jews and Gentiles are guilty of committing grave sin, Jews have an advantage over the Gentiles because God gave them divine revelation. As N. T. Wright and A. T. Robertson point out, Paul's use of the peculiar phrase "the oracles of God" may mean Paul was talking not about Scripture per se but about the general concept of divine revelation.[46]

In any case, if this passage meant the Jews were entrusted with determining the canonical status of all written divine revelation, then the New Testament would not be canonical, because the majority of Jews rejected it.[47] Indeed, if the beliefs of non-Christian Jews were normative for Christians, then we would have to exclude the entire New Testament from the canon. The early Christians, who wrote and

[45] Adele Berlin and Maxine Grossman, eds., *The Oxford Dictionary of the Jewish Religion* (New York: Oxford University Press, 2011), 125.

[46] N. T. Wright says Paul uses this word to refer to Israel's commission to share the law with the Gentiles. He writes, "Nowhere else in early Christian writings are Israel's scripture designated as 'Gods oracles'.... Israel was 'entrusted with [what the Gentile nations might have perceived as] divine oracles.'" N. T. Wright, *Pauline Perspectives: Essays on Paul* (Minneapolis: Fortress Press, 2013), 491. A. T. Robertson says this may just refer to "the commands and promises of God". A. T. Robertson, *Word Pictures in the New Testament: The Epistles of Paul*, vol. 4 (Nashville, TN: Broadman, 1931), 33.

[47] Discussions of second-century Judaism and the Old Testament canon usually bring up the so-called Jewish Council of Jamnia (or Yavne) that closed the Old Testament canon in A.D. 90. Modern scholarship, while allowing for the possibility that discussions about the canon took place at Jamnia, has abandoned the theory that this council authoritatively closed the canon of the Hebrew Bible. For a good overview, see Jack P. Lewis, "Jamnia Revisited", in *The Canon Debate*, ed. Lee M. McDonald and James A. Sanders (Grand Rapids, MI: Baker Academic, 2002).

received the New Testament, did not view the canon in their day as being closed, and from a Christian point of view, the decision of later non-Christian Jews cannot determine the biblical canon.

## Pre-Nicene Church Fathers (A.D. 90–A.D. 325)

Protestant apologists usually say a significant number of Church Fathers rejected the deuterocanonical books, so modern Christians are right to doubt the validity of these books. Of the Christians who wrote before the Council of Nicaea, two are usually mentioned: Melito, the bishop of Sardis (a town that now lies in present-day western Turkey), and Origen.

At the beginning of the first century, Melito wrote a work entitled *Extracts*, which the Protestant historian Philip Schaff calls "a collection of testimonies to Christ and Christianity ... in which appeal was made from the Old Testament—the common ground accepted by both parties".[48] The *Extracts* has been lost, but the fourth-century historian Eusebius quoted its introduction where Melito says he "went East and came to the place where these things were preached and done, [and] learned accurately the books of the Old Testament".[49]

Melito's list of the Old Testament books lacks the deuterocanonicals, but this is not surprising given that many second-century Jews rejected the deuterocanonical books. The Protestant citation of Melito only helps their case if Melito was listing the *Christian* canon of the Old Testament. But because Melito was composing a defense of Christ from sources Jews would accept, we would expect Melito's canon in his *Extracts* to reflect what Jews in his time accepted. In *Hebrew Scripture in Patristic Biblical Theory*, Edmon Gallagher says, "Most scholars have been willing to attribute [Melito's] list ultimately to Jewish Sources."[50]

---

[48] Philip Schaff and Henry Wace, *A Select Library of Nicene and Post-Nicene Fathers of the Christian Church*, 2nd series, vol. 1, *Eusebius* (New York: Christian Literature, 1886), 206.

[49] Eusebius, *Church History* 4.26.14.

[50] Edmon Gallagher, *Hebrew Scripture in Patristic Biblical Theory* (Leiden; Boston: Brill Academic Publishers, 2012), 23. Even Roger Beckwith, who defends the Protestant position on the Old Testament, says that the similarities between Melito's list and the Jewish canon represent "exceptional knowledge of Jewish tradition" in the allegedly Palestinian churches Beckwith claims Melito visited instead. Beckwith, *Old Testament Canon of the New Testament Church*, 185.

The fact that Melito went all the way to Israel (or the "eastern place") instead of asking the Jews in Sardis about the Old Testament canon shows, as we noted earlier, that there was not a consensus among second-century Jews about the canon of the Hebrew Bible. McDonald says, "Not all Josephus scholars agree with Josephus's account that all Jews everywhere both know and would die for these twenty-two sacred books.... Why did [Melito] not go across the street and talk to the nearest Jew to find out, if the matter was well known long before his time?"[51]

What about Origen? He often cited apocryphal works but was careful to distinguish them from Scripture.[52] When he referred to Sirach, Wisdom, Judith, deuetro-Daniel, and Maccabees, however, he called these books "holy scripture" or "scripture".[53] He said Tobit is read "in all the churches"[54] and used deutero-Daniel in a theological discussion with Julius Africanus.[55]

The only place where Origen is said to have "denied" the deuterocanonical books is a fragment recorded in Eusebius where Origen says, "The canonical books, as the Hebrews have handed them down, are twenty two; corresponding with the number of their letters."[56] Origen then lists the modern Hebrew canon but without the minor prophets (which may have been omitted as a typographical error).

The problem with relying on Origen's list is that it is an allegorical explanation for the number of books in the Old Testament canon as *handed down by the Jews*, not Christians. Origen even makes a habit of "investigating the Jewish Scriptures, and comparing them with ours, and noticing their various readings".[57] As Geofrey Hahneman says in his study of the biblical canon, "Both lists that Melito and Origen

---

[51] Lee Martin McDonald, *Formation of the Bible: The Story of the Church's Canon* (Peabody, MA: Hendrickson Publishers, 2012), 50.

[52] For example, he said, "Books which bear the name Enoch do not at all circulate in the Churches as divine." Origen, *Against Celsus* 5.54. It turns out, however, that this is not correct. The book of Enoch was accepted as Scripture by some early Christians, including Irenaeus (*Against Heresies* 4.16.2) and Origin's older contemporary, Tertullian (*On Idolatry* 15). It is also accepted as canonical by some Christians today (i.e., Abyssinians).

[53] Michuta, *Case for the Deuterocanon*, 150–60.

[54] Origen, *Epistle to Africanus* 13

[55] Ibid., 11.

[56] Eusebius, *Church History* 6.25.

[57] Origen, *Epistle to Africanus* 5.

presented are clearly Jewish catalogues and not Christian ones."[58] He
then makes this observation:

> [Origen] noted, for instance, that the Jews did not use Tobit and
> Judith, to which the churches did appeal (*Ad Africanum* 13.3). Origen
> appears to have suggested confinement by Christians to the Jewish
> canon only for polemical purposes with Jewish opponents (*Ad Africa-
> num* 5.13). A similar need may lie behind Melito's list for he is known
> to have made a collection of testimonies from the Jewish canon (Euse-
> bius, He 4.26.12,14).[59]

Another point to mention is that if being present in either Melito's
or Origen's lists were necessary for canonicity, then Esther and Lamentations would be disqualified since they are absent from both lists.
In *The Old Testament in Early Christianity*, Earl Ellis leans toward the
probability that Esther "was not recognized as Scripture by Melito's
informants".[60]

Finally, the weakness of citing Origen's and Melito's lists is
exposed when we compare them to the seventy-plus citations of
the deuterocanonical books that can be found in the works by the
pre-Nicene Fathers Clement of Rome, Irenaeus, Athenagoras,
Clement of Alexandria, Methodius, and Cyprian (not to mention
the dozens of citations found in Origen's own works).[61] Jerome even
tells us that at the Council of Nicaea the deuterocanonical work of
Judith was considered to be a part of the canon of Scriptures.[62] As the
Anglican scholar J. N. D. Kelly said, for the great majority of the early
Church Fathers, "the deuterocanonical writings ranked as scripture
in the fullest sense."[63]

---

[58] Geofrey Hahneman, *The Muratorian Fragment and the Development of the Canon* (Oxford:
Clarendon Press, 1992), 77.

[59] Ibid.

[60] Earl Ellis, *The Old Testament in Early Christianity* (Eugene, OR: Wipf and Stock, 2003), 11.

[61] For a list of citations, see Michuta, *Case for the Deuterocanon*, 113–19 and 138–60.

[62] This can be found in Jerome's prologue to Judith in the Vulgate. I owe this observation
to Jimmy Akin; see his article "The First Ecumenical Council on the Book of Judith?", *Catholic Answers Magazine*, August 13, 2013.

[63] J. N. D. Kelly, *Early Christian Doctrines* (New York: HarperCollins, 1978), 55. In response
to Kelly, Geisler and MacKenzie say this is "out of sync with the facts just cited by Beckwith"
(*Roman Catholics and Evangelicals*, 162), but I've shown that it is actually Beckwith who has
overstated his case, and so Kelly's verdict is vindicated by modern scholarship on the Old
Testament canon in patristic thought.

## Post-Nicene Church Fathers (A.D. 325–A.D. 600)

According to Roger Beckwith, who wrote an academic treatment on the Old Testament canon, when the Church Fathers cite the deuterocanonical books, many "do not give any indication that the book is regarded as Scripture".[64] But modern scholarship has shown Beckwith to be mistaken in his approach. David A. deSilva, who ultimately denies the inspiration of the deuterocanonical books, admits:

> Those who speak of the New Testament authors only rarely alluding to the books of the Apocrypha or admitting only "an occasional correspondence of thought" (Beckwith 1985: 387) are saying more about their ideological convictions about the apocrypha than about actual usage and influence, which actually are quite substantial.[65]

This same "substantial usage" can be seen in works by the Church Fathers; for example, Cyril of Jerusalem refers to Baruch as "the prophet", cites Baruch 3:35–37 in defense of the deity of Christ, and includes Baruch in the writings of Jeremiah in his list of the canon.[66] Athanasius likewise called Wisdom and Judith "Scripture" and appealed to Wisdom 7:25–27 as evidence for the deity of Christ.[67] But if that's true, then why did Cyril tell his catechumens to "read the two and twenty books [of the Hebrew canon] but have nothing to do with the apocryphal writings"?[68] Why did Athanasius not include the deuterocanonical books in his list of the canon of Scripture?

Regarding Cyril, he divided the Old Testament Scripture into three groups: the protocanonical works that catechumens should read, books of "secondary rank" that catechumens should avoid, and books "not read in Churches"[69] that catechumens should also avoid. The fact that Cyril wanted those who were new to the faith to avoid the deuterocanonical books does not prove they were noncanonical. According to Gallagher, "Cyril himself uses and cites Wisdom and Sirach. Cyril's canon list was written for catechumens, and so he may have intended

---

[64] Beckwith, *Old Testament Canon of the New Testament Church*, 387.
[65] DeSilva, *Introducing the Apocrypha*, 22.
[66] St. Cyril of Jerusalem, *Catechetical Lectures* 4.35, 11.15.
[67] St. Athanasius, *De Sententia Dionysii* 9.15. See also Michuta, *Case for the Deuterocanon*, 120.
[68] St. Cyril of Jerusalem, *Catechetical Lectures* 4.35.
[69] Ibid. 4.36.

his prohibition to apply to them alone, as those who are unable to properly separate the wheat from the chaff."[70]

Athanasius uses the same division in his festal letter and even places Baruch alongside protocanonical books like Jeremiah. He did not reject the inspiration of the deuterocanonical books, because, as we've seen, he called them "Scripture" and used the book of Wisdom in his defense of orthodox Christology. Athanasius recognized that these books were disputed by the Jews of his time but still said those who seek further catechesis should read them. And, as with Melito and Origen, if being present in one of Cyril's or Athanasius' lists is a necessary condition for canonicity, then Esther would be disqualified (it is absent from Athanasius' list) alongside Revelation, which is absent from Cyril's list.

The other major post-Nicene Father that Protestant apologists cite is Jerome. Luther, for example, appealed to Jerome's rejection of the deuterocanon in his debate with Johann Eck when Eck cited Second Maccabees in his defense of purgatory.[71] But Jerome did accept the deuterocanonical portions of the book of Daniel and defended those portions against critics like Rufinus.[72] It's true that Jerome claimed that the deuterocanonical books were not canonical, but he still included them in his Latin Vulgate translation since to do otherwise would have incited tremendous backlash from the Christian community at large where they were very popular.[73]

What drove Jerome to dismiss these books, then, was not a tradition delivered from the apostles entrusted to the Church. Instead, it

[70] Gallagher, *Hebrew Scripture in Patristic Biblical Theory*, 29.

[71] Ariel Hessayon, "The Apocrypha in Early Modern England", in *The Oxford Handbook of the Bible in Early Modern England, C. 1530–1700*, ed. Kevin Killeen, Helen Smith, and Rachel Willie (Oxford: Oxford University Press, 2015), 135.

[72] He writes, "What sin have I committed in following the judgment of the churches? But when I repeat what the Jews say against the Story of Susanna and the Hymn of the Three Children, and the fables of Bel and the Dragon, which are not contained in the Hebrew Bible, the man who makes this a charge against me proves himself to be a fool and a slanderer." St. Jerome, *Against Rufinus* 2.33.

[73] Consider this episode when Jerome made an uncommon translation of a passage in the book of Jonah: "When the bishop of Oea (modern Tripoli) introduced Jerome's recent rendering into his community service, Augustine worriedly related, the congregation nearly rioted. (At issue, perhaps, was the identity of the vine under which the prophet Jonah had rested—a 'gourd' so the traditional version, or an 'ivy' so Jerome; Letter 75.7, 22; Jonah 4:6)." Paula Fredriksen, *Augustine and the Jews: A Christian Defense of Jews and Judaism* (New Haven, CT: Yale University Press, 2010), 289.

was his belief in the superiority of what would later develop into the Hebrew Masoretic text. Indeed, this text is the authoritative manuscript tradition of the Hebrew Bible among nearly all Jews today, and it lacks the deuterocanonical books. Jerome believed that the Greek Septuagint of his day was simply a loose translation of these proto-Masoretic texts. He claimed that it was only from these Hebrew texts that the "true" Old Testament documents could be translated. But according to Megan Hale Williams in her study of Jerome's scholarship:

> The seemingly commonsense notion that in order to establish a correct text of the Hebrew scriptures, one ought to turn to the language in which they were composed, becomes a choice not between original and copy but between two independent textual traditions, each with its own history.... Jerome's privileging of the Hebrew text used by the Jews, together with its attendant traditions of interpretation, as the ultimate sources of biblical truth was by no means a simple recognition of scientific fact. Rather, it was an idiosyncratic insight, which allowed Jerome to construct for himself a unique position as an authority on the scriptures.[74]

Since Jerome was mistaken about the reliability and textual tradition of the Septuagint, this refutes his claim that the true Hebrew canon could be found only in manuscripts that lacked the deuterocanonical books. It also refutes Protestant apologists who cite later medieval theologians, along with biblical commentaries, that rejected the deuterocanonical books simply because they followed Jerome's erroneous argument about the Hebrew text.[75]

## Manuscript Evidence

Geisler and MacKenzie claim that not all of the deuterocanonical books are present in the oldest, most complete manuscripts of the

[74] Megan Hale Williams, *The Monk and the Book: Jerome and the Making of Christian Scholarship* (Chicago: University of Chicago Press, 2008), 71.

[75] These include figures Protestant apologists frequently cite such as Cardinal Cajetan (1469–1534) and Cardinal Ximenes (1436–1517), and commentaries such as the *Glossa Ordinaria*, which was a popular collection of "glosses" or annotations written in manuscripts of the Latin Vulgate.

Bible, which typically come from the fourth and fifth centuries.[76] These manuscripts are called a codex or codices and, unlike scrolls, they contained bounded pages, which makes them a precursor to modern books. But the Codex Alexandrinus (A.D. 400–A.D. 440) does contain all of the deuterocanonical books, and those books are placed next to the other protocanonical books. They aren't relegated to the manuscript's appendix with truly apocryphal works like the Psalms of Solomon.

The Codex Vaticanus (A.D. 300–A.D. 325) lacks only First and Second Maccabees, a point Geisler and MacKenzie think is decisive for their argument,[77] yet they fail to mention that this codex also lacks the letters to Timothy, Titus, and Philemon. Like Vaticanus, Codex Sinaiticus (A.D. 330–A.D. 360) is missing only two deuterocanonical books, which is not surprising, given that Sinaiticus also lacks the majority of the Pentateuch as well as entire historical books, including Joshua, Samuel, and Kings.

The abundant presence of the deuterocanonicals in these manuscripts is evidence in favor of their canonicity and inspired nature. That is why shortly after this time these writings were affirmed as being canonical at the regional councils of Hippo (393) and Carthage (397) and then the later ecumenical councils of Second Nicaea (787), Florence (1442), and Trent (1546).[78] Ultimately, our confidence in the canonicity of these books (as well as the rest of the biblical canon) comes from our confidence in the Catholic Church's authority to preserve and teach the contents of Sacred Tradition. Therefore, we must now turn our attention to the evidence for the infallible authority God gave to the Catholic Church.

[76] Geisler and MacKenzie, *Roman Catholics and Evangelicals*, 162.

[77] Ibid.

[78] Council of Carthage, canon 24; Council of Florence, eleventh session; Council of Trent, fourth session, Decree concerning the Canonical Scriptures. The first canon of the Second Council of Nicaea does not explicitly describe the canon, but it does affirm the promulgations from earlier regional councils, including the 397 Council of Carthage and the later Council of Carthage in 419.

# 4

# The New Testament Canon

To say a piece of writing is *inspired* means it has God as its author. To say a piece of writing is *canonical* means it is part of a rule of faith for the Church. Since the Council of Trent, the seventy-three books of the Catholic Bible are each considered the *inspired* word of God and each equally belongs to the *canon* of Scripture. However, the understanding of the contents of the canon developed over time, both in the Old Testament (as we saw in chapter 3) and in the New Testament. Debate over the New Testament canon even took place during the Reformation, as is evident in Luther's original preface to the Letter of James (1522), which said:

> St. James' epistle is really an epistle of straw, compared to the others, for it has nothing of the nature of the gospel about it.... I cannot include [James] among the chief books, though I would not thereby prevent anyone from including or extolling him as he pleases, for there are otherwise many good sayings in him.[1]

Luther removed this description from future editions, but he still moved James, along with the Letter to the Hebrews, to the back of his translation of the Bible. While this may seem like merely a piece of historical trivia, it raises deep questions about the authority of Scripture. If Luther and other Reformers believed they had the authority to alter the Old Testament canon, could they have also altered the New Testament canon in accordance with the differing levels of value they gave to the books it contained? Could a group of

[1] Martin Luther, *Luther's Works*, 35:397.

twenty-first-century scholars alter the canon of Scripture if they felt they had the same authority as Luther or Calvin?[2]

Catholics can say Christ's Church infallibly defined the contents of the biblical canon and so no one can change the fact that these books are sacred and canonical, but Protestants cannot avail themselves of such a solution. Instead, they must present a justification for an infallible canon of Scripture even though the only infallible rule of faith for Protestants is Scripture itself. Given the seemingly inherent contradiction in such a task, it's no wonder that James White says, "For many, the issue of the canon is the Achilles heel of scriptural sufficiency."[3]

## The Problem of the Canon

If Scripture is the "final court of appeal" or "the only infallible rule of faith", then on what basis does a Christian determine whether certain writings are or are not Scripture? If one appeals to an authority outside of Scripture, that authority becomes at least equal in authority to Scripture. For many Protestants this is unacceptable, or as the Calvinist scholar Richard Gaffin says, "It would destroy the New Testament as canon, as absolute authority."[4]

On the other hand, appealing to Scripture alone to answer the question, What belongs in Scripture? involves circular reasoning. It reveals that you already know the answer to the question you're

---

[2] The Jesus Seminar was a group of about 150 critical scholars whose methods cast doubt on the historical reliability of the New Testament. One member named Hal Taussig released a volume called *A New New Testament: A Bible for the 21st Century Combining Traditional and Newly Discovered Texts* (Boston: Houghton Mifflin, 2013), which included such Gnostic writings as the Gospel of Thomas. Most conservative scholars responded to this publication as being a silly, passing fad (as one article is entitled), but if Protestant Luther and other intellectuals of the sixteenth century could alter the canon of Scripture, why can't scholars today follow suit? For an example of a response by a conservative scholar, see Daniel Wallace, "A New New Testament: Are You Serious?", March 23, 2013, available at The Aquilareport. com, http://theaquilareport.com/a-new-new-testament-are-you-serious/.

[3] James R. White, *Scripture Alone: Exploring the Bible's Accuracy, Authority and Authenticity* (Bloomington, MN: Bethany House, 2004), 98.

[4] Richard Gaffin, "The New Testament as Canon", in *Inerrancy and Hermeneutic*, ed. Harvey M. Conn (Grand Rapids, MI: Baker, 1988), 170. Cited in Michael Kruger, *Canon Revisited: Establishing the Origins and Authority of the New Testament Books* (Wheaton, IL: Crossway, 2012), 88.

asking. In the face of this dilemma a Protestant might avoid the question entirely, an approach of which the Reformed theologian Douglas Wilson provides a sober analysis:

> The problem with contemporary Protestants is that they have no doctrine of the Table of Contents. With the approach that is popular in conservative evangelical circles, one simply comes to the Bible by means of an epistemological lurch. The Bible "just is," and any questions about how it got here are dismissed as a nuisance. But time passes, the questions remain unanswered, the silence becomes awkward, and conversions of thoughtful evangelicals to Rome proceed apace.[5]

Before we examine the various proposals Protestants have put forward to solve "the canon dilemma", we must distinguish the property of being inspired from the property of being canonical.

The distinction between inspiration and canonicity is important because some Protestants think Catholics believe that the Church "created the Bible" in the sense of causing human writings to become Scripture. Ron Rhodes says, "Let us not forget that God *determines* the canon, but human beings *discover* the canon. God *regulates* the canon, but human beings *recognize* the canon [emphasis in original]."[6] F. F. Bruce likewise says that when the Church listed the books of the canon at the Council of Carthage (A.D. 397), "it did not confer upon them any authority which they did not already possess."[7]

But Catholics agree that the Church does not determine the canon in the sense of causing certain books in it to become inspired. According to Yves Congar,

> It is not that the Church and her Magisterium actually create the canon; even less do they endow Scripture with its authority, as mistakenly rather than intentionally certain Catholic apologists have sometimes maintained. With this dogma, as with the others, Church and

---

[5] Douglas Wilson, "A Severed Branch", *Credenda Agenda* 12, no. 1 (2012), http://www.credenda.org/archive/issues/12-1thema.php.

[6] Ron Rhodes, *Reasoning from the Scriptures with Catholics* (Eugene, OR: Harvest House Publishing, 2000), 59.

[7] F. F. Bruce, *The Books and the Parchments* (London: Pickering Inglis, 1950), 111. Cited in Rhodes, *Reasoning from the Scriptures*, 59.

Magisterium simply recognize the truth established by God's action, submit to it and, since they are responsible for it, *proclaim it with authority* [emphasis added].[8]

The Church does not determine the canon in the sense of choosing which writings are inspired—God does that when he chooses to create Scripture and give human writings divine authority. But the Church also doesn't *merely* recognize Scripture or use fallible methods in order hopefully to "discover" the contents of the canon. Instead, God *determines* the canon while the Church authoritatively *declares* the canon.

However, since Catholics do not believe in *sola scriptura*, the nature of the canon did not have to be resolved immediately as the truths of the faith were taught by the Magisterium, who possessed the word of God in written and unwritten forms. Eventually the issue of the canon was settled through a progressive process that would not have been possible without the Church authoritatively declaring the contents of the canon based on her reception of them through Sacred Tradition.

## The History of the Canon

The testimony of the earliest apostolic Fathers shows that they not only lacked a closed canon of Scripture, but they relied on oral testimony to complement these written accounts. Papias, writing in A.D. 125, sought the testimony of those who knew the apostles and says, "I imagined that what was to be got from books was not so profitable to me as what came from the living and abiding voice."[9] First-century works such as the *Didache* and the First Epistle of Clement seem to use the Gospel of Matthew, but more often they support their teachings with citations from the Old Testament or oral tradition.[10]

In the second century, Ignatius of Antioch and Polycarp used the Gospel of Matthew, some of Paul's letters, and (in Polycarp's

---

[8] Yves Congar, *The Meaning of Tradition* (San Francisco: Ignatius Press, 2004), 110.

[9] Some have misinterpreted this to mean that Papias valued oral tradition over Scripture. For a good treatment on this issue, see Richard Bauckham, *Jesus and the Eyewitnesses: The Gospels as Eyewitness Testimony* (Grand Rapids, MI: Wm. B. Eerdmans, 2006), 12–37.

[10] It's also possible that Matthew used the *Didache* as a source. See Alan Garrow, *The Gospel of Matthew's Dependence on the Didache* (London: Bloomsbury Academic, 2013).

case) Hebrews and some of the Catholic letters. In contrast, Justin says that when Christians gathered on Sunday, "the memoirs of the apostles or the writings of the prophets are read", but no mention is made of Paul's letters.[11] Justin Martyr also quotes every canonical Gospel (and references Revelation), but he never makes a clear reference to Paul's writings.

At the end of the second century Irenaeus said that, among gospel writings, the four canonical Gospels "alone are true and reliable". But Tatian, a disciple of Justin Martyr, published a very popular harmony of the four Gospels called the Diatessaron (literally "through the four") that redacted parts of the canonical Gospels (such as Luke's genealogy) and added traditions from noncanonical gospels.

Irenaeus did cite the remainder of the New Testament with the exception of Second Peter, Second and Third John, and Jude, but he also called the *Shepherd of Hermas* Scripture.[12] Even though Irenaeus is the first author to use the term "New Testament", he does not describe any authoritative list that describes the contents of the New Testament. According to McDonald, the Christian message "was [Irenaeus'] 'canon' and he limited this message to the apostolic tradition resident in the church." He adds:

> The establishing of a closed canon of inspired scriptures, however, was not Irenaeus's primary concern, but rather to defend the Christian message with all the tools at his disposal. He sought to root his teaching in the apostolic teaching and tradition that, he argued, was passed on in the church through the succession of bishops as well as by the authority of both the Old Testament and New Testament.[13]

In order to establish a widespread acceptance of the canon during the second century, some Protestant apologists appeal to a manuscript called the Muratorian Fragment, which was discovered by Lodovico Antonio Muratori in the eighteenth century. It is an eighth-century Latin text that appears to be a copy of a Greek original that some scholars date to the middle of the second century. Rather than being a canonical list, the fragment describes the books of the New

[11] St. Justin Martyr, *First Apology* 67.
[12] Cited in Eusebius, *Church History* 5.8.2–8.
[13] Lee Martin McDonald, *The Biblical Canon: Its Origin, Transmission, and Authority* (Grand Rapids, MI: Better Academic, 2007), 296.

Testament and, according to the Reformed scholar Michael Kruger, "suggests that by the end of the second century the canon is at a fairly mature stage".[14]

First, even if this were an early articulation of the canon, it still doesn't match the modern New Testament canon. The fragment begins with a description of Luke's Gospel and continues to describe the rest of the New Testament books except for Hebrews, First and Second Peter, James, and one of John's letters (the Gospels of Matthew and Mark are also omitted, but they were probably included in the original manuscript, whose beginning has been lost). The Muratorian canon also includes the deuterocanonical book of Wisdom and the apocryphal gospel of Peter and says the *Shepherd of Hermas* ought to be read but not in public liturgies because it was written after the time of the apostles.

Second, there are good reasons to believe that the Muratorian Fragment comes not from the second century, but from the fourth century.[15] The fragment doesn't mention any apocryphal gospels, even as rejected texts, which makes sense in a fourth-century context where they were not as popular. Kruger also notes that it is puzzling that the book of Wisdom is included in a description of the New Testament canon but attributes this to a "widespread practice" of listing disputed books after canonical ones.[16] But the only examples Kruger cites are from the fourth century, including works by Saint Athanasius, and manuscripts including the Codex Sinaiticus and the Codex Alexandrinus. This provides further evidence that the Muratorian canon contains a fourth-century list of sacred books rather than a second-century list.

The strongest evidence that the fragment comes from the second century is that the author says, "Hermas wrote the Shepherd very recently, in our times, in the city of Rome, while bishop Pius, his brother, was occupying the [episcopal] chair of the church of the

---

[14] Michael J. Kruger, *The Question of Canon: Challenging the Status Quo in the New Testament Debate* (Downers Grove, IL: InterVarsity Press, 2013), 163.

[15] The classic defense of this theory can be found in Albert C. Sundberg Jr., "Canon Muratori: A Fourth Century List", in *Harvard Theological Review* 66 (1973): 1–41. An updated defense can also be found in Geofrey Hahneman, *The Muratorian Fragment and the Development of the Canon* (Oxford: Clarendon Press, 1992).

[16] Kruger, *Canon Revisited*, 231.

city of Rome." Pius I's pontificate lasted between 140 and 154, but in the *Shepherd of Hermas* an angel instructs its titular character to "write two little books, and shalt send one to Clement". If this Clement is the third successor of Peter, or Clement of Rome, then the *Shepherd* could not have been written after the first century. That this is Clement of Rome is buoyed by the fact that the angel says Clement will send the letter "to the foreign cities, for this is his duty", which corresponds with the possibility that Clement was corresponding secretary among the elders in the Roman Church (see chapter 6, footnote 4).

The fact that the fragment refers to the *Shepherd* being written "very recently, in our times" (*nuperrime temporibus nostris*) does not mean the fragment comes from even the same century as the *Shepherd*, since Irenaeus uses a similar phrase in reference to events that happened a century before he wrote. In his study of the social setting in post-apostolic Christianity, New Testament professor Harry O. Maier says the key phrase in question "may refer not to the lifetime of the author of the fragment, but to the post-apostolic period".[17]

Finally, there are no parallels to the Muratorian canon in any second-century literature, but the fragment does contain parallels to fourth-century documents, which supports a later date. For example, second-century authors considered the *Shepherd of Hermas* to be inspired and no restrictions were placed on where it could be read, but restrictions on the *Shepherd* can be found in fourth-century works. O. Maier concludes, "The anti-canonical references to the *Shepherd* in the Muratorian Canon are more consonant with a later than an earlier date. A later date and the writer's apologetic concern seriously impugn the accuracy of the Muratorian Canon composer's remark concerning the date of the *Shepherd*."[18]

The third century reveals a similar absence of a universally recognized canon of Scripture. In the previous chapter we saw that Origen listed the books of the Old Testament canon, but he does not do the same with the New Testament canon. Tertullian and Clement of

---

[17] Harry O. Maier, *The Social Setting of the Ministry as Reflected in the Writings of Hermas, Clement and Ignatius* (Ontario: Wilfrid Laurier University Press, 2002), 57.
[18] Ibid., 58.

Alexandria also fail to attest to the existence of a widely recognized canon, and neither author cites some of the Catholic epistles, including James or Second Peter. Metzger also notes that Clement

> speaks of Plato as being "under the inspiration of God". Even the Epicurean Metrodorus uttered certain words "divinely inspired". It is not surprising then that [Clement] can quote passages as inspired from the epistles of Clement of Rome and of Barnabas, the Shepherd of Hermas, and the Apocalypse of Peter.[19]

At the beginning of the fourth century Eusebius speaks of the "accepted writings" as comprising the Gospels, Acts, the first letters of John and Peter, and Paul's letters (which aren't named). He says disputed writings that are still accepted by many include James, Jude, Second Peter, Second and Third John, and Revelation. Works like the *Shepherd of Hermas* and some of the apocryphal gospels were "rejected", but he admits that Christians of Jewish descent are "are especially delighted" with the Gospel of the Hebrews.[20]

According to F. F. Bruce, "Athanasius is the first writer known to us who listed exactly the twenty-seven books which traditionally make up the New Testament in catholic and orthodox Christianity, without making any distinction of status among them."[21] This can be found in his 39th Festal Letter, written in A.D. 367, though many of Athanasius' Eastern contemporaries such as Saint Gregory of Nazianzus and Amphilocius either left out Revelation or said many people considered it to be "spurious". But Revelation, along with the rest of the traditional New Testament, can be found in the canons that were promulgated at the synod in Rome held under Pope Damasus (382) and the regional councils of Hippo (393) and Carthage (397) held in North Africa.

While there would still be disputes about some of these books in the centuries that followed (these councils did not have infallible authority), one notices a greater unity about the canon after these councils rendered their decisions. The renowned Protestant New Testament

---

[19] Bruce Metzger, *The Canon of the New Testament: Its Origin, Development, and Significance* (Oxford: Oxford University Press, 1997), 134.

[20] Eusebius, *Church History* 3.25.

[21] F. F. Bruce, *The Canon of Scripture* (Downers Grove, IL: IVP Academic, 1988), 209.

scholar F. F. Bruce says that "Augustine, like Jerome, inherited the canon of scripture as something 'given.' It was part of the Christian faith which he embraced at his conversion in 386."[22] In 405 Bishop Exuperius of Toulouse (located in modern-day France) sent a letter to Pope Innocent I requesting clarification on the canon of Scripture, and he received the same list issued at the previous councils that was further ratified at another synod held in Carthage in 419.

The Church recognizes what writings are the word of God and, unlike the Protestant position on this issue, declares with infallible authority from Christ which books belong in the canon. The *Catechism* says as much when it teaches that "it was by the apostolic Tradition that the Church discerned which writings are to be included in the list of the sacred books" (*CCC* 120).

Can Protestants present a way for the early church (with a lowercase "c") to have "discovered" the canon of Scripture while still affirming that the canon they discovered constitutes an infallible rule of faith? Let's examine four criteria Protestants have used to accomplish that task: subjective criteria, objective criteria, self-authenticating criteria, and fallible criteria.

## Subjective Criteria

Some Protestants claim that Christians can know which books are inspired and which are not through a subjective, internal witness that the Holy Spirit provides them. These apologists might cite John 10:27, where Jesus says, "My sheep hear my voice, and I know them, and they follow me."[23] According to advocates of the subjective view, a Christian can know the writings of the New Testament are inspired because God reveals that truth to each believer. The early twentieth-century Reformed theologian Charles Briggs said:

> The divine authority of the Canon, and of every writing in the Canon, [is] a question between every man and his God.... The Spirit of God bears witness by and with the particular writing or part of a writing, in

---

[22] Ibid., 209.

[23] Quoted in Kruger, *Canon Revisited*, 88. Indeed, in his book on the canon, the chapter on a self-authenticating canon is called "My Sheep Hear My Voice".

the heart of the believer, removing every doubt and assuring the soul
of its possession of the truth of God.[24]

One can't help but notice that this approach to the canon bears a
striking resemblance to "Mormon epistemology". When Mormon
missionaries share their faith, they usually ask prospective converts to
read the Book of Mormon (or excerpts of it) and then pray to God
and ask if the book is true. Mormons try to ground this practice biblically by citing James 1:5: "If any of you lacks wisdom, let him ask
God, who gives to all men generously and without reproaching, and
it will be given him."

This verse merely assures us that God will give wisdom to those
who pray, not that he will give them a private revelation of what
books belong in the Bible. This doctrine, however, is really derived
from another Latter-Day Saints Scripture called *Doctrine and Covenants*, which says if the Book of Mormon is true, reading it "will
cause that your bosom will burn within you" (9:8). But both Mormon and Protestant appeals to the witness of the Holy Spirit alone to
determine if a writing is inspired suffer from the same flaws.

First, while the Bible tells us to test everything (1 Thess 5:21)
and even gives specific tests to determine if prophets are genuine
(Deut 18:21–22), it never tells us to pray and rely on our feelings
to determine if a certain writing is inspired. James 1:5 refers to
seeking *wisdom*, or practical moral principles for living a holy life,
and John 10:27 is about believing in the Person of Christ for salvation. Neither verse is about recognizing divine inspiration through
the revelation of the Holy Spirit. Scripture even describes cases
where a prophet failed to recognize God's voice, such as when
Samuel mistook God's voice for Eli (1 Sam 3) or when a man
of God was deceived by a fellow prophet who claimed to speak for
God (1 Kings 13:18).[25]

Most believers who read the census accounts in Numbers or the
instructions for offering sacrifices in Leviticus do not feel a "burning
in the bosom" from the Holy Spirit, but that would not disprove

[24] Charles Briggs, *Church Unity: Studies of Its Most Important Problems* (New York: Charles
Scribner's Sons, 1909), 161.

[25] James Akin, "The Two Canons: Scripture and Tradition", EWTN.com, 1996, https://
www.ewtn.com/library/answers/2canons.htm.

the inspired nature of these books. Conversely, some people feel as if God is speaking to them through non-Christian literature or even preachers who say they've received "a word from the Lord".

Also, if this criterion were true, then every person who ever accepted the deuterocanonical books of Scripture (including Church Fathers and saints whom many Protestants admire) would either be sheep that failed to hear Christ's voice or sinners who did not belong to Christ's flock at all. If they, from a Protestant perspective, could be deceived into thinking a particular book was inspired, then how do Protestants know they haven't fallen into the same error?

Finally, this approach to the canon doesn't reflect the way most Christians come to believe that the Bible is inspired. Many Christians have not read the entire Bible, and those who have read it usually have not sought the Holy Spirit's help in authenticating every part of every book or letter they've read. Most Christians believe the Bible is inspired simply because they accept the testimony of other Christians who believe in the Bible and were "in Christ before" them (Rom 16:7).

The subjective approach to establishing the canon should remind us of the warning from the prophet Jeremiah: "The heart is deceitful above all things, and desperately corrupt; who can understand it?" (Jer 17:9). The lesson we learned from our investigation of *sola scriptura* bears repeating: relying on subjective feelings in order to establish a rule of faith only produces a "blueprint for anarchy".[26]

## Objective Criteria

In order to escape the perils of subjectivism, some Protestants put forward objective criteria for determining the canon that do not carry with them the judgment of an infallible church endowed with Christ's authority.

Martin Luther wrote in his preface to the letters of James and Jude, "This is the true test of all books, when we see whether or not they preach Christit.... Whatever does not teach Christ, that is not apostolic, even though St. Peter or St. Paul taught it; again, what preaches

---

[26] Patrick Madrid, "Sola Scriptura: A Blueprint for Anarchy", EWTN.com, accessed July 8, 2017, https://www.ewtn.com/library/scriptur/solascri.txt.

Christ would be Apostolic."[27] But this is not a necessary condition for canonicity, nor is it even a sufficient one. A simple gospel tract or a painting of the Crucifixion could be said to "preach Christ", yet those works are not inspired. The Third Letter of John, on the other hand, never even mentions the name of Christ, yet it is considered to be the inspired word of God.

Some Protestants might say this is a problem with Luther's ambiguous criterion to determine the canon, not the use of objective criteria in general. According to F. F. Bruce in his book *The Canon of Scripture*, the early Church used the criteria of apostolic authority, antiquity, orthodoxy, and catholicity or universal reception in order to recognize if a book was inspired. The Protestant apologist may ask, "Why can't Christians today use these same criteria to justify the authority of the canon apart from the authority of the Church?"

First, any claim that a certain set of criteria should determine the canon still involves a subjective judgment. For example, why shouldn't Luther's criteria of "preaching Christ" be joined to Bruce's criteria? Second, it's true that the Church used these criteria, among others, when determining which traditions about the canon were apostolic in origin. But that doesn't mean these criteria can be applied by anyone apart from the Church's judgment in order to create the same infallible New Testament canon found in today's Bibles.

Consider, for example, the criteria of apostolic authority or authorship. It isn't a sufficient condition for being considered canonical. Paul wrote letters we do not possess (1 Cor 5:9), and many Protestants say that if one of those letters were ever discovered, they would not consider it to be Scripture because, even though an apostle wrote it, this writing had not been "left to the church".[28] However, if the early Church could choose not to recognize an apostolic writing as being canonical, then what's to prevent the modern Church from doing the same? Could the "Church" merely decide that *portions* of the New Testament, such as those that seem contradictory or offend modern sensibilities, are not canonical? If the early Church did not have

---

[27] Paul Althaus, *The Theology of Martin Luther* (Minneapolis: Fortress Press, 1966), 83.

[28] "Even if we were to discover Paul's lost letter in the desert sands today, we would not place it into the canon as the twenty-eighth book. Instead, we would simply recognize that God had not preserved this book to be a permanent foundation for the church." Kruger, *Canon Revisited*, 97.

apostolic authority, then there is no reason for the modern Church to continue to abide by decisions with which it no longer agrees.

Apostolic authority also isn't a necessary condition for being canonical, since Mark and Luke were not apostles and their Gospels do not claim to have any connection to the apostles (Mark's role as Peter's interpreter and Luke's role as Paul's traveling companion are known through tradition). The Letter to the Hebrews was once attributed to Paul, but is now widely understood to be non-Pauline. If apostolic authorship alone makes the New Testament distinct from any other canon of literature, then several New Testament books that do not have apostles as authors would have to be removed from the Bible.

A Protestant might say there is at least an apostolic *tradition* behind Mark, Luke, and Hebrews that justifies their inclusion in the canon. However, it's inconsistent for a Protestant to base the identity of the Scriptures that serve as his foundational authority (or *sola scriptura*) solely on tradition and then say *sola scriptura* requires him to reject any doctrines he thinks are only found in tradition. And such a move doesn't give him the New Testament canon we have today, because it would also include writings from Church Fathers such as Clement of Rome, Polycarp, and Ignatius since tradition associates these men with the apostles (Clement with Peter and Polycarp and Ignatius with John).

The other criteria also fail to generate automatically the traditional canon because these writings, along with works like the *Didache*, would be included under the criteria of antiquity since they were written in the first century or (in the case of Ignatius) immediately afterward. They also pass the criteria of orthodoxy, which becomes a problematic criterion since one must rely on a tradition to know what orthodoxy is before Scripture can be tested to see if it is orthodox and true to the faith handed down from the apostles.

In the second century the heretic Marcion accepted only the Gospel of Luke and some of Paul's letters because he believed only these writings were "orthodox". Tertullian attacked Marcion's canon but not through any appeal to a widely recognized canon from which Marcion had deviated.[29] McDonald says of Tertullian, "Nowhere in his extant writings, however, do we find any specific listing or

---

[29] See Tertullian, *Against Marcion* 5.

identification of precisely what was in Tetrullian's Old Testament or
New Testament."[30] According to Bruce,

> Where the interpretation of the Bible was at issue, there was a ten-
> dency to maintain that only the catholic church had the right to inter-
> pret it, because the Bible was the church's book; but in the Marcionite
> controversy an answer had to be given to the more fundamental ques-
> tion: What is the Bible? ... If they had not given much thought to the
> limits of holy writ previously, they had to pay serious attention to the
> question now.[31]

That leaves us with the criteria of "catholicity" or "universal
reception by the Church". Robert Godfrey says, "The self authenticating character of the canon is demonstrated by the remarkable
unanimity reached by the people of God on the canon."[32] First,
even if the canon had been universally accepted in the early Church,
it is inconsistent for Protestants to adopt this tradition from that
time period but not others that were universally accepted like the
Real Presence of Christ in the Eucharist (see chapter 8), baptismal
regeneration (see chapter 9), and the possibility of losing salvation
(see chapter 12).

But as we've already seen, there was no universal reception of
today's canon among believers in the first few centuries of Christian
history. Such a consensus only later grew out of the authoritative
teaching of the Catholic Church. According to McDonald, "The
notion of a closed New Testament canon was not a second-century
development in the early church, and there were still considerable
differences of opinion about what should comprise that canon even
in the fourth and fifth centuries."[33] Craig Allert agrees and also notes
that "this has direct implications for the argument that the early
church appealed to the Bible and the Bible alone for its doctrine: one

---

[30] McDonald, *Biblical Canon*, 304.
[31] Quoted in Bruce, *Canon of Scripture*, 129.
[32] Robert Godfrey, "What Do We Mean by Sola Scriptura?", in *Sola Scriptura! The Protestant Position on the Bible* (Morgan, PA: Soli Deo Gloria Publications, 1995), 19. A similar
argument can be found in Roger Nicole, "The Canon of the New Testament", *Journal of the
Evangelical Theology Society* 40, no. 2 (June 1997).
[33] McDonald, *Biblical Canon*, 383.

cannot properly speak of a Bible in the first several centuries of the church's existence."[34]

Those who merely rely on the Church's acceptance of the canon also have no reason to say the canon is infallible if the Church that promulgated the canon (in their eyes) was not infallible. Some Protestants attempt to do this, but before we examine their arguments we should address one other way to justify the canon apart from the teaching authority of the Catholic Church.

## Self-Authenticating Criteria

Calvin said, "Scripture indeed is self-authenticated; hence it is not right to subject it to proof and reasoning." But how is Scripture self-authenticated? Calvin explains:

> How shall we be persuaded that it came from God without recurring to a decree of the church? It is just the same as if it were asked, how shall we learn to distinguish light from darkness, white from black, sweet from bitter? Scripture bears upon the face of it as clear evidence of its truth, as white and black do of their color, sweet and bitter of their taste.[35]

For some Protestants, Scripture is capable of authenticating itself through a mixture of subjective criteria (such as the witness of the Holy Spirit) and objective criteria (such as the written and historical elements associated with Scripture). One recent attempt to justify a self-authenticating canon can be found in Kruger's book *Canon Revisited*. In chapter 3 Kruger proposes a model for the canon that would "let the canon have a voice in its own authentication."[36]

Kruger does not mean we should merely accept the Bible's claim to be the word of God (a claim that, by the way, many books of the Bible do not make for themselves). Instead he says, "A self-authenticating canon is not just a canon that claims to have authority, nor is it simply a canon that bears internal evidence of authority, but

[34] Craig D. Allert, *A High View of Scripture? The Authority of the Bible and the Formation of the New Testament Canon* (Grand Rapids, MI: Baker Academic, 2007), 51.

[35] John Calvin, *Institutes of the Christian Religion* 1.7.2.

[36] Kruger, *Canon Revisited*, 89.

one that guides and determines how that authority is to be established."[37] For Kruger, the canon authenticates itself through divine providence (God allows some books to remain in existence to be authenticated and others to be lost), divine qualities (beauty, efficacy, and harmony), and divine confirmation through the witness of the Holy Spirit.

First, the witness of the Holy Spirit *would* reliably establish the canon of Scripture *if* the Holy Spirit chose to give such revelations to individuals. However, we've shown that the Bible does not promise this kind of revelation will be given to individuals and so it cannot serve as an alternative foundation for the New Testament canon. However, Kruger uses an analogy to argue that if these criteria are combined, they can authenticate God's revelation. He asks, "If the created world (general revelation) is able to speak clearly that it is from God, then how much more so would the canon of scripture (special revelation) speak clearly that it is from God?"[38]

In other words, the world authenticates the fact that it has a divine author because it contains divine qualities (beauty, harmony, efficacy) that we are able to recognize with help from the Holy Spirit. Why can't the books of the Bible authenticate themselves in a similar way?

The reason is that the conclusion that God is the author of creation is not reached merely because the world is beautiful or harmonious. Instead, the fact that an orderly universe exists at all instead of nothing demands an explanation that only a necessary being like God could provide. The Scripture verses that show we can recognize God through his creation, such as Romans 1:20 and Psalm 19:1, do not refer to the beauty of creation testifying to God. They instead refer to God's power being displayed in his mighty craft, or they speak of effects that only an all-powerful God could create.

The same is not true for the Bible and our understanding that it has a divine author. Unlike the Qur'an, the Bible never claims to be something that only God could create.[39] While the Bible does

---

[37] Ibid., 91.

[38] Ibid., 99.

[39] One of the proposed evidences for the Qur'an is human inability to produce prose that matches it in elegance or beauty. One verse this is derived from is Sura 2:23, which says, "If you are in doubt about what We have sent down upon Our Servant [Muhammad], then produce a surah the like thereof and call upon your witnesses other than Allah, if you should be truthful."

contain beautiful prose and gripping stories, so do many other ancient and modern pieces of sacred and secular literature. Perhaps that's why Kruger says canonicity also requires works to have apostolic origins and reception in the early Church, but we've seen the limits of applying the criteria of apostolicity and catholicity on their own toward determining the canon.

Indeed, Kruger's claim that the canon of Scripture "speaks more clearly" that it is from God than the natural world does is patently false. While the early Church unanimously agreed that God created the entire world (even in the face of Gnostic heretics who thought otherwise), they did not possess a similar agreement over the canon of Scripture. Instead, the Church intervened and settled this disagreement, a fact that some Protestant apologists admit when they construct their justification of the New Testament canon.

## Fallible Criteria

In *The Shape of Sola Scriptura*, Keith Mathison admits that the kind of arguments we've just considered present a "devastating criticism" toward those who try to create a canon of Scripture from Scripture alone. He says those who attempt this task "can say that only scripture is authoritative, but they can't say with any authority exactly what scripture is. Any attempt to authoritatively define a canon, or table of contents, is automatically a denial of solo scriptura."[40]

Mathison thinks that his understanding of *sola scriptura*, which gives some authority to tradition (as opposed to *solo scriptura*), is immune to this devastating criticism. However, this immunity comes at a price because Mathison admits that while he recognizes tradition has authority when determining doctrine and practice, it does not have infallible authority over those areas, and so traditions could be mistaken. Mathison isn't concerned, though, because "it is logically and theologically possible for any fallible individual or church to make an inerrant [i.e., true] statement. The point is this: the fallibility of the church does not mean she *must* always err, it only means she can err [emphasis in original]."[41] In other words, the Church gave us the canon, but that doesn't mean the Church is infallible, because even

---

[40] Keith Mathison, *The Shape of Sola Scriptura* (Moscow, ID: Canon Press, 2001), 314.
[41] Ibid., 315.

fallible entities can make correct decisions (or "a broken clock is right twice a day").

The prominent Calvinist scholar R. C. Sproul makes a similar argument when he contrasts the Roman Catholic view of the canon as "an infallible collection of infallible books" with what he proposes as a Protestant view that the canon is "a fallible collection of infallible books". Sproul admits, "It is possible that the church erred in its compilation of the books found in the present Canon of Scripture." This does not undermine his confidence in the accuracy of the canon, however, because "it is one thing to say that the church *could* have erred; it is another thing to say that the church *did* err [emphasis in original]."[42]

But if, as these apologists claim, the Church could have made mistakes in selecting the books of the New Testament, then this undermines the idea that the books of the Bible can be regarded as an infallible rule of faith. They can't merely say that there's no reason to think the Church got the canon wrong. How do they know it didn't? To that question they have no clear answer. In fact, these apologists take different (and sometimes completely opposite) approaches to defending the inerrancy of Scripture than they do with defending the inerrancy of the canon of Scripture, as we will see.

First, the Danish systematic theologian G. C. Berkouwer rejected the view that the Bible should be an infallible authority like the pope (or what he called a "paper pope", to borrow a term from Gotthold Lessing). In response to Berkouwer's claim that Scripture can be fallible but still communicate divine revelation, R. C. Sproul says this approach leaves us without an answer to "the question of the degree of biblical trustworthiness. Is the Bible altogether and completely trustworthy? If so, then what is wrong with the categories of verbal inspiration and inerrancy?"[43] We could ask the same question of the canon to Sproul: Is the canon altogether and completely trustworthy? If so, then what is wrong with the category of infallibility for the Church that pronounced the canon?

Likewise, in *Scripture Alone* White says, "The foundation of the certainty of our knowledge of the canon is based upon God's

---

[42] R. C. Sproul, *Scripture Alone: The Evangelical Doctrine* (Phillipsburg, NJ: P&R Publishing, 2005), 42.

[43] Ibid., 67.

purposes in giving Scripture, not upon alleged authority of any eccle-sial body." He goes on to argue that the Church was "a *means* to establish widespread knowledge of [the] canon so *that* Scripture will function as He decreed it to function [emphasis in original]."[44] But in the same book White says it "makes no sense" for God to use errant Scriptures as a means to establish widespread knowledge of infallible gospel truths. He declares, "*Infallible teaching is not derived from errant foundations* [emphasis in original]."[45] But doesn't that mean the infal-lible teaching of the canon can only be derived from the foundation of an infallible church that cannot err when it defines doctrine, or the Catholic Church?

Third, other apologists claim that if the fallible Jewish leaders before Christ could pass on an infallible Old Testament canon, then why couldn't a fallible church pass on an infallible New Testament canon to Christians? Protestant apologist Eric Svendsen says of Jesus and the New Testament writers:

> They were faced with the same situation as Evangelicals today; namely, adherence to a canon of scripture preserved until the Reformation by a corrupt ecclesial body. Jesus, the apostles, and the rest of the New Testament writers were able to place complete confidence in such a canon. Yet they would be able to do this only on the assumption that the Holy Spirit occasionally gives infallible guidance, especially where it concerns recognition and preservation of his word, and in spite of the fallibility of the agents he uses.[46]

There are several responses to be made. First, the New Testament says nothing about Jesus or the New Testament writers discerning the Old Testament canon through the guidance of the Holy Spirit. They simply had an awareness of the books of the Old Testament as "the Scriptures" through the tradition they had received.

Second, as we saw in the previous chapter, there also wasn't a single canon of Scripture that all Jews recognized before or shortly after Christ. Unless Svendsen and other apologists who make this

---

[44] White, *Scripture Alone*, 107.

[45] Ibid., 73.

[46] Eric Svendsen, *Evangelical Answers: A Critique of Current Roman Catholic Apologists* (Atlanta: New Testament Restoration Foundation, 1999), 94–95.

argument are comfortable with Christians disagreeing about the New Testament canon as much as the Sadducees, Pharisees, and Essenes disagreed on the Old Testament canon, then this solution will not be palatable to them.

## The Church and the Canon

Calvin objected to the idea that the canon of Scripture derives its authority from the Church because, according to him, "It is utterly vain, then, to pretend that the power of judging Scripture so lies with the church and that its certainty depends upon churchly assent."[47] But Calvin's justification for the canon simply replaces "the church" with "the individual" and derives its certainty from the individual's assent to what he thinks the Holy Spirit has revealed (or "illumined by his power") to him.

Kruger presents a more potent objection, saying that even though his approach to the canon may seem to be circular, any approach to determining the canon of Scripture will seem to be circular. He writes, "All models have prior theological convictions about what Scripture is (or is not), and this in turn determines the manner in which canon is authenticated. But where do these prior theological convictions about Scripture come from if not from Scripture itself?"[48]

The answer, as we've seen, is that we do not have to confine God's revelation to the written word alone. In the early Church there were several competing traditions about the nature of the Christian canon. There were also several traditions about what constituted the essential elements of the orthodox understanding of the Christian faith. Fortunately, the Church Christ founded used her authoritative judgment to determine which of these traditions were apostolic and which allegedly sacred writings came from the apostles and corresponded to the orthodox understanding of the Deposit of Faith they left us.

But how do we know the Church has authority if not from Scripture itself? Kruger asks, "How does the Roman Catholic Church establish its *own* infallible authority? If the Roman Catholic Church believes that infallible authorities (like the Scriptures) require external

---

[47] John Calvin, *Institutes of the Christian Religion* 1.7.2.
[48] Kruger, *Canon Revisited*, 99.

authentication, then to what authority does the church turn to establish the grounds for its own infallible authority?"[49]

One answer can be found in Karl Keating's book *Catholicism and Fundamentalism*, where the author offers a "spiral argument" in defense of the inspiration of Scripture. Keating is clear that he does not offer a circular argument that says, "The Bible is inspired because of what the Church says, and the Church is authoritative because of what an inspired Bible says." Instead, he writes, "On the first level we argue to the reliability of the Bible insofar as it is history. From that we conclude that an infallible Church was founded. And then we take the word of that infallible Church that the Bible is inspired."[50]

It is beyond the scope of this book to defend the historical reliability of the Bible, but since most Protestant apologists believe in the Bible's historical reliability, it is a claim we need not defend to establish the authority of the Catholic Church. Instead, we will assume that the Bible is reliable and that it describes how Christ founded an authoritative, infallible Church. We will examine the biblical and historical evidence that the Catholic Church is this same Church in the next few chapters.

[49] Ibid., 46.

[50] Karl Keating, *Catholicism and Fundamentalism: The Attack on "Romanism" by "Bible Christians"* (San Francisco: Ignatius Press, 1988), 126.

Part II

What Is the Church?

# 5

# The Papacy, Part I

The Westminster Confession says, "There is no other head of the Church but the Lord Jesus Christ. Nor can the Pope of Rome, in any sense, be head thereof" (25.6). Luther, Calvin, later Reformers, and even a few Protestants today not only deny the pope's authority—they think he is the antichrist.[1] The eighteenth-century Puritan pastor Cotton Mather said, "In the Pope of Rome, all the characteristics of that Antichrist are so marvelously answered that if any who read the Scriptures do not see it, there is a marvelous blindness upon them."[2]

But the pope is not a sinister agent of Satan, nor is he an all-knowing, sinless king over his fellow Christians. Rather, the pope is an imperfect human being God chooses to inherit the office Saint Peter first held—that is, the pastor of the entire Church. Just as Saint Paul called himself a father to Christians in his care (1 Cor 4:15), Peter's successor is called pope, which is derived from a Greek word for "father" (*papas*). According to the *Catechism*, quoting *Lumen Gentium*,[3]

The *Pope*, Bishop of Rome and Peter's successor, "is the perpetual and visible source and foundation of the unity both of the bishops and of the whole company of the faithful" (*LG* 23). "For the Roman Pontiff, by reason of his office as Vicar of Christ, and as pastor of the entire Church has full, supreme, and universal power over the whole

---

[1] See, for example, Martin Luther, *First Principles of the Reformation*, and John Calvin, *Institutes of the Christian Religion* 4.7.25. Against this charge we would point out that 1 John 2:22 says that the antichrist "denies that Jesus is the Christ", but no pope is recorded as ever having done this.

[2] Cotton Mather, *The Fall of Babylon*. Cited in Stephen J. Vicchio, *The Legend of the Antichrist: A History* (Eugene, OR: Wipf and Stock, 2009), 210.

[3] *Lumen Gentium* (*LG*) is Vatican Council II's Dogmatic Constitution on the Church (November 21, 1964).

Church, a power which he can always exercise unhindered" (*LG* 22).
(*CCC* 882)

## Prince of the Apostles

In order to establish the doctrine of the papacy, we will show that
Peter had unique authority as the leader of the early Church. In addition, this authority was passed on to his successors who now serve as
the pope or the bishop of Rome. Before we examine the evidence
for Peter's authority, however, we must dispatch a common objection: How could Peter have been the first pope when Scripture never
refers to him with papal titles like "pope" or "the Vicar of Christ"?

The answer is that Peter can be a pope even if Scripture does not
use that title for him, just as God can be a Trinity even though Scripture does not contain the words "Trinity" or "Triune". In both cases
nonbiblical terms are used to clarify and understand biblical doctrines.

For example, a vicar is one who acts as an agent or representative
for a sovereign leader. So, when Jesus tells the apostles, "He who
hears you hears me" (Lk 10:16), he makes them his vicars. In the third
century Saint Cyprian said Jesus addressed this statement not only to
the apostles, but to all the Church's leaders as the apostle's successors.[4]
One example of the specific *vicar*ious role Peter played for Christ
would be his condemnation of Ananias, who withheld money from
the apostles. Ananias lied to Peter, but Peter charged Ananias with
lying to God (Acts 5:3-4). Scott Hahn says, "As judge Peter acted as
Christ's vicar. To lie to Peter was to lie to God himself."[5]

Peter had unique authority both as the leader of the apostles and
of the nascent Church. Peter's role as "chief apostle" is evident in
that he is mentioned in the Gospels more than every other apostle
*combined*, often speaks for the whole group, and is placed first in every
formal list of the apostles (Mt 10:2). Peter was also the recipient of

---

[4] "Nor do I boast of these things, but with grief I bring them forward, since you constitute
yourself a judge of God and of Christ, who says to the apostles, and thereby to all chief rulers,
who by vicarious ordination succeed to the apostles: He that hears you, hears me; and he that
hears me, hears Him that sent me; and he that despises you, despises me, and Him that sent
me." St. Cyprian, *Epistle* 68.4.

[5] Scott Hahn, *Reasons to Believe: How to Understand, Explain, and Defend the Catholic Faith*
(New York: Doubleday, 2007), 133.

the revelation that Jesus is the Son of the God (Mt 16:17–19), Jesus preached from Peter's boat (Lk 5:3), and Peter was the first man Jesus appeared to after the Resurrection (Lk 24:34; 1 Cor 15:5). The angel at the tomb even instructed the women there to "tell [Jesus'] disciples and Peter that he is going before [them] to Galilee" (Mk 16:7).

Those who try to downplay Peter's role among the apostles often seem to grasp at straws. This includes suggesting that Peter is mentioned first in apostolic lists because he was the oldest or the first one called.[6] However, John 1:42 tells us Andrew was called before Peter, and John was traditionally believed to be the youngest apostle, yet he is not listed last.[7] Instead, these lists rank the apostles in order of importance, with Judas being the least important and Peter being the most. For example, Matthew 10:2 says, "The names of the twelve apostles are these: first [Greek, *protos*], Simon, who is called Peter ..." John MacArthur says, "[*Protos*] doesn't refer to the first in a list; it speaks of the chief, the leader of the group."[8]

Some Protestant apologists grant that Peter held a place of prominence in the early Church. They deny, however, that this prominence was equivalent to primacy or that Peter had authority over the other apostles. It's true that prominence does not *equal* primacy, but it does provide *evidence* for Peter's primacy. This is especially the case when that evidence is joined to texts that explicitly teach Petrine primacy—for example, Matthew 16:18–19, John 21:25, and Acts 15.

## The Rock

When Jesus first met Peter, he promised that Peter would "be called Cephas" (Jn 1:42), an Aramaic word that means "rock". This promise was fulfilled in Matthew 16:18–19, which records in its Greek text how Jesus changed Simon's name to *Petros* (Peter), which means *rock*. Jesus said, "You are Peter, and on this rock I will build my Church,

---

[6] For example, White says this fact about Peter's place in the apostolic lists "may simply reflect his being the oldest, or the first called". James R. White, *The Roman Catholic Controversy* (Minneapolis: Bethany House, 1996), 108.

[7] Norman Geisler agrees that John "was probably the youngest disciple" and attributes his ability to outrun Peter to the Lord's tomb to his youth (Jn 20:4). See Norman Geisler, *Popular Survey of the New Testament* (Grand Rapids, MI: Baker Books, 2007), 103.

[8] John MacArthur, *Twelve Ordinary Men* (Nashville, TN: Thomas Nelson, 2002), 38.

and the gates of Hades shall not prevail against it. I will give you the keys of the kingdom of heaven, and whatever you bind on earth shall be bound in heaven, and whatever you loose on earth shall be loosed in heaven."

The fact that Simon's name was changed indicates he was given a divine commissioning. Whenever God changes someone's name, it signifies a person's new mission. For example, when Abram became Abraham his new mission was summarized in a name that means "the father of a multitude of nations" (Gen 17:5). The fact that Simon's name was changed to the word "rock", and Jesus says he will build his Church on "rock", cannot be a coincidence. The Protestant biblical scholar Oscar Cullmann calls this an "obvious pun",[9] while Craig Keener says, "[Jesus] plays on Simon's nickname, 'Peter,' which is roughly the English 'Rocky': Peter is 'rocky,' and on this rock Jesus would build his Church."[10]

Protestant objections to this interpretation frequently try to prove that the rock on which Jesus builds the Church is something other than Peter, such as Peter's confession of faith. However, biblical symbols can refer to more than one thing (cf. Rev 17:9–10), and so the two are not exclusive. In fact, the *Catechism of the Catholic Church* says that the rock in this passage can also refer to Peter's confession of faith and not just Peter himself (*CCC* 424). Thus, what the critic must do is show the rock *cannot* be Peter, not that it *can* be something else.

Some Protestants say the rock must be Christ, and he alone, because Paul said Christ is the only foundation of the Church (1 Cor 3:11) and "the Rock was Christ" (1 Cor 10:4). McCarthy goes so far as to say that the name "rock" is symbolically applied only to God in Scripture and so it cannot refer to Peter in Matthew 16:18.[11] But this is false. Jesus unmistakably refers to Simon Bar-Jona as Cephas/Peter/Rock—so the term "rock" *must* be used for more than just God in Scripture.

---

[9] Oscar Cullmann, *Theological Dictionary of the New Testament*, vol. 6, ed. Gerhard Kittel (Grand Rapids, MI: Wm. B. Eerdmans, 1969), 98.

[10] Craig Keener, *The Gospel of Matthew: A Socio Rhetorical Commentary* (Grand Rapids, MI: Wm. B. Eerdmans, 2009), 426.

[11] James McCarthy, *The Gospel according to Rome* (Eugene, OR: Harvest House Publishers, 1995), 241.

Further, in 1 Corinthians 10:4 Paul was referring to Christ being the rock Moses struck that, according to Jewish legend, followed the Israelites through the desert. Paul did not mean every rock in Scripture was Christ because Isaiah says Abraham was a rock from which the Jewish people were hewn (Is 51:1). This also refutes McCarthy's claim that no one besides God is ever called "rock" in Scripture.

What about 1 Corinthians 3:11? Biblical symbols can be used in more than one way, and in that passage Christ is indeed the Church's foundation. But in Ephesians 2:20 Paul uses the foundation metaphor differently and says the apostles are the foundation of the Church. George Salmon, a critic of Catholicism whose arguments against papal infallibility will be examined in the next chapter, writes of this kind of argument, "The same metaphor may be used to illustrate different truths, and so, according to circumstances may have different significations."[12] Cullmann says that the interpretation of the rock solely referring to a confession of faith is "inconceivable", given that in this passage "there is no reference here to the faith of Peter."[13]

Those who claim that the rock can only be Peter's confession of faith often claim that there is a difference in meaning between Peter's name (*petros*) and the rock upon which the Church would be built (*petra*). But this argument, whose roots can be traced back to William Cathcart's *The Papal System*, is based on a flawed understanding of Greek vocabulary. The Protestant biblical scholar D. A. Carson says, "Although it is true that *petros* and *petra* can mean '[small] stone' and 'large rock' respectively in earlier Greek, the distinction is largely confined to poetry."[14] John Calvin even said, "There is no difference of meaning, I acknowledge, between the two Greek words *petros* and *petra*."[15]

Moreover, that Jesus was not making a distinction between *petros* and *petra* can be seen in the fact that Jesus was probably speaking

---

[12] George Salmon, *The Infallibility of the Church* (Dublin: University Press, 1888), 332.

[13] Cullmann, *Theological Dictionary of the New Testament*, 98. I owe this observation to Tim Staples.

[14] D. A. Carson, "Matthew", in *The Expositor's Bible Commentary*, vol. 8, ed. Frank E. Gaebelein (Grand Rapids, MI: Zondervan, 1984). Cited in Jimmy Akin, *A Daily Defense* (San Diego: Catholic Answers Press, 2016), kindle edition.

[15] John Calvin, *Commentary on Matthew, Mark, and Luke*, vol. 2, trans. William Pringle (Edinburgh: Calvin Translation Society, 1845), 295.

Aramaic, not Greek. In Matthew 16:17, Jesus referred to Simon with the Aramaic expression "Bar-Jona", or son of Jonah. John 1:42 describes Jesus' promise that Simon would be given the new name Cephas. Carson informs us that in the early Eastern Church the Syriac translation of the Bible (which is linguistically similar to Aramaic) did not use different words to translate *petros* and *petra*.[16] As Cullmann says, "Petra=Kepha=petros".[17]

Some Protestant apologists remain undaunted in their quest to keep Peter from being "the rock". McCarthy asks, "Why did not the Holy Spirit just repeat the word *petros*, as Catholic defenders speculate he did in the Aramaic?"[18] The answer is he could have, but there are compelling reasons for the Holy Spirit, along with the human author he inspired, not to repeat the word *petros*. Carson offers one explanation: "The Greek makes the distinction between *petros* and *petra* simply because it is trying to preserve the pun, and in Greek the feminine *petra* could not very well serve as a masculine name."[19]

Other Protestant apologists who accept that *petros* and *petra* have no difference in meaning try to exploit the difference between the personal pronoun in which Jesus refers to Peter ("*you* are Peter") and the demonstrative adjective in which Jesus refers to the rock ("on *this* rock").[20] They say that if Jesus was referring to Peter, he would have said, "You are Peter, and upon you, the rock, I will build my church." But this is not true. It is perfectly possible for one person to refer to someone using a personal pronoun like "you" and then refer to the same person using a demonstrative adjective like "this". For example, a man might tell his beloved, "You are the light of my life, and this light shines more brightly than the sun."

Even though they reject the doctrine of the papacy, Protestant biblical scholars admit that Jesus declared Peter to be the rock upon which the Church is built. According to Carson, "Many have attempted to avoid identifying Peter as the rock on which Jesus builds his church yet if it were not for Protestant reactions against extremes of Roman Catholic interpretations, it is doubtful whether many would have

[16] Carson, "Matthew", 368.
[17] Cullmann, *Theological Dictionary of the New Testament*, 98.
[18] McCarthy, *Gospel according to Rome*, 242.
[19] Carson, "Matthew", 368.
[20] White, *Roman Catholic Controversy*, 118.

taken 'rock' to be anything or anyone other than Peter."[21] Cullmann
bluntly declares, "Roman Catholic exegesis is right and all Protestant
attempts to evade this interpretation are to be rejected."[22]

Did the Fathers of the Church believe that Peter was the rock on
which the Church is built? The first testimony to Peter as the rock
(that at least has survived to the present day) comes from Tertullian,
who wrote in the early third century, "The Lord said to Peter, 'On
this rock I will build my Church.... Upon *you*, he says, I will build
my Church; and I will give to *you* the keys, not to the Church."[23]
Additional citations confirming Peter is the rock in Matthew 16:18
can be found in writings by Cyprian, Ambrose, Jerome, and Pope
Leo the Great.[24] Also, in his *Homilies on John*, Augustine says, "Peter,
that Rock, answered with the voice of all, Lord, to whom shall we
go? You have the words of eternal life."[25]

Some Protestant apologists claim that Augustine changed his mind
about Peter being the rock and took back this claim in a work called
*Retractations*.[26] Some readers erroneously assume this work is called *Re-
tractions* and believe that Augustine is correcting most of what he
previously wrote, but that is not the case. Patristic scholar William Jurgens explains, "Augustine had very little to retract, and the
meaning of Retractationes is Reconsiderations, Revisions, Second
Thoughts, or, as I have called it, Corrections. With the Corrections,
Augustine again invented a new literary genre: a summation and criticism of his own writings."[27]

Augustine did not deny that Peter is the rock on whom the Church
is built. He even acknowledged that his teacher, Saint Ambrose, held
that view. In *Retractations* Augustine offered an alternative interpretation of what the words could mean. He writes, "For 'Thou art Peter'
and not 'Thou art rock' was said to him. But 'the rock was Christ,'

[21] Carson, "Matthew", 368.

[22] Cullmann, *Theological Dictionary of the New Testament*, 108.

[23] Tertullian, *On Modesty*, 21.

[24] St. Cyprian, *Unity of the Catholic Church* 4; St. Ambrose, *Faith* 5.57; St. Jerome, *Letter* 1.5.2;
St. Leo the Great, *Letter* 10.1. Cited in Jimmy Akin, *The Fathers Know Best: Your Essential Guide
to the Teachings of the Early Church* (San Diego: Catholic Answers Press, 2010), 190–93.

[25] St. Augustine, *Tractates on John* 11.5.

[26] White, *Roman Catholic Controversy*, 121–22.

[27] William Jurgens, *The Faith of the Early Fathers*, vol. 3 (Collegeville, MN: Liturgical Press,
1979), 163.

in confessing whom, as also the whole Church confesses, Simon was called Peter. But let the reader decide which of these two opinions is the more probable."[28] The early twentieth-century archbishop (and future cardinal) Rafael Merry del Val offered this excellent rejoinder to those who would use this part of Augustine's work to discredit the doctrine of the papacy:

> If St. Augustine had rejected the commonly accepted interpretation given by his great teacher St. Ambrose, he would not have left the reader his choice. Nor could he have left us that choice.... Whichever interpretation [he] may have preferred, he does not retract, or suggest retracting the doctrine of the supremacy of St. Peter, a doctrine which he had repeatedly put forward in his writings, like the other Fathers before him, and in regard to which he leaves us no choice.[29]

## The Keeper of the Keys

Jesus did not intend for Peter's office of leadership to lapse when Peter died. As we'll see, Jesus' declaration of Peter as the foundation of the Church would be similar to the Continental Congress saying to George Washington, "You are president, and upon the/this president, we will build our nation."

One clue that Jesus is speaking of an office of leadership in the Church, and not just a man to lead it, is that Jesus tells Peter, "I will give you the keys of the kingdom" (Mt 16:19). This is an allusion to Isaiah 22:22 and its description of Israel's chief steward. In ancient Israel the king had absolute authority over his kingdom, but he would select a chief steward or vizier to oversee his house, especially when he was away. Isaiah 22 describes how Israel's wicked chief steward Shebna was replaced with the righteous man Eli'akim. Verse 22 says Eli'akim would have "the key of the house of David; he shall open, and none shall shut; and he shall shut, and none shall open".

Just as King Hezekiah gave Eli'akim authority to oversee his house, Christ gave Peter authority to oversee his Church (i.e., the

---

[28] Augustine, *The Retractations*, trans. Sister M. Inez Bogan (Washington, DC: Catholic University of America Press, 1999), 90–91.

[29] Rafael Merry del Val, *The Truth of Papal Claims* (St. Louis, MO: B. Herder, 1902), 46.

"keys of the kingdom"). According to F. F. Bruce, "What about the 'keys of the kingdom'? The keys of a royal or noble establishment were entrusted to the chief steward.... So in the new community which Jesus was about to build, Peter would be, so to speak, chief steward."[30]

Receiving the "keys of the kingdom" also included the authority to "bind" and "loose", which is a rabbinic expression that refers to the act of determining official doctrine and practice. According to R. T. France, "The terms [binding and loosing] thus refer to a teaching function, and more specifically one of making halakhic pronounce-ments [i.e., relative to laws not written down in the Jewish Scriptures but based on an oral interpretation of them] which are to be 'binding' on the people of God."[31] The Lutheran professor Tord Fornberg likewise says, "Peter stands out as a kind of chief Rabbi who binds and looses in the sense of declaring something to be forbidden or permitted. Peter is looked upon as a counterpart to the High Priest. He is the highest representative for the people of God."[32]

## The Shepherd

Matthew's Gospel describes the promise that Peter would be the foundation of the Church and receive Christ's authority to oversee it. The epilogue to John's Gospel (21:1–19) reveals the fulfillment of that promise through Jesus' commissioning of Peter to be the shepherd of his flock.

The scene begins with Jesus appearing to the disciples who are fishing and have failed to catch anything. Jesus, whom the disciples don't recognize, calls out to them and encourages them to cast their net out one more time. They catch a huge quantity of fish (153 to be exact), whereupon they recognize Jesus, which spurs Peter to leap into the sea and quickly reunite with his master. Then, after eating

---

[30] F. F. Bruce, The Hard Sayings of Jesus (Downers Grove, IL: IVP Academic, 1983), 143–44.

[31] R. T. France, Matthew: Evangelist and Teacher (Grand Rapids, MI: Zondervan, 1989), 247. Cited in Scott Butler, Norman Dahlgen, and David Hess, Jesus, Peter & the Keys A Scriptural Handbook on the Papacy (Goleta, CA: Queenship Publishing, 1996), 54.

[32] Tord Fornberg, "Peter: The High Priest of the New Covenant", Southeast Asia Journal of Theology 4 (1986): 113. Cited in Hahn, Reasons to Believe, 221.

breakfast, John describes Peter and Jesus engaging in a conversation where Jesus tells Peter to "feed my lambs", "tend my sheep", and "feed my sheep" (vv. 15–17). Peter is thus commissioned to provide spiritual care ("feed my sheep") and leadership ("tend my sheep") to Christ's Church.

Protestants often say this passage only describes Peter being reinstated to his role as a faithful apostle rather than Peter being given authority over the other apostles.[33] Catholics agree that Jesus' three questions around the fire in this scene give Peter the opportunity to atone for his threefold denial of Christ that he made near a fire during the Lord's trial (Mk 14:66–72; Lk 22:54–62; Jn 18:15–18; cf. Mt 26:69–75). Where we and other scholars disagree is that this is not the only purpose of Peter and Jesus' conversation. In his monograph on Peter's role in John's Gospel, Bradford Blaine Jr. says,

> Although the three professions of love do allow him to mitigate some of the damage of the three denials, they function primarily as warrants for the three pastoral responsibilities he receives: feeing lambs, tending sheep, and feeding sheep. I concur with [the biblical scholar Herman Ridderbos] that, "Jesus has sought not so much Peter's triple retraction of his denial, and even less to embarrass him again before the other disciples; it is rather what awaits Peter in the future that prompts Jesus to reinforce his ties with him as never before."[34]

Jesus does not give a similar command to any of the other disciples, or as the Protestant scholar Joachim Jeremias observes, "Only in John 21:15–17, which describes Peter's appointment as a shepherd by the Risen Lord, does the whole church appear to have been in view as the sphere of activity."[35] David A. deSilva likewise notes that "Peter is the one commissioned to tend the sheep and feed them; the Beloved Disciple [whom the text presents as the author of John's Gospel] is

---

[33] Ron Rhodes, *Reasoning from the Scriptures with Catholics* (Eugene, OR: Harvest House Publishing, 2000), 116.

[34] Bradford Blaine Jr., *Peter in the Gospel of John: The Making of an Authentic Disciple* (Atlanta: Society of Biblical Literature, 2007), 170.

[35] Joachim Jeremias, in Kittel, *Theological Dictionary of the New Testament*, 498. Cited in Steve Ray, *Upon This Rock: St. Peter and the Primacy of Rome in Scripture and the Early Church* (San Francisco: Ignatius Press, 1999), 49.

not given any specific commission or responsibility for the church in that scene or any other."[36]

## Opposing Biblical Evidence

Even critics of the papacy admit that these passages *seem* to teach that doctrine. D. A. Carson says that when the Petrine texts in John 21 and Matthew 16 are conjoined, "the argument [for Petrine primacy] gains a certain plausibility."[37] Of course, these scholars find something else in Scripture that, in their opinion, negates the concept of the papacy, so it is those texts we must now examine.

Some critics claim that Jesus' failure to answer the apostles' question of who among them was the greatest (Mk 9:34; Lk 9:46; 22:24) with "Peter; he's the pope" is evidence against Peter's primacy.[38] Others say the fact that the apostles were arguing at all over the question shows that they did not believe the title of "greatest" belonged to Peter. However, the apostles' inability to understand Peter's unique role among them does not refute the doctrine of the papacy any more than their inability to understand the necessity of the Crucifixion (even after Jesus said it was necessary) refutes the doctrine of the atonement.

In addition, Christ's answer that "the leader" will become "as one who serves" (Lk 22:26) was aimed at keeping the apostles from seeing their leader as a privileged king who would lord his authority over others. If the Protestant position on the papacy were correct, we would expect Jesus to say something like, "There is no greatest among you for you are all sheperds of my flock." Instead, Jesus indicated that the greatest must act as the servant of all. That is why since the sixth century popes have called themselves *servus servorum Dei*, or "servant of the servants of God".

Jesus then continues his teaching by reminding the apostles that he is a servant to them (Lk 22:27), each of whom will have prominent

[36] David A. deSilva, *An Introduction to the New Testament: Contexts, Methods & Ministry Formation* (Downers Grove: InterVarsity Press, 2004), 432.

[37] D. A. Carson, *The Gospel according to John* (Grand Rapids, MI: Wm. B. Eerdmans, 1991), 678.

[38] White, *Roman Catholic Controversy*, 109.

places in his kingdom (vv. 28–30). Continuing this same discourse (which is not interrupted until verse 35), Jesus singles out Peter and prays for him so that his faith may not fail and he would strengthen his brethren (vv. 31–32). Peter will be a leader, but one who serves others instead of being served. This also explains why Peter refers to himself in 1 Peter 5:1–2 as a fellow elder, and not as the leader of the Church.[39]

In this passage Peter is heeding his own advice to "clothe your-selves ... with humility toward one another" (5:5). Peter's address to his fellow elders does not undermine his authority over the other elders any more than the president's address to "my fellow Ameri-cans" undermines the presidency. Besides, Paul referred to himself as a servant using the Greek word *diakonoi*, which in other contexts refers to deacons (see 1 Cor 3:5; 2 Cor 11:23; 1 Tim 3:12), and even said he was "the very least of all the saints" (Eph 3:8)—but that did not detract from his authority as an apostle.

White says that if the papacy were an office in the Church, then Paul would have placed it before the office of apostle in his list of ecclesial ministries in 1 Corinthians 12:28: "God has appointed in the Church first apostles, second prophets, third teachers, then workers of miracles, then healers, helpers, administrators". White writes, "First the Pope, Peter, and *then* the Apostles is simply not the biblical order."[40] But the pope is not an office above apostle or bishop—the pope is one of the bishops and Peter was one of the apostles, even though he had authority over the Church as her leader. Paul himself recognized that among the apostles James, Peter, and John had unique roles as "pillars" of the Church (Gal 2:9), yet Paul does not say in 1 Corinthians 12:28, "First the pillars, and then apostles, and then ..."

Indeed, three chapters earlier when Paul makes an argument for the permissibility of traveling with wives, he refers to the same right held by "the other apostles and the brethren of the Lord and Cephas" (9:5). Notice that Peter is distinguished from the other apostles and

[39] Robert M. Zins, *Romanism: The Relentless Roman Catholic Assault on the Gospel of Jesus Christ!* (Huntsville, AL: White Horse Publications, 1995), 138. Rhodes, *Reasoning from the Scriptures*, 116–17.

[40] White, *Roman Catholic Controversy*, 110.

even Jesus' own kin and is ranked in ascending order among them. Finn Damgaard, in his study of Peter, says that throughout his letters "Paul exploits Peter's authority in order to highlight his own ministry."[41] The fact that Paul has to contend with a faction in Corinth that pledged its loyalty to Peter (1 Cor 1:12) further demonstrates Peter's authority in the early Church.

Finally, some Protestant apologists appeal to Acts 15 and claim that the first ecumenical council in Jerusalem was invoked and decided through the authority of James rather than Peter. But while James had a prominent place at the council, it was Peter who proposed a divinely revealed dogma that the council would later settle upon. Verse 7 tells us that "after there had been much debate" Peter rose and addressed the assembly. In the same verse, he recounted how "God made choice among you, that by my mouth the Gentiles should hear the word of the gospel and believe", indicating his special role.

Paul and Barnabas then spoke and added support to Peter's revelation. James concluded the gathering with a pastoral proposal for Christians to abstain from blood and meat sacrificed to idols, lest Jewish converts be scandalized. This proposal was accepted, but it was not a dogmatic declaration, since Paul allowed the Church in Corinth to eat meat sacrificed to idols just a few years later (1 Cor 8:8–9).

## Peter in Rome

Some Protestants claim that Peter was never in Rome, much less that he was the city's bishop. Reformed apologist Lorraine Boettner says, "There is in fact no New Testament evidence, nor any historical proof of any kind, that Peter was in Rome."[42] The earliest example of this claim comes from Marsilius of Padua (1275–1342), who said of Peter, "It cannot be proved by Scripture that he was bishop of Rome or, what is more, that he was ever at Rome."[43] However,

---

[41] Finn Damgaard, *Rewriting Peter as an Intertextual Character in the Canonical Gospels* (New York: Routledge, 2016), 28.

[42] Lorraine Boettner, *Roman Catholicism* (Phillipsburg, NJ: Presbyterian and Reformed Publishing, 1962), 117. Cited in Karl Keating, *Catholicism and Fundamentalism: The Attack on "Romanism" by "Bible Christians"* (San Francisco: Ignatius Press, 1988), 199–200.

[43] Thomas Craughwell, *St. Peter's Bones: How the Relics of the First Pope Were Lost and Found ... and Then Lost and Found Again* (New York: Random House, 2013), 96.

there is not only strong evidence that Peter was in Rome, but that Peter's remains lie beneath Vatican City. According to the *Oxford Dictionary of Saints*, "It is probable that the tomb [of Peter] is authentic. It is also significant that Rome is the only city that ever claimed to be Peter's place of death."[44]

When it comes to evidence from the New Testament, most commenters focus on how Peter ends his first letter. He writes, "She who is at Babylon, who is likewise chosen, sends you greetings; and so does my son Mark" (1 Pet 5:13). Since the time of Calvin some Protestants have taken the name "Babylon" to mean that Peter, the apostle to the Jews, was evangelizing the Jewish population in the actual city of Babylon, which was located in what is now modern-day Iraq.[45]

However, there was a sizable Jewish population in Rome given that the emperor expelled the Jews from Rome in A.D. 19 and again in A.D. 49. Neither the first expulsion nor the second one caused the city to become permanently vacant of either Jews or Christians who were thought to be Jews. Indeed, Paul's extended treatment of Jewish responses to the gospel in his Letter to the Romans demonstrates conclusively that there was a Jewish population in the city a few years after Emperor Claudius' expulsion in A.D. 49. Josephus also tells us that by the time of Claudius the Jews had left Babylon for Seleucia.[46] Sean McDowell, an Evangelical apologist who has written the definitive treatment on the fate of the twelve apostles, says:

> The Old Testament city of Babylon was in ruins, so [Peter] could not have been referring to that city. Rather, it was a relatively common cryptic name for Rome, the enemy of God. Like the Hebrews exiled in the Babylon of the Old testament, Christians in Rome felt

---

[44] David Farmer, *The Oxford Dictionary of Saints* (New York: Oxford University Press, 2011), 353.

[45] "As to the place from which he wrote, all do not agree. There is, however, no reason that I see why we should doubt that he was then at Babylon, as he expressly declares." John Calvin, *Commentaries on the Catholic Epistles*, trans. John King (Altenmuster, Germany: Jazzybee Verlag, 2012), kindle edition.

[46] Josephus, *Antiquities of the Jews* 18.9.8–9. Cited in Ben Witherington, *Letters and Homilies for Hellenized Christians: A Socio-Rhetorical Commentary on 1–2 Peter* (Downers Grove, IL: InterVarsity Press, 2007), 248.

themselves exiles in a foreign land, a sinful city that oppressed the people of God.[47]

Jewish literature, such as the Sibylline Oracles and 4 Baruch, as well as Christian literature, such as the book of Revelation, all used the name Babylon in reference to Rome.[48] The early Church Fathers Ignatius and Irenaeus also agree that Peter was in Rome.[49] A priest named Gaius who lived during Irenaeus' time told a heretic named Proclus that "the trophies of the apostles" (i.e., their remains) were buried at Vatican Hill.[50] McDowell concludes, "It is historically very probable that Peter was in Rome for at least some period of time."[51] D. A. Carson and Douglas Moo propose the more specific hypothesis that Peter was "in Rome about 63 (the probable date of 1 Peter)".[52]

## Papal Infallibility

The doctrine of papal infallibility teaches that the pope has a special grace from God that protects him from binding the Church to believe error. This grace is related to the general grace Christ gives the Church that prevents the entire college of bishops, as well as the faithful as a whole, from falling into error. For the purposes of our

[47] Sean McDowell, *The Fate of the Apostles: Examining the Martyrdom Accounts of the Closest Followers of Jesus* (New York: Routledge, 2016), 59. According to the Protestant theologian Wayne Grudem, "By referring to Rome as 'Babylon,' Peter was carrying through the imagery of the church as the new people of God or the new Israel, which he uses throughout this letter." Wayne Grudem, *1 Peter* (Grand Rapids, MI: Wm. B. Eerdmans, 1988), 34.

[48] "'Babylon' was the Jewish code name for Rome, as is perfectly clear from many references (2 Bar. 11:1–2: 67:7; 2 Esd. 3:1–28; Sib. Or. 5:143, 157–160; cf. Rev. 14:8: 16:19: 17:18: 18:2–24). It is a term Peter could expect a Jewish Christian audience to understand without further explanation." Witherington, *Letters and Homilies for Hellenized Christians*, 248.

[49] St. Ignatius of Antioch told the Christians in Rome he would not command them in the same way Peter had previously commanded them (*Letter to the Romans* 4). At the end of the second century, St. Irenaeus wrote, "The blessed apostles [Peter and Paul], having founded and built up the church [of Rome], they handed over the office of the episcopate to Linus." *Against Heresies* 3.3.3. See also the copious citations in David Eastman, *The Ancient Martyrdom Accounts of Peter and Paul* (Atlanta: Society of Biblical Literature, 2016).

[50] Eusebius, *Church History* 2.25.5.

[51] Sean McDowell, *Fate of the Apostles*, 60.

[52] D. A. Carson and Douglas Moo, *An Introduction to the New Testament*, 2nd ed. (Grand Rapids, MI: Zondervan, 2009), 180.

discussion, however, we will examine only the aspects of infallibility that directly pertain to the office of the papacy. The *Catechism* puts it this way:

> Christ endowed the Church's shepherds with the charism of infallibility in matters of faith and morals.... "The Roman Pontiff, head of the college of bishops, enjoys this infallibility in virtue of his office, when, as supreme pastor and teacher of all the faithful—who confirms his brethren in the faith—he proclaims by a definitive act a doctrine pertaining to faith or morals" (*LG* 25). (*CCC* 890–91)

There are several important clarifications that must be made when it comes to this doctrine. First, infallibility does not include impeccability, or protection from sinning in general. Every pope has been a sinner, and a few were notorious for the grave sins they committed during their pontificates. Instead, infallibility means the pope will be kept from binding the Church to doctrinal error *in spite* of his moral failings.

Second, the pope is infallible when he "definitively" proclaims a doctrine or makes what is called an ex cathedra (Latin, "from the chair") statement related to faith or morals or when he proclaims definitively certain truths that are connected with faith and morals (e.g., the validity of an ecumenical council). When the pope does this, he is said to derive his authority from the chair or teaching office of Saint Peter. However, if the pope is speaking as a private theologian, or even issuing a magisterial document that does not explicitly make a dogmatic definition, then his teaching is not protected by infallibility.

Third, papal infallibility is not a positive protection that guarantees the pope will always have the right answers for every problem the Church faces. Instead, it is a negative protection that keeps the pope from binding the Church to believe error. In this case, infallibility might often manifest itself by *preventing* the pope from publicly speaking as opposed to empowering him to speak correctly on a certain doctrine.

This clarification answers the common retort that if the pope were infallible, then "why doesn't he just infallibly settle every controversy the Church faces?"[53] For the same reason that an inerrant Scripture

---

[53] "We cannot help but ask why the popes of Rome have failed to do their studying and call upon this alleged power to protect them from error to explain to the waiting world the 'official' interpretation of Jesus Christ on all the passages of the Bible." Zins, *Romanism*, 138.

does not explicitly reveal the answers to those same controversies: God has chosen not to reveal himself in this way. The pope must learn about issues that face the Church like everyone else and is free to abstain from weighing in on a theological or moral dispute.

What's interesting is that Protestant definitions of scriptural inerrancy contain similar qualifications to Catholic definitions of papal infallibility. Geisler says, for example, that the inerrancy of Scripture is limited only to what was written in the Bible's original autographs, which exempts copyist errors from the scope of inerrancy. He also says that inerrancy does not require the Bible to use scientific language, exact numbers, or even record the exact words Jesus or the apostles used on certain occasions.[54]

I don't disagree with some of the points Geisler makes about Scripture's inerrancy. Rather, I point them out to rebut Protestants like Geisler who claim that the doctrine of papal infallibility contains "so many" qualifications that it becomes useless as a guide for the Church.[55] If Protestants are allowed to qualify their defense of Scripture, then Catholics should be allowed the same right to qualify their defense of the papacy.

## Infallibility and Scripture

Matthew 16:18 says the "gates of Hades [Hell]" will never prevail against the Church, so it makes sense that the pastor of Christ's Church will never steer it into hell by dogmatically teaching heresy. Luke 22:31–32 records Jesus telling Peter, "Satan demanded to have you, that he might sift you like wheat, but I have prayed for you that your faith may not fail; and when you have turned again, strengthen your brethren." The original Greek in the passage shows that Satan demanded to sift "you", or all the apostles, but Jesus prayed specifically for Peter and his faith not to fail.[56]

---

[54] See, for example, Norman Geisler and William Roach, *Defending Inerrancy: Affirming the Accuracy of Scripture for a New Generation* (Grand Rapids, MI: Baker Books, 2011), 296–302.

[55] "Once all the qualifications are placed on infallibility, both in theory and in practice, it is defrocked of its glory." Norman L. Geisler and Ralph E. MacKenzie, *Roman Catholics and Evangelicals: Agreements and Differences* (Grand Rapids, MI: Baker Books, 1995), 216–17.

[56] In Luke 22:31–32 Jesus prays, "Simon, Simon, behold, Satan demanded to have you [Greek, *hymas*, second person plural] that he might sift you like wheat, but I have prayed for you [Greek, *sou*, second person singular] that your faith may not fail; and when you have turned again, strengthen your brethren."

Rhodes says, "This verse has nothing to do with papal infallibility.... Jesus' prayer for Peter is in keeping with his general inter-
cessory ministry for all believers (Rom 8:34, Heb. 7:25, see also
John 17:15)."[57] But in those passages Jesus does not pray that every
believer's faith "might not fail" (Greek, *me eklipe*) like he does for
Peter. Nor is a single believer charged with strengthening the faith of
others. While they try to soften the passage's meaning, the Protestant
authors of the *Dictionary of Jesus and the Gospels* admit,

> Peter, despite his failure, is implicitly singled out for special leader-
> ship. Again, the emphasis is not so much on transfer of authority as
> on mission. Peter is to care for the disciples much as Jesus has. This
> anticipates Peter's role in Acts where he will be the leader of the
> early church.[58]

J. N. D. Kelly agrees that "Peter was the undisputed leader of the
youthful church."[59] Most Protestants would also admit that Peter was
at least infallible when he wrote First and Second Peter, or that those
epistles have no errors. Catholics simply believe that, as the leader of
the Church, neither Peter nor any of his successors ever bound the
Church to heresy or error.

It's true that Christ once called Peter "Satan" (Mt 16:23) for saying
in response to Jesus' prediction of his death at the hands of the Jewish leaders, "God forbid, Lord! This shall never happen to you" (Mt
16:22). Jesus' rebuke was a serious one, but it fails to disprove papal
infallibility because Peter was not making a doctrinal declaration. He
was assuming the traditional Jewish view that the Messiah would
conquer rather than suffer, and Jesus corrected him on that point. In
fact, Jesus needed to rebuke Peter publicly because in that instant, as
he often did, Peter spoke for all the apostles and would become the
leader of the entire Church. According to Albright and Mann, in
their Anchor Bible commentary on Matthew,

---

[57] Rhodes, *Reasoning from the Scriptures*, 115.

[58] R. W. Paschal Jr., "Farewell Discourse", in *Dictionary of Jesus and the Gospels*, ed. Joel
B. Green, Scot McKnight, and I. Howard Marshall (Downers Grove, IL: InterVarsity Press,
1992), 231.

[59] J. N. D. Kelly, *Oxford Dictionary of the Popes* (New York: Oxford University Press,
1986), 1.

To deny the pre-eminent position of Peter among the disciples or in the early Christian community is a denial of the evidence.... The interest in Peter's failures and vacillations does not detract from the pre-eminence; rather, it emphasizes it. Had Peter been a lesser figure his behavior would have been of far less consequence.[60]

The most common argument against Peter's infallibility is Paul's rebuke of Peter in Galatians 2:11–14. R. T. Kendall, for example, admits that Protestants "overreact" to Matthew 16:18 and says he has no problem admitting Peter is the rock on whom the Church is built in that passage.[61] However, he says that passage does not teach that Peter was infallible and believes such an idea is contradicted by Galatians 2:11. In that verse Paul says, "When Cephas [Peter] came to Antioch I opposed him to his face, because he stood condemned." What had Peter done to earn Paul's ire? The apostle explains:

For before certain men came from James, [Cephas] ate with the Gentiles; but when they came he drew back and separated himself, fearing the circumcision party. And with him the rest of the Jews acted insincerely, so that even Barnabas was carried away by their insincerity. But when I saw that they were not straightforward about the truth of the gospel, I said to Cephas before them all, "If you, though a Jew, live like a Gentile and not like a Jew, how can you compel the Gentiles to live like Jews?"

This encounter between Peter and Paul does not disprove papal infallibility, because Paul was rebuking Peter's personal behavior, not his teaching. As the Reformed theologian Thomas Schreiner puts it, "Peter and Paul still agreed *theologically* [emphasis in original]. Paul rebukes Peter because the latter acted *against* his convictions."[62]

Some Protestants try to impugn Peter and say he erred in his teaching since he was "not straightforward about the truth of the gospel". But the text means, "They were not walking uprightly

---

[60] W. F. Albright and C. S. Mann, *The Anchor Bible: Matthew* (New York: Doubleday, 1971), 195. Cited in Ray, *Upon This Rock*, 34.

[61] R. T. Kendall, *The Parables of Jesus: A Guide to Understanding and Applying the Stories Jesus Told* (Grand Rapids, MI: Chosen Books, 2006), 144.

[62] Thomas R. Schreiner, *Galatians* (Grand Rapids, MI: Zondervan, 2010), 145.

according to the truth of the Gospel." Verse 14 uses the Greek word *orthopodousin*, from which we get the English word "orthopedics". Once again, it was Peter's actions that were being criticized, not his teaching.[63]

But even if Saint Peter did have infallible authority over the apostolic Church, how do we know this authority was passed on to his successors? How do we know that the subsequent bishops of Rome inherited a primacy of authority and charism of infallibility that was first entrusted to Peter? To answer that question we must proceed beyond the biblical evidence and examine the historical evidence for the papacy.

---

[63] Geisler and MacKenzie write, "It is difficult to exonerate Peter from the charge that he led believers astray—something the infallible pastor of the church would never do! The Catholic response that Peter was only infallible in his *ex cathedra* words and not his actions, rings hollow when we remember that 'actions speak louder than words.'" Geisler and MacKenzie, *Roman Catholics and Evangelicals*, 211. But papal infallibility does not mean a pope's actions will not cause scandal; it just means the pope will not bind believers to accepting erroneous doctrine. And since choosing where to have a meal does not communicate declarations of doctrine, this incident does not disprove papal infallibility.

# 6

# The Papacy, Part II

Even if Peter had authority over the universal Church, that does not mean his successors retained his same authority. In chapter 7 we will examine the biblical evidence for the general idea of apostolic succession. For now, we will examine the historical evidence for the particular claim that Peter's authority was passed on to his successors, the bishops of Rome.

## Evidence for Papal Primacy

Our earliest writing from a pope after Peter comes from Clement of Rome, whom Tertullian says Peter ordained and Irenaeus describes as Peter's third successor.[1] Sometime in the latter half of the first century Clement responded to a dispute in the Church of Corinth through a letter now known as the First Epistle of Clement (1 Clement), which discussed the unjust dismissal of several leaders in the local church.

Some apologists say Clement was merely writing in a tone of "fraternal correction", and this letter provides no evidence that the bishop of Rome had any special primacy among other bishops.[2] But the fact that Rome was specifically sought out to resolve this dispute and charged the Corinthians to obey the words of the Holy Spirit shows that Rome was not a mere "brother church", but a church with unique prestige and influence among all others. Philip Schaff goes further and describes this letter as "the first example of the exercise of a sort of papal authority." He goes on to say the Roman Church

[1] St. Irenaeus, *Against Heresies* 3.3.3; Tertullian, *Prescription against Heretics* 32.
[2] "The First Epistle of Clement is simply an example of the overall concern which individual churches took for the well being and care of one another." William Webster, *The Church of Rome at the Bar of History* (Carlisle, PA: Banner of Truth Trust, 1995), 57.

gives advice, with superior administrative wisdom, to an important church in the East, dispatches messengers to her, and exhorts her to order and unity in a tone of calm dignity and authority, as the organ of God and the Holy Spirit. This is all the more surprising if St. John, as is probable, was then still living in Ephesus, which was nearer to Corinth than Rome.[3]

In fact, the writings of Pope Clement, along with Pope Soter (A.D. 167–174), were so popular that they were read in the Church alongside Scripture.[4] In response, Webster claims that

> the writing of such a letter does not, in and of itself, suggest that there is any issue of primacy involved. Ignatius of Antioch, who died between 112 and 116 A.D., also wrote letters to different churches, including the church at Rome, rebuking, exhorting and giving instruction. Does this mean that Ignatius had a right of jurisdiction over these churches? Surely not, for that would mean that he had a right of jurisdiction over the Church at Rome itself.[5]

With the exception of his letter to Rome, Ignatius' letters were all written to communities in western Asia Minor, over which he may have had influence given that he was the bishop of the nearby historic see of Antioch. But while Ignatius rebukes and gives instruction to these churches in matters like avoiding heresy or remaining in union with the bishop, he does not do the same in his letter to the Romans. Instead, Ignatius primarily asks the Roman Church not to save him from martyrdom. He also tells them, "I do not, as Peter and Paul,

---

[3] Philp Schaff, *History of the Christian Church*, vol. 2 (New York: Charles Scribner's Sons, 1901), 158. Cited in Steve Ray, *Upon This Rock: St. Peter and the Primacy of Rome in Scripture and the Early Church* (San Francisco: Ignatius Press, 1999), 132.

[4] Eusebius, *Church History* 4.23.9. Some say 1 Clement's use of plural pronouns is evidence that a group of presbyters served as the leaders at Rome rather than a single bishop. However, the use of the magisterial or royal "we" was popular from even before the time of Christ and has been used by popes until modern times. Paul himself used the plural "we" when addressing the Corinthians, but this did not nullify his unique authority as an apostle (1 Cor 1:23; 2 Cor 1:24). Second, it's possible Clement was still an elder at Rome when he wrote this letter as the Roman Church's personal corresponding secretary. This doesn't disprove the existence of a single bishop in Rome at that time any more than a papal secretary writing about what "we" or "the Vatican" believes about a subject disproves the existence of the current bishop of Rome.

[5] Webster, *Church of Rome at the Bar of History*, 57.

issue commandments unto you," and commends this church because it has "never envied any one; you have taught others".[6]

Another feature that is not found in his other letters is Ignatius' effusive praise for the Roman Church. He declares that she is "worthy of praise, worthy of obtaining her every desire, worthy of being deemed holy".[7] Ignatius also says the Church at Rome "presides in love" (Greek, *prokathemenon tes agapes*), which translators have rendered "having the presidency of love"[8] and "preeminent in love".[9] The language of "presiding" is also found in Ignatius' letter to the Church in Magnesia where he says, "Your bishop presides in the place of God."[10]

Some scholars, especially Eastern Orthodox ones, claim that this phrase merely refers to the superior generosity of the Roman Church, but it seems to imply more than that. Earlier in the prologue of his letter, Ignatius refers to Rome "presiding in the country of the Romans", using the same Greek word (*prokathemai*), thus indicating a ruling role. Ignatius uses the word "preside" only in a clerical context, and non-Christian literature generally uses the word in conjunction with concrete entities like cities rather than abstract ideas like love.[11] In his study of the papacy, A. Edward Siecienski says that at the very least, "Rome's preeminence is simply accepted by both [Ignatius] and (presumably) his readers without debate or explanation."[12]

This preeminence can be seen in the second century when Saint Irenaeus protested Pope Victor I's decision to excommunicate an entire region of churches. While Irenaeus felt such a decision was not prudent, he never doubted the pope had the authority to impose such a punishment on churches outside of his local bishopric. Irenaeus even said that in the face of heresy it was important to seek out churches that were the custodians of apostolic tradition—specifically, "the very great, the very ancient, and universally known Church

---

[6] St. Ignatius of Antioch, *Letter to the Romans* 4.3.

[7] St. Ignatius of Antioch, *Epistle to the Romans*, Greeting.

[8] J. B. Lightfoot, *The Apostolic Fathers: Part II* (London: Macmillan, 1855), 554.

[9] Kirsopp Lake, *The Apostolic Fathers*, vol. 1 (London: William Heinemann, 1919), 225.

[10] St. Ignatius of Antioch, *Letter to the Magnesians* 6.

[11] Ray, *Upon This Rock*.

[12] A. Edward Siecienski, *The Papacy and the Orthodox: Sources and History of a Debate* (New York: Oxford University Press, 2017), 146.

founded and organized at Rome by the two most glorious apostles, Peter and Paul".[13]

Irenaeus put this advice into practice when he visited Victor's predecessor Eleutherius in order seek his appraisal of the Montanist heresy.[14] In fact, Irenaeus declared in his work *Against Heresies* that "it is a matter of necessity that every Church should agree with this Church, on account of its preeminent authority, that is, the faithful everywhere, inasmuch as the tradition has been preserved continuously by those [faithful men] who exist everywhere."[15] According to the Methodist scholar John Lawson:

> The prestige of Rome is based upon the circumstance that her Church was founded by the two greatest Apostles, i.e. it is connected with the nature of the message she has to declare: with her authority, in fact … the *potentior principalitas* of the Roman Church is, then, the possession in a unique and supreme degree of that which is the possession of the whole Church.[16]

The third-century ecclesial writer Tertullian refers to Rome as the location of the apostolic thrones (Latin, *cathedrae*) and the place where "our authority derives".[17] He also asked if the Lord withheld any knowledge from Peter, who "is called the rock on which the church should be built, who also obtained the keys of the kingdom of heaven, with the power of loosing and binding in heaven and on earth".[18] Tertullian connects Rome's authority with Peter and Paul, saying, "How happy is its church, on which apostles poured forth all their doctrine along with their blood!"[19]

In response to this, some critics quote Tertullian's later writings where he argues that Peter's authority was not passed on to his

---

[13] St. Irenaeus, *Against Heresies* 3.3.2.

[14] J. N. D. Kelly, *A Dictionary of Popes* (Oxford: Oxford University Press, 2010), 11.

[15] St. Irenaeus, *Against Heresies* 3.3.2. There is some dispute among scholars about key terms in this passage like "preeminent authority [*potentior principalitas*]" because they derive from a Latin copy of Irenaeus' original Greek text.

[16] John Lawson, *The Biblical Theology of Saint Irenaeus* (Eugene, OR: Wipf and Stock, 2006), 275.

[17] Tertullian, *Prescription against Heretics* 36.

[18] Ibid., 22.

[19] Ibid.

successors. In one passage Tertullian claims, "For this power is Peter's personally, and after that it belongs to those who have the spirit."[20] But this writing comes from Tertullian's later Montanist period, where he rejected the authority of the Catholic Church and substituted it with the authority of private, ecstatic prophecies (hence Tertullian's claim that Peter's authority now resided with anyone who "had the Spirit"). According to Siecienski, "Whereas the orthodox Tertullian had seen bishops as heirs of the apostles and thus central to his understanding of the church, the montanist Tertullian believed the true church could not be bound by such institutional structures."[21]

Unlike Tertullian, his contemporary Saint Cyprian remained faithful to the Church throughout his whole life and recognized the important role the Roman bishop played in preserving apostolic succession and Church unity. Cyprian writes in *On the Unity of the Church*, "A primacy is given to Peter, whereby it is made clear that there is but one Church and one chair.... If he desert the chair of Peter upon whom the Church was built, can he still be confident that his is in the Church?"[22]

In the second edition of this work Cyprian makes this primacy more implicit but still begins what he calls an "easy proof for faith" with Scripture passages about Peter from Matthew 16 and John 21. Cyprian says that in John 20 the authority to bind and loose was also given to all the apostles, but he says concerning Christ:

> That He might set forth unity, He arranged by His authority the origin of that unity, as beginning from one. Assuredly the rest of the apostles were also the same as was Peter, endowed with a like partnership both of honor and power; but the beginning proceeds from unity.... Does he who does not hold this unity of the Church think that he holds the faith?[23]

This shift in tone over the course of a few years parallels Cyprian's shifting relationship with the bishop of Rome. On the one hand, Cyprian praised Rome, especially Pope Cornelius, when that

[20] Tertullian, *On Modesty* 21. Cited in Siecienski, *Papacy and the Orthodox*, 149.
[21] Ibid.
[22] St. Cyprian, *Treatise 1 (On the Unity of the Church)*, 4.
[23] Ibid.

Church stood against his detractors in Carthage, where he served as bishop. On the other hand, he strongly disagreed with Cornelius' successor Pope Stephen over whether heretics and schismatics needed to be rebaptized prior to reconciling with the Church. Cyprian believed rebaptism was necessary and upheld a local Carthaginian custom attesting to the practice. Stephen, however, held to the older and more widespread view that one's baptism remains valid even if he falls into heresy or schism (which is still the view of the Church today).

The pontiff and the African bishop exchanged heated letters with one another over the subject, which may explain Cyprian's later downplaying of papal authority in the second edition of On the Unity of the Church. The Orthodox scholar Nicholas Afanassief astutely says Cyprian "has left us a literary heritage broken by frequent self contradiction, which has been a matter for controversy from then until the present day".[24] We will discuss Cyprian's views of Rome's authority in more detail later, but for now Afanassief's observation about the Carthaginian bishop is helpful for our inquiry. He says that even though Cyprian believed all the bishops shared one kind of equal authority (a position with which Catholics agree), "the place given by [Cyprian] to the Roman Church did raise it above the 'harmonious multitude.'"[25]

Moving on to the fourth century, the regional Council of Sardica affirmed the right of bishops to appeal a dispute with their colleagues to the bishop of Rome, who has unique authority to judge such matters.[26] Both Saint Basil the Great and Athanasius sought the intervention of Rome in their disputes with Arian bishops in the Eastern empire. When Saint Jerome sought Pope Damasus' counsel about a dispute over the rightful claimant to the See of Antioch, he said, "As I follow no leader save Christ, so I communicate with none but your blessedness, that is with the chair of Peter. For this, I know, is the rock on which the church is built!"[27]

---

[24] Nicholas Afanassief, "The Church which Presides in Love", in The Primacy of Peter Primacy: Essays in Ecclesiology and the Early Church, ed. John Meyendorff (Crestwood, NY: St. Vladirmir's Press, 1992), 98. Cited in Ray, Upon This Rock, 181.

[25] Ibid.

[26] Council of Sardica, canons 3–5.

[27] St. Jerome, Letter 15 to Pope Damasus 2.

In response to this, some apologists cite Jerome's letter to Evangelus, where Jerome says, "Wherever there is a bishop, whether it be at Rome or at Engubium, whether it be at Constantinople or at Rhegium, whether it be at Alexandria or at Zoan, his dignity is one and his priesthood is one."[28]

Catholics agree that every bishop equally shares in being a successor of the apostles even if he is the shepherd of a geographically small or relatively recent addition to the Church (such as a rural, missionary territory). This is similar to saying every Supreme Court justice is equal with his colleague in virtue their being justices of the Court, even though only one of them is the Chief Justice. According to papacy scholar Dom John Chapman, "St. Jerome's point is that bishops have exactly the same powers by their ordinations, whatever the immense difference in their jurisdiction."[29] This corresponds to this excerpt from Jerome's treatise against Jovinianus:

> The Church was founded upon Peter: although elsewhere the same is attributed to all the Apostles, and they all receive the keys of the kingdom of heaven, and the strength of the Church depends upon them all alike, yet one among the twelve is chosen so that when a head has been appointed, there may be no occasion for schism.[30]

In the next century the status of the pope as the authoritative successor of Peter can be seen in the Council of Chalcedon, where, after a public recitation of Pope Leo's letter, the bishops in attendance proclaimed, "Peter has spoken through Leo!"[31] J. N. D. Kelly concludes, "By the middle of the fifth century the Roman church had established, de jure as well as de facto, a position of primacy in the West, and the papal claims to supremacy over all bishops of Christendom had been formulated in precise terms."[32]

---

[28] St. Jerome, *Letter 146 to Evangelus* 1.

[29] Dom John Chapman, *Studies on the Early Papacy* ([Place of publication not identified] Ex Fontibus Company, 2015; originally published in 1898), 109.

[30] St. Jerome, *Against Jovinianus* 1.26.

[31] Jaroslav Pelikan, *The Christian Tradition: A History of the Development of Doctrine*, vol. 1, *The Emergence of the Catholic Tradition (100–600)* (Chicago: University of Chicago Press, 1971), 148.

[32] J. N. D. Kelly, *Early Christian Doctrines* (New York: HarperCollins, 1978), 410.

## Historical Arguments against the Papacy

Some critics claim that the humble bishops of Rome would have looked nothing like modern popes who move through throngs of people via the "popemobile". In one sense that's true, but the first humble house churches would have looked nothing like modern Protestant "mega churches". Since that doesn't disprove Evangelical theology, changes in papal customs do not disprove Catholic theology. In another sense, the early popes were approached by crowds of people, and, in Peter's case, some of these people hoped his shadow would fall on them so that they would be healed of their infirmities (Acts 5:15); so there is a historical precedent for the adulation the current pontiff often receives.

Other critics, such as Geisler and MacKenzie, claim that the existence of multiple claimants to the papacy (or antipopes) is evidence against the doctrine of the papacy. They write, "How can there be two infallible and opposing popes at the same time?"[33] But this is a straw man of the Catholic position. Catholics do not hold that there were ever two legitimate popes at once, much less that both were infallible. Instead, there have been rare occasions in Church history when, after the election of one pope, another individual began falsely claiming to be pope and was able to attract a significant following.[34] But just as the existence of forged or counterfeit Scriptures does not disprove the existence of God's inspired word, the existence of "papal pretenders" does not disprove the divine origins of the office of the papacy.

Other apologists attempt to disprove the papacy by citing specific historical examples of the Fathers apparently denying the pope's authority. According to William Webster, "No father denies that Peter had a primacy or that there is a Petrine succession." Webster qualifies this admission, however, by saying that "the issue is how the fathers interpreted those concepts. They simply did not hold to

[33] Norman L. Geisler and Ralph E. MacKenzie, *Roman Catholics and Evangelicals: Agreements and Differences* (Grand Rapids, MI: Baker Books, 1995), 217.
[34] Geisler and MacKenzie are aware of this but still claim that this is only a "theoretical solution" because "the faithful have no way to know for sure which [pope] is the right one." Ibid. But that assumes Christ did not establish a Church through which believers can know which pope is authentic and which is not. If Geisler and MacKenzie believe the Holy Spirit can help believers know which writings are authentic Scripture and which are not then what would prevent the Holy Spirit from guiding the Church in a similar way?

the Roman Catholic view of later centuries that primacy and succession were 'exclusively' related to the bishops of Rome."[35] For example, Webster says, " 'The chair of Peter' was a term that applied to all bishops no matter what See they were in and all were the successors of Peter."[36] In other words, Cyprian's claims of unity coming from the chair of Peter refer to the bishops as a whole, and not to the pope in particular. Webster then says of Cyprian:

> His view is similar to that of Augustine's in maintaining that Peter is a symbol of the principle of unity. The entire episcopate, according to Cyprian, is the foundation of the Church.... All of the bishops constitute the Church and rule over their individual areas of responsibility as co-equals.[37]

But while Cyprian did object to some aspects of Rome's authority, it is inaccurate to say he believed all the bishops held equal authority. Cyprian urged Pope Stephen to excommunicate the heretic Marcianus of Arles even though the man lived in Gaul, which had its own bishops. When Stephen threatened Cyprian with excommunication, Cyprian did not deny that the pope had the authority to carry out such a punishment. Afanassief, who rejects the Catholic view of the papacy, provides a more accurate summary of Cyprian's views on Roman primacy:

> According to Cyprian, every bishop occupies Peter's throne (the Bishop of Rome among others), but the See of Peter is Peter's throne par excellence. The Bishop of Rome is the direct heir of Peter, where as the others are heirs only indirectly, and sometimes only by the mediation of Rome. Hence Cyprian's insistence that the Church of Rome is the root and matrix of the Catholic Church.[38]

Calvin likewise believed Cyprian taught that "the bishopric of Christ alone is universal", but he adds the further claim that Pope Gregory the Great "execrates the name of universal bishop as profane,

---

[35] William Webster, personal email cited in Ray, *Upon This Rock*, 13.
[36] Webster, *Church of Rome at the Bar of History*, 50.
[37] Ibid., 49.
[38] Nicholas Affanassieff, "The Church which Presides in Love", 98.

nay, blasphemous, and the forerunner of the anti-Christ".[39] Geisler and MacKenzie also claim that Gregory said this and declare that any claim of being a universal bishop entails "the corruption of the church, and perhaps even the work of the Antichrist".[40]

What these apologists are referring to is Pope Gregory the Great's dispute with John the Faster, the patriarch of Constantinople, over the latter's use of the title "universal bishop". In condemning the title "universal bishop", Gregory didn't deny that one bishop had primacy over all the others. In his twelfth epistle Gregory explicitly says Constantinople was subject to the authority of the pope.[41]

Instead, Gregory denied that the pope or any bishop that served a metropolitan area (like a patriarch in the East) was the bishop of every *individual territory* and the bishops under his authority were merely agents acting on his behalf. Such a view would rob one's brother bishops of their legitimate authority, even though they were still subject to Gregory in virtue of his being Peter's successor. As Gregory says in his twenty-first epistle, "As to what they say of the Church of Christ, who doubts that it is subject to the Apostolic See?"[42] J. N. D. Kelly rightly concludes that "Gregory argued that St. Peter's commission [e.g., in Matthew 16:18–19] made all churches, Constantinople included, subject to Rome."[43]

## History and Papal Infallibility

Protestant apologists who attempt to refute the doctrine of papal infallibility usually claim that the doctrine came into existence long after the apostles and was therefore not a part of the apostolic Deposit of Faith. Or, they try to present instances of popes who allegedly promulgated heretical doctrine, which would refute the claim that every pope receives the charism of infallibility.

---

[39] John Calvin, "Articles of Faith", in *Tracts and Treatises of John Calvin*, vol. 1, trans. Henry Beveridge (Eugene, OR: Wipf and Stock, 2002), 112.

[40] Geisler and MacKenzie, *Roman Catholics and Evangelicals*, 206.

[41] It states, in part: "For as to what they say about the Church of Constantinople, who can doubt that it is subject to the Apostolic See, as both the most pious lord the emperor and our brother the bishop of that city continually acknowledge?" St. Gregory the Great, *Registrum Epistolarum*, book 9, letter 12.

[42] St. Gregory the Great, *Letters of Gregory* 9.12.

[43] Kelly, *Dictionary of Popes*, 64.

Concerning the apostolic origins of papal infallibility, although the language of papal infallibility took time to develop, that doesn't prevent it from being a part of the Deposit of Faith. Language used to define doctrines like the Trinity and original sin also took time to develop, but the doctrines they describe existed at the beginning of Church history. Papal infallibility was not formally defined until 1870 at the First Vatican Council, but its development can be traced long before that point. For example, in the sixteenth century Saint Francis de Sales said the pope "cannot err when he is in cathedra, that is, when he intends to make an instruction and decree for the guidance of the whole Church, when he means to confirm his brethren as supreme pastor, and to conduct them into the pastures of the faith".[44]

The Fathers at Vatican I cited a profession made at the thirteenth-century Second Council of Lyon that said, in part, "The Holy Roman Church possesses the supreme and full primacy and principality over the whole Catholic Church.... If any questions arise concerning the faith, it is by her judgment that they must be settled."[45] The Protestant scholar Mark Powell places the modern doctrine's origin in the fourteenth century but admits that it "was itself part of a long development of papal claims".[46]

In 622 an Eastern monk named Saint Maximus the Confessor said of "the most holy Church of the Romans" that "it is in no way overcome by the gates of Hades according to the very promise of the Savior, but holds the keys of the orthodox confession and faith in Him.... It shuts up and locks every heretical mouth that speaks unrighteousness against the Most High."[47] In 517 Pope Hormisdas said that in "the Apostolic See the Catholic religion has always been preserved unblemished."[48] We should also consider the witness of Saint Cyprian and his description of heretics who

---

[44] St. Francis de Sales, *The Catholic Controversy*, trans. Henry Benedict Mackey ([Place of publication not identified] Aeterna Press, 2015), 186.

[45] Vatican I, *Pastor Aeternus* 4.2.

[46] Mark Powell, *Papal Infallibility: A Protestant Evaluation of an Ecumenical Issue* (Grand Rapids, MI: Wm. B. Eerdmans, 2009), 34.

[47] St. Maximus the Confessor, *Opuscula theologica et polemica*, 11. Cited in Siecienski, *Papacy and the Orthodoxy*, 202.

[48] Vatican I, *Pastor Aeternus* 4.2.

bear letters from schismatic and profane persons to the throne of Peter, and to the chief church whence priestly unity takes its source; and not to consider that these were the Romans whose faith was praised in the preaching of the apostle, to whom faithlessness could have no access.[49]

These patristic and conciliar texts don't contain explicit affirmations of papal infallibility as they were defined at Vatican I. They do contain implicit affirmations that the Roman Church, led by the bishop of Rome, possessed a unique authority that could be relied upon in the face of heresy. According to Lawson:

> To saint Irenaeus Rome was most certainly an authority none must question, as she cannot be imagined as ever in error. The word "infallible" to some extent begs the question, for the use of it imports into the discussion the results of later definition. It is nevertheless a word which is difficult to do without. With this proviso we may say that Irenaeus regarded Rome as the very corner-stone and typification of a whole structure of ecclesiastical infallibility.[50]

Concerning the claim that certain popes were fallible, we must remember that infallibility only protects the pope from formally defining something that is theologically or morally erroneous. So, for example, immoral behavior on the part of pontiffs does not refute the doctrine of papal infallibility.[51]

Infallibility also does not protect the pope (or the Church as a whole) from making errors in regard to the administration of ecclesiastical punishments. For example, the nineteenth-century critic George Salmon says, "The history of Galileo makes short work of the question: Is it possible for the Church of Rome to err in her interpretation of scripture or to mistake in what she teaches to be an essential part of the Christian faith? She *can* err, for she *has* erred" [emphasis in original].[52] But this objection, along with similar appeals to the trial of Galileo, does not disprove papal infallibility.

---

[49] St. Cyprian, *Epistle* 54.14.

[50] Lawson, *Biblical Theology of Saint Irenaeus*, 276.

[51] Particularly egregious examples can be found in the "pornocracy" of the tenth century. See Kelly, *Dictionary of Popes*, 120.

[52] George Salmon, *The Infallibility of the Church* (London: John Murray, 1888), 253.

Even if the pope erred in his treatment of Galileo and acted unjustly toward him, that is a moot point because infallibility does not prevent the pope from acting in a sinful or imprudent manner. Contrary to what Salmon asserts, the pope never infallibly defined how Scripture was to be interpreted nor did he infallibly condemn Galileo's astronomical conclusions. While a case can be made that the tribunal that censured Galileo acted prudently against Galileo's unproven science and erroneous views of biblical exegesis, such a case does not need to be made here. The trial and eventual house imprisonment of Galileo never involved all of the elements that are necessary for a papal teaching to be considered infallible, so this case does not disprove the doctrine of papal infallibility.

## Alleged Cases of Papal "Fallibility"

Protestants who believe some popes did teach error usually cite the examples of Liberius (352–366), Zosimus (417–418), Vigilius (537–555), and Honorius (625–638). But when we examine the facts related to each of these popes we see that none of them taught heresy in a way that was binding for the entire Church (i.e., they did not promulgate an *ex cathedra* statement).

Liberius has the dubious honor of being the first pope not to be canonized, due in part to the claim that he endorsed an Arian creed. But Liberius was a strong opponent of Arianism, and when the Arian-sympathizing Emperor Constantius rebuked him for his solitary support of Bishop Athanasius, Liberius reminded him that Shadrach, Meshach, and Abednego stood alone against Nebuchadnezzar. Liberius' defiance eventually motivated the emperor to send him into exile in Thrace (an area that lies in modern-day Greece and Turkey). Two years later Liberius gave in to the pressure of his circumstances whereupon he excommunicated Athanasius and signed a creed that, according to Cambridge historian Eamon Duffy, "did not actually repudiate the Nicene Creed, [but] weakened it with the meaningless claim that the Logos was 'like the father in being' and in all things".[53]

This case does not disprove papal infallibility for several reasons.

[53] Eamon Duffy, *Saints and Sinners: A History of the Popes*, 4th ed. (New Haven, CT: Yale University Press, 2015), 33.

First, there is doubt that Liberius was released because he signed any creeds. He may have been returned to Rome because the people refused to accept the authority of the antipope Felix II. While some Church Fathers said Liberius signed an Arian creed, this may have come from Arian propaganda as there is no record of Emperor Constantius ever saying Liberius signed the creed, which would have been to the emperor's benefit to publicize as widely as possible.[54]

Second, as we saw with Galileo, infallibility does not protect the pope from incorrect juridical decisions like excommunicating someone without just cause. It also does not apply to cases where the pope is coerced or does not freely choose to exercise his office. Even Salmon admits that the pope was coerced into signing this creed, saying, "In his heart, I doubt not, he condemned Arianism."[55] Finally, even if Liberius did sign these creeds, they were not formally heretical but merely failed accurately and unambiguously to teach Catholic doctrine. As we will see in the other examples Protestant apologists put forward, a failure to teach the truth is not synonymous with being guilty of teaching heresy.

Our next example is Pope Zosimus (417–418), who, according to Svendsen, "received confessions of faith from both Pelagius and Ceolestius [also spelled Caelestius], officially declared them orthodox, reproved the African bishops who condemned them, and subsequently changed his mind upon discovering that his predecessor (Innocent I) had also condemned these men."[56] But is that what really happened?

In 431 the Council of Ephesus declared as heresy the Pelagian belief that man could attain moral perfection apart from grace in this life. But in 417 Pope Zosimus met with Pelagius' disciple Caelestius, whom Zosimus' predecessor, Innocent I, had previously condemned. Augustine tells us that Caelestius sent a letter to the pope saying he had not definitively reached an answer on the matters under which he had been condemned and that he was willing to be corrected by the pontiff on these matters. Augustine records Caelestius saying, "If

[54] Patrick Madrid, *Pope Fiction: Answers to 30 Myths & Misconceptions about the Papacy* (Rancho Santa Fe, CA: Basilica Press, 1999), 145–47.

[55] Salmon, *Infallibility of the Church*, 423.

[56] Eric Svendsen, *Evangelical Answers: A Critique of Current Roman Catholic Apologists* (Atlanta: New Testament Restoration Foundation, 1999), 25.

by chance any error of ignorance has crept in upon us being but men, it may be corrected by your decision."[57]

Unfortunately, as Dom John Chapman writes in his study of the papacy, "The mistake of Pope Zosmius, and it was serious enough, was to believe Caelestius was sincere in his submission."[58] Pelagius sent a similar letter to Innocent that only reached Rome by the time of Zosimus' pontificate, which the pope also considered to be a sincere profession of faith. Philip Schaff, while deriding the notion of papal infallibility, admits that "[Augustine] opposed Pope Zosmius, when, deceived by Pelagius, he declared him sound in the faith."[59]

In response to both letters, Zosimus wrote a letter to the African bishops stating they had been hasty in their condemnation of the men. Alarmed at this pronouncement, the African bishops met and urged Pope Zosmius to reconsider his ruling on the Pelagian heretics. He did and in an encyclical entitled *Trattoria* (of which a few excerpts survive in Augustine's writings) Pope Zosimus upheld the African council's decision and formally condemned Pelagianism.[60]

This was not an example, as Webster asserts, of a pope being "instructed by bishops on a major doctrinal issue, and subsequently submitting himself to their judgment" (even if it were, infallibility does not preclude the pope from receiving and agreeing with counsel from his brother bishops).[61] Neither is it an example, as Svendsen claims, of the pope reversing a decision merely because he became aware of the actions of his predecessor. Instead, this was an example of a pope reinstating alleged heretics to communion with the Church and then later reversing that decision after the heretics' ruse was discovered. Pope Zosimus never infallibly defined any of the specific *tenets* of Pelagianism when he accepted these heretics into the Church, so this case does not refute papal infallibility.[62]

[57] Dom John Chapman, *Bishop Gore and the Catholic Claims* (New York: Longmans, Green, 1905), 80.

[58] Chapman, *Studies on the Early Papacy*, 163.

[59] Philip Schaff, *The Creeds of Christendom*, vol. 1 (New York: Cosimo Books, 2007; original publication 1877), 175.

[60] For *Trattoria* see *Nicene and Post-Nicene Fathers: First Series*, ed. Philip Schaff, vol. 5 (New York: Cosmo Classics, 2007), xlviii.

[61] Webster, *Church of Rome at the Bar of History*, 65.

[62] This answers Svendsen's reply that "Zosimus made positive declarations about heretical doctrine" since the pope was issuing judgments about individuals based on confessions of faith that were orthodox but not accurate. Svendsen, *Evangelical Answers*, 60.

What about Vigilius? According to Keith Mathison, the Second Council of Constantinople (A.D. 553) condemned a collection of writings called the Three Chapters because they allegedly promoted the heresy of Nestorianism, or the belief that Jesus was a union of two separate Persons, one divine and the other human. Vigilius refused to agree with the council's condemnation but later retracted his position and condemned these writings. Mathison says, "What we have here is a pope who publicly and officially changes his mind on Christology, a doctrine central to the Christian faith."[63]

But Mathison is mistaken because Pope Vigilius never taught christological errors or changed his mind on that subject. He only changed his mind about condemning certain heretics during a historical affair that is more complicated than Mathison makes it out to be.

In 544 (or late 543) Emperor Justinian condemned Theodore of Mopsuestia along with writings from Theodore of Cyrus and Ibas, the bishop of Eddesa (the writings that became known as the Three Chapters). This was done in order to help bring Monophysite heretics back into the Church. The Western bishops worried that condemning these writings would undermine the authority of the Council of Chalcedon, where Theodoret and Ibas had been brought back into union with the Church.[64] In fact, the Eastern patriarchs agreed to condemn the Three Chapters only if Vigilius did as well, but he refused. This prompted the emperor to have Vigilius taken by force from Rome to Constantinople.

After being imprisoned for a year, in 548 Vigilius issued a *judicatum* (Latin for "verdict") that said the Three Chapters should be condemned. However, the backlash among the Latin bishops was so intense that Vigilius retracted his condemnation and the emperor agreed to hold a council to decide the matter. Vigilius agreed to this solution provided that the emperor refrained from involving himself in any further theological disputes.

However, in 551 Justinian broke his word and issued a new edict that condemned the Three Chapters, an edict which Vigilius wanted withdrawn. This council, the fifth ecumenical one in the Church's

---

[63] Keith Mathison, *The Shape of Sola Scriptura* (Moscow, ID: Canon Press, 2001), 220.

[64] Aaron Riches, *Ecce Homo: On the Divine Unity of Christ* (Grand Rapids, MI: Wm. B. Eerdmans, 2016), 84.

history, was eventually held in Constantinople, though Vigilius refused to attend because of the lack of Western bishops in attendance. According to J. N. D. Kelly:

> [Vigilius] issued on 14 May [553] his First Constitution, condemning 60 propositions attributed to Theodore but not his person and declining to anathematize Theodoret and Ibas on the grounds that they had died in the peace of the Church and, if they had held erroneous opinions they had done so in good faith. It was a skillful manifesto, but Justinian rejected it.[65]

The council, heavily influenced by Justinian, condemned the Three Chapters in its eighth session. Sixth months later the aged, ailing, and still imprisoned Vigilius wrote to Patriarch Eutychius and withdrew his refusal to condemn the Three Chapters. A few months later he issued a new constitution that fully approved the council's decisions. The emperor then set Vigilius free, whereupon he died from complications related to gallstones on the journey back to Rome.[66]

A more complete description of this episode shows that Vigilius never taught either the Nestorian heresy or any other error. The decision to refrain from condemning certain writings or persons (like the Three Chapters) is not the same as endorsing everything in those writings. One may have a prudent reason for not publicly condemning a heretical writing such as if, as happened in this case, some of the heretics in question later reconciled with the Church. Vigilius may have been guilty of cowardice or inconsistency, but he was not guilty of officially teaching heresy.

## The Case of Honorius

That leaves us with Honorius, who is by far the favorite example among critics who say some popes did teach error and contradicted their alleged charism of infallibility. According to Protestant apologist Todd Baker, "Pope Honorius (625–638 A.D.) was condemned after his death as a heretic for his monothelite belief (the doctrine that

---

[65] Kelly, *Dictionary of Popes*, 59.
[66] Duffy, *Saints and Sinners*, 57.

Christ had only one will) by the Third Council of Constantinople held in 680 A.D."[67] In order to determine if this charge is accurate, we must examine two aspects of the case of Pope Honorius—his allegedly heretical writings and the condemnation he received at the Third Council of Constantinople.

In 619 the patriarch of Constantinople, Sergius I, developed a Christology that he hoped would bring Monophysite heretics into communion with the Church. He did not explicitly reject the Chalcedonian decree that Christ has two natures (which the Monophysites rejected). He did, however, put forward the theory that Christ had one will in order to help the Monophysites see that the Church did not embrace the opposing error of Nestorianism. After all, he must have thought, "If Christ had only one will, then he could not be two persons." But if Christ lacked either a divine will or a human will, then he could not fully possess a human and a divine nature. As a result, both parties rejected Sergius' compromise, and so the patriarch wrote to Pope Honorius in order to gather his opinion on the matter.

In his letter to Honorius, Sergius questioned the pope about the use of language describing Christ as having "one operation" or "two operations" and suggested that the Church refrain from using both terms until the Monophysites could be brought back into the fold. In his reply to Sergius, Honorius agreed that both expressions should be avoided but then says at one point, "We acknowledge one will of our Lord Jesus Christ, for evidently it was our nature and not the sin in it which was assumed by the Godhead, that is to say, the nature which was created before sin, not the nature which was vitiated by sin." While Sergius and other Monothelites seized on this statement as an endorsement of Monothelitism, that is not necessarily what the pope intended to convey.

Notice Christ is said to have "one will" because he was without sin. Since human nature that is free from sin always obeys God according to his will, one can say that Christ had "one will" in the sense that he never contradicted the Father's will. This would be akin to saying that two different people are "of one mind" even though they have two distinct minds that are in harmonious agreement. The

[67] Todd Baker, *Exodus from Rome: A Biblical and Historical Critique of Roman Catholicism*, vol. 1 (Bloomington, IN: iUniverse, 2014), kindle edition.

non-Catholic historian Jaroslav Pelikan says Honorius' opposition to the idea that Christ had two wills "was based on the interpretation of 'two wills' as 'two contrary wills.' He did not mean that Christ was an incomplete human being."[68] Laurent Cleenewerck, an Eastern Orthodox priest, offers this assessment:

> I do not think that Honorius was an ontological monothelite. His letter is very reminiscent of the language of St. Gregory of Nazianzen "the Theologian," although very unwise and unguarded in the context of the seventh century. In 641, Pope John IV attempted to explain Honorius' teaching by stressing that "when he confessed one will of our Lord, only meant to deny that Christ had a will of the flesh, of concupiscence, since he was conceived and born without stain of sin."[69]

Even if Honorius did endorse Monothelitsm in this letter to Sergius, that would not mean he contradicted the charism of infallibility. Papal infallibility protects the pope only when he intends to define dogma and can allow for a pope to express theologically incorrect views. In the fourteenth century Pope John XXII taught in a series of sermons the erroneous view that the dead do not attain the Beatific Vision until the Last Judgment (similar to the false teaching of soul sleep). The pope eventually retracted his view shortly before his death, but his case is not considered as evidence against papal infallibility (even by most critics of papal infallibility) because the pope was speaking as a "private theologian" and not defining a doctrine that was binding upon the whole Church.

In anticipation of a reply like this, Baker says that some Catholic apologists "claim Honorius did not teach in his official capacity as the Pope speaking ex cathedra from the chair of St. Peter". He then cites Webster's insistence that the decrees of the sixth ecumenical council "condemn Honorius as a heretic in his official capacity as pope, not as a private individual".[70] But it is a false dichotomy to say the pope

---

[68] Jaroslav Pelikan, *The Christian Tradition: A History of the Development of Doctrine*, vol. 2, *The Spirit of Eastern Christendom (600–1700)* (Chicago: University of Chicago Press, 1977), 151.

[69] Laurent Cleenewerck, *His Broken Body: Understanding and Healing the Schism between the Roman Catholic and Eastern Orthodox Churches* (Washington, DC: Euclid University Consortium Press, 2008), 195.

[70] Baker, *Exodus from Rome*, kindle edition.

either speaks ex cathedra or speaks as merely a private individual or theologian. The pope usually speaks in his official capacity as pope without making ex cathedra statements, and some of those could be erroneous (such as John XXII's erroneous public sermons). The question before us is rather, did Honorius intend to define Monothelitsm as a binding belief for the universal Church? According to Dom John Chapman, the answer is no.

> Honorius addressed Sergius alone, and it is by no means evident that he intended his letter to be published as a decree. Further, he does not appeal, as popes habitually appealed on solemn occasions, to his apostolic authority, to the promise to Peter, to the tradition of his Church. Lastly, he neither defines nor condemns, utters no anathema or warning, but merely approves a policy of silence.[71]

That leaves us with the question of the condemnation of Honorius at the Third Council of Constantinople (680–681). In its sixteenth session the council declared, "To Honorius, the heretic, anathema!" and in its definition of faith it said the devil found in Honorius a "suitable instrument" to be employed in "raising up for the whole Church the stumbling-blocks of one will and one operation". In its thirteenth session the council said, "We define that there shall be expelled from the holy Church of God and anathematized Honorius who was some time Pope of Old Rome, because of what we found written by him to Sergius, that in all respects he followed his view and confirmed his impious doctrines."[72]

The council did not define that Honorius erred by binding the faithful to believe in Monothelitism. It did condemn him for following Sergius' view and causing this heresy to be spread throughout the Church. Pope Leo II confirmed the council's decrees but added the detail that Honorius was anathematized because he "did not illuminate this apostolic see with the doctrine of apostolic tradition, but permitted her who was undefiled to be polluted by profane teaching".[73] In a letter to the bishops of Spain he said that Honorius

---

[71] Dom John Chapman, *The Condemnation of Pope Honorius* (London: Catholic Truth Society, 1907), 16.

[72] Darwell Stone, *The Christian Church* (New York: Edwin S. Gorham, 1906), 375.

[73] Salmon, *Infallibility of the Church*, 428.

"did not extinguish the flame of the heretical doctrine in its rise, as it became the apostolical authority, but fomented it by negligence".[74]

In other words, Pope Leo II confirmed the council's decrees to mean that Honorius deserved to be anathematized because he failed to correct a heresy and helped it to spread through his ambiguous letter to Sergius. But failing to lead the Church as one ought is not the same as infallibly teaching something that is false. It only proves that, like Saint Peter before him, God uses men who possess a mixture of virtue and vice to serve the Church as pope. However, God promises to strengthen these men, like he strengthened Peter, and in spite of their weaknesses he will use his divine power and limitless grace to ensure that neither they nor anyone else will cause the gates of hades to prevail against the Church.

[74] Jaroslav Pelikan, *The Christian Tradition: A History of the Development of Doctrine*, vol. 2, *The Spirit of Eastern Christendom (600–1700)* (Chicago: University of Chicago Press, 1977), 152.

# 7

# The Priesthood

Pop quiz: Which sacrament turns shepherds into wolves, servants into tyrants, and churchmen into something worse than what we normally find in the world of men? According to Martin Luther, it is the sacrament of holy orders, or the priesthood.[1]

If one wanted to strike at the heart of Catholic authority, like Luther did, it would make sense to attack the legitimacy of the Catholic priesthood since, without it, sacraments like the Eucharist and reconciliation would not exist. That's why in place of priests ordained by those who had apostolic authority, Luther claimed that every believer was a priest who stood in equal status with every other believer. He writes:

> Because we are all priests of equal standing, no one must push himself forward and take it upon himself, without our consent and election, to do that for which we all have equal authority. For no one dare take upon himself what is common to all without the authority and consent of the community.[2]

Is the Catholic priesthood an invention of the pope as Luther claimed? Or did Christ give us priests so that the Church would have not only the sacraments, but leaders with the authority to shepherd his flock until the Second Coming? To answer that question we must

---

[1] "The sacrament of ordination has been and still is an admirable device for establishing all the horrible things that have been done hitherto in the church, and are yet to be done. Here Christian brotherhood has perished, here shepherds have been turned into wolves, servants into tyrants, churchmen into worse than worldlings." Martin Luther, *The Babylonian Captivity of the Church*, *1520*, ed. Erik H. Hermann (Minneapolis: Fortress Press, 2016), 115.

[2] Martin Luther, "To the Christian Nobility of the German Nation", in *Three Treatises*, 2nd ed., trans. Charles M. Jacobs (Minneapolis: Fortress Press, 1990), 14.

look to the Old Testament priesthood that has been fulfilled in the Catholic Church.

## The Ministerial Priesthood

The Old Testament priesthood existed in three degrees: a universal priesthood or "kingdom of priests" to which every member of the Old Covenant belonged (Ex 19:6), a ministerial priesthood that offered sacrifices on behalf of the people (Ex 28:1–2), and a high priest who offered sacrifices for all of God's people, including his fellow priests (Lev 1). Each one of these priesthoods has been fulfilled in the New Covenant, a fact Protestants agree with regarding the universal priesthood (1 Pet 2:5) and the high priesthood that Christ holds forever (Heb 4:14–16).

But many Protestants reject the idea of a sacramental, ministerial priesthood because they believe this aspect of the Old Covenant was done away with in light of Christ becoming our new high priest.[3] Since Christ is the one mediator between God and man (1 Tim 2:5), and he is superior to the former priests who were many in number (Heb 7:23), they say there are no longer any other priests except for Jesus Christ.

However, Hebrews is speaking of the *high priests* who were many in number, not priests in general. The New Testament does not teach that there is now only one priest, Jesus Christ, because all Christians belong to a royal priesthood (1 Pet 2:9). They can intercede for one another without detracting from Christ, who is our one mediator of redemption (1 Tim 2:1–5). In fact, Peter was quoting the Old Testament's description of the people belonging to a royal priesthood (Ex 19:5–6). If the Old Testament's description of Israel having a universal priesthood did not prevent the existence of ministerial priests in that age, then Peter's application of this passage does not prevent the existence of ministerial priests in the New Testament.[4]

In fact, the English word "priest" is a shortened form of the Greek word *presbuteros*, which modern translations usually render as "elder".

---

[3] Other Protestants, like Anglicans, would disagree with only some aspects of the Catholic ministerial priesthood, but not with the idea of a ministerial priesthood itself.
[4] Thanks to Jimmy Akin for pointing this out.

This word can refer to one who is older than most, but in many cases it refers to officials within the Jewish (Mt 27:1) and Christian (Acts 14:23) communities. In response to this, Protestant apologists point out that the elders of the New Testament were not called *hiereus*, which was the Greek word that was applied to Jewish and even pagan priests. They claim instead that these men were elders who functioned as revered teachers but did not offer sacrifices or communicate forgiveness of sins.[5]

But in Romans 15:16 Paul describes his own ministry with a variant of the word *hiereus*. He writes of the grace from God that makes him "a *minister* of Christ Jesus to the Gentiles in the *priestly* service [*hierourgounta* = 'priestly work'] of the gospel of God, so that the *offering* of the Gentiles may be acceptable, sanctified by the Holy Spirit [emphasis added]". Notice that Paul doesn't refer to the laity as being fellow priests like him. Instead, they were a sacrifice that he and other ministers offered to God. According to the Protestant authors Rosalind Brown and Christopher Cocksworth,

> Some Christians find this embarrassing and prefer to speak about ministers, pastors, and parsons, or are more comfortable with more occupational descriptions like vicar, rector or chaplain.... For our part we do not think that it is so easy to dismiss the nomenclature as a semantic mistake precisely because the presbyter's ministry among the priestly people of God takes on certain priestly characteristics.[6]

## The Forgiveness of Sins

One example of a "priestly characteristic" found in Christ's ministerial priesthood is communicating the forgiveness of sins. The ministerial priests of the Old Covenant were responsible for offering sacrifices that atoned for the people's sins. Those sacrifices, however,

---

[5] "The Greek word for elder here is presbuteros or presbyter in English.... It is translated Priest, which is an untruth. The Greek word for Priest is 'hierus.'" Larry Ball, *Escape from Paganism: How a Roman Catholic Can Be Saved* (Victoria, BC: Trafford Publishing, 2008), 161–62. Ball does admit, however, that when the term "elder" was applied to Jews, in some cases it referred to members of the Sanhedrin, some of whom were priests.

[6] Rosalind Brown and Christopher Cocksworth, *On Being a Priest Today* (Cambridge, MA: Cowley Publications, 2004), 29–30.

were not effective in themselves (Heb 10:4), but with the advent of Christ's definitive sacrifice the forgiveness offered through his ministers becomes effectual. This forgiveness is experienced through what is called the sacrament of reconciliation or confession.

The *Catechism* teaches that even though the celebration of this sacrament has changed over time, two fundamental elements have always remained. These include the acts of contrition and confession made by the person seeking forgiveness of sins and the acts of "the Church, who through the bishop and his priests forgives sins in the name of Jesus Christ and determines the manner of satisfaction, also prays for the sinner and does penance with him. Thus the sinner is healed and re-established in ecclesial communion" (*CCC* 1448).

Biblical support for this sacrament can be found in John 20:22–23, where, after Jesus' declaration that he is sending the apostles just as the Father has sent him, he breathes on the apostles and says, "Receive the Holy Spirit. If you forgive the sins of any, they are forgiven; if you retain the sins of any, they are retained." Note that John 20:22 says Jesus breathed on the apostles before granting them authority to forgive sins. This is the same word used in the Septuagint's account of God's breathing life into Adam, a fact that led C. K. Barrett to conclude "that John intended to depict an event of significance parallel to that of the first creation of man cannot be doubted; this was the beginning of the new creation."[7]

The *Catechism* says that while it is God alone who forgives sins, "he entrusted the exercise of the power of absolution to the apostolic ministry which he charged with the 'ministry of reconciliation' (2 Cor 5:18)" (*CCC* 1442).

Protestants usually claim that in John 20:23 Jesus was giving the apostles the power only to *preach* the forgiveness of sins rather than the ability to communicate the forgiveness of sins.[8] According to this interpretation, if a person accepted the gospel, the apostles preached then that his sins would be forgiven, but if he did not accept the gospel, the apostles preached then that his sins would be retained. Other

[7] C. K. Barrett, *The Gospel according to St. John: An Introduction with Commentary and Notes on the Greek Text*, 2nd ed. (Philadelphia: Westminster Press, 1978), 570.

[8] Lorraine Boettner, *Roman Catholicism* (Phillipsburg, NJ: Presbyterian and Reformed Publishing, 1962), 209.

apologists claim that because the Greek word rendered "have been forgiven" (*aphiami*) is in the perfect tense and passive voice, this means the apostles were announcing that Christ only had already forgiven a person's sins.[9] But this interpretation is untenable for several reasons.

In John's Gospel Jesus rarely refers to the preaching of the apostles, and the subject is not mentioned in this chapter. In verse 23 Jesus simply said, "If you forgive the sins of any, they are forgiven." Jesus' use of the perfect tense means that once the apostles forgave someone's sins, those sins would now be forgiven because of the apostles' actions. This is comparable to Jesus' declaration about the sinful woman who anointed his head at the house of Simon the Pharisee. He said, "Her sins, which are many, are forgiven [*aphiami*], for she loved much" (Lk 7:47). Note that Jesus said the woman's sins were forgiven *after* she performed actions that demonstrated her love for him. New Testament professor James Barker says the grammar of this passage "conveys that God concurs with the disciples' decision, and the perfect [tense] aspect signifies the enduring significance of the disciples' decisions".[10] Saint John Chrysostom understood John 20:23 in the same way and said, "What priests do here below God ratifies above."[11]

The Baptist scholar George Beasley-Murray admits that John's Gospel "is directed to the Church, wherein believers stand continually in need of forgiveness of sins". Concerning John 20:23, he writes, "[When] dealing with sin and guilt an authoritative word of forgiveness is required from a representative of the Lord."[12] This contradicts Geisler and MacKenzie's claim that "this ministry of forgiveness and reconciliation was not limited to any special class known as 'priests' or 'clergy' (2 Cor. 3–5)."[13] However, when Paul speaks of how God "gave us the ministry of reconciliation" (2 Cor 5:18), he is not referring to Christians in general but to apostles like himself.

[9] Ron Rhodes, *Reasoning from the Scriptures with Catholics* (Eugene, OR: Harvest House Publishing, 2000), 117–18.

[10] James Barker, *John's Use of Matthew* (Minneapolis: Fortress Press, 2015), 54.

[11] St. John Chrysostom, *On the Priesthood* 3.5. Cited in ibid.

[12] G. R. Beasley-Murray, *Baptism in the New Testament* (Grand Rapids, MI: Wm. B. Eerdmans, 1973), 384.

[13] Norman L. Geisler and Ralph E. MacKenzie, *Roman Catholics and Evangelicals: Agreements and Differences* (Grand Rapids, MI: Baker Books, 1995), 289.

## The Confession of Sins

Other critics object to the sacrament of confession by appealing to 1 John 1:9: "If we confess [Greek, *homologōmen*; root *homologeō*] our sins, he is faithful and just, and will forgive our sins and cleanse us from all unrighteousness." They say that there is no mention of any need for a public confession to a priest and that we need only confess our sins directly to God. But the context of the passage concerns what we say or confess to other people rather than what we communicate to God. The previous verse, "If we say we have no sin, we deceive ourselves, and the truth is not in us," and the following verse, "If we say we have not sinned, we make him a liar, and his word is not in us," describe believers speaking to one another. In fact, aside from Hebrews 13:15, *homologeō* is never used to describe confessing *anything* to God, and in John's writings it is always used to describe confessing a belief to other men.[14]

The nineteenth-century Anglican New Testament scholar Brooke Westcott (who helped create the Greek New Testament that scholars still study today) said that the phrase "confess our sins" means "not only acknowledge them, but acknowledge them openly in the face of men".[15] The Johannine New Testament scholar David Rensberger writes in his recent commentary on John's letters,

> Confession of sin was generally public (Mark 1:5; Acts 19:18; Jas 5:16; Did 4:14; 14:1), and that may well be the case here. The use of the plural "sins" (rather than "sin," as in 1:8) is a reminder that not just an abstract confession of sinfulness but the acknowledgement of specific acts is in mind.[16]

---

[14] Here's a breakdown of how it's used in the New Testament outside of 1 John 1:9: God's promise he spoke to Abraham (Acts 7:17); Jesus confessing to damned hypocrites what their fate will be (Mt 7:23); John the Baptist confessing to the Jewish leaders that he is not the Christ (Jn 1:20); the Jewish leaders not confessing aloud their internal belief in Jesus (Jn 12:42); Christians confessing their beliefs to other people (Mt 10:32; Lk 12:8; Jn 9:22; Acts 24:14; Rom 10:9–10; 1 Tim 6:12; Tit 1:16; 1 Jn 2:23; 4:2, 15); non-Christians making promises, declarations, or confessions of belief/disbelief to other people (Mt 14:7; Acts 23:8; Heb 11:13; 1 Jn 4:3; 2 Jn 1:7).

[15] Brooke Westcott, *The Epistles of St. John* (New York, Macmillan, 1902), 23.

[16] David Rensberger, *Abingdon New Testament Commentary 1, 2, 3 John* (Nashville, TN: Abingdon Press, 1997), 54.

Notice Rensberger's citation of the *Didache*, which was a first-century catechism. It gave believers the following instruction: "In your gatherings, confess your transgressions, and do not come for prayer with a guilty conscience" (4:14). Scholars tend to date First John as being written in the late '90s and the *Didache* as having been written at the same time or even earlier. It makes sense, therefore, to connect John's instruction to "confess your sins" with the context of public confession in the early Church described in the *Didache*.

Father Raymond Brown reached the same conclusion in his Anchor Bible commentary on First John. After listing the public confession of sins in the Old Testament that John is alluding to (Lev 5:5–6; Prov 28:13; Sir 4:25–26; Dan 9:20), he writes, "All the parallels and background given thus far suggest that the Johannine expression refers to a public confession rather than a private confession by the individual to God."[17] Indeed, another passage in the New Testament that instructs Christians to confess their sins is James 5:16, which says, "Therefore confess your sins *to one another* [emphasis added], and pray for one another, that you may be healed. The prayer of a righteous man has great power in its effects."

The word rendered "confess" in this passage is *exomologeó*, and, while it does refer to confessing praise or thanksgiving directly to God (Mt 11:25; Lk 10:21; Rom 14:11), it never refers to confessing sins to God. Like *homologeó*, this verb primarily describes public confessions or declarations to other humans (e.g., Lk 22:6; Acts 19:8; Rom 15:9; and Phil 2:11—though this last verse might also refer to confessing belief in Jesus directly to God as well as to other men). The two verses prior to this passage even describe sins being forgiven through priests administering the sacrament of anointing of the sick:

> Is any among you sick? Let him call for the elders of the Church, and let them pray over him, anointing him with oil in the name of the Lord; and the prayer of faith will save the sick man, and the Lord will raise him up; and if he has committed sins, he will be forgiven.

[17] Raymond Brown, *The Epistles of John* (New York: Doubleday, 1982), 208. Other Protestant commenters admit that public confession is a possible way to interpret this verse even if they don't accept it as the verse's primary meaning. See Robert Yarbough *1, 2, 3 John* (Grand Rapids, MI: Baker Academic, 2008), 63.

In describing this sacrament the *Catechism*, quoting this passage, says, "This assistance from the Lord by the power of his Spirit is meant to lead the sick person to healing of the soul, but also of the body if such is God's will. Furthermore, 'if he has committed sins, he will be forgiven' (Jas 5:15)" (*CCC* 1520). In the third century Origen commented on this passage saying that remission of sins could be received when a sinner "is not ashamed to make known his sin to the priest of the Lord". He then writes, "What the Apostle James says is fulfilled in this," thus connecting the presbyter of James 5:14–16 to the "priest of the Lord" to whom one confesses his sins.[18]

In both the sacrament of confession and anointing of the sick, the priest does not directly heal or forgives sin but he becomes the means by which a person receives healing or forgiveness. Most Protestants would agree with this thinking on something like baptism since they usually deny the validity of self-baptism (something Catholics also deny). Those who believe in baptismal regeneration correctly point out that while God alone takes away sin, God does not *act* alone when he takes away a person's sins through baptism. Instead, God works through other believers who baptize on his behalf. The same principle applies when God uses a minister to forgive a person's sins through confession as well as through baptism.

But in order for the apostles to know if someone needs reconciliation with God or if the person's sins should be retained, they would have to know what the person's sins were. Barring some kind of revelation from God, this knowledge could come only from a person confessing his sins aloud. As Saint Cyprian of Carthage put it in A.D. 251, "With grief and simplicity confess this very thing to God's priests, and make the conscientious avowal, put off from them the load of their minds, and seek out the salutary medicine even for slight and moderate wounds."[19]

## Apostolic Succession and Leadership

Some Protestants claim that "the Church" is merely the invisible union that exists between all baptized Christians, and there is no

---

[18] *Homilies on Leviticus*, trans. Gary Wayne Barkley (Washington, DC: Catholic University of America Press, 1990), 47–48.

[19] St. Cyprian, *The Lapsed* 28.

visible, authoritative hierarchy. In one sense, this invisible church does exist. According to the Vatican's Congregation for the Doctrine of the Faith (CDF), "The Church of Christ is present and operative in the churches and ecclesial Communities not yet fully in communion with the Catholic Church, on account of the elements of sanctification and truth that are present in them." But the CDF also points out that

> Christ "established here on earth" only one Church and instituted it as a "visible and spiritual community" (cf. Second Vatican Council, Dogmatic Constitution *Lumen gentium*, 8.1).... This Church, constituted and organised in this world as a society, subsists in the Catholic Church, governed by the successor of Peter and the Bishops in communion with him.[20]

Christ's church "subsists" in the Catholic Church in the sense that the "perduring, historical continuity and the permanence of all the elements instituted by Christ" can be found only in the Catholic Church.[21] That is why the apostles and their successors were tasked with maintaining this historical continuity and ensuring the Church would remain, as Saint Paul described it, "the pillar and bulwark of the truth" (1 Tim 3:15). That's also why Jesus prayed not only for the apostles but "for those who believe in me through their word" (Jn 17:20). He specifically prayed that "they may become perfectly one, so that the world may know that you have sent me and have loved them even as you have loved me" (Jn 17:23). According to the Reformed minister Peter Leithart,

> Division *cannot* [emphasis in original] be the final state of Christ's church.... If the Gospel is true, this division is at best provisional. Jesus prayed that we would be "perfected in unity," and this unity must be visible enough for the world to notice and conclude that the Father sent Jesus.[22]

[20] Congregation for the Doctrine of the Faith, "Responses to Some Questions regarding Certain Aspects of the Doctrine on the Church" (June 29, 2007), http://www.vatican.va /roman_curia/congregations/cfaith/documents/rc_con_cfaith_doc_20070629_responsa -quaestiones_en.html.
[21] Ibid.
[22] Peter Leithart, *The End of Protestantism: Pursuing Unity in a Fragmented Church* (Grand Rapids, MI: Brazos Press, 2016), kindle edition.

But the way to ensure that this unity would remain in the Church requires authorities who could settle disputes among Christians. When we read the New Testament, we find that the apostles set about establishing these authorities under the titles of bishop (or overseer, Greek, *episkopos*), priest (or elder, Greek, *presbuteros*), and deacon (or minister/servant, Greek, *diakonos*). It took time for these offices to develop their technical meanings, so in the New Testament we see apostles being described as elders (1 Pet 5:1) and even deacons (Eph 3:7).[23] However, by A.D. 110 the threefold division of the Church's hierarchy was firmly established in places as far away as western Turkey, as evidenced by Saint Ignatius of Antioch, who said:

> It is therefore necessary that, as you indeed do, so without the bishop you should do nothing, but should also be subject to the presbytery [or elders], as to the apostle of Jesus Christ, who is our hope, in whom, if we live, we shall [at last] be found. It is fitting also that the deacons, as being [the ministers] of the mysteries of Jesus Christ, should in every respect be pleasing to all.[24]

The New Testament likewise records how Paul instructed Titus to appoint elders in Crete (Tit 1:5) and warned Timothy "not [to] be hasty in the laying on of hands" (1 Tim 5:22). Paul's advice to Timothy is a reference to ordination, given that Paul also told Timothy, "Do not neglect the gift you have, which was given you by prophetic utterance when the elders laid their hands upon you" (1 Tim 4:14).[25] Luther claimed, however, that these instructions were not evidence of priestly ordination but rather of congregational organization. He writes:

> Neither Titus nor Timothy nor Paul ever instituted a priest without the congregation's election and call. This is clearly proven by the sayings in Titus 1[:7] and 1 Timothy 3[:10], "A bishop or priest should be blameless," and, "Let the deacon be tested first." Now Titus could

---

[23] Jimmy Akin, *A Daily Defense* (San Diego: Catholic Answers Press, 2016), 316.

[24] St. Ignatius of Antioch, *Letter to the Trallians* 2.

[25] "The earliest Jewish Christians would have been familiar with laying on of hands for ordination before it was practiced among themselves (1 Tim. 4:14)." Craig Keener, *Acts: An Exegetical Commentary*, vol. 2, *3:1–14:28* (Grand Rapids, MI: Baker Academic, 2013), kindle edition.

not have known which ones were blameless; such a report must come from the congregation, which must name the man.²⁶

Yet the New Testament never hints that the community is the one to choose these men. Instead, it talks about how the apostles "appointed elders for them in every church" (Acts 14:23). It expects overseers like Timothy and Titus first to get to know candidates for ordination and assess whether they are blameless, but it does not envision the congregation electing its leaders. Instead, the laity is instructed to "obey your leaders and submit to them; for they are keeping watch over your souls, as men who will have to give account" (Heb 13:17). Jesus said that, as a last resort, in the case of a fellow Christian who sins against you, you should "tell it to the Church; and if he refuses to listen even to the Church, let him be to you as a Gentile and a tax collector" (Mt 18:17).

Some argue that this is simply the local church, or the community of local Christians responding to a pragmatic issue, and not indicative of the existence of one church with authority over believers. But Jesus did not say "tell it to *your* church." He spoke of *the* Church, which implies that the believers were to be united organizationally as well as doctrinally. Without this organizational union, an excommunicated sinner or heretic could simply walk down the street to the next church that welcomes him. But according to D. A. Carson:

> Only "church" (*ekklesia* in the singular) is used for the congregation of all believers in one city, never "churches"; one reads of churches in Galatia [a region, not a city] but of the church in Antioch or Jerusalem or Ephesus. Thus it is possible, though not certain, that a single elder may have exercised authority in relation to one house group—a house group that in some cases constituted part of the city wide church—so that the individual elder would nevertheless be one of many in that citywide "church" taken as a whole.²⁷

The succession of the apostles' authority to bishops, priests, and deacons is even more evident in the writings of the first generation

---

²⁶ Martin Luther in *Word and Sacrament III*, ed. Robert H. Fischer, vol. 39 of *Luther's Works*, ed. Jaroslav Pelikan and Helmut T. Lehmann (Philadelphia: Fortress Press, 1961), 312.

²⁷ D. A. Carson, "Church Authority", in *Evangelical Dictionary of Theology*, 2nd ed. (Grand Rapids, MI: Baker, 2001), 250.

of Christians who lived after the death of the apostles. In Clement's letters to the Corinthians he writes:

> Our apostles also knew, through our Lord Jesus Christ, that there would be strife on account of the office of the episcopate. For this reason, therefore, inasmuch as they had obtained a perfect fore-knowledge of this, they appointed those [ministers] already mentioned, and afterwards gave instructions, that when these should fall asleep, other approved men should succeed them in their ministry.[28]

In the second century Saint Ignatius exhorted Christians to "do all things with a divine harmony, while your bishop presides in the place of God, and your presbyters in the place of the assembly of the apostles."[29] Saint Irenaeus likewise taught that

> it is incumbent to obey the presbyters who are in the Church—those who, as I have shown, possess the succession from the apostles; those who, together with the succession of the episcopate, have received the infallible charism of truth, according to the good pleasure of the Father.[30]

Geisler and MacKenzie seem to admit the strength of the evidence for apostolic succession because their only response to it is "simply because a teaching existed early in church history that does not make it true."[31] That is correct, but in the absence of compelling evidence to the contrary (which Geisler and MacKenzie never offer), we are justified in rejecting the claim that the early Church was an egalitarian gathering of believers who were united only through an invisible bond of Christian brotherhood. Instead, as J. N. D. Kelly observes,

---

[28] St. Clement of Rome, *1 Clement* 44.

[29] St. Ignatius of Antioch, *Epistle to the Magnesians*, 6

[30] St. Irenaeus, *Against Heresies* 4.26.2.

[31] Geisler and MacKenzie, *Roman Catholics and Evangelicals*, 293. Svendsen also seems to sense the strength of this evidence and in response claims that citing the Fathers in support of apostolic succession constitutes an act of fallaciously "begging the question". Eric Svendsen, *Evangelical Answers: A Critique of Current Roman Catholic Apologetics* (Atlanta: New Testament Restoration Foundation, 1997), 80. But quoting the Fathers on this or any doctrine presents evidence for the antiquity of that doctrine; it is not a circular argument in favor of the doctrine. The same objection could be turned against Svendsen whenever he or any other Protestant apologist tries to marshal the witness of the Church Fathers in defense of the historicity of one of their doctrines.

"What these early Fathers were envisioning was almost always the empirical, visible society: they had little or no inkling of the distinction between a visible and invisible Church."[32]

Before we continue to the evidence for the ministerial priesthood from the Bible's description of the leadership roles assigned to these men, we should address two aspects of the priesthood Protestants object to: the practice of calling priests "father" and the discipline of clerical celibacy.

## "Call No Man Your Father"

Some Protestants condemn the practice of calling priests "father" by citing Jesus' command to "call no man your father on earth, for you have one Father, who is in heaven" (Mt 23:9). Of course, if this command were taken literally, Christians could not even call their own biological fathers "father". That's why most Protestants who advance this objection say Jesus meant we should not refer to anyone with the *spiritual* title "father", but this interpretation is untenable.

Jesus was not condemning the idea of earthly or spiritual fatherhood but the practice of giving some people, like the Pharisees who sought public approval (Mt 23:6–7), honor and fatherly respect that was due to God alone. Calling people spiritual fathers in and of itself isn't wrong, because a few years after this command was given, Stephen, who was filled with the Holy Spirit, addressed his Jewish audience as "brethren and fathers" (Acts 7:2). Ron Rhodes even admits that spiritual fatherhood is not wrong, saying, "In the New Testament the apostle Paul was a spiritual father to young Timothy (1 Cor. 4:15) and referred to Timothy as 'my dear son' (2 Tim. 1:2)."[33]

In 1 John 2:12–13 John says, "I am writing to you, little children, because your sins are forgiven for his sake. I am writing to you, fathers, because you know him who is from the beginning." John is not addressing either literal children or biological fathers, but

---

[32] J. N. D. Kelly, *Early Christian Doctrines* (New York: HarperCollins, 1978), 190.

[33] Rhodes, *Reasoning from the Scriptures*, 113. Rhodes still tries to condemn the practice of calling priests "father" by claiming that Catholics use that title "in a much more exalted sense—a sense requiring holy reverence and unquestioned obedience". Ibid. But wouldn't the Corinthians have owed Paul obedience and "holy reverence" as their spiritual father? Also, when Catholics call priests "father", that does not require unquestioned obedience or placing a priest's authority on the same plane with God's authority.

believers who differed in maturity and leadership roles. According to Warren Wiersbe, "The 'fathers,' of course, are mature believers who have an intimate personal knowledge of God."[34] Concerning Matthew 23:9, the Evangelical author Walter Kaiser Jr. says:

> If the local Catholic priest is known throughout the community as Father Jones, I am simply being silly if I persist in calling him something else. If I stop to think what is meant by my calling him Father Jones, I shall probably conclude that he is not my father in any sense but that he is no doubt a real father in God to his own congregation. "Father" in this sense is synonymous with "Pastor"; the former views the congregation as a family, the latter as a flock of sheep.[35]

Finally, this interpretation of Matthew 23:9 fails when we apply its same principles to the previous verse: "You are not to be called rabbi, for you have one teacher, and you are all brethren." The Hebrew word *rabbi* means "my master, my teacher" and describes one who had mastered the meaning of the Torah. Jesus says no one should be called rabbi, not because Christians have only one master (that is addressed in verse 10), but because Christians have only one teacher (Greek, *didaskalos*).

But the English word "doctor" comes from the Latin word *docere*, which means "teach". It's just another word for teacher and, in the modern sense of the word, it refers to someone who has *mastered* a certain discipline (or received a doctoral degree). If Matthew 23:9 forbids granting someone the spiritual title of father, then Matthew 23:8 would forbid grating someone the spiritual title of teacher, including Protestant theologians who have earned doctoral degrees. Therefore, Matthew 23:9 does not prove that Catholics violate the teachings of Jesus by calling priests "father".

## "The Husband of One Wife"

According to the *Catechism*, priestly celibacy is a discipline found in the Western Church for those who are "called to consecrate

[34] Warren W. Wiersbe, *Be Real (1 John): Turning from Hypocrisy to Truth* (Colorado Springs, CO: David C. Cook, 2009), 77.

[35] Walter Kaiser Jr., *Hard Sayings of the Bible* (Downers Grove, IL: InterVarsity Press, 2010), 359.

themselves with undivided heart to the Lord and to 'the affairs of the Lord' (1 Cor 7:32)" (*CCC* 1579). Eastern Catholic churches maintain a tradition that allows for married priests, but, as is also the custom in the Western Church, those who hold the office of bishop must be unmarried. Since it is a discipline that was introduced later in Church history by the Church's authority, the presence of married clergy in Scripture does not refute it.

This discipline is also not an arbitrary one but follows Paul's teaching that a married man is anxious about pleasing his wife whereas the unmarried man is anxious about pleasing the Lord (1 Cor 7:32–34). In fact, both Saint Paul and Jesus practiced celibacy, so taking vows of celibacy would follow Saint Paul's command to "be imitators of me, as I am of Christ" (1 Cor 11:1).

Some Protestant apologists, however, claim Paul condemned celibacy, calling it a part of the "doctrines of demons" taught by those who "forbid marriage and enjoin abstinence from foods" (1 Tim 4:1, 3). In fact, Paul said that "a bishop must be above reproach, the husband of one wife" (1 Tim 3:2), which means, according to Todd Baker, "Rome blatantly contradicts scripture by demanding their bishops and priests must be unmarried celibates."[36]

First, Paul's letter to Timothy contains an exhortation to stand against Gnostic heresies that held that marriage itself was evil—not a blanket prohibition on celibacy. The Gnostics believed there were two gods: a good one who created the universe and an evil one that created the material world. They believed that salvation came by attaining secret, spiritual knowledge (or in Greek, *gnosis*), and by abstaining from evil, material things such as meat and marriage. In 1 Timothy 6:20 Paul may be making a pun related to the Gnostics when he warns Timothy to "avoid the godless chatter and contradictions of what is falsely called knowledge [Greek, *gnoseos*], for by professing it some have missed the mark as regards faith." The Protestant scholar William Barclay says of this passage:

> If matter is evil, the body is evil; and the body must be despised and held in check. Therefore Gnosticism could and did result in strict

---

[36] Todd Baker, *Exodus from Rome: A Biblical and Historical Critique of Roman Catholicism*, vol. 1 (Bloomington, IN: iUniverse, 2014), kindle edition.

abstinence. It forbade marriage, instincts of the body were to be suppressed. It laid down strict food laws, for the needs of the body must as far as possible be eliminated. So the pastorals speak of those who forbid marriage and who demand abstinence from foods (1 Tim. 4:3). The answer to these people is that everything which God has created is good and is to be received with thanksgiving (1 Tim. 4:4).[37]

The Catholic Church does not teach that marriage or eating meat is evil. In fact, it is because these things are good and pleasurable that it is praiseworthy when someone abstains from them to serve the Church for a season (such as during a Lenten fast) or for the remainder of an entire lifetime as in the case of clerical celibacy.[38] The fact that Paul desired that all could be celibate like him (1 Cor 7:7) makes it highly implausible that he would have condemned voluntary vows of celibacy.

However, Baker claims that while Paul had Gnostics in mind, "his warning is against all prohibition of marriage in general for whatever reason."[39] But that is not true, because Paul spoke of young widows who "when they grow wanton against Christ they desire to marry, and so they incur condemnation for having violated their first pledge" (1 Tim 5:11–12). In Romans 7:2 Paul teaches that widows are free to remarry, so the condemned widows in 1 Timothy 5:12 must have violated a pledge or vow to remain celibate.

Some commenters try to avoid this conclusion, but their exegesis is unconvincing. For example, Wiersbe writes, "This pledge must not be interpreted as a 'vow of celibacy,' nor should we look on this group of ministering widows as a 'special monastic order.' There seemed to be an agreement between the widows and the church that they would remain widows and serve the Lord."[40] It's true this

---

[37] William Barclay, *The Letters to Timothy, Titus, and Philemon*, 3rd ed. (Louisville, KY: Westminster John Knox Press, 2003), 33–34.

[38] Those who would also press this verse into their condemnation of Catholic fasting should remember that Jesus said, "When [not 'if'] you fast, anoint your head and wash your face, that your fasting may not be seen by men but by your Father who is in secret; and your Father who sees in secret will reward you" (Mt 6:17–18). Jesus taught that fasting is an appropriate spiritual discipline and not a "doctrine of demons".

[39] Baker, *Exodus from Rome*.

[40] Warren W. Wiersbe, *Be Faithful (1 & 2 Timothy, Titus, Philemon): It's Always Too Soon to Quit!* (Colorado Springs, CO: David C. Cook, 2009), 79.

text does not refer to a general call to celibacy or an encouragement
for the never married to remain unmarried—though both Jesus and
Paul encourage that (Mt 19:12, 1 Cor 7:8). But there is no difference
between "a vow of celibacy" and "an agreement to remain a widow"
that incurs condemnation if broken.

In regard to 1 Timothy 3:2, this verse does not require that bishops
or other members of the clergy be married, nor does it disprove the
discipline of celibacy. If this verse were taken literally, then widowed
pastors as well as holy celibates like Paul or even Jesus, whom Peter
calls the "Bishop of your souls" (1 Pet 2:25, KJV), could not be
bishops. Instead, the curious detail that bishops must be the husband
of *one* wife rather than that they simply be *married* signifies that Paul
does not want the bishop to be a source of scandal due to an irregular
marriage situation.

The Protestant apologist Gregg Allison agrees that this phrase
"must mean something other than that an elder must be married to
qualify to serve in this office" since it contradicts Paul's praise of celibate men who can give the Lord their undivided interest.[41] Allison
opts for the view that Paul is saying a bishop must be faithful to his
wife, but other commenters believe Paul is saying men who have
remarried are not fit to be bishops. Either way, Paul is not restricting
the sacrament of holy orders only to those who currently possess the
sacrament of matrimony. (In the ancient Church, sometimes married
men were ordained priests, but in the West it was generally the case
that such men were to live as "brother and sister" with their wives
after ordination. In other words, for instances in which clerical celibacy was not observed, clerical continence was to be.)

Finally, Baker dredges up the canard that priestly celibacy is
responsible for the clergy sexual abuse crisis that took place in the
late twentieth century. He claims, "There are more reported cases on
file of sexual abuse committed by Roman Catholic priests, than those
involving clergy from denominations where ministers are allowed to
marry."[42] While it does not affect the biblical and historical roots of
celibacy, such a blatant falsehood that harms the reputations of priests

<hr />

[41] Gregg Allison, *Sojourners and Strangers: The Doctrine of the Church* (Wheaton, IL: Crossway, 2012), 214.

[42] Baker, *Exodus from Rome*, kindle edition.

must be answered. Ernie Allen, the director of the National Center for Missing and Exploited Children, said in an interview with *Newsweek* magazine about the abuse scandal:

> We don't see the Catholic Church as a hotbed of this or a place that has a bigger problem than anyone else. I can tell you without hesitation that we have seen cases in many religious settings, from traveling evangelists to mainstream ministers to rabbis and others.[43]

Insurance companies that cover sexual abuse claims as part of their liability insurance do not charge higher premiums for the Catholic Church, indicating that denominations with married clergy do not have lower rates of abuse.[44] According to the textbook *Sex Crimes: Patterns and Behavior*, "Many pedophiles of all types have adult sexual outlets. Many are married. Some have been known to marry women with children in order to have access to the children."[45] In fact, according to Hofstra University researcher Charol Shakeshaft, "The physical sexual abuse of students in [public] schools is likely more than 100 times the abuse by priests."[46]

The actions of the small number of priests who abused children, as well as the decisions of some bishops to transfer those priests and rely on psychological treatments instead of criminal prosecution, have caused great harm to innocent lives and great scandal to the Church. But these sinful acts do not prove that *celibacy* is sinful or that it was a motivating factor in the recent clerical abuse scandal.

## Principles for the Priesthood

In the first volume of his *Systematic Theology*, the nineteenth-century Presbyterian theologian Charles Hodge wrote:

---

[43] Pat Wingert, "Priests Commit No More Abuse than Other Males", *Newsweek*, April 7, 2010, http://www.newsweek.com/priests-commit-no-more-abuse-other-males-70625.

[44] Ibid.

[45] Stephen T. Holmes and Ronald M. Holmes, *Sex Crimes: Patterns and Behavior*, 3rd ed. (Thousand Oaks, CA: SAGE Productions, 2009), 117. I would also note that the clergy sexual abuse cases were usually examples of ephebophilia, or attraction to adolescents, not pedophilia or attraction to pre-pubescent children.

[46] Tom Hoopes, "Has Media Ignored Sex Abuse in Schools?", CBSNews.com, August 24, 2006, http://www.cbsnews.com/news/has-media-ignored-sex-abuse-in-school/.

All the principles on which the doctrine of the priesthood of the Christian clergy rests are false. It is false that the ministry are a distinct class from the people, distinguished from them by supernatural gifts, conveyed by the sacrament of orders. It is false that the bread and wine are transmuted into the body and blood of Christ. It is false that the Eucharist is a propitiatory sacrifice applied for the remission of sins and spiritual benefits.[47]

We have shown, however, that the clergy of the New Testament were a distinct class entrusted with sacramental responsibilities that were carried out under the authority of the apostles. We have not yet discussed the most important of these responsibilities: the offering of the sacrifice of the Eucharist. Hodge correctly points out that this is one of the, if not the most, foundational principles upon which the ministerial priesthood rests. In order to show that Christ's ministers are priests in the fullest sense of the word, we must show that the Mass they celebrate is an example of a propitiatory sacrifice and the Eucharist they consecrate at Mass truly becomes the Body and Blood of Jesus Christ.

[47] Charles Hodge, *Systematic Theology*, vol. 1 (New York: Charles Scribner, 1872).

# 8

# The Eucharist and the Mass

As the Reformation spread throughout Europe, a German prince named Philip I convened a meeting in Marburg, Germany, in order to unify the various Protestant political states. In order to achieve this union, Philip understood the value of establishing religious harmony among the different Protestant churches. But after four days of intense debate and discussion, there remained one doctrine that the attendees could not agree on: the nature of the Eucharist.

Martin Luther held to a view that he came to call "a sacramental union", which means that at the Consecration Christ is present "in, with, and under" the bread and wine.[1] Ulrich Zwingli, on the other hand, taught that the Eucharist symbolizes the Body and Blood of Christ, but it doesn't actually contain the Body and Blood of Christ.[2] While the parties could not reach a consensus about what the Eucharist is, in their later writings these two did agree on what the Eucharist was *not*.

Zwingli said, "That his body is literally eaten is far from the truth and the nature of faith."[3] Luther called the terminology Catholics used to describe the change of bread and wine into the Body and Blood of Christ "an absurd and unheard-of juggling with words".[4]

---

[1] Martin Luther, "Confession Concerning Christ's Supper", in *Word and Sacrament III*, ed. Robert H. Fischer, vol. 37 of *Luther's Works*, ed. Jaroslav Pelikan and Helmut T. Lehmann (Philadelphia: Fortress Press, 1961), 299–300.

[2] Philip Schaff, *The Creeds of Christendom: The History of Creeds*, vol. 1 (New York: Harper and Brothers, 1919), 375.

[3] Ibid.

[4] Martin Luther, "The Babylonian Captivity of the Church", in *Works of Martin Luther*, vol. 2, ed. Henry Ester Jacobs and Adolph Spaeth (Philadelphia: A.J. Holman, 1915), 190.

Calvin, who was not at Marburg, later went so far as to claim that belief in the Real Presence of Christ in the Eucharist was "a devil's doctrine".[5]

In order to defend the Church's teaching on the Eucharist, we must focus on two claims that are articulated in the *Catechism*: (1) it is by the conversion of the bread and wine into Christ's Body and Blood that Christ becomes present in the sacrament of the Eucharist, and (2) the sacrifice of the Mass makes present the one sacrifice of Christ that, in doing so, takes away sin (*CCC* 1375). Let's begin with the latter claim that the Mass is a propitiatory sacrifice, or a sacrifice that is able to take away sins (similar to *expiation*).

## The Sacrifice of the Mass

The Eucharist was instituted at the Last Supper " 'in order to perpetuate the sacrifice of the cross throughout the ages until he should come again' (*SC* 47)"[6] (*CCC* 1323). According to the *Catechism*,

> The sacrifice of Christ and the sacrifice of the Eucharist are *one single sacrifice* [emphasis in original].... "In this divine sacrifice which is celebrated in the Mass, the same Christ who offered himself once in a bloody manner on the altar of the cross is contained and is offered in an unbloody manner ... this sacrifice is truly propitiatory" (Council of Trent [1562]: *Doctrina de ss. Missae sacrificio*, c. 2: DS 1743). (*CCC* 1367)

At the Last Supper Jesus instructed the disciples to receive bread and wine that he called his body and blood and to "do this in remembrance of me" (*Touto poieite eis tan eman anamnesin* [Lk 22:19; 1 Cor 11:24]). The verb *poieo* means "do" or "make", but it can also mean "to offer" and is used in the Septuagint in a sacrificial context (Ex 29:28; Lev 9:7; Ps 66:15). According to J. N. D. Kelly,

---

[5] "The devil knowing that our Lord has left nothing to his Church more useful than the holy sacrament, has after his usual manner labored from the beginning to contaminate it by errors and superstitions." John Calvin, *Short Treatise of the Lord's Supper*, 33, http://www.the-highway.com/supper1_Calvin.html.

[6] *SC* is the abbreviation for *Sacrosanctum Concilium*, Vatican II's Constitution on the Sacred Liturgy (December 4, 1963).

It was natural for early Christians to think of the Eucharist as a sacrifice. The fulfillment of prophecy demanded a solemn Christian offering, and the rite itself was wrapped in the sacrificial atmosphere with which our Lord invested the Last Supper. The words of institution, "Do this" (*touto poieite*), must have been charged with sacrificial overtones for second-century ears; Justin at any rate understood them to mean, "Offer this."[7]

Many Protestants believe the Eucharist (or what they often call "The Lord's Supper") is not an offering of Christ's actual body. Rather, it is a memorial meal where bread and wine are consumed in obedience to Christ's command to "do this in remembrance of me." According to Ron Rhodes, "The word remembrance literally means 'bring to mind,' not 'ingest into the stomach.'"[8] But this interpretation assumes that it is the believer who does the "remembering".

Joachim Jeremias has shown that the Greek word rendered "remembrance" (*anamnesin*) refers to more than just a purely spiritual recollection. In the Greek translation of Numbers 10:10 found in the Septuagint, *anamnesin* (and its Hebrew equivalent *zekher*) is used to describe sacrifices that "shall serve you for remembrance [*anamnesis*] before your God". Hebrews 10:3 says, "In these sacrifices there is a reminder of sin year after year." In both cases the sacrifices that are mentioned cause *God* (in a figurative sense) to remember something about his people. Therefore, according to Jeremias, the inclusion of *anamnesis* in Luke 22:19 (and 1 Corinthians 11:24) means Jesus instructed believers to do this, "that God may remember me". He continues:

> This means that the command to repeat the rite is not a summons to the disciples to preserve the memory of Jesus and be vigilant ("repeat the breaking of bread so that you may not forget me"), but it is an eschatologically oriented instruction: "Keep joining yourselves together as the redeemed community by the table rite, that in this way

---

[7] J. N. D. Kelly, *Early Christian Doctrines* (New York: HarperCollins, 1978), 196–97. Cited in Jimmy Akin, *The Fathers Know Best: Your Essential Guide to the Teachings of the Early Church* (San Diego: Catholic Answers Press, 2010), 299.

[8] Ron Rhodes, *Reasoning from the Scriptures with Catholics* (Eugene, OR: Harvest House Publishing, 2000), 184.

God may be daily implored to bring about the consummation on the [Second Coming]."[9]

Since *poieo* can have sacrificial connotations, Jesus' command in Luke 22:19 can be understood to mean, "Offer this memorial sacrifice to God for me." In addition, Jesus was instituting a fulfillment of the Passover, whose celebration "made present" in a mystical way the events of the Exodus. Therefore, through the new Passover the Eucharist would make Christ's sacrifice present for all future believers. According to the non-Catholic scholar Anthony Thiselton:

> The Passover *Seder* enables Jewish households *to participate in* the deliverance of the Passover *as if they were "there."* The Eucharist enables Christians *to participate in* the deliverance of the cross *as if they were "there."* They are *contemporaneous sharers in the drama* [emphasis in original].[10]

That Christians believed the Eucharist was a sacrifice for God is also evident in Paul's teaching to the Corinthians. He warned that they "cannot drink the cup of the Lord and the cup of demons" nor can they "partake of the table of the Lord and the table of demons" (1 Cor 10:21).

In the previous verses Paul describes Jewish (v. 18) and pagan sacrifices (v. 20) before he speaks about Christians partaking in the Body and Blood of the Lord in a similar way. According to Evangelical authors Robert Bowman Jr. and J. Ed Komoszewski, "The expression 'table of the LORD' is an Old Testament expression for the altar, which the prophet Malachi warned against defiling (Mal. 1:7, 12)."[11] This refutes the objection that Paul is not talking about a Christian altar upon which Christ is offered merely because he uses the Greek word for table.[12]

---

[9] Joachim Jeremias, *The Eucharistic Words of Jesus* (New York: Charles Scribner and Sons, 1966), 255.

[10] Anthony C. Thiselton, *The Hermeneutics of Doctrine* (Grand Rapids, MI: Wm. B. Eerdmans, 2007), 528.

[11] Robert M. Bowman Jr. and J. Ed Komoszewski, *Putting Jesus in His Place: The Case for the Deity of Christ* (Grand Rapids, MI: Kregel Publications, 2007), 165.

[12] Rhodes, *Reasoning from the Scriptures*, 206.

## "Once for All" Sacrifice

Most Protestant apologists who deny that the Mass is a sacrifice usually cite the Letter to the Hebrews and its reference to Christ's sacrifice being "once for all" (10:10), or "a single offering" (10:14). According to Protestant apologists John Ankerberg and John Weldon,

> Christ is pictured as having accomplished his work once for and for all and having sat down at the right hand of the Father (Heb. 1:3; 8:1). The finality of Christ's sacrifice stands in stark contrast with the Catholic conception of the constant "renewal" of that sacrifice in the mass.... How can the mass apply a forgiveness of sins that was already fully earned by Christ on the cross and applied to the believer at the very point of saving faith?[13]

Catholics agree that Christ was sacrificed *once* on the Cross and no longer has to suffer or offer a bloody sacrifice. Hebrews teaches that Christ's one *bloody* sacrifice on the Cross accomplishes what the many animal sacrifices of the Old Covenant could not accomplish. But this does not mean that Christ, in his glorified body, does not continue to offer himself as a living sacrifice to the Father just as we offer ourselves to God (Rom 12:1). The Council of Trent made this distinction in its twenty-second session, saying, "Forasmuch as, in this divine sacrifice which is celebrated in the Mass, that same Christ is contained and immolated in an unbloody manner, who once offered Himself in a bloody manner on the altar of the cross."[14]

Hebrews 7:24–25 says of Christ, "He holds his priesthood permanently, because he continues for ever. Consequently he is able for all time to save those who draw near to God through him, since *he always lives to make intercession for them* [emphasis added]." If Christ were "a priest forever", it would follow that Christ always fulfills his priestly duty by offering his one sacrifice to the Father on our behalf. The existence of continuing heavenly sacrifices can also be found in Hebrews 9:23, which says that "it was necessary for the copies of

[13] John Ankerberg and John Weldon, *Protestants & Catholics: Do They Now Agree?* (Eugene, OR: Harvest House Publishers, 1995), 81.

[14] "On the Sacrifice of the Mass", The Council of Trent, September 17, 1563, chap. 2, www.thecounciloftrent.com/ch22.htm.

the heavenly things to be purified with these rites, but the heavenly things themselves with better sacrifices than these."

In his commentary on Hebrews, George Buchanan says Protestant scholars such as him "have had trouble with these passages, because Christ's 'once for all' sacrifice on earth was thought to make all other sacrifices unnecessary". But he notes that

> since the heavenly archetype functions just as its earthly imitation, it seemed reasonable for the heavenly high priest to offer sacrifices in heaven. These sacrifices, of course, must be better than their earthly counterparts, but their function is to cleanse "the heavenly things" (Heb 9:23).[15]

Once again, the author of Hebrews rejects the idea that Christ would have to "suffer repeatedly since the foundation of the world" (Heb 9:26). But he also acknowledges the existence of other heavenly sacrifices as well as the fact that Christ presents himself to the Father where he "appear[s] in the presence of God on our behalf" (Heb 9:24). According to the Anglican bishop Stephen Sykes,

> Christ *continually* [emphasis in original] intercedes with his blood in the presence of God on behalf of sinners.... If that sacrifice is being eternally pleaded on behalf of sinners by the exalted Christ in the heavens, it is but a short step to say that the prayer of the Christian body at the Eucharist joined with that of Christ, its head, is itself offering of a sacrifice.[16]

Finally, in Hebrews 13:10 the author says, "We have an altar from which those who serve the tent have no right to eat." Those who "serve the tent" are the Jewish priests who serve in the Jerusalem Temple (which was probably still in existence when Hebrews was written). Modern interpreters who deny that this is a reference to a literal,

---

[15] George Wesley Buchanan, *The Book of Hebrews: Its Challenge from Zion* (Eugene, OR: Wipf and Stock, 2006), 301. Cited in Jimmy Akin, "Jesus' 'Once for All' Sacrifice", Jimmy Akin.com, accessed July 11, 2017, http://jimmyakin.com/jesus-once-for-all-sacrifice. (I also owe the explanation of the Mass via bloody and unbloody sacrifices to Jimmy Akin.)

[16] Cited in Steve Walton, "Sacrifice and Priesthood in Relation to the Christian Life and Church in the New Testament", in *Sacrifice in the Bible*, ed. Roger T. Beckwith and Martin J. Selman (Eugene, OR: Wipf and Stock, 2004), 147.

Eucharistic altar usually base this on the assumption that Hebrews teaches there are no more sacrifices. But we've shown that Hebrews acknowledges the existence of multiple, unbloody heavenly sacrifices, so there is no reason those heavenly realties would not have earthly counterparts. The Protestant scholar Victor Pfitzner says:

> The assertion that the theology of Hebrews excludes any sacramental dimension is questionable. Further sacrifices for atonement from sin are rejected, but 13:9–10 does not rule out the eating of a Christian sacrificial meal. Care must be exercised so as not to interpret Hebrews through Paul, but it is interesting to note that Paul, by analogy, connects the altar of Israel with the table of the Lord (1 Cor. 10:18, 21).[17]

Other arguments against the Mass claim that it contradicts the efficacy of Christ's sacrifice on the Cross. James White asks, "Can a person approach Calvary a thousand times, seeking forgiveness, and yet die 'impure,' so as to have to suffer in purgatory before entering God's presence? If not, then the Mass cannot be the *same* sacrifice as that of Calvary."[18] In a similar vein, Ankerberg and Weldon cite Hebrews 10:18, which says, "Where there is forgiveness of these, there is no longer any offering for sin." They then ask, "If there is no longer a sacrifice for sin, what can possibly be the purpose of Mass as a sacrifice for sins?"[19]

The answer, as we've seen, is that there is no longer a *bloody* sacrifice for sin. There will never be a "re-crucifixon" of Christ. But (contra Ankerberg, Weldon, and White) the one bloody sacrifice of Christ is applied to different people in different ways, a fact many Protestants also accept. For example, the author of Hebrews says that if a believer goes on sinning deliberately after receiving the truth, "there no longer remains a sacrifice for sins" (10:26). Christ is not sacrificed again, but his one sacrifice must remain after the Crucifixion in some form so that it can accomplish its salvific purpose.

In addition, the Bible teaches that Christ's sacrifice atoned not just for our sins, but for those of the whole world (1 Jn 2:2), which is why God is called "the Savior of all men, especially of those who believe"

[17] Victor Pfitzner, *Hebrews* (Nashville, TN: Abingdon Press, 1997), 204.

[18] James R. White, *The Roman Catholic Controversy* (Minneapolis: Bethany House, 1996), 166.

[19] Ankerberg and Weldon, *Protestants & Catholics*, 81.

(1 Tim 4:10). But this does not mean that all people will be saved, because Christ's sacrifice must be applied to an individual in order for it to be efficacious in saving that person.

In regard to White's argument, his claim that the sacrifice of the Mass does not re-present the sacrifice of Calvary because those who partake of it can still be potentially lost proves too much. After all, many Protestants believe one can partake of that sacrifice through faith and still die an apostate. Of course, White and other Reformed apologists believe Christ died only for the elect and that these people cannot lose their salvation. But this means that White's argument against the Mass now relies on doctrines to support it that most Protestants, including some Calvinists, reject. This includes the doctrine of limited atonement, which is denied by some Calvinists, and eternal security, which is denied by many Protestants more broadly (and which we will examine in chapter 12). Since we will show that eternal security is false and the limited atonement is plainly contradicted by Scripture's testimony that Christ died for all men, this means White's argument against the Mass does not succeed.[20]

## Historical Evidence for the Sacrifice of the Mass

According to Geisler and MacKenzie, the description of the Mass as a sacrifice "is found as early as Gregory the Great (c. A.D. 540–604) ... 'This notion of the mass as sacrifice eventually became standard doctrine of the Western church—until it was rejected by Protestants in the sixteenth century.' "[21] But the historical record indicates that the Eucharist was understood as a sacrifice from the beginning. For example, one of the earliest nonbiblical references to the Eucharist being offered as a sacrifice can be found in the *Didache*, which is from the first century. It says:

[20] See, for example, 1 John 2:2: "He is the expiation for our sins, and not for ours only but also for the sins of the whole world"; also, 1 Timothy 4:10: "We have our hope set on the living God, who is the Savior of all men, especially of those who believe." For a reply to Calvinist rebuttals of these verses see *The Grace of God and the Will of Man: A Case for Arminianism*, ed. Clark H. Pinnock (Grand Rapids, MI: Zondervan, 1989), 57–96.

[21] Norman L. Geisler and Ralph E. MacKenzie, *Roman Catholics and Evangelicals: Agreements and Differences* (Grand Rapids, MI: Baker Books, 1995), 266.

But every Lord's day gather yourselves together, and break bread, and give thanksgiving after having confessed your transgressions, that your sacrifice may be pure. But let no one that is at variance with his fellow come together with you, until they be reconciled, that your sacrifice may not be profaned. For this is that which was spoken by the Lord: In every place and time offer to me a pure sacrifice; for I am a great King, says the Lord, and my name is wonderful among the nations.[22]

Ignatius references this sacrificial gathering when he exhorts his audience to "Take heed, then, to have but one Eucharist. For there is one flesh of our Lord Jesus Christ, and one cup to [show forth] the unity of His blood."[23] In his study of the Christian concept of sacrifice, Huub van de Sandt says, "The text in Didache 14 does not teach that the Eucharist is a sacrifice [thusia] but seems to take this idea for granted. It is used as an argument for maintaining that Christians should participate in this sacrifice only with an unpolluted conscience."[24]

Early Christians also believed the Mass was a sacrifice because it fulfilled the prophecy found in Malachi 1:11, which says, "In every place incense is offered to my name, and a pure offering; for my name is great among the nations, says the LORD of hosts." Justin Martyr said this prophecy was fulfilled when Christians "in every place offer sacrifices to Him, i.e., the bread of the Eucharist, and also the cup of the Eucharist".[25] Indeed, Justin's description of Christian liturgy in his letter to the Roman emperor closely parallels elements that are still found in the Catholic Mass, such as the prayers of the faithful, the exchange of peace, and the "great amen" (along with the Consecration of bread and wine).[26]

---

[22] Didache 14.

[23] St. Ignatius of Antioch, Epistle to the Philadelphians 4.

[24] Huub van de Sandt, "Baptism and Holiness: Two Requirements Requiring Participation in the Didache's Eucharist", in The Didache: A Missing Piece of the Puzzle in Early Christianity, ed. Jonathan A. Draper and Clayton N. Jefford (Atlanta: Society of Biblical Literature, 2015), 157–58.

[25] St. Justin Martyr, Dialogue with Trypho 41.

[26] "He gives praise and glory to the Father of the universe, through the name of the Son and of the Holy Ghost, and offers thanks at considerable length for our being counted worthy to receive these things at His hands. And when he has concluded the prayers and thanksgivings, all the people present express their assent by saying Amen." St. Justin Martyr, First Apology 65.

While discussing the Last Supper, Irenaeus said Christ "gives us as the means of subsistence the first-fruits of His own gifts in the New Testament, concerning which Malachi, among the twelve prophets, thus spoke beforehand".[27] Saint Cyprian explicitly describes how our previous arguments about Christ's priesthood naturally entail the continual offering of his sacrifice to the Father:

> For if Jesus Christ, our Lord and God, is Himself the chief priest of God the Father, and has first offered Himself a sacrifice to the Father, and has commanded this to be done in commemoration of Himself, certainly that priest truly discharges the office of Christ, who imitates that which Christ did; and he then offers a true and full sacrifice in the Church to God the Father, when he proceeds to offer it according to what he sees Christ Himself to have offered.[28]

William Webster admits that Cyprian believed the Mass was a propitiatory sacrifice, but he says that is only because "the Church at this time was drifting from reliance on God's grace in Jesus Christ to a theology which included the concept of human works."[29] Webster claims that the early Fathers before Cyprian believed the Mass was merely a sacrifice of praise and thanksgiving. Of course, the *Catechism* also describes the Mass as a "sacrifice of praise in thanksgiving" (*CCC* 1359), so we should not be surprised to find this language among early Christians (the word "eucharist" even means "thanksgiving").

According to eminent Church history scholar Everett Ferguson, "Although Justin identified the sacrifice primarily with the prayers (Dial. 117), he also spoke of the bread and cup as the sacrifice (Dial 41). Irenaeus more explicitly spoke of the bread and cup as an oblation of the first fruits of creation (Here. 4.17.5)."[30] In his study on Luther, the Mennonite scholar Harry Loewen wrote, "The church fathers Justin Martyr, Irenaeus, Tertullian, and Cyprian seemed to

---

[27] St. Irenaeus, *Against Heresies* 4.17.5.

[28] St. Cyprian, *Epistle* 62.14.

[29] William Webster, *The Church of Rome at the Bar of History* (Carlisle, PA: Banner of Truth Trust, 1995), 126.

[30] Everett Ferguson, "Sacrifice", in *Encyclopedia of Early Christianity*, 2nd ed. (New York: Routledge, 1999), 1070.

believe in the sacrificial nature of the mass and held either to transubstantiation or consubstantiation."[31]

Given the abundance of this ancient evidence, it's not surprising that Luther wrote in *The Babylonian Captivity of the Church*, "What shall we say, then, about the canon of the mass and the sayings of the Fathers? ... It would yet be the safer course to reject them all rather than admit that the mass is a work or a sacrifice."[32]

## Defining the Real Presence

One common objection to the real, bodily presence of Christ in the Eucharist goes something like this: "How can you say the Eucharist becomes the Body and Blood of Christ when it still looks like bread and wine? A scientist can examine these specimens and show you at the molecular level how no change has taken place, so why do you believe anything at Mass has transformed into something else?" But this objection contains a misunderstanding of the doctrine, not a refutation of it.

Catholics agree that upon Consecration the bread and wine at Mass do not *visibly transform* into the Body and Blood of Jesus Christ. Instead, the substance of the bread and wine become the substance of the Body and Blood of Christ while the form or accidents of the bread and wine (what we observe with our senses) remain. The Council of Trent put it this way:

> Because Christ our Redeemer said that it was truly his body that he was offering under the species of bread, it has always been the conviction of the Church of God, and this holy Council now declares again, that by the consecration of the bread and wine there takes place a change of the whole substance of the bread into the substance of the body of Christ our Lord and of the whole substance of the wine into the substance of his blood. This change the holy Catholic Church has fittingly and properly called transubstantiation.[33]

[31] Harry Loewen, *Luther and the Radicals: Another Look at Some Aspects of the Struggle between Luther and the Radical Reformers* (Ontario: Wilfrid Laurier University, 1974), 40.

[32] Martin Luther, *Works of Luther: With Introductions and Notes*, ed. Henry Eyster Jacobs and Adolph Spaeth (Philadelphia: A.J. Holman, 1915), 213.

[33] Council of Trent (1551): DS 1642; cf. Mt 26:26ff.; Mk 14:22ff.; Lk 22:19ff.; 1 Cor 11:24ff. Cited in *CCC* 1376.

Since at the Last Supper Jesus did not say of the bread, "This represents my body" or "This contains my body", but simply, "This is my body," the concept of *transubstantiation* best explains the miracle God achieves through the Eucharist. The term "transubstantiation" itself was first used in a magisterial document in 1215 when the Fourth Lateran Council described how "his body and blood are truly contained in the sacrament of the altar under the forms of bread and wine, the bread and wine having been *changed in substance* [emphasis added; Latin, *transsubstantiatio*], by God's power, into his body and blood, so that in order to achieve this mystery of unity we receive from God what he received from us."[34]

This does not mean that the *idea* of transubstantiation was unknown before the thirteenth century. In the fourth century Gregory Nyssa described the change in the bread and wine at Consecration as "*transelementation*" (Greek, *metastoicheiosis*), which refers to a restructuring of an object's fundamental elements.[35] The fact that this belief was later called *transubstantiation* does not refute its apostolic origins, because many doctrines are later clarified with postbiblical language. For example, the term *homoousios* (same substance) was first prominently used to address the christological controversies surrounding the Council of Nicaea (A.D. 325), but that does not mean Christians who lived before the council did not believe that the Father and the Son were each equally God.

Finally, if the Eucharist were the substance of Christ's Body and Blood, then wouldn't consuming the Eucharist be an act of cannibalism? It would not, because cannibalism involves destroying human flesh through chewing and digestion in order to extract nutrients from it. However, the Body of Christ is not damaged when the Eucharist is consumed, nor is it digested since whenever the appearances of bread and wine cease to exist, the substance of Christ's Body and Blood ceases to exist as well. Besides, if consuming the Eucharist were cannibalism, then Protestants who celebrate "the Lord's Supper" would still be guilty of practicing *symbolic* cannibalism. But since

---

[34] "Confession of Faith", Fourth Lateran Council, in Decrees of the Ecumenical Councils, trans. Norman P. Tanner (1990), http://www.ewtn.com/library/councils/lateran4.htm.

[35] Albert J.D. Walsh, *The Eucharist's Biographer: The Liturgical Formation of Christian Identity* (Eugene, OR: Wipf and Stock, 2012), 14–15.

Christ would never command us to engage in either literal or symbolic evils, it follows that consuming the Eucharist is not cannibalism.

## Biblical Evidence for the Real Presence

Jesus celebrated Passover at the Last Supper (Mt 26:18–19), but the Gospels do not record him discussing the meaning of the Passover lamb or the story of the Exodus. Instead, they record Jesus speaking about his Body and Blood and the inauguration of the New Covenant. This would make sense if Jesus considered *himself* to be the Passover lamb that his disciples would eat in the bread and wine he offered them. In fact, Paul says, "Christ, our Paschal [Passover] Lamb, has been sacrificed" (1 Cor 5:7), and John the Baptist called Jesus "the Lamb of God, who takes away the sin of the world" (Jn 1:29).

Paul also told the Corinthians, "The cup of blessing which we bless, is it not a participation in the blood of Christ? The bread which we break, is it not a participation in the body of Christ?" (1 Cor 10:16). He also warned that anyone who "eats the bread or drinks the cup of the Lord in an unworthy manner will be guilty of profaning the body and blood of the Lord" (1 Cor 11:27). This profaning of the Eucharist was so severe that it incurred a judgment that resulted in many of the Corinthians becoming sick or dying (1 Cor 11:29–30).

Another important text to discuss when analyzing the evidence for the Real Presence of Christ in the Eucharist is the bread of life discourse in John 6. When examining this chapter we must remember, as Craig Keener says, "Many Jewish people were also hoping for a new exodus led by a new Moses—complete with new manna, or bread from heaven."[36] This hope was revealed in the crowd's exclamation, "This is indeed the prophet who is to come into the world!" (Jn 6:14), which refers to Deuteronomy 18:15 and its promise that God would raise up a prophet like Moses from among the Israelites.

The late first-century apocalypse of Second Baruch demonstrates the Jewish belief that at the Messiah's coming, "the treasury of manna shall again descend from on high, and they will eat of it in those years, because these are they who have come to the consummation

---

[36] Craig Keener, *The IVP Bible Background Commentary: New Testament*, 2nd ed. (Downers Grove, IL: IVP Academic, 2014), 53.

of time."[37] Jesus repeatedly says he is the bread that has come down
from heaven, or the new manna, and then explicitly says this bread he
will give is his flesh for the life of the world. He then says:

> Truly, truly, I say to you, unless you eat the flesh of the Son of man
> and drink his blood, you have no life in you; he who eats my flesh and
> drinks my blood has eternal life, and I will raise him up at the last day.
> For my flesh is food indeed, and my blood is drink indeed. He who
> eats my flesh and drinks my blood abides in me, and I in him. As the
> living Father sent me, and I live because of the Father, so he who eats
> me will live because of me. (Jn 6:53–57)

John tells us that "after this many of his disciples drew back and
no longer walked with him" (Jn 6:66). If they drew back because
they thought Jesus was requiring actually eating his flesh instead of
belief in him, then Jesus could have corrected them. Indeed, earlier in
John's Gospel when the disciples mistook Jesus' figurative reference
to food for a literal one, he corrected them (Jn 4:31–34). But in John
6 Jesus did nothing to stem the tide of disciples who left him. Jesus
even asks the remaining disciples, "Will you also go away?" (v. 67)
instead of explaining to them the symbolic meaning of his teaching
that others failed to grasp.

Consider also when Jesus warned the disciples about the teaching
of the Jewish leaders. The disciples thought Jesus was speaking about
literal bread until he corrected them, saying, "How is it that you fail
to perceive that I did not speak about bread? Beware of the leaven of
the Pharisees and Sadducees." Matthew then adds this detail: "They
understood that he did not tell them to beware of the leaven of bread,
but of the teaching of the Pharisees and Sadducees" (Mt 16:11–12).

Some Protestant apologists say Jesus' teaching in this discourse is
purely symbolic because in John's Gospel Jesus also says, "I am the
door" (Jn 10:7) or "I am the vine" (Jn 15:5). According to Geisler
and MacKenzie, "Roman Catholic scholars do not take these statements literally, even though they come from the same book that
records 'This is my body!' It is, therefore, not necessary to take Jesus

---

[37] 2 Bar 29:8. Cited in Brant Pitre, *Jesus and the Jewish Roots of the Eucharist* (New York: Doubleday, 2011), 181.

literally when he said 'this is my body' or 'eat my flesh.' "[38] But unlike in those statements, Jesus never says, "Truly, truly, I tell you my body is a true door and my hands are real knobs," in the same manner as he says, "My flesh is food indeed, and my blood is drink indeed" (6:55).

Other apologists claim that Jesus taught that the words "eating" and "drinking" in verses 53–57 are synonymous with the words "believing" and "coming" that he uses earlier in the discourse. Robert Zins says verse 35 is "the controlling verse" for exegesis because Jesus says, "I am the bread of life; he who comes to me shall not hunger, and he who believes in me shall never thirst."[39] White, on the other hand, points to verse 47 ("he who believes has eternal life") and says this shows "eating=believing".[40]

But verse 47 does not say "believing" is the same thing as "eating", and verse 35 actually parallels "believing" with "drinking". In John 6 Jesus does not teach that believing in him and consuming him are synonymous but rather that the former is a *prerequisite* for the latter. That's why the *Didache* records how early Christians were prohibited from giving the Eucharist to the unbaptized (which Catholics still practice today).

The idea that "believing" and "coming" are synonymous with "eating" and "drinking" is complicated by the fact that Jesus commanded us to drink his *blood* rather than his *water*, which was a metaphor he used earlier in John's Gospel (Jn 4:10–15). Jesus' command makes sense only if he was referring to the Eucharist he identified at the Last Supper with his Body and Blood, the latter of which he presented under the form of drinkable wine.

Finally, Ulrich Zwingli (and many Protestants since him) claimed that John 6:63 settles the matter because Jesus said, "It is the Spirit that gives life, the flesh is of no avail; the words that I have spoken to you are Spirit and life."[41] According to this argument, Jesus meant for his words to be taken in a "spiritual context", and he taught that literal flesh does not communicate eternal life. But if that's true, then

---

[38] Geisler and MacKenzie, *Roman Catholics and Evangelicals*, 261–62.

[39] Robert M. Zins, *Romanism: The Relentless Roman Catholic Assault on the Gospel of Jesus Christ!* (Huntsville, AL: White Horse Publications, 1995), 119.

[40] White, *Roman Catholic Controversy*, 171.

[41] John W. Riggs, *The Lord's Supper in the Reformed Tradition* (Louisville, KY: Westminster John Knox Press, 2015), 62.

why did the Word become flesh (Jn 1:14) and atone for the sins of the world through the death of that flesh on a cross?

Jesus is saying that fleshly, earthly ways of understanding do not save someone but rather spiritual, heavenly ways of understanding. Later in John's Gospel Jesus chides the Pharisees because they "judge according to the flesh" (Jn 8:15). The word "spirit" (*pneuma*) does not mean "figurative" or "symbolic", but in this context it more closely means "life-giving". Jesus even refers to the spiritual reality that lay behind his words in the previous verse when he asks his critics, "What if you were to see the Son of man ascending where he was before?" (6:62). Raymond Brown summarizes Jesus' message thusly: "It is not the dead body or flesh of Jesus which will be of benefit in the Eucharist, but his resurrected body full of the Spirit of Life."[42]

## Historical Evidence for the Real Presence

Did the early Christians believe that the Eucharist was merely a symbol of Christ? The Protestant scholar Darwell Stone says, "Throughout the writings of the Fathers there is unbroken agreement that the consecrated bread and wine are the body and blood of Christ, and that the Eucharist is a sacrifice."[43] J.N.D. Kelly likewise says, "Eucharistic teaching, it should be understood at the outset, was in general unquestioningly realist, i.e., the consecrated bread and wine were taken to be, and were treated and designated as, the Savior's body and blood."[44] A short survey of the Fathers readily confirms these conclusions.

Saint Ignatius of Antioch said that heretics "confess not the Eucharist to be the flesh of our Savior Jesus Christ, which suffered for our sins, and which the Father, of His goodness, raised up again."[45] Justin Martyr said the Eucharistic prayer at Mass changes the bread and wine so it becomes "the flesh and blood of that Jesus who was made flesh".[46] Origen taught that the Eucharist was a new kind of

---

[42] Raymond Brown, *The Gospel according to John*, vol. 1 (New York: Anchor Bible, 1966). Cited in Pitre, *Jesus and the Jewish Roots of the Eucharist*, 219–20.
[43] Darwell Stone, *The Holy Communion* (London: Longmans, Green, 1904), 37.
[44] Kelly, *Early Christian Doctrines*, 198. Cited in Akin, *Fathers Know Best*, 292.
[45] St. Ignatius of Antioch, *Epistle to the Smyrnaeans* 7.
[46] St. Justin Martyr, *First Apology* 66.

manna because "the flesh of the Word of God is 'true food,' just as he himself says: 'My flesh is truly food and my blood is truly drink [Jn 6:55].' "[47]

Webster claims that even though the apostolic Fathers of the first two centuries "identified the elements with the body and blood of Christ, and referred the Eucharist as a sacrifice", they did not believe the substance of the bread and wine changed leaving only accidents behind.[48] Therefore, the Church Fathers did not subscribe to the doctrine of transubstantiation. Webster claims that this is evident in writers such as Irenaeus, who he says "implied that at consecration, though the elements are no longer common bread and wine, they do not lose the nature of being bread and wine".[49]

But just as the early Fathers did not have a precise theological framework for discussing dogmas like the Trinity or original sin, they did not have a precise theological framework for discussing dogmas like the Eucharist. Their references to bread and wine existing after Consecration do not contradict these same writers' assertion that this bread and wine has truly become the Flesh and Blood of Jesus Christ. The nature of the Eucharist, according to Jaroslav Pelikan,

> did not become the subject of controversy until the ninth century. The definitive and precise formulation of the crucial doctrinal issues concerning the Eucharist had to await that controversy and others that followed even later.... The effort to cross-examine the fathers of the second or third century about where they stood in the controversies of the ninth or sixteenth century is both silly and futile.[50]

Irenaeus says that if heretics were right and there were no salvation in the flesh, then neither "is the cup of the Eucharist the communion of His blood, nor the bread which we break the communion of His body".[51] Irenaeus argued against the Gnostic denial of the

---

[47] Origen, *Homily on Numbers* 7.2.2. Cited in Origen, *Homilies on Numbers*, trans. Thomas P. Scheck, ed. Christopher A. Hall (Downers Grove, IL: InterVarsity Press, 2009), 26.

[48] Webster, *Church of Rome at the Bar of History*, 117.

[49] Ibid.

[50] Jaroslav Pelikan, *The Christian Tradition: A History of the Development of Doctrine*, vol. 1, *The Emergence of the Catholic Tradition (100–600)* (Chicago: University of Chicago Press, 1971), 167.

[51] St. Irenaeus, *Against Heresies* 5.2.2.

resurrection of the body by pointing out how God causes bread and wine to become the Body and Blood of Christ and through the consumption of which we will receive immortality. According to J. N. D. Kelly, "Irenaeus teaches that the bread and wine are really the Lord's body and blood. His witness is, indeed, all the more impressive because he produces it quite incidentally while refuting the Gnostic and Docetic rejection of the Lord's real humanity."[52]

Since the doctrine of transubstantiation had not yet been defined, we should not expect the Church Father's description of the Eucharist to conform to this idea (just as we should not expect the Father's descriptions of the Trinity to conform to later theological ideas like "circumincession", which refers to the unique way the three Persons of the Trinity dwell in one another). However, what we do find does not support the position of many Protestants who claim that the Eucharist is *merely* a symbol.

Some apologists cite Church Fathers and ecclesial writers who spoke of the Eucharist as a "sign" or "symbol", but those writers did not mean the Eucharist was *only* a sign or symbol of Christ's Body. As Kelly says, "According to ancient modes of thought a mysterious relationship existed between the thing symbolized and its symbol, figure or type, the symbol in some *was* the thing symbolized. Again, the verb *repraesentare*, in Tertullian's vocabulary, retained its original significance of 'to make present.'"[53] Webster even admits that "as time passed clearer descriptions of the Eucharist as the transformation of the elements into the literal body and blood of Christ emerged in the writings of the Fathers such as Cyril of Jerusalem, Gregory of Nyssa, Gregory Nazianzen, Chrysostom and Ambrose."[54]

Concerning Augustine's view of the Eucharist, the bishop of Hippo said, "What you see is the bread and the chalice.... But what your faith obliges you to accept is that the bread is the Body of Christ and the chalice the Blood of Christ."[55] In regard to Christ's offering of his body, he says, "Christ was carried in his own hands when, referring to his own body, he said, 'This is my body' [Mt 26:26]. For

---

[52] Kelly, *Early Christian Doctrines*, 198. Cited in Akin, *Fathers Know Best*, 292.

[53] Kelly, *Early Christian Doctrines*, 212.

[54] Webster, *Church of Rome at the Bar of History*, 120.

[55] St. Augustine, *Sermons* 227. Cited in Akin, *Fathers Know Best*, 297.

he carried that body in his hands."[56] In *City of God* Augustine says of Christ, "He is both the Priest who offers and the Sacrifice offered."[57] But how do we reconcile this with Webster's claim that Augustine believed "Christ's physical body could not literally be present in the sacrament of the Eucharist because he is physically at the right hand of God in heaven and will be there until he comes again"?[58]

In that homily Augustine taught that Christ is not present in a *purely* bodily way in the Eucharist, or as he says of the Church's teaching on the subject, "by faith it holds, not with eyes beholds him". Christ is not present in the Eucharist in the same way as he was present with his disciples, but he is still truly present in the bread and wine that is consecrated at Mass. Saint Thomas Aquinas addressed this objection to the Eucharist by noting that "Christ's body is not in this sacrament in the same way as a body is in a place, which by its dimensions is commensurate with the place; but in a special manner which is proper to this sacrament."[59]

Given that Christ's glorious, resurrected body could transcend spatial locations by passing through solid objects (Jn 20:19), disappearing from sight (Lk 24:31), and ascending into heaven (Acts 1:9), we should not be surprised that Christ could make his body sacramentally present in the Eucharist.

---

[56] St. Augustine, *Explanations of the Psalms* 33.1.10. Cited in Akin, *Fathers Know Best*, 297.
[57] St. Augustine, *City of God* 10.20.
[58] Webster, *Church of Rome at the Bar of History*, 121.
[59] St. Thomas Aquinas, *Summa Theologica* III, q. 75, a. 1.

Part III

How Am I Saved?

# 9

# Baptism

"What a great, excellent thing Baptism is, which delivers us from the jaws of the devil and makes us God's own, suppresses and takes away sin, and then daily strengthens the new man; and is and remains ever efficacious until we pass from this estate of misery to eternal glory."[1] These may sound like the words of a Catholic saint, but they actually come from Martin Luther. Luther's words are similar to the *Catechism*'s declaration that baptism "not only purifies from all sins, but also makes the neophyte 'a new creature,' an adopted son of God, who has become a 'partaker of the divine nature' (2 Cor 5:17; 2 Pet 1:4; cf. Gal 4:5–7), member of Christ and co-heir with him (cf. 1 Cor 6:15; 12:27; Rom 8:17), and a temple of the Holy Spirit (1 Cor 6:19)" (*CCC* 1265).

While Catholics, Eastern Orthodox, Lutherans, Pentecostals, and many other Christians believe baptism takes away sin and is necessary for salvation, some Protestants deny this doctrine. According to Ron Rhodes, "Baptism is basically a public profession of faith. It says to the whole world, 'I'm a believer in Christ and have identified my life within him.'"[2] For Protestants like Rhodes, baptism is an ordinance instituted by Christ (and so it must be carried out), but it does not remit sin or make someone a spiritually regenerate member of the Body of Christ.[3]

---

[1] Martin Luther, *The Large Catechism*, "Holy Baptism", BookofConcord.org, accessed July 13, 2017, http://bookofconcord.org/lc-6-baptism.php.

[2] Ron Rhodes, *Reasoning from the Scriptures with Catholics* (Eugene, OR: Harvest House Publishing, 2000), 168.

[3] Not all Protestants believe that baptism is an ordinance that must be carried out in obedience to Jesus' command. For example, the Salvation Army does not encourage its members to be baptized. See http://www.waterbeachsalvationarmy.org.uk/what-to-know-more/why-does-the-salvation-army-not-baptise-or-hold-communion/.

However, the biblical and patristic evidence supports what the majority of Christians have long believed: baptism saves us from sin and makes everyone who receives it, including infants, members of the Body of Christ.

## The Evidence from Peter

In the first sermon given after Pentecost, Peter told a crowd in Jerusalem that God raised Jesus of Nazareth from the dead and that "God has made him both Lord and Christ, this Jesus whom you crucified" (Acts 2:36). Luke tells us that when the crowd heard this, "they were cut to the heart, and said to Peter and the rest of the apostles, 'Brethren, what shall we do?'" (Acts 2:37). Peter then replied:

> Repent, and be baptized every one of you in the name of Jesus Christ for the forgiveness of your sins; and you shall receive the gift of the Holy Spirit. For the promise is to you and to your children and to all that are far off, every one whom the Lord our God calls to him. (Acts 2:38–39)

According to Everett Fergusson in his study of baptism in the first five centuries of Church history, "The double command of Acts 2:38 seems straightforward enough that repentance and being baptized both have as their purpose the forgiveness of sins."[4] However, some critics of baptismal regeneration say that because "those who received [Peter's] word" were baptized (Acts 2:41), this means it is the preaching of the gospel that remits sins and not baptism.[5]

But Peter was speaking to a crowd of adults that first had to accept his teaching's veracity (or "receive his word") before they could comply with his command to repent and be baptized. Receiving the gospel is a necessary condition for salvation among those who are capable of receiving it, but is not a sufficient condition for salvation. Hebrews 4:2 describes unbelievers who hear the good news of God's plan of salvation, but because they lack faith, this preaching "did not

---

[4] Everett Fergusson, *Baptism in the Early Church: History, Theology and Liturgy in the First Five Centuries* (Grand Rapids, MI: Wm. B. Eerdmans, 2009), 168.

[5] Norman L. Geisler and Ralph E. MacKenzie, *Roman Catholics and Evangelicals: Agreements and Differences* (Grand Rapids, MI: Baker Books, 1995), 481.

benefit them". Along with hearing the "word", or the gospel, one must respond to it with repentance, faith, and baptism.

Other apologists claim that the word "for" (Greek, *eis*) in the clause "for the forgiveness of sins" refers to the forgiveness of sins being the cause of baptism rather than its effect. For example, "I took an umbrella to work today for (because of) the rain" would be an example of "for" being used in a causal sense. The rain did not happen because I brought the umbrella; rather, the rain caused me to bring the umbrella to work. In contrast, "I took sleeping pills on the plane for (in order to achieve) a good night's rest" would be an example of "for" being used in an efficacious sense. Sleeping didn't cause me to grab the pills before I went to the airport; I took the pills with me so I could acquire sleep on the plane. Those who reject baptismal regeneration say Peter is using the word "for" in a causal sense, or, we are baptized because we have already been forgiven of our sins. A person is not baptized in order to receive the forgiveness of his sins.[6] The nineteenth-century Baptist preacher Charles Spurgeon described the purpose of baptism after the forgiveness of sins in this way:

> Baptism is the avowal of faith; the man was Christ's soldier, but now in baptism he puts on his regimentals. The man believed in Christ, but his faith remained between God and his own soul. In baptism he says to the baptizer, "I believe in Jesus Christ:" he says to the Church, "I unite with you as a believer in the common truths."[7]

However, the causal "for" (Greek, *eis*) is not the default use of this preposition in the New Testament. In fact, Fergusson says this interpretation of Acts 2:38 "has been thoroughly refuted".[8] The renowned

[6] Edward Dalcour provides a good summary of arguments like this made by the influential Greek grammarians J. R. Mantey and A. T. Robertson: "[Mantey] argued that the preposition *eis* ("for") could be causal, hence the passage could read: 'And Peter said to them, "Repent, and be baptized—each one of you—at the name of Jesus Christ because of/for/unto the forgiveness of sins.'" In other words, the preposition *eis* should be translated "because of," or "in view of", not "in order to" or "for the purpose of forgiveness of sins." Edward Dalcour, *A Definitive Look at Oneness Theology: Defending the Tri-Unity of God* (Lanham, MD: University Press of America, 2004), 112.

[7] Charles Spurgeon, "The Sermon on Baptismal Regeneration". Cited in Lewis A. Drummond, *Spurgeon: Prince of Preachers* (Grand Rapids, MI: Kregel Publications, 1992), 800.

[8] Fergusson, *Baptism in the Early Church*, 168. See, for example, Ralph Marcus, "On Causal eis", *Journal of Biblical Literature* 70 (1951): 129–30.

Greek scholar Daniel Wallace, who rejects the doctrine of baptismal regeneration, says that the "ingenious solution of a causal [*eis*] lacks conviction" and has no basis in altering the grammar of the passage.[9] In response to J. R. Mantey's popularization of this argument, the Evangelical scholar Murray Harris writes in his work *Prepositions and Theology in the Greek New Testament*:

> Although there are as many as 15 instances where *eis* could be construed as causal, in no case is *eis* in itself unambiguously causal; alternative and preferential renderings always present themselves.... Mantey has not adduced any convincing example from extra biblical Hellenistic Greek where *eis* expresses "immediate and direct cause."[10]

According to Robert Stein, "Although some have sought to interpret the expression 'for [*eis*] the forgiveness of your sins' as 'in the hope of forgiveness' or 'because of your forgiveness,' it is best to interpret the expression as indicating the purpose of repentance-baptism."[11] This makes sense of the crowd's desire to seek forgiveness for being accomplices in the death of the Messiah. When they asked, "What shall we do?" the crowd was eager to hear a way to have their sins forgiven, not a way to show God had already forgiven them. Acts 2:38 shows that baptism is the way to *receive* the forgiveness of sins, not the way merely to *demonstrate* God's forgiveness of our sins. The other key Petrine passage related to baptism is 1 Peter 3:20–21, which says,

> When God's patience waited in the days of Noah, during the building of the ark, in which a few, that is, eight persons, were saved through water. Baptism, which corresponds to this, now saves you, not as a removal of dirt from the body but as an appeal to God for a clear conscience, through the resurrection of Jesus Christ.

---

[9] Daniel Wallace, *Greek Grammar: Beyond the Basics* (Grand Rapids, MI: Zondervan, 1996), 371. Wallace says that the shift from second person plural to third person singular and then back to the second person plural could make it acceptable to say *eis* is subordinate to repent rather than to baptize (i.e., repent *with reference* to your sins). But the subtlety and awkwardness of the phrase counts against it being the intended meaning (ibid., 370).

[10] Murray J. Harris, *Prepositions and Theology in the Greek New Testament* (Grand Rapids, MI: Zondervan, 2012), 91.

[11] Robert H. Stein, "Baptism in Luke-Acts", in *Believer's Baptism*, ed. Thomas R. Schreiner and Shawn D. Wright (Nashville, TN: B&H Publishing, 2006), 49.

According to Lutheran scholar Robert Kolb, "The apostle Peter was direct and simple.... Baptism fulfills what God promised to his Old Testament people. It gives salvation, that is, new life in Christ."[12] Even scholars who deny baptismal regeneration agree that this view of 1 Peter 3:21 "maximizes the typological correspondence between the flood and Christian baptism".[13] One critic admits, "Interpretation of this verse has been plagued by Protestant fear of finding in it a basis for the doctrine of 'baptismal regeneration.'"[14]

Is there any good reason to deny the salvific efficacy of baptism that at least *seems* to flow from this verse?

Geisler and MacKenzie claim that baptism saves us only from "a bad conscience", or the guilt that comes from refusing to follow Jesus' command to be baptized. They also claim that the floodwaters, or the thing to which baptism is said to correspond, were not what made Noah righteous. That's because Noah was called righteous before the flood, so if the floodwaters didn't make Noah righteous, then the waters of baptism can't make us righteous either.[15] But this interpretation misses the whole point of Peter's comparison.

Peter is not comparing the salvation of Noah's soul to the salvation of our souls. He is comparing the fact that the occupants of the Ark were saved from physical death through water to the fact that the baptized are saved from spiritual death through water. According to Kittel's *Theological Dictionary*, "The request for a good conscience ... is to be construed as a prayer for the remission of sins."[16]

Other critics of baptismal regeneration point out that Peter qualifies his statement by saying that baptism does not remove "filth from the flesh". Instead, baptism provides an opportunity to make an appeal to God for a clean conscience through the Resurrection of Christ. Baptism may provide the opportunity to be saved, but it is the Resurrection of Christ and faith in him that actually saves us. Thomas Nettles claims, "The text says that baptism does not remove the moral filth natural to life in this body. It affirms rather that we

---

[12] Robert Kolb, "Lutheran View: God's Baptismal Act as Regenerative", in *Understanding Four Views on Baptism*, ed. John H. Armstrong (Grand Rapids, MI: Zondervan, 2007), 91.

[13] Karen H. Jobes, *1 Peter* (Grand Rapids, MI: Baker Academic, 2005), 253.

[14] I. Howard Marshall, *1 Peter* (Downers Grove, IL: InterVarsity Press, 1991), 130.

[15] Geisler and MacKenzie, *Roman Catholics and Evangelicals*, 486.

[16] Heinrich Greeven, "*eperotema*", in *Theological Dictionary of the New Testament*, vol. 2, ed. Gerhard Kittel (Grand Rapids, MI: Wm. B. Eerdmans, 1964), 688.

know that God has dropped his charges of condemnation against us because of Christ."[17]

However, Peter is not saying that at baptism it is a person's appeal to God for a clean conscience that saves him. Neither does Peter refer to any "dropping of charges" or removal of "moral filth" (Peter uses only the Greek word *rhupos*, which means "dirt as refuse differentiated from soil").[18] Peter explicitly says "baptism now saves you" because *the act of baptism* is the appeal to God for a clear conscience. As former Cincinnati Bible College and Seminary professor Jack Cottrell notes, "Even though it does not save through its physical element of action, it is still *baptism* that saves [emphasis in the original]."[19]

The water of baptism does not possess a magical property that saves us apart from God's grace, nor does it simply take away ritual impurities or physical imperfections from our skin (i.e., "filth of the flesh"). Instead, as the renowned Lutheran scholar Oscar Cullmann puts it, "Just as ordinary water takes away the physical uncleanness of the body so the water of baptism will take away sins."[20]

Finally, some critics say Peter did not believe in baptismal regeneration, because he acknowledged that some unbaptized Gentiles received the Holy Spirit (Acts 10:44–48). Specifically, Peter said, "Can any one forbid water for baptizing these people who have received the Holy Spirit just as we have?" (v. 47). Critics of baptismal regeneration say the fact that these people received the Holy Spirit apart from baptism proves baptism is not necessary for salvation.[21]

However, God is not bound by the sacraments he created, so he is free to impart his grace to anyone in any way he deems fit.[22] Many

---

[17] Thomas Nettles, "Baptism as a Symbol of Christ's Saving Work", in Armstrong, *Understanding Four Views on Baptism*, 38.

[18] William F. Arndt, Frederick W. Danker, and Walter Bauer, *A Greek-English Lexicon of the New Testament and Other Early Christian Literature*, 3rd ed. (Chicago: University of Chicago Press, 2000), 908.

[19] Jack Cottrell, *Baptism: A Biblical Study* (Joplin, MO: College Press Publishing, 1989), 147.

[20] Oscar Cullmann, *Baptism in the New Testament*, Studies in Biblical Theology, no. 1 (London: SCM Press, 1950), 11.

[21] Geisler and MacKenzie, *Roman Catholics and Evangelicals*, 485.

[22] See *CCC* 1257. God's ability to dispense grace apart from the sacraments also explains how the good thief on the cross could be saved without being baptized (Lk 23:43), which some critics invoke. See also my discussion of the good thief in chapter 13.

Protestants believe that children who die before making an act of faith can be saved, but this would not prove that faith is not necessary for salvation. It would prove only that God is merciful and the "Gentile Pentecost" in Acts 10 was an example of God's mercy extending to all people regardless of their religious or ethnic heritage. According to Fergusson,

> The baptism of the Holy Spirit in the case of Cornelius, instead of eliminating the need for water baptism, was the justification for administering it (10:47–48). That Peter commanded water baptism shows the norm: if these Gentiles received the Holy Spirit, then they have to be baptized in water. The implication of [Acts 11:17] is that God would have been hindered in giving salvation if they were denied baptism.[23]

## The Evidence from Paul

After Christ told Paul that Paul was persecuting him (Acts 22:7), Paul asked Jesus in verse 10, "What shall I do, Lord?" (which parallels the crowd's response to Peter's baptismal preaching after Pentecost). But unlike Peter's response to the crowd, Jesus did not give Paul any instructions on how to be forgiven of his sins. Instead, Jesus allowed Paul to be blinded and instructed him to go to Damascus and await further instructions (Acts 22:10). When Ananias met Paul in Damascus, he said Jesus sent him so that Paul would regain his sight and be filled with the Holy Spirit. Then Ananias laid hands upon Paul and restored his sight. He then said to Paul, "Why do you wait? Rise and be baptized, and wash away your sins, calling on his name" (Acts 22:16).

Some critics say Paul's conversion narrative proves he had been forgiven of his sins long before his baptism. They say Paul's calling Jesus "Lord" and Ananias' calling Paul "brother" (v. 13) show that Paul was a regenerate Christian before his baptism.[24] The nineteenth-century theologian Charles Hodge said, "No one can believe that [Paul] was under the wrath and curse of God, during the three days which intervened between his conversion and his baptism. He did

[23] Fergusson, *Baptism in the Early Church*, 177.
[24] Geisler and MacKenzie, *Roman Catholics and Evangelicals*, 485.

not receive baptism in order that his sins should be washed away; but as the sign and pledge of their forgiveness."[25]

However, it was common for Jews to call each other brother (Acts 7:2), and the title "Lord" (Greek, *kurios*) can be used to address an authority figure without claiming that figure is divine (see Mt 27:63). Likewise, in Matthew 27:63, the Pharisees address Pontius Pilate as a Kyrie, or Lord, but almost all English translations render the word, "Sir". In John 4:11 the Samaritan woman at the well uses *kurios* in this fashion when she addressed Jesus, which most translations render as "Sir" rather than "Lord". Hodge's interpretation also strains credulity given that for three days God had cursed Paul—with blindness. Paul prayed and fasted for some answer to his predicament and did not find one until the arrival of Ananias. The plain meaning of this verse is that Paul's sins were forgiven, or "washed away", through the waters of baptism.

Denver Seminary professor Bruce Demarest even admits that "a superficial reading of Acts 22:16 might suggest that baptism effects regeneration."[26] He claims, however, that it was not baptism that washed away Paul's sins but Paul's calling on the name of the Lord. But the "washing away" of the sins is unmistakably connected to the application of water in baptism. In Greek the passage literally records Ananias saying, "Be baptized and wash away the sins of you" (*baptisai kai apolousai tas hamartias sou*). The phrase "having called on the name of the Lord" is a qualifier added to the paired actions of baptism and washing away sins.

In fact, Paul's calling on the name of the Lord proves he was not saved the moment he met Jesus on the road to Damascus, because Paul associates calling on the name of the Lord with the beginning of our salvation (Rom 10:13). On the other hand, Paul does not limit our salvation *only* to calling on the name of the Lord. He also associates our salvation with the Resurrection and links that reality to our union with Christ or our being "in Christ". This union is made possible through baptism as Paul wrote in Romans 6:3–5:

---

[25] Charles Hodge, *Systematic Theology*, vol. 3 (Grand Rapids, MI: Wm. B. Eerdmans, 1940). Cited in Ronald Nash, *When a Baby Dies: Answers to Comfort Grieving Parents* (Grand Rapids, MI: Zondervan, 1999), 54.

[26] Bruce Demarest, *The Cross and Salvation: The Doctrine of Salvation* (Wheaton, IL: Crossway Books, 1997), 296.

Do you not know that all of us who have been baptized into Christ Jesus were baptized into his death? We were buried therefore with him by baptism into death, so that as Christ was raised from the dead by the glory of the Father, we too might walk in newness of life. For if we have been united with him in a death like his, we shall certainly be united with him in a resurrection like his.

Paul connects our hope of resurrection with Christ to our initial union with his death—and he associates that union with the baptism that buried us into Christ's death. In commenting on a similar passage, John Calvin said, "Paul proves us to be the sons of God, from the fact that we put on Christ in baptism."[27] According to Douglas Moo, who teaches the New Testament at Wheaton College,

A few scholars have denied any reference to water baptism here, arguing that "baptize" means "immerse" in a metaphorical sense, or that Paul refers to "baptism in the spirit," or that he uses "baptize" as a metaphor for incorporation into the body of Christ. But, without discounting the possibility of allusions to one or more of these ideas, a reference to water baptism is primary. By the date of Romans "baptize" had become almost a technical expression for the rite of Christian initiation by water, and this is surely the meaning the Roman Christians would have given the word.[28]

Paul also told Titus that God "saved us, not because of deeds done by us in righteousness, but in virtue of his own mercy, by the washing of regeneration and renewal in the Holy Spirit" (Tit 3:5). The fact that this verse does not contain the word "baptism" (Greek, *baptisma*) does not refute its connection to baptismal regeneration. It speaks of the *loutro* of regeneration, a Greek noun that first referred to a bath or place of bathing. The Methodist scholar Laurence Stookey says this passage uses language "which is undeniably baptismal",[29] and, according to Fergusson, "The washing is not figurative (such a

---

[27] John Calvin, *Institutes of the Christian Religion* 15.6. Calvin is referring in this passage to Galatians 3:27: "For as many of you as were baptized into Christ have put on Christ."

[28] Douglas Moo, *The Epistle to the Romans* (Grand Rapids, MI: Wm. B. Eerdmans, 1996), 359.

[29] Laurence Hull Stookey, *Baptism: Christ's Act in the Church* (Nashville, TN: Abingdon Press, 1982), 108.

usage would be unprecedented) for the work of the holy Spirit.....
The theological ideas of the passage are elsewhere associated with
baptism, which is indicated here by washing."[30]

In response to these verses, some critics say Paul did not believe in
baptismal regeneration, because he was thankful that he baptized only
the households of Crispus and Gaius (1 Cor 1:14). Ronald Nash says,
"If Paul believed and taught that baptism was absolutely essential to
the new birth, his failure to baptize more than two people in Corinth
is an odd thing to boast about."[31] Critics like Nash also cite Paul's
declaration that "Christ did not send me to baptize but to preach
the gospel" (1 Cor 1:17) as evidence that baptism is not connected
to the gospel.[32]

What these critics fail to appreciate, however, is that in the preceding verses Paul lamented about dissension in the Church caused by
neophytes inappropriately pledging their loyalty to the person who
baptized them (1 Cor 1:10–14). Paul was thankful that he did not
have many believers pledging themselves to him in this way, because
he only baptized a few people. According to a Protestant author who
rejects the doctrine of baptismal regeneration, "Paul is not denying
how very important baptism is; rather, he is denying that baptism
bonds the candidate to the person performing it."[33]

Likewise, Paul's report that "Christ did not send [him] to baptize
but to preach the gospel" (1 Cor 1:17) does not prove that the act of
baptism has no connection to the gospel Paul preached. As we will
see, Jesus preached the necessity of baptism (Jn 3:5) and oversaw
many baptisms without personally baptizing anyone (Jn 4:2). Paul's
decision personally to take part in only a few baptisms does not disconnect baptism from the gospel any more than a decision to only
personally disciple a few people would disconnect discipleship from
the gospel (Mt 28:19).

Finally, Rhodes incredibly claims that "when the desperate Philip-
pian jailer asked Paul what he must do to obtain salvation and have

[30] Fergusson, *Baptism in the Early Church*, 163.

[31] Nash, *When a Baby Dies*, 49.

[32] Nettles, "Baptism as a Symbol of Christ's Saving Work", 33. See also Geisler and Mac-
Kenzie, *Roman Catholics and Evangelicals*, 481–82.

[33] John D. Castelein, "Believers' Baptism as the Biblical Occasion of Salvation", in Armstrong, *Understanding Four Views on Baptism*, 55.

eternal life, Paul said nothing about baptism. He merely said, 'Believe in the Lord Jesus and you shall be saved' (Acts 16:31). Simple and to the point!"[34] Acts 16:31 says, "Believe in the Lord Jesus, and you will be saved, *you and your household* [emphasis added]." But the next two verses then describe Paul's sharing of "the word of the Lord" (v. 32) and how the jailer "was baptized at once, with all his family" (v. 33).

## The Evidence from Jesus

The Gospel of John describes how the Pharisee Nicodemus came to Jesus at night to confess his belief in Jesus' divine mission. The two then had this exchange:

> Jesus answered him, "Truly, truly, I say to you, unless one is born anew, he cannot see the kingdom of God." Nicodemus said to him, "How can a man be born when he is old? Can he enter a second time into his mother's womb and be born?" Jesus answered, "Truly, truly, I say to you, *unless one is born of water and the Spirit, he cannot enter the kingdom of God* [emphasis added]. That which is born of the flesh is flesh, and that which is born of the Spirit is spirit. Do not marvel that I said to you, 'You must be born anew.'" (3:3–7)

We will discuss the historical evidence for baptism shortly, but for now, our analysis of the verse "unless one is born of water and the Spirit, he cannot enter the kingdom of God" (v. 5) cannot neglect the fact that every Church Father who cited the verse before the Council of Nicaea agreed that it referred to baptismal regeneration. In the second century Justin Martyr spoke of converts who "are brought by us where there is water, and are regenerated in the same manner in which we were ourselves regenerated.... They then receive the washing with water. For Christ also said, Unless you be born again, you shall not enter into the kingdom of heaven."[35]

Protestants who deny baptismal regeneration usually rely on one of two alternative interpretations of the phrase "born of water and the Spirit".

[34] Rhodes, *Reasoning from the Scriptures*, 164.
[35] St. Justin Martyr, *First Apology* 61.

First, they claim that Jesus' reference to water is a reference to our biological birth and the breaking of the amniotic sac and the fluid that is released. This would mean a person must be born twice—once through a natural process (water) and again through a supernatural process (spirit)—in order to enter the kingdom of God.[36] But the Bible never refers to biological birth as the process of being "born of water".

According to D. A. Carson, "There are no ancient sources that picture natural birth as 'from water', and the few that use 'drops' to stand for semen are rare and late."[37] Instead, the Bible uses phrases like "born of the flesh" to describe natural birth. Jesus even uses this phrase to refer to biological birth in the very next verse. According to the Baptist theologian Stanley K. Fowler, "The grammar of the statement seems to link water and spirit closely as two aspects of the same birth (in that the two nouns are objects of one preposition)."[38] Jesus is not saying you must be born first from amniotic fluid and then be born again of the Holy Spirit. Jesus is instead saying a person must be "born of water and the Spirit", or be baptized.[39]

Another approach involves interpreting the water to be synonymous with the word of God or the Holy Spirit.[40] Even though Paul refers to the Church being washed with the word (Eph 5:26), the Bible never identifies "water" with Scripture. It's true that the Spirit is compared to water, but that is usually in a poetic context or with a modifying adjective. For example, in the Gospel of John, Jesus refers to the Spirit as "living water" rather than just "water" (7:37–39).

Those who object to the traditional interpretation of John 3:5 usually say that as a Jew, Nicodemus would have had no understanding of Christian baptism and no reason to associate Jesus' command

[36] Ben Witherington, *John's Wisdom: A Commentary on the Fourth Gospel* (Louisville, KY: Westminster John Knox Press, 1995), 97.

[37] D. A. Carson, *The Gospel according to John* (Grand Rapids, MI: Wm. B. Eerdmans, 1991), 191.

[38] Stanley K. Fowler, *Rethinking Baptism: Some Baptist Reflections* (Eugene, OR: Wipf and Stock, 2015), 27.

[39] Ferguson says, "The preposition 'of' governs both water and Spirit; the birth has a Water-spirit, forming a conceptual unity. There is only one birth, not two." Fergusson, *Baptism in the Early Church*, 143.

[40] Geisler and MacKenzie, *Roman Catholics and Evangelicals.*

with baptism.[41] Moreover, they say, Jesus' teaching that the Spirit's movements are as mysterious as the wind's (Jn 3:8) wouldn't be true if we attain God's spirit through the easily observable act of baptism.[42]

However, John 1:19–34 refers to the Baptist's testimony about Jesus' baptism. Jesus' conversation with Nicodemus also ends with a description of Jesus and his disciples going into Judea to baptize (Jn 3:22). Associating a baptismal meaning with John 3:5 naturally fits the context in which the passage is found. Plus, as a teacher of Israel (Jn 3:9–10), Nicodemus should have known that for those in the messianic age God had already promised, "I will sprinkle clean water upon you, and you shall be clean from all your uncleannesses" (Ezek 36:25). This sprinkling would give God's people "a new heart" that would allow them "to observe [God's] ordinances" (Ezek 36:26–27).

Concerning the second argument, it's true that baptism is a reality we can see, but so are public confessions of faith, which no Protestant would say are antithetical to the sovereign actions of the Holy Spirit. The desire to confess our faith in Christ and the desire to be baptized both come from the same source—the mysterious moving of the Holy Spirit. That some people confess faith in Jesus and are baptized is the product of the Holy Spirit's invisible action on their hearts. Thus Jesus concludes by saying, "So it is with every one who is born of the Spirit" (Jn 3:8).

Moreover, John the Baptist said that the Messiah's baptism would be superior to his baptism because it would be a purifying one that conveyed the Holy Spirit (Mt 3:11). The Jewish historian Josephus believed that John's baptism was an external sign of interior repentance that could not, by itself, take away sin.[43] Even if John's baptism did communicate the forgiveness of sins, it did not communicate the Holy Spirit in the same manner as Christian baptism does (Acts 2:38). Therefore, if Christian baptism does not spiritually regenerate

[41] Carson, Gospel according to John, 192.

[42] "If the new birth could be called down by baptism, which is not even mentioned in the context, what should we do with John 3:8, which states clearly that the Spirit is free?" Robert M. Zins, Romanism: The Relentless Roman Catholic Assault on the Gospel of Jesus Christ! (Huntsville, AL: White Horse Publications, 1995), 87.

[43] "The washing [with water] would be acceptable to him, if they made use of it, not in order to the putting away [or the remission] of some sins [only], but for the purification of the body; supposing still that the soul was thoroughly purified beforehand by righteousness." Josephus, Antiquities of the Jews 18.5.2.

the one being baptized, then it would hardly be different from John's baptism to which it is supposed to be superior.[44]

In fact, the weight of the biblical evidence in favor of baptismal regeneration is so strong that even scholars from traditions that reject this doctrine don't deny its biblical foundations. In his exhaustive study of baptism, the Baptist scholar G. R. Beasley-Murray writes:

> In the light of the foregoing exposition of the New Testament representations of baptism, the idea that baptism is a purely symbolic rite must be pronounced not alone unsatisfactory but out of harmony with the New Testament itself. Admittedly, such a judgment runs counter to the popular tradition of the Denomination to which the writer belongs.... The extent and nature of the grace which the New Testament writers declare to be present in baptism is astonishing for any who come to the study freshly with an open mind.[45]

## The Historical Evidence

The abundant biblical evidence for baptismal regeneration also explains the unanimous acceptance of this doctrine before the Protestant Reformation. According to J. N. D. Kelly, "From the beginning baptism was the universally accepted rite of admission to the Church.... As regards its significance, it was always held to convey the remission of sins."[46]

The first-century work *Shepherd of Hermas* describes how Christians "descended into the water and received remission of [their] former sins".[47] The *Epistle of Barnabas* says the prophets predicted of

---

[44] Jesus also taught in Mark 16:16 that "he who believes and is baptized will be saved; but he who does not believe will be condemned." Protestants who deny that this passage is canonical should at least recognize it as an early witness to Christian belief in baptismal regeneration. Those who do recognize this passage's canonicity but reject baptismal regeneration usually claim that because Jesus only ties condemnation to a lack of belief, it follows that it is only belief that saves a person and not baptism. But if that were true, then why did Jesus mention baptism at all? Imagine if Jesus had said, "He who believes and repents will be saved; but he who does not believe will be condemned." Unlike those who do not believe, people who truly believe in Christ will accompany their belief with appropriate actions like repentance and baptism.

[45] G. R. Beasley-Murray, *Baptism in the New Testament* (Grand Rapids, MI: Wm. B. Eerdmans, 1973), 263.

[46] J. N. D. Kelly, *Early Christian Doctrines* (New York: HarperCollins, 1978), 193–94.

[47] *The Shepherd* 2.4.3.

Israel "that they should not receive that baptism which leads to the remission of sins".[48] The *Didache* even commands, "Let no one eat or drink of your Thanksgiving (Eucharist), but they who have been baptized into the name of the Lord."[49] Nothing, not even faith in Christ, justified an unbaptized person's reception of the Eucharist.

Irenaeus quoted John 3:5 saying that just as Naaman was cleansed of leprosy through water, Christians are lepers in sin who are cleansed with sacred water that makes them "spiritually regenerated as new-born babes".[50] He also says that the power to baptize given to the apostles in Matthew 28:19 was "the power of regeneration into God".[51] Citations from the early Church Fathers, including Origen, Tertullian, Cyril, Gregory of Nyssa, Chrysostom, Athanasius, and Augustine, can also be produced in favor of baptismal regeneration.[52] William Webster admits that "the doctrine of baptism is one of the few teachings within Roman Catholicism for which it can be said that there is a universal consent of the Fathers."[53]

## Infant Baptism

In Romans 9:11 Paul refers to Jacob and Esau when "they were not yet born and had done nothing either good or bad". Scripture teaches that very young children are incapable of committing personal sins, but it does not teach that they are free from all association with sin. That's because original sin is the deprivation of original holiness and justice that is communicated to every descendant of Adam and Eve (*CCC* 404, 417) but is restored through baptism. According to the *Catechism*,

> Born with a fallen human nature and tainted by original sin, children also have need of the new birth in Baptism to be freed from the

---

[48] *Epistle of Barnabas* 11.

[49] *Didache* 9.

[50] St. Irenaeus, *Fragment* 34.

[51] St. Irenaeus, *Against Heresies* 3.17.1.

[52] See, for example, Tertullian, *On Baptism* 1; St. Athanasius, *Letter 49 to Dracontius* 4.558; and St. Gregory of Nyssa, *On the Baptism of Christ* 5.519. For a more comprehensive series of citations, see Stephen K. Ray, *Crossing the Tiber: Evangelical Protestants Discover the Historic Church* (San Francisco: Ignatius Press, 1997), 131–74.

[53] William Webster, *The Church of Rome at the Bar of History* (Carlisle, PA: Banner of Truth, 1995), 95.

power of darkness and brought into the realm of the freedom of the children of God, to which all men are called. The sheer gratuitousness of the grace of salvation is particularly manifest in infant baptism. The Church and the parents would deny a child the priceless grace of becoming a child of God were they not to confer Baptism shortly after birth. (*CCC* 1250)

Some Protestants who reject baptismal regeneration still baptize infants because they believe children of any age who have believing parents should be a part of the New Covenant, and baptism is the means of entering the New Covenant even if it doesn't take away sin.[54] For example, even though most contemporary Reformed Baptists reject infant baptism, the historic Westminster Confession of Faith affirmed it, saying, "Not only those that do actually profess faith in and obedience unto Christ, but also the infants of one, or both, believing parents, are to be baptized" (28.4).

Protestants who deny infant baptism usually claim that baptism is an ordinance that is given to those who have been spiritually regenerated, which they say cannot happen (or cannot be known to have happened) until a person makes an act of faith. But this argument for "believer's baptism" fails in light of the evidence we've seen for the role baptism plays in washing away sin and uniting us to Christ.

If all people stand in need of spiritual regeneration, and baptism were capable of spiritually regenerating anyone, it logically follows that infants ought to be baptized. When the disciples attempted to keep infants from being brought to Jesus, he responded by saying, "Let the children come to me, and do not hinder them; for to such belongs the kingdom of God" (Lk 18:16). Some object that an act of willing, which infants cannot perform, is necessary for baptism to be spiritually regenerative. But the Bible never says baptism requires an act of willing, and the Gospels record several occasions where Jesus healed someone because others willed for the person to be healed.

To the centurion who sought healing for his paralyzed servant, Jesus said, "Let it be done for you as you have believed" (Mt 8:13). Mark 2:5 tells us that, concerning the men who lowered the paralytic

---

[54] For a defense of this view, see Gregg Strawbridge, *The Case for Covenantal Infant Baptism* (Phillipsburg, NJ: P&R Publishing, 2003).

through a roof where Jesus was speaking, "when Jesus saw *their faith* [emphasis added], he said to the paralytic, 'Child, your sins are forgiven.'" The faith of those who baptize an infant is sufficient for the child to receive sanctifying grace, but the child's own faith must still be cultivated over time so that this grace can be more efficacious in his life (*CCC* 1231).

This parallels the rite of circumcision in the Old Testament that made a child part of the Old Covenant but did not obviate the need for further instruction in the faith. In fact, Colossians 2:11–12 connects circumcision with baptism. Paul says, "You were circumcised with a circumcision made without hands, by putting off the body of flesh in the circumcision of Christ; and you were buried with him in baptism, in which you were also raised with him through faith in the working of God, who raised him from the dead." In the Greek text of the phrase "the circumcision of Christ; and you were buried with him in baptism", the Greek word rendered "and", or *kai*, is not present. The passage literally reads, "You were circumcised with ... the circumcision of Christ; having been buried with him in baptism."

Making baptism the replacement of circumcision corresponds to the Bible's teaching that the New Covenant is superior to and more inclusive than the Old Covenant (Gal 3:28; Heb 8:6). If children before the age of reason could not be baptized (and thus could not receive the sign of the New Covenant), then this would make the New Covenant an *inferior* replacement for the Old Covenant, to which they previously belonged. As Peter said of baptism and its ability to forgive sin, "the promise is to you and to your children and to all that are far off, every one whom the Lord our God calls to him" (Acts 2:39). Martin Luther simply said, "We now have baptism instead of circumcision."[55]

Not only does Jesus describe the kingdom of God as belonging to children; the New Testament also contains multiple occasions where entire households are baptized (Acts 16:31–34; 1 Cor 1:16). While none of them explicitly describe infants being baptized, it is likely that they were. These passages show that there was a principle of baptizing whole households in the early Church, and some

---

[55] Martin Luther, *The Babylonian Captivity of the Church 1520: The Annotated Luther Study Edition*, ed. Paul W. Robinson (Minneapolis: Fortress Press, 2016), 100.

households undoubtedly contained children below the age of reason. Thus, contrary to what some critics argue, the absence of an explicit example of infant baptism from Scripture does not prove that the practice is unbiblical.[56]

For infant baptism to be unbiblical, particularly in light of the parallel with circumcision, we would need passages stating or clearly implying that children are *not* to be baptized, and these we do not have. In the absence of such prohibitions, we should apply Paul's principle of liberty among believers in matters that are not sinful or contrary to the gospel (Rom 14:5).

Neither is there any evidence that the early Church prohibited this practice. R. C. Sproul says, "The fact that the practice of infant baptism seems to have spread to the whole Christian community within a hundred years with no known protest is a further indication that the acceptability of giving infant children the covenant sign was simply assumed by the early Church."[57]

Robert Zins claims that the earliest author to mention infant baptism was Tertullian and he opposed it.[58] But in the early third century, when Tertullian was writing, Hippolytus advised his readers: "And they shall baptize the little children first. And if they can answer for themselves, let them answer. But if they cannot, let their parents answer or someone from their family."[59] Origen said, "The Church has received the tradition from the apostles to give baptism even to little children. For they to whom the secrets of the divine mysteries were committed were aware that in everyone was [original] sin's innate defilement, which needed to be washed away through water and the Spirit."[60]

---

[56] There is also no record in the New Testament of anyone being married in a church in the presence of a minister or the baptism of children whose parents are believers, but the absence of these descriptions does not prove any of these practices are unbiblical, including infant baptism.

[57] R. C. Sproul, *What Is Baptism?* (Grand Rapids, MI: Reformation Trust Publishing, 2011), 68.

[58] Zins, *Romanism*, 94.

[59] Hippolytus, *The Apostolic Tradition* 21.4. Translation found in Gregory Dix and Henry Chadwick, *The Treatise on the Apostolic Tradition of St Hippolytus of Rome, Bishop and Martyr* (New York: Routledge, 2006; original publishing, 1937), 33.

[60] Origen, *Commentary on Romans* 5.9. This translation can be found in Thomas Scheck, *Origen: Commentary on the Epistle to the Romans Books 1–5* (Washington, DC: Catholic University of America Press, 2001), 367.

Tertullian objected to infant baptism, but he did not deny that infants could be validly baptized. Instead, he argued it was *preferable* to delay their baptism so that its ability to remit sins completely could be used to full effect.[61] This is also evident in his advice that unmarried people wait until marriage to be baptized because of the temptation to sin before that point.[62] Philip Schaff says, "Among the fathers, Tertullian himself not excepted—for he combats only its expediency—there is not a single voice against the lawfulness and the apostolic origin of infant baptism."[63] Tertullian's disciple Cyprian firmly supported infant baptism, a fact Augustine recounts in this way:

> [Cyprian] was not inventing any new doctrine, but preserving the firmly established faith of the Church; and he, along with some of his colleagues in the episcopal office, held that a child may be properly baptized immediately after its birth.[64]

## Baptism, Faith, and Works

Some who oppose baptismal regeneration and infant baptism argue that because human works do not save us, and baptism is a work, it follows that baptism does not save us. They might even cite Titus 3:5 in their favor because it says, "[God] saved us, not because of deeds done by us in righteousness [which they say includes baptism], but in virtue of his own mercy, by the washing of regeneration and renewal in the Holy Spirit."

It is true that our initial salvation, or when we first become justified in God's eyes, is received by grace through faith (Eph 2:8–9).

---

[61] Zin quotes Tertullian as saying, "Let them become Christians when they have become able to know Christ," but he leaves out a crucial justification Tertullian makes: "Why does the innocent period of life hasten to the remission of sins?" (*On Baptism* 18). Later theologians and Fathers of the Church who saw the need to baptize children as soon as possible rejected Tertullian's belief in the need to delay baptism.

[62] Tertullian writes, "For no less cause must the unwedded also be deferred—in whom the ground of temptation is prepared, alike in such as never were wedded by means of their maturity, and in the widowed by means of their freedom—until they either marry, or else be more fully strengthened for continence. If any understand the weighty import of baptism, they will fear its reception more than its delay: sound faith is secure of salvation" (*On Baptism* 18).

[63] Philip Schaff, *History of the Christian Church* (New York: Charles Scribner's Sons, 1891), 259.

[64] St. Cyprian, *Letter* 166.8.23.

The critic's error, however, can be demonstrated by reversing his own argument. Since baptism saves us (1 Pet 3:21), and no work brings about our initial salvation in Christ, it follows therefore that baptism is *not* a work or mere righteous deed. Martin Luther said as much in his own defense of baptism:

> Yes, our works, indeed, avail nothing for salvation; Baptism, however, is not our work, but God's (for, as was stated, you must put Christ-baptism far away from a bath-keeper's baptism). God's works, however, are saving and necessary for salvation, and do not exclude, but demand, faith; for without faith they could not be apprehended.[65]

The fact that the vast majority of Christians baptize babies who are incapable of doing anything to merit their own salvation, including having faith in Christ, demonstrates the Church's conviction that we are saved by God's grace. Whether it is an adult who seeks baptism, or parents who seek baptism for their child, these people do not earn salvation through a work. They instead have faith in God's promise that baptism takes away sin and unites them to Christ so they can live out their faith.

In reading the work of Protestant apologists who deny baptismal regeneration, one comes across a familiar pattern. The author is convinced that we are saved by "faith alone", and faith only includes a personal trust in Christ and not any corresponding external actions, including baptism. Ronald Nash says, "There is only one necessary condition for salvation, and that is faith in Jesus Christ.... We can approach the so-called problem texts with confidence that they cannot possibly teach baptismal regeneration."[66]

In order properly to address this and other issues related to our salvation, we must now examine the second pillar of the Protestant Reformation: *sola fide*, or justification by faith alone.

---

[65] Luther, *Large Catechism*, "Holy Baptism".
[66] Nash, *When a Baby Dies*, 48.

# Justification, Part I

Martin Luther once said, "Our righteousness is dung in the sight of God. Now if God chooses to adorn dung, he can do so. It does not hurt the sun, because it sends its rays into the sewer."[1] How does God take putrid dung like us and make it capable of dwelling in the "rays" of his love for all eternity?

Chris Castaldo says that one time when Luther made this comparison, snow began to fall, and the dung disappeared from sight. Luther then allegedly said, "That is how God sees us in his Son, Jesus Christ. While we remain full of sin, in Christ we are clothed with perfect righteousness and therefore we are acceptable in God's sight."[2] While this story about Luther may be apocryphal, its lesson has a historical basis.

## Protestant Views of Justification

John Calvin said, "Every one who would obtain the righteousness of Christ must renounce his own."[3] The Reformers taught that God covers sins with Christ's righteousness, and this justification is received *sola fide*, or "by faith alone", a rallying cry that became the material principle of the Protestant Reformation.

Before we continue, however, I should note that it is not accurate to speak of *the* Protestant view of justification. Indeed, one major publisher has released a book called *Justification: Five Views*, four of which

---

[1] *Luther's Works*, 34:184.

[2] Christopher A. Castaldo, *Holy Ground: Walking with Jesus as a Former Catholic* (Grand Rapids, MI: Zondervan, 2009), 117.

[3] John Calvin, *Institutes of the Christian Religion* 3.11.3.

are from Protestants.[4] Likewise, Catholic theologians have articulated the Church's teaching on justification in different ways, but there is much more uniformity among their views because the Magisterium has defined the essential elements of this doctrine.[5] However, there are several common elements among Protestant views of justification that can be compared to Catholic teaching on this subject.

One of these elements is the nature of the righteousness by which we are justified. Protestants often describe the act of justification as taking place in a legal or forensic context where God declares the sinner to be righteous or "not guilty" of sin. Protestants typically believe this declaration does not intrinsically change the sinner himself (just as the rays of the sun do not change the dung they shine upon), but they change the sinner's relationship with God. This is made possible through an *imputation* of Christ's righteousness that covers sin rather than an *infusion* of Christ's righteousness that blots out or removes it. Protestants agree that our sanctification, or personal holiness, increases in this life through the working of the Holy Spirit, but most believe that our justification, or righteousness before God, does not increase. According to John MacArthur, "Justification is a one-time *event*; sanctification is an ongoing *process*. Justification frees us from the *guilt* of sin, sanctification from the *pollution* of sin [emphasis in original]."[6]

Another common element is the *means* by which we receive Christ's righteousness. Martin Luther described the principle of justification "by faith alone" this way:

> All have sinned and are justified without merit [freely, and without their own works or merits] by His grace, through the redemption that is in Christ Jesus, in His blood, Rom. 3:23f. Now, since it is necessary to believe this, and it cannot be otherwise acquired or apprehended by any work, law, or merit, it is clear and certain that this faith alone justifies us.[7]

---

[4] James K. Beilby and Paul Rhodes Eddy, eds., *Justification: Five Views*, with contributions by Michael F. Bird et al. (Downers Grove, IL: InterVarsity Press, 2011).

[5] See, for example, the canons of the sixth session of the Council of Trent on justification.

[6] John F. MacArthur, *The Gospel according to the Apostles* (Nashville, TN: Thomas Nelson, 2005), 90.

[7] Martin Luther, *Smalcald Articles* 2.1.3–4; available online at http://bookofconcord.org /smalcald.php.

## Catholic Views of Justification

When people compare Protestant and Catholic views on justification, some inaccurately say, "Protestants believe in justification by 'faith alone', but Catholics believe in justification by 'faith and works'." However, magisterial documents, including the canons of the Council of Trent and the *Catechism of the Catholic Church*, do not use the phrase "justified by faith and works".[8] Instead, Catholics distinguish between the initial moment of our justification and the process of justification that continues throughout our lives. The best way to illustrate this distinction would not be Luther's dunghill but another analogical example.

Imagine a group of malnourished, filthy street children who are one day approached by a wealthy man and given the opportunity to be adopted into his family. Some of the children reject his offer because they don't want to abandon the decrepit conditions to which they've grown accustomed. Others, however, accept his offer and are then adopted into the man's family. The father takes these children home and washes them clean from the filth of their former way of life. He then instructs them in how to live to be good people.

The children who reject the wealthy man's offer would be like people who reject God's gift of God's forgiveness and are never justified. In contrast, the children who accept the man's offer would be like believers who hear God's offer of salvation, accept it, and are then baptized and catechized so they can live out their new life in Christ. The *Catechism* describes this initial justification as follows: "Moved by grace, man turns toward God and away from sin, thus accepting forgiveness and righteousness from on high. 'Justification is not only the remission of sins, but also the sanctification and renewal of the interior man' (Council of Trent [1547]: DS 1528)" (*CCC* 1989).

Notice in our analogy that the children do nothing to earn or merit the man's initial offer of adoption. They only choose to accept or reject it. The fact that they submit to being washed when he brings them home doesn't mean they "earned" the right to live with him. Instead, they obeyed the man in accordance with the gift of adoption

---

[8] Jimmy Akin, *A Daily Defense* (San Diego: Catholic Answers Press, 2016), 222.

he gave them. Likewise, the *Catechism* teaches that "*no one can merit the initial grace* [emphasis in original] of forgiveness and justification, at the beginning of conversion" (*CCC* 2010). The Council of Trent likewise taught that through baptism believers "are made innocent, immaculate, pure, harmless, and beloved of God, heirs indeed of God, but joint heirs with Christ; so that there is nothing whatever to [hinder] their entrance into heaven."[9]

When believers submit to baptism (either for themselves or their children), they do not merit the graces they receive through that sacrament. However, the process of justification also has an ongoing element that can be increased through our own actions. Jimmy Akin compares this element of our justification to the qualities of light.[10]

One quality of the light would be purity, or the whiteness of a lamp's light. At baptism we are made free from sin and capable of entering into heaven, or we receive pure righteousness from God. But another quality of a lamp's light is its intensity. A lamp might radiate pure, white light either dimly or brightly. Likewise, a justified person might do good works that increase the radiance of the righteousness he received from God. A believer who does not do good works, then, would fail to heed Jesus' command to "let your light so shine before men, that they may see your good works and give glory to your Father who is in heaven" (Mt 5:16).

We must remember that this increase of righteousness would not be something the believer *earned* through any of the good works he performed. Just as the adoptive father of the street children is not obligated to give his children rewards when they obey him, God is not obligated to reward our obedience to him. But, as God's adopted children, our obedience genuinely pleases him, and so he freely rewards us with grace that increases our justification and helps us attain eternal life. Therefore, we can say, as the Council of Trent does, that good works "cause" an increase in justification, not in the sense of *earning* justification but in the sense of *meriting* it.

Consider the fourth-century Church Father Hilary of Poitiers, who said, "Payment is not the same thing as a gift because it is owed for work rendered, whereas God has freely granted his grace to everyone

---

[9] Council of Trent, fifth session, Decree on Original Sin.
[10] Akin, *Daily Defense*, 257.

by the justification of faith."[11] This corresponds to the Catholic view of justification since the *Catechism* says, "There is no strict right to any merit on the part of man" (*CCC* 2007). If there were such a strict right to God's grace, then God would, in a sense, be morally obligated to provide grace just as employers are morally obligated to provide employees monetary compensation.

God's giving of grace in response to good works is not a wage that is earned. It is instead a reward that is merited in the same way a father might reward his child's good conduct at school without being *obligated* to reward him. In the third century Saint Cyprian said, "We must obey his precepts and warnings, that our merits may receive their reward."[12] The Reformed pastor Nick Needham makes the following observation:

> Hilary of Poitiers, while recognizing merits in the sense of virtues that obtain divine reward, also makes it clear that the reward is ultimately gracious in nature: "For the very works of righteousness would not suffice to merit perfect blessedness, unless in our righteous will the mercy of God overlooked the defects of human changes and impulses.... Through the mercy of God, more will follow than is merited."[13]

While Fathers like Hilary strongly taught that salvation was not earned and that it was first received by grace through faith, they also emphasized the importance that works play in our salvation. Saint Augustine said, "We feel that we should advise the faithful that they would endanger the salvation of their souls if they acted on the false assurance that faith alone is sufficient for salvation or that they need not perform good works in order to be saved."[14]

Martin Luther testifies to the fact that Augustine did not teach justification by faith alone when he says, "At first I devoured, not

[11] St. Hilary of Poitiers, *Commentary on Matthew* 20.7. Cited in *St. Hilary of Poitiers Commentary on Matthew*, trans. D. H. Williams (Washington, DC: Catholic University of America Press, 2012), 212.

[12] St. Cyprian, *Treatise* 1.15.

[13] Nick Needham, "Justification in the Early Church Fathers", in *Justification in Perspective: Historical Developments and Contemporary Challenges*, ed. Bruce L. McCormack (Grand Rapids, MI: Baker Academic, 2006), 53.

[14] St. Augustine, *On Faith and Works* 14.21. Cited in St. Augustine, *On Faith and Works*, trans. Gregory Lombardo (Paulist Press, 1988), 28.

merely read, Augustine. But when the door was opened for me in Paul, so that I understood what justification by faith is, it was all over with Augustine."[15] Similarly the Dutch Reformed theologian Louis Berkhof says, "The writings of the early Church fathers contain very little respecting the doctrine of sanctification. A strain of moralism is quite apparent in that man was taught to depend for salvation on faith and good works."[16]

We must stress, however, that salvation comes not by a mere combination of faith and works that earns one's place before God. Rather, it comes from receiving God's offer of salvation through faith and then obeying God's commandments as his adopted children, which results in good works. The *Catechism* says that "filial adoption, in making us partakers by grace in the divine nature, can bestow *true merit* [emphasis in original] on us as a result of God's gratuitous justice" (*CCC* 2009).[17] This corresponds to the biblical doctrine of rewards, which is evident in Paul's promise that God "will render to every man according to his works: to those who by patience in well-doing seek for glory and honor and immortality, he will give eternal life" (Rom 2:6–7).

Of course, like all analogies, the one with the street children isn't perfect, because the children, to some degree, perform good works on their own, without an infusion of grace from their adoptive father (though, one could argue their new upbringing has enabled them to perform works they otherwise would not have been able to perform while living on the street). But the *Catechism* teaches that "*the charity of Christ is the source in us of all our merits* [emphasis in original] before God.... The saints have always had a lively awareness that their merits were pure grace" (*CCC* 2011).

The analogy can also be continued in the fact that these children will probably disobey their new father. Most of the time this will be in minor matters that hurt but do not destroy their relationship with him (just as venial sins blemish but do not kill God's grace in our souls). Unfortunately, in some cases the children may rebel against

---

[15] *Luther's Works*, 54:49–50.

[16] Louis Berkhof, *Systematic Theology* (Grand Rapids, MI: Wm. B. Eerdmans, 1996), 529.

[17] Moved by the Holy Spirit and by charity, *we can then merit* for ourselves and for others the graces needed for our sanctification, for the increase of grace and charity, and for the attainment of eternal life.

their father so severely that they end up leaving his home and returning to their squalid, former way of life (just as believers who commit mortal sins lose the grace of justification). Fortunately, God is merciful and, as the Parable of the Prodigal Son shows (Lk 15:11–32), will welcome his children back from spiritual death if they return to him with contrite hearts.

## Common Ground?

To summarize where we are at so far, Protestants usually believe justification involves a single moment where we are clothed in the righteousness of Christ. This imputed righteousness covers our sins but does not change our souls. Catholics, on the other hand, believe justification is *both* an event *and* a process that begins in one unmerited moment and continues throughout our lives as Christ's righteousness is infused into our souls and helps us become holy just as God is holy.

Catholics believe in a *restorative* view of justification rather than a purely *forensic* or *legal* view. God certainly declares us to be righteous, but just as God's declaration "Let there be light" (Gen 1:3) created actual light, God's declaration of our justification creates actual righteousness in those he justifies. The *Catechism* says, "With justification, faith, hope, and charity are poured into our hearts, and obedience to the divine will is granted us" (*CCC* 1991).

But do we receive this justification by faith alone? Because the scope of the doctrine of justification is too wide to address in the space we have, our discussion of the Protestant/Catholic debate over it will primarily focus on the key element of *sola fide*, or whether justification is only received through faith alone.

During one of his Wednesday audiences, Pope Benedict XVI said, "Luther's phrase: '*faith alone*' is true, if it is not opposed to faith in charity, in love."[18] We will explore in more detail in the next chapter what Pope Benedict meant by this statement, but for now our analysis will show that justification is not received through the classical Protestant understanding of "by faith alone". Instead, when the believer cooperates with God's grace and lives out his faith in Christ, his free

[18] Pope Benedict XVI, General Audience (November 19, 2008), https://w2.vatican.va /content/benedict-xvi/en/audiences/2008/documents/hf_ben-xvi_aud_20081119.html.

acts of charity and obedience contribute to his ongoing justification. They obey Saint Paul's teaching that the hope of our justification is found in "faith working through love" (Gal 5:6).

## The Teachings of Jesus

At a 2010 conference John Piper gave a lecture entitled "Did Jesus Preach Paul's Gospel?"[19] Scot McKnight says of Piper's approach, "The order—asking if Jesus fits Paul!—might rankle many Bible readers and historians, but such questions about the Bible are not inappropriate."[20] The Evangelical author Alan Stanley, however, asks an important question: "Why is it that Jesus must be reconciled to Paul as if Paul were the benchmark? If anyone should be the benchmark, should it not be Jesus himself?"[21]

So what did Jesus teach about justification?

In Matthew 12:36–37 Jesus said, "On the day of judgment men will render account for every careless word they utter; for by your words you will be justified, and by your words you will be condemned." Alan Stanley notes that this parallels the instruction in James 2:12 to "speak and so act as those who are to be judged under the law of liberty." He writes, "Clearly Jesus knows of a justification that will take place in the 'day of judgment' and it is likely James is speaking of the same judgment, that is, all people will be judged on the basis of their works vis-à-vis their eternal destiny."[22]

Protestants usually claim that Jesus means our words are indicative of the content of our hearts, and so it is our hearts (and the faith they contain) that will be judged rather than our words or actions themselves. But in Revelation 2:23 Jesus says, "I am he who searches mind and heart, and I will give to each of you as your works deserve."[23]

---

[19] John Piper, "Did Jesus Preach Paul's Gospel?" (Ligonier Ministries' 2010 Pastors Conference, St. Andrew's Chapel, Sanford, FL), http://t4g.org/media/2010/06/did-jesus-preach -pauls-gospel-session-vi-2/.

[20] Scot McKnight, "Jesus vs. Paul", *Christianity Today*, December 3, 2010, http://www .christianitytoday.com/ct/2010/december/9.25.html.

[21] Alan P. Stanley, *Did Jesus Teach Salvation by Works? The Role of Works in Salvation in the Synoptic Gospels* (Eugene, OR: Wipf and Stock, 2006), 3.

[22] Ibid., 311.

[23] In his final teaching recorded in the Bible, Jesus likewise says, "I am coming soon, bringing my recompense, to repay every one for what he has done" (Rev 22:12).

Jesus does not render a judgment based solely on what our *hearts* deserve, but also on what our *works* deserve.

Does this contradict Jesus' parable about the Pharisee who boasted of his works and the lowly tax collector who simply prayed, "God, be merciful to me a sinner" (Lk 18:13)? Jesus said the tax collector was justified "rather than" the Pharisee (Lk 18:14), a statement Calvin seized upon as evidence that faith rather than works justifies us.[24] But this parable doesn't teach the sufficiency of faith for justification; it teaches the necessity of repentance. According to the Calvinist theologian Richard Gaffin Jr.,

> There is nothing wrong with what the Pharisee prays. It is a prayer of thanksgiving to God for the thoroughly commendable deeds enumerated.... What is wrong and deeply flawed is what is missing (and present in the tax collector's prayer): a heartfelt confession of his own sinfulness and guilt, and acknowledgement that ultimately, despite the undeniable difference in their behavior, he is "even like this tax collector."[25]

When Jesus explains this parable, he does not say the tax collector was justified rather than the Pharisee because the former did not rely on works for his justification. Instead, the Pharisee was not justified because he was guilty of the sin of pride, whereas the tax collector was humble and recognized his need to repent. Jesus even explains *why* the tax collector rather than the Pharisee was justified, telling us, "For every one who exalts himself will be humbled, but he who humbles himself will be exalted" (Lk 18:14)—indicating it is the tax collector's humble, repentant attitude that is the distinguishing factor. In fact, in the next chapter an actual tax collector, Zacchaeus, repents of his wrongdoings and seeks forgiveness from Jesus. It is only after Zacchaeus declares he will pay back everyone

---

[24] "He who acknowledges that he is guilty and convicted, and then proceeds to implore pardon, disavows all confidence in works; and Christ's object was to show that God will not be gracious to any but those who betake themselves with trembling to his mercy alone." John Calvin, *Commentary on a Harmony of the Evangelists, Matthew, Mark, and Luke*, trans. Rev. William Pringle, vol. 2, Christian Classics Ethereal Library, commentary for Luke 18:13, accessed July 14, 2017, https://www.ccel.org/ccel/calvin/calcom32.ii.xxxvii.html.

[25] Richard Gaffin Jr., "Justification in Luke-Acts", in *Right with God: Justification in the Bible and the World*, ed. D. A. Carson (Eugene, OR: Wipf and Stock, 2002), 124.

he defrauded that Jesus tells him, "Today salvation has come to this house" (Lk 19:9).

Consider also Jesus' answer to the following question: "What good deed must I do, to have eternal life?" (Mt 19:16). Rather than merely say, "Have faith in God", or "Believe in me", Jesus tells the young man, "If you would enter life, keep the commandments" (Mt 19:17). This does not mean Jesus denied that faith plays a part in our justification. In John 6:28 the crowd asks Jesus, "What must we do, to be doing the works of God?" to which Jesus replied, "This is the work of God, that you believe in him whom he has sent" (Jn 6:29). But it would be a mistake to conclude, as John MacArthur does, that verses like these make it "easy to demonstrate from Jesus' evangelistic ministry that He taught sola fide".[26] Jesus exhortation to "believe in him" doesn't mean we must *only* believe in him, just as Jesus' exhortation to "keep the commandments" doesn't mean we must *only* keep the Ten Commandments.

MacArthur also claims that because Jesus said to several people in the Gospels, "Your faith has made you well" (Mk 5:34; 10:52; cf. Lk 7:50), it follows that "all those healings were object lessons on the doctrine of justification by faith alone."[27] But just because a passage speaks about faith, it does not follow that it is talking about justification by faith *alone*, or even *justification*. We cannot conclude from these texts that individuals who had faith that Jesus the prophet could heal them were justified. In fact, Jesus' rebuke of the nine lepers who failed to return and thank God as the Samaritan did provides further evidence that our actions also contribute to our growth in righteousness. Just because faith in Jesus saved someone from a temporal harm, this does not mean they possessed faith that saved them from eternal harms.

Finally, MacArthur cites John 5:24 because Jesus said, "He who hears my word and believes him who sent me, has eternal life; he does not come into judgment, but has passed from death to life." But just four and five verses later Jesus says that at the final judgment, "All who are in the tombs will hear his voice and come forth, those who have done good, to the resurrection of life, and those who have

[26] John MacArthur, "Jesus' Perspective on Sola Fide", Grace to You, last modified July 8, 2017, https://www.gty.org/library/articles/A192/jesus-perspective-on-sola-fide.
[27] Ibid.

done evil, to the resurrection of judgment." Matthew's description of Jesus at the final judgment casting out the goats who failed to feed, clothe, visit, and care for "the least of these my brethren" (Mt 25:40), and receiving the sheep who did do these things also shows that acts of charity and obedience do play a role in our justification (Mt 25:31–46).

Jesus did not teach that salvation came from man obeying God's law apart from God's grace. But neither did Jesus teach that salvation consists *only* of being justified by faith in him. In *Did Jesus Teach Salvation by Works?* Alan Stanley provides the following answer to his book's titular question:

> [If] we mean final or eschatological salvation and post-conversion works originating from God himself, then, yes, Jesus did teach salvation by works—in the same way that James taught justification by works [emphasis in the original].[28]

## The Teaching of James

Ever since the Reformation, the Letter of James has been considered one of the most controversial witnesses to the Bible's teaching on justification. Luther put it this way:

> That epistle of James gives us much trouble, for the papists embrace it alone and leave out all the rest. Up to this point I have been accustomed just to deal with and interpret it according to the sense of the rest of Scriptures.... If they will not admit my interpretations, then I shall make rubble also of it. I almost feel like throwing Jimmy into the stove, as the priest in Kalenberg did.[29]

Luther was referring to an episode in the German village of Kalenberg, where a priest burned wooden statues of the apostles in order to provide warmth for a visiting duchess. Luther's temptation to burn the actual Letter of James reveals a conflicted relationship he had with this piece of Scripture. His original 1522 preface for the

---

[28] Stanley, *Did Jesus Teach Salvation by Works?*, 333.
[29] *Luther's Works*, 3:317.

letter derided it as an "epistle of straw", though he later admitted that James "promulgates the laws of God".[30] The source of Luther's conflict was James' repeated affirmations that works are necessary for a person's justification.

Far from teaching the idea that we are saved apart from works, James 2:17 says, "Faith by itself, if it has no works, is dead." Verse 21 refers to how Abraham and Rahab were justified by their works. In fact, the only passage in the New Testament that contains the phrase "faith alone" (Greek, *pisteos monon*) is James 2:24: "You see that a man is justified by works and not by faith alone." In response to these passages Protestant apologists usually adopt two strategies, both of which involve redefining key words in the letter.

First, they say James' reference to "faith" is to an empty, dead, or inauthentic faith. It is not the same kind of faith that Paul says is capable of justifying us apart from works of the law (Rom 4:15). Second, Protestants often say James is talking about what justifies or makes us righteous before men or other people—not what justifies us before God. If justification were a one-time event before God, then Abraham could not be justified when he obeyed the command to offer up Isaac (Jas 2:21; Gen 22:1–14), because he had already been justified when he first believed in God (Rom 4; Gen 15:6). Instead, Abraham's obedience to God must have merited the praise of men, rather than the righteousness of God.

But is this what James means by the terms "faith" and "justify"?

The primary section we are concerned with is James 2:14–26, but we should not ignore the other parts of this letter. Prior to this passage James is addressing fellow Christians and speaks of their faith being tested by trials, which will make them "perfect and complete" (1:4). This faith involves a complete trust in God, but James does not say it is the faithful man who will receive "the crown of life" (1:12). Instead, it is the man who has endured life's tests and trials and is a doer of the word and not a mere hearer who will receive such a reward. James also says true religion is not merely a confession of faith but is evident in those who "visit orphans and widows in their affliction, and . . . keep oneself unstained from the world" (1:27).

---

[30] Ibid., 35:362.

James then makes his only reference to faith in Christ where he warns those who "hold the faith of our Lord Jesus Christ" that they should "show no partiality" especially toward the wealthy (2:1). James says that we "fulfil the royal law" and "do well" when we love our neighbors as ourselves (2:8). Let's begin with verse 14, which says, "What does it profit, my brethren, if a man says he has faith but has not works? Can his faith save him?"

Some defenders of *sola fide* claim that James is referring to someone who "says" or "claims" he has faith and not to someone who actually has faith. This person has an empty or dead faith that is incapable of saving him. These individuals bolster this interpretation by translating the word "faith" (*he pistis*) in the second clause as "that faith" or "such faith". In these translations James asks, "Can this kind of faith [i.e., a dead faith] save a person?" The paraphrase of this passage in the extremely loose Bible translation known as *The Message* summarizes what most Protestants think James is saying: "Does merely talking about faith indicate that a person really has it?"

In regard to James 2:14, John MacArthur says, " 'If someone says' is the phrase that governs the interpretation of the entire passage."[31] But if that's true, then the conclusion of *sola fide* derived from this passage becomes extremely tenuous. That's because while *he pistis* can be translated as "that faith", it literally means "the faith" or "faith", as can be seen in the KJV's translation, "can faith save him?" James is not concerned with whether someone has the right kind of faith. He always affirms the concept of faith as being good even if it is incomplete without the separate concept of works. Scot McKnight says, "No matter how hard we Protestants might try to work this out, the bottom line for James is having works."[32]

According to White, "The point is the same all the way through: deedless faith is not saving faith."[33] But James is not teaching about the importance of having "saving faith" over what Protestants might call dead, deedless, or inauthentic faith. The phrase "saving faith" is never even found in the Letter of James (or anywhere in the Bible). That James is not talking about a false kind of faith becomes obvious

[31] John MacArthur, *James* (Nashville, TN: Thomas Nelson, 2007), 124.
[32] Scot McKnight, *The Letter of James* (Grand Rapids, MI: Wm. B. Eerdmans, 2011), 228.
[33] James R. White, *The God Who Justifies* (Bloomington, MN: Bethany House, 2001), 331.

when one substitutes "dead/deedless/inauthentic faith" for the word
"faith" as it is used in the rest of this section of the letter.[34] Notice
what it does to James 2:17-20:

> So *dead faith* by itself, if it has no works, is dead. But some one will
> say, "You have *deedless faith* and I have works." Show me your *deed-
> less faith* apart from your works, and I by my works will show you
> my *deedless faith*. You believe that God is one; you do well. Even the
> demons believe—and shudder. Do you want to be shown, you foolish
> fellow, that *inauthentic faith* apart from works is barren?

When James says, "Faith by itself, if it has no works, is dead,"
he is not saying, "A dead faith is one that has no works whereas a
living faith is one that does have works." James does not speak of
dead or inauthentic faith but only "faith". For example, James 2:19
says, "You believe that God is one; you do well. Even the demons
believe—and shudder." Belief in monotheism is good but on its own
it does not bring about salvation. Moreover, as Scot McKnight notes,
James connects the act of believing with those who "affirm some
kind of 'orthodox' faith in Jesus Christ, the glorious one (Jas. 2:1)."[35]
This means even belief in *Christian* monotheism is insufficient for
salvation if it does not have works.

At this point some will argue that James is criticizing people who
have *mere* intellectual belief. They may assent to the truths of theology like demons that know God's true nature, but like those same
demons they refuse to submit to or have faith *in* God. But once again,
read the passage and substitute "mere intellectual assent" for the word
"faith". James would be saying there are people who boast of mere
intellectual assent (v. 14) and claim to demonstrate mere intellectual
assent by works (v. 18). James would also be saying that Abraham's
mere intellectual assent was active with his works (which would no
longer be *mere* intellectual assent). Jimmy Akin sharply illustrates the
real issue in James: "The faith isn't the problem; its being *alone* is
the problem [emphasis in original]."[36]

---

[34] Jimmy Akin, *The Drama of Salvation* (San Diego: Catholic Answers Press, 2014), kindle
edition.

[35] McKnight, *Letter of James*, 177.

[36] Akin, *Drama of Salvation*.

James 2:26 says, "For as the body apart from the spirit is dead, so faith apart from works is dead." For James what makes faith "alive" is not the presence of authenticity or a genuine commitment to God—it's works! Just as the spirit is distinct from the body and is what gives it life, works are distinct from faith and they are what make that faith alive. James is not telling people to have a faith that will necessarily produce good works; he is telling those with genuine faith to bring this faith to life by choosing to do good works. Works are not, as some Protestants allege, the automatic consequence of an authentic or genuine faith.

One popular way of describing this idea about works is found in the phrase "We are justified by faith alone, but faith is never alone." The Westminster Confession puts it this way: "Faith, thus receiving and resting on Christ and His righteousness, is the alone instrument of justification: yet is it not alone in the person justified, but is ever accompanied with all other saving graces, and is no dead faith, but works by love" (11.2). In other words, we are justified or made righteous by faith alone, but everyone who is justified will, of necessity, perform good works.

However, James does not say he who is justified does good works; he says, "A man is justified by works and not by faith alone" (Jas 2:24). The Bible is full of warnings not only to refrain from doing evil deeds, but also to refrain from failing to do good deeds. James himself says, "Whoever knows what is right to do and fails to do it, for him it is sin" (Jas 4:17). To defend the idea that those with faith must also choose to do good works, James presents two examples: Abraham who offered Isaac on the altar and Rahab who protected the spies in Jericho. Concerning Abraham he said:

> Was not Abraham our father justified by works, when he offered his son Isaac upon the altar? You see that faith was active along with his works, and faith was completed by works, and the Scripture was fulfilled which says, "Abraham believed God, and it was reckoned to him as righteousness"; and he was called the friend of God. You see that a man is justified by works and not by faith alone. (Jas 2:21–24)

Many Protestants claim that James used the word "justify" in a different way than Paul used the word. Calvin, for example, claimed that James was referring to Abraham being justified before men on account of his good works, whereas Paul spoke of the time when Abraham was justified before God by faith alone.[37] But despite the popularity of this explanation, many exegetes (including Protestant ones) find it unconvincing.

First, Genesis 22:5 says Abraham and Isaac went away from his servants to conduct the sacrifice. The text gives no evidence that anyone witnessed this act or that Abraham was esteemed in other men's eyes for his behavior. Robert Zins points out that "the word 'shown' is not in the passage," and concludes that "it may be stretching things too far to say that Abraham was 'shown to have been justified' when he offered Isaac."[38] Thomas Schreiner likewise says, "There is no evidence that justification here relates to justification before people rather than God. When James uses the words 'save' and 'justify,' he has in mind one's relationship with God."[39]

Another explanation is that James is speaking of justification in the sense of a general *vindication* of righteousness rather than a divine *declaration* of righteousness. John Ankerberg and John Weldon claim, "James uses the word 'justified' in the same sense Jesus did in Luke 7:35." In that verse Jesus said, "Wisdom is justified by all her children," from which the authors conclude, "Abraham's works *vindicated* his faith."[40] Even if there were no other people to witness it, Abraham's actions proved he had faith that justifies apart from works.

---

[37] "That we may not then fall into that false reasoning which has deceived the Sophists, we must take notice of the two fold meaning, of the word justified. Paul means by it the gratuitous imputation of righteousness before the tribunal of God; and James, the manifestation of righteousness by the conduct, and that before men, as we may gather from the preceding words, 'Shew to me thy faith,' etc. In this sense we fully allow that man is justified by works, as when any one says that a man is enriched by the purchase of a large and valuable chest, because his riches, before hid, shut up in a chest, were thus made known." John Calvin, *Commentaries on the Catholic Epistles*, trans. and ed. Rev. John Owen, Christian Classics Ethereal Library, commentary for James 2:21, accessed July 13, 2017, https://www.ccel.org/ccel/calvin/calcom45.vi.html.

[38] Robert M. Zins, *Romanism: The Relentless Roman Catholic Assault on the Gospel of Jesus Christ!* (Huntsville, AL: White Horse Publications, 1995), 179.

[39] Thomas R. Schreiner, *Faith Alone—The Doctrine of Justification* (Grand Rapids, MI: Zondervan, 2015), 205.

[40] John Ankerberg and John Weldon, *Protestants & Catholics: Do They Now Agree?* (Eugene, OR: Harvest House Publishers, 1995), 36.

The problem with this response is that there is no contradiction in saying Abraham's works both demonstrated that he had faith and also increased his righteousness before God. Plus, James 2:22 doesn't say Abraham's faith was *shown* or *demonstrated* by works, but rather, "You see that faith was active along with his works, and faith was completed by works." Verse 23 says Genesis 15:6 ("Abraham believed God, and it was reckoned to him as righteousness") was "fulfilled" when Abraham offered his son on the altar. This doesn't mean Abraham's faith was revealed only decades later when he offered Isaac on the altar. Instead, it means that Abraham's life was one of *continual belief* that resulted in his choosing to obey God and perform good works that pleased him (Heb 11:8–12 describes how Abraham did many good works "by faith"). According to Protestant scholar Ben Witherington,

> The concept of righteousness at least in James 2:23 seems to be Jewish— not "counted/considered righteous" but "declared to *be* [emphasis in original] righteous," that is, righteous by means of deeds. Abraham's belief was belief in action. The point of James's argument, then, has nothing to do with a forensic declaration of justification.[41]

## A Catholic View of "Faith and Works"

The point of using Abraham as an example is revealed in 2:24, where James concludes, "You see that a man is justified by works and not by faith alone." Protestant attempts to get around this verse usually present the same alternative definitions for "faith" we discussed earlier— but none of them work. If "faith" merely means "dead faith", then James would be saying, "A man is justified by works and not by dead faith alone." This would imply that a person is justified by a combination of "dead faith" and "works". Protestants usually counter by saying that James cannot be using Paul's definition of "justify" in reference to authentic faith, because if he were, then he would be contradicting Paul.

Catholics agree that Paul and James use the word "justify" in different ways, so there is no contradiction, but we disagree with the

---

[41] Ben Witherington, *Letters and Homilies for Jewish Christians: A Socio-Rhetorical Commentary on Hebrews, James and Jude* (Downers Grove, IL: InterVarsity Press, 2007), 478.

Protestant claim that James is not talking about justification before God. Instead, James is talking about an increase in a believer's *ongoing* justification before God. That's why he uses the example of a believer like Abraham to prove his point (as well as Rahab, who may have been more relatable to an audience that did not want to compare themselves to a spiritual giant like Abraham).

As we will see in the next chapter, when Paul is speaking about justification apart from works, he is talking about justification apart from obedience to the Law of the Old Testament as a form of maintaining a Jewish identity. That's why James uses Abraham's first acceptance of faith in Genesis 15, before God gave him the Old Covenant's sign of circumcision, to prove his point. According to Witherington,

> James is not dealing with works of the law as a means to become saved or as an entrance requirement (he never speaks of "works of the law"); rather, he is dealing with the conduct of those who already believe. He is talking about the perfection of faith in its working out through good works.... [If we take] James 2:24 as referring to that final verdict of God on one's deeds and life work, then even Paul can be said to have agreed.[42]

In its discussion of justification, the Council of Trent cites James 2:24 only when it talks about an increase in ongoing justification. It said, "Faith co-operating with good works, increase in that justice which they have received through the grace of Christ, and are still further justified."[43] But Trent also taught that the grace of initial justification does not come from works or any kind of merit. It said we are justified freely by faith, "because that none of those things which precede justification—whether faith or works—merit the grace itself of justification. For, if it be a grace, it is not now by works, otherwise, as the same Apostle says, grace is no more grace [Rom 11:6]."[44]

As we will see in the next chapter, Catholic teaching on justification not only does not contradict the writings of Saint Paul (or "The Apostle"); it is firmly supported by those same writings.

---

[42] Ibid.
[43] Council of Trent, sixth session, chapter 10.
[44] Council of Trent, sixth session, chapter 8.

# II

# Justification, Part II

Now that we've reviewed what Jesus and James taught about the doctrine of justification, we are ready to examine Saint Paul's writings on the subject. These writings are important because many Protestants stake the majority, if not the entirety, of their defense of *sola fide* on them. In his book *Faith Alone*, R. C. Sproul focuses almost entirely on Paul and never provides a detailed analysis of Jesus' teachings on justification.[1] James White says, "We must allow the primary expositor of this issue, in this case, the Apostle Paul, to speak first; his epistles to the Romans and Galatians must define the issues."[2]

However, one element of Pauline scholarship in the past few decades called "the New Perspective on Paul" (NPP) has helped support the Church's historic understanding of justification as it is taught in Paul's letters.[3] Defenders of the NPP are usually Protestants who do not accept the totality of the Catholic position on justification. Their insights, however, clear up misconceptions about Paul that have been used to criticize Catholic teaching on justification. Although, one of the view's defenders admits, "NPP versions of salvation seem closer to the Roman Catholic view than to Luther's."[4]

---

[1] While Sproul cites Romans and Galatians about three dozen times, he cites the four Gospels only seven times, and none of those citations involves a comprehensive discussion of Jesus' views on justification. R. C. Sproul, *Faith Alone: The Evangelical Doctrine of Justification* (Grand Rapids, MI: Baker Books, 1995), 261.

[2] James R. White, *The Roman Catholic Controversy* (Minneapolis: Bethany House, 1996), 147.

[3] Due to the disagreements between the defenders of NPP, it may be more accurate to call it the new *perspectives* on Paul.

[4] Kent L. Yinger, *The New Perspective on Paul: An Introduction* (Eugene, OR: Wipf and Stock, 2011), 81.

## The New Perspective on Paul

In 1977 E. P. Sanders published a book called *Paul and Palestinian Judaism*,[5] which helped launch the "new perspective". It showed how scholars since the Reformation had misunderstood both first-century Judaism and Paul's view of justification. NPP advocates like Sanders, N. T. Wright, and James Dunn (the latter of whom coined the term "New Perspective on Paul") showed how many Protestants anachronistically read sixteenth-century debates between the Reformers and the Catholic Church back into Paul's arguments.

According to this "old perspective", the Jews of Paul's time tried to earn God's favor by performing "good works" in accordance with the Law of Moses. As long as their good deeds outweighed their sins, they would be saved. But since no one could know if he had done enough good deeds, people fell into despair about losing salvation or became arrogant and failed to understand the gravity of their sins. In response, Paul taught that salvation could not be earned through works but could only be received through faith. It's no surprise that the Reformers identified themselves with Paul and his theology of "justification by faith alone" and identified the Church, with its sacraments and rules, with Paul's opponents who believed in "works-righteousness" salvation. Defenders of the NPP, however, challenged these long-held assumptions.

After an exhaustive study of Second Temple Judaism, Sanders came to the conclusion that the Jews in Paul's time never believed a person could earn his salvation by performing a certain number of good works. Instead, first-century Jews believed their salvation came through grace because God freely chose them, primarily through birth, to become members of his covenant. These Jews did not perform works to be saved, but obeyed the Law in order to remain in God's covenant. If they broke the Law, then there were means to make atonement for sin and receive them back into the covenant (Sanders calls this theological framework "covenantal nomism").[6]

[5] E. P. Sanders, *Paul and Palestinian Judaism: A Comparison of Patterns of Religion* (Philadelphia: Fortress Press, 1977).

[6] Sanders defines it as "the view that one's place in God's plan is established on the basis of the covenant and that the covenant requires as the proper response of man his obedience to its commandments, while providing the means of atonement for transgression." Ibid., 75.

The works first-century Jews performed didn't earn their salvation but showed others they were God's chosen people. In fact, Dunn calls things like circumcision or observance of kosher laws "badges" rather than "works" because while they demonstrated a person was saved, they were not a way to "earn" salvation. The Law was seen not as a burden that condemned Jews, but as a gift that protected them and brought them closer to God. In the same address where Pope Benedict XVI said, "Luther's phrase: *'faith alone'* is true, if it is not opposed to faith in charity, in love,"[7] Benedict explains how this can be in ways that parallel the NPP.

Benedict says that for Paul, "The word 'Law' meant the Torah in its totality, that is, the five books of Moses." As the ancient world became increasingly Hellenistic (or Greek), Jews became pressured to abandon their ancient customs and give up their belief in the one true God. So, according to Benedict, "It was necessary to create a wall of distinction, a shield of defence to protect the precious heritage of the faith; this wall consisted precisely in the Judaic observances and prescriptions."[8]

Prior to his conversion, Paul agreed with this view of salvation and correctly recognized the Law as a blessing to Israel. The NPP shows that Paul was not a man wracked with guilt over a law he could not keep who rejoiced in being set free from it by faith in Christ alone. That was how *Luther* saw Paul because Luther was projecting his own struggles onto the apostle he studied. According to one historian, Luther suffered from "attacks of doubt that made him utterly despair of God's love.... At such moments even the rustling of dried leaves in a forest sounded like the legions of hell coming to seize his soul" (one confessor even scolded the scrupulous Luther to "stop calling every fart a sin").[9]

But James Dunn points out that "in passages where Paul speaks explicitly about his pre-conversion experience there is no hint whatsoever of any such agony of conscience."[10] Rather, Paul boasted of

[7] Pope Benedict XVI, General Audience (November 19, 2008), https://w2.vatican.va/content/benedict-xvi/en/audiences/2008/documents/hf_ben-xvi_aud_20081119.html.

[8] Ibid.

[9] James M. Kittelson, *Luther the Reformer: The Story of the Man and His Career*, 2nd ed. (Minneapolis: Fortress Press, 2016), 22.

[10] James Dunn, *The New Perspective on Paul* (Grand Rapids, MI: Wm. B. Eerdmans, 2007), 195.

how he was advanced in Judaism beyond many his own age (Gal 1:13), and as to righteousness under the law, he was "blameless" (Phil 3:6).[11] According to Pope Benedict, after Paul's encounter with Christ, he saw that the "wall" formed by the Law "is no longer necessary; our common identity within the diversity of cultures is Christ, and it is he who makes us just. Being just simply means being with Christ and in Christ. And this suffices. Further [Jewish] observances are no longer necessary."[12]

Paul's complaint wasn't that his fellow Jews were trying to earn their standing before God through good works. Rather, his complaint was that they preached the need to become a Jew (or enter into God's Old Covenant) before one could become a Christian and enter into God's New Covenant. Acts 15:1 describes how "some men came down from Judea and were teaching the brethren, 'Unless you are circumcised according to the custom of Moses, you cannot be saved.'" According to Dunn in his book *The New Perspective on Paul*,

> What [Paul] is concerned to exclude is the *racial* not the *ritual* expression of faith; it is *nationalism* which he denies not *activism* [emphasis in original]. Whatever their basis in the scriptures, these works of the law had become identified as indices of Jewishness, as badges betokening race and nation.... What Jesus had done by his death and resurrection, in Paul's understanding, is to free the grace of God in justifying from its nationalistically restrictive clamps for a broader experience (beyond the circumcised Jew) and a fuller expression (beyond concern for ritual purity).[13]

Through faith in Christ entry into the covenant was now open to everyone: both Jews and Gentiles. If a ritual requirement like circumcision or observance of the dietary laws was necessary for salvation, then Gentiles could not be saved because, by accepting these requirements for covenant membership, they would become Jews and cease to be Gentiles. While Luther and the Reformers claimed that Paul believed good works were like filthy rags in God's eyes (cf.

---

[11] The classic work on this subject is Krister Stendahl, "The Apostle Paul and the Introspective Conscience of the West", *Harvard Theological Review* 56, no. 3 (July 1963): 199–215.

[12] Benedict XVI, General Audience.

[13] Dunn, *New Perspective on Paul*, 115.

Is 64:6), according to Sanders, "Paul was entirely in favor of good works. The works he had in mind, against which he was polemicizing in Galatians and Romans, were those works that make you Jewish and distinguished you from Gentiles."[14] Even non-Christian New Testament scholars agree, such as Bart Ehrman, who said that

> when Paul speaks of "works" he is explicitly referring to "works of the law," that is, observance of Jewish rules governing circumcision, the Sabbath, kosher foods, and the like. When James speaks of works, he means something like "good deeds." Paul himself would not argue that a person could have faith without doing good deeds.[15]

The problem for Paul was not people who chose works over grace in order to become right with God. The problem was people who chose grace given to a chosen people who obeyed the Torah (or Jews) over grace being given to all people who have faith in Christ and subsequently obey "the law of Christ" (Gal 6:2; 1 Cor 9:21).

Now that we have a better understanding of the real source of conflict for Paul, we can examine his view on justification. Since this is a lengthy and multifaceted topic that would require a large book in its own right to address completely, we will have to limit our scope to the verses that are most often cited in defense of justification by faith alone.

## Justification in Romans

Paul begins his argument in Romans by saying he is not ashamed of the gospel, "For in it the righteousness of God is revealed through faith for faith; as it is written, 'He who through faith is righteous shall live'" (Rom 1:17). After Luther came to the conclusion that this text taught justification by faith alone, he said, "I felt that I was altogether born again and had entered paradise itself through open gates."[16] The

---

[14] Michael Barnes Norton, "An Interview with E. P. Sanders: 'Paul, Context, & Interpretation'", *Journal of Philosophy and Scripture* 2 no. 2 (Spring 2005), http://philosophyandscripture.org/Issue2-2/Sanders/Sanders.html.

[15] Bart D. Ehrman, *Peter, Paul and Mary Magdalene: The Followers of Jesus in History and Legend* (New York: Oxford University Press, 2006), 167.

[16] Michael A. Mullett, *Martin Luther* (New York: Routledge, 2004), 60.

problem with this interpretation, however, is that Luther and most Protestants have primarily understood "faith" to be synonymous with "belief".

As Pope Benedict XVI points out, we can be justified by "faith alone" if faith includes charity and is lived out in love. The NPP contributes to Benedict's thesis because it shows that a significant element of Paul's conception of "faith" (Greek, *pistis*) includes the concept of "faithfulness". Faith includes not just trust or confidence in someone, but obedience to that person because he is so trustworthy. According to New Testament scholar Don Garlington,

> Righteousness is, by definition, conformity to the covenant relationship; it *consists of* [emphasis in original] a faithful obedience to the Lord whose will is enshrined in the covenant. Yet the beginning of "faithfulness" is "faith." In keeping with the Hebrew term *'emunah*, the Greek noun translated faith, *pisti* is two-sided: faith and faithfulness. Given this set of data, righteousness does consist of *pistis* in the expansive sense of *'emunah*, that is, covenant conformity.[17]

Romans 1:17 quotes Habakkuk 2:4, which also uses the Hebrew word *'emunah*. Protestant translations often render this Old Testament verse, "The righteous (or just) will live by faith." But the RSV (both Catholic and non-Catholic editions) provides a clearer translation: "He who through faith is righteous shall live." Paul did not believe righteousness came from faith alone, but from a faith that was lived out in righteous deeds. This is evident in his Letter to the Romans where Paul reminds his audience that God "will render to every man according to his works: to those who by patience in well-doing [Greek, *ergou agathou*, literally "good work"] seek for glory and honor and immortality, he will give eternal life" (2:6–7). Paul then promises:

> There will be tribulation and distress for every human being who does evil, the Jew first and also the Greek, but glory and honor and peace for every one who does good, the Jew first and also the Greek.... It is not the hearers of the law who are righteous before God, but the doers of the law who will be justified. (2:9–10, 13)

---

[17] Don Garlington, *Studies in the New Perspective* (Eugene, OR: Wipf and Stock, 2008), 143.

It is not the Jews who hear the Law preached in the Temple who will be justified. Instead, those who actually do what the Law requires, including the Gentiles, will be the ones who will be justified. The fact that the Gentiles were not given the Mosaic Law is irrelevant because, according to Paul, "what the law requires is written on their hearts" (Rom 2:15). This requirement does not include things like circumcision or kosher observance, but rather the most important parts of the Law found in the moral code that even the Gentiles understand.

Protestant interpretations of these passages sometimes assume that because Paul allegedly teaches justification by faith alone, these verses don't describe justification or reward because of good works. Instead, they must refer to a hypothetical that is impossible to fulfill such as, "Doers of the Law will be justified, but no one can perfectly obey the Law; therefore, no one will be justified by it."[18] But Romans 2:6–13 can't consist only of impossible hypotheticals, because verses 8 and 9 promise that evildoers will be punished for their sins, something Protestants agree God will do at the final judgment. In addition, Paul's Jewish audience knew God would not give someone eternal life just because he did good works. According to Dunn in his commentary on Romans, "The thought that no one could stand before God on his own terms, in his own strength, or could hope for acquittal on the merit of his own deeds, was thoroughly Jewish."[19]

A better explanation of these passages is that Paul is talking about the increase of righteousness that takes place *after* one enters into God's covenant on *God's* terms rather than trying to stand before God on one's *own* terms. N. T. Wright says, "Paul, in company with mainstream second-Temple Judaism, affirms that God's final judgment will be in accordance with the entirety of a life led—in accordance, in other words, with works."[20] Dunn further says that Romans 2:13

---

[18] "What Paul claims is theoretically possible in [Rom] 2:13 he denies as a possibility in practice in [Rom 3:20]." Douglas Moo, *Encountering the Book of Romans: A Theological Survey* (Grand Rapids, MI: Baker, 2002), 65.

[19] James Dunn, *Word Biblical Commentary: Romans 1–8*, vol. 38A (Nashville, TN: Thomas Nelson, 1988), 153.

[20] N. T. Wright, "New Perspectives on Paul" (2003), in *Pauline Perspectives: Essays on Paul, 1978–2013* (Minneapolis: Fortress Press, 2013), 281.

and 3:20 (which we will address momentarily) stand "against the view that Paul sees justification simply as an act which marks the beginning of a believer's life, as a believer."[21]

That Paul sees justification as a process is crucial to understanding his argument because, even though doers of the Law will be justified, in the next chapter Paul makes a striking claim about the Law and its ability to justify a person.

In the third chapter of Romans, Paul dispels the notion that the Jews, simply in virtue of being Jews, possessed a special kind of righteousness. While the Jews had the benefit of being the recipients of divine revelation (v. 2), they are still not better off than non-Jews. That's because, quoting from Psalm 14:3, Paul says, "None is righteous, no, not one" (Rom 3:10). This can't mean there are no righteous individuals, because the Psalmist also says that "God is with the generation of the righteous" (Ps 14:5). Instead, it means that no one is righteous simply by virtue of belonging to one group or the other. All people, "both Jews and Greeks, are under the power of sin" (Rom 3:9). Paul then says that "no human being will be justified in [God's] sight by works of the law, since through the law comes knowledge of sin" (Rom 3:20).

The term "works of the law" cannot be synonymous with the "good work" done by the individual Paul described in the previous chapter who would be rewarded with eternal life. Instead, in this context "works of the law" means works done in order to obey what was found in the Mosaic Law (or the Torah). In the Greek Septuagint the Hebrew word *Torah* (which means something "teaching") was called "*nomos*" or "Law". That Paul is speaking of works associated specifically with the Torah can be seen in verses that Protestants often cite in defense of justification by faith alone. Paul writes,

> [God] justifies him who has faith in Jesus. Then what becomes of our boasting? It is excluded. On what principle? On the principle of works? No, but on the principle of faith. For we hold that a man is justified by faith apart from works of law. Or is God the God of Jews only? Is he not the God of Gentiles also? (Rom 3:26–29)

[21] Dunn, *Word Biblical Commentary: Romans 1–8*, 153. Thanks to Jimmy Akin for this reference.

Ankerberg and Weldon claim, "Since Paul says that a man is justified by faith *apart* from the works of the law, then one can only
conclude that justification must be by faith alone. There are no other
options."[22] In his translation of Romans 3:28, Luther added the word
"alone" to make this point clear, even though the word "alone"
(Greek *monos*) is not in the Greek text of Romans 3:28. But adding
the word "alone" doesn't clarify the passage's meaning; it changes it.

If I say, "A man is made healthy by medicine apart from quack
cures," that is not the same as saying, "A man is made healthy by
medicine alone apart from quack cures." Medicine divorced from
exercise and healthy diet cannot make someone healthy, just as faith
divorced from charity and obedience cannot make someone justified. The only way such a translation could be defended would be
by claiming, as Ankerberg, Weldon, and Luther do, that the terms
"faith" and "works of law" include all the ways a person is justified.
Therefore, if justification is done apart from works of Law, then
only faith is left to justify a person. As Luther says, "When all works
are so completely rejected—which must mean faith alone justifies—
whoever would speak plainly and clearly about this rejection of works
will have to say 'Faith alone justifies and not works.'"[23]

But the context of this passage makes it clear that Paul is not identifying "works of law" with human effort in general. In the next two
verses Paul says, "Or is God the God of Jews only? Is he not the God
of Gentiles also? Yes, of Gentiles also, since God is one; and he will
justify the circumcised on the ground of their faith and the uncir-
cumcised through their faith" (Rom 3:29–30). Paul's point is that all
people, both Jews and Gentiles, enter the New Covenant through
faith in Christ. They do not need to bear any marks of the Old Covenant like circumcision in order to receive initial justification in the
New Covenant. They also do not have to obey the Torah in order
to remain in the New Covenant.

The "boasting" Paul refers to in verse 27 is not self-righteous pride
in moral conduct that earned a person's place before God. Instead,

[22] John Ankerberg and John Weldon, *Protestants & Catholics: Do They Now Agree?* (Eugene,
OR: Harvest House Publishers, 1995), 32.
[23] Larry D. Mansch and Curtis H. Peters, *Martin Luther: The Life and Lessons* (Jefferson,
NC: McFarland, 2016), 150.

it was *nationalistic* pride that came from being called by God to be among his chosen people. Since entry into the Covenant now comes through faith rather than obedience to a law one's ancestors had been given, there is no room to boast; everyone stands equally before God in the New Covenant (Gal 3:28). As proof that God justifies by faith rather than adherence to the law, Paul offers the example of Abraham being "reckoned righteous" when he believed God's promise in Genesis 15 that he would have innumerable descendants:

> For if Abraham was justified by works, he has something to boast about, but not before God. For what does the Scripture say? "Abraham believed God, and it was reckoned to him as righteousness" [Gen 15:6]. Now to one who works, his wages are not reckoned as a gift but as his due. And to one who does not work but trusts him who justifies the ungodly, his faith is reckoned as righteousness. (Rom 4:2–5)

Protestant apologist John Armstrong says, "The whole point here, as in verse 5, is this—God reckons righteousness, i.e. He imputes it, to those who believe solely on the basis of their whole-hearted trustful reliance upon the gracious and kind promises of God."[24] Calvin goes even further claiming that "even saints [or those who have been justified] cannot perform one work which, if judged on its own merits, is not deserving of condemnation."[25] But the point of Romans 4 is that someone can become right with God without being circumcised, not that righteousness before God comes through faith alone.

Paul isn't talking about boasting of morally good works, since those would give someone grounds to boast before God of what he had done in his name. Instead, he is talking about boasting of one's place before God to the Gentiles, which a person could not do with God any more than an orphan could boast to his new adoptive parents about his being adopted as an infant. Romans 2:23 even describes Jews who "boast in the law [Torah]", which is something Abraham could not do because, aside from not having the Torah,

---

[24] John Armstrong, "Justification by Faith *Alone*: The Sufficiency of Faith for Justification", in *Justification by Faith Alone*, ed. Don Kistler (Morgan, PA: Soli Deo Gloria Publications, 1995), 140.

[25] John Calvin, *Institutes of the Christian Religion* 3.14.9.

God accepted him on account of his humble faith and not something like his ancestors' relationship with God.

N. T. Wright says the discussion in Romans 4:4–5 about people "earning a reward" is not a condemnation of being justified by good deeds. Instead, "[Paul] is ruling out any suggestion that Abraham might have been 'just the sort of person God was looking for,' so that there might be some merit prior to the promise, in other words, some kind of 'boast.' "[26] This passage in Romans does not teach that justification occurs in a single moment apart from works, because, as James says, Abraham was justified decades later when he offered Isaac on the altar.

In addition, Abraham was justified years *before* God made a covenant with him in Genesis 15 when he answered God's first call to follow him into a strange land in Genesis 12. Hebrews 11:8 says Abraham did so through a faith by which, according to verse 2, "men of old received divine approval." This means Abraham was approved, became right, or was "justified" years before God made his covenant with him in Genesis 15:6. This shows justification occurs throughout the life of a person who "lives by faith", and not in a single act of faith.

Romans 4 also does not deny the truth that God rewards our good works. Remember, God isn't obligated to reward our works even though he chooses to do so out of his gracious love for us. But that doesn't mean believers cannot increase their righteousness before God through good works. The denial of this possibility usually stems from the assumption that justification occurs in a single moment by faith alone. For example, Romans 5:1 says, "Since we are justified by faith, we have peace with God through our Lord Jesus Christ." This does not mean, however, that justification is an irrevocable, completely past reality.

The United States has peace with Japan, but that doesn't mean a future act of aggression could not undo this peace.[27] In Romans 5:9 Paul connects past justification with future salvation by asking how

---

[26] N. T. Wright, *Justification: God's Plan & Paul's Vision* (Downers Grove, IL: InterVarsity Press, 2009), 220.

[27] Jimmy Akin makes this point with a similar example in his article "Justification and Peace with God", JimmyAkin.com, accessed July 14, 2017, http://jimmyakin.com/justification -and-peace-with-god.

"much more shall we be saved by him from the wrath of God". In Romans 6:16 Paul implicitly describes a *future* justification when he writes, "Do you not know that if you yield yourselves to any one as obedient slaves, you are slaves of the one whom you obey, either of sin, which leads to death, or of obedience, which leads to righteousness [*dikaiosynen*]?"

Paul uses *dikaiosynen* to describe the righteousness or justification that was credited to Abraham because of his faith (Rom 4). This means one can translate the end of Romans 6:16 as speaking of a person who becomes a slave of "obedience, which leads to *justification*". Luther even described justification as a process when he wrote, "Daily we sin, daily we continue to be justified, just as daily the Physician knows to heal the sickness, until it is healed."[28] This progressive justification, which Catholics believe is increased when one performs good works through God's grace, culminates in a "final justification". According to Azusa Pacific University professor B.J. Oropeza,

> In Romans, as in Galatians, those who believe the gospel message are initially made righteous/justified [*dikaiosynen*: Rom 1:17], but their final righteousness/justification will not take place until the second coming of Christ. Moreover, the righteousness in which they participate during the present era does not guarantee their final righteousness at the [end of the world]. They must persevere and not reject faith.[29]

## Justification in Galatians

In his Letter to the Galatians, Paul was angry that his audience was deserting the gospel he preached (Gal 1:6). After defending his apostolic credentials, Paul explains the false gospel that some of the "foolish Galatians" accepted (3:1). It appears that while the community started out in the Spirit, they are "now ending with the flesh" (Gal

---

[28] Martin Luther, WA [Weimar edition, Weimar Ausgabe] 39.I:122, 8–15. Cited in Mark A. Seifrid, "Luther Melancthon and Paul on the Question of Imputation", in *Justification: What's at Stake in the Current Debates*, ed. Mark Husbands and Daniel J. Treier (Downers Grove, IL: InterVarsity Press, 2004), 145.

[29] B.J. Oropeza, *Jews, Gentiles, and the Opponents of Paul: Apostasy in the New Testament Communities*, vol. 2, *The Pauline Letters* (Eugene, OR: Wipf and Stock, 2012), 150.

3:3), by returning to Jewish ritual practices or "works of the law" (Gal 3:2, 5). Paul berates the Galatians for this decision, saying:

> A man is not justified by works of the law but through faith in Jesus Christ, even we have believed in Christ Jesus, in order to be justified by faith in Christ, and not by works of the law, because by works of the law shall no flesh be justified. (Gal 2:16).

> All who rely on works of the law are under a curse; for it is written, "Cursed be every one who does not abide by all things written in the book of the law, and do them." (Gal 3:10)

Some Catholic apologists have argued that Paul is condemning works related only to ceremonial aspects of the Torah, such as circumcision. This is a time-tested approach given that Calvin said of this passage, "The papists, misled by Origen and Jerome ... assert, that by 'the works of the law' are meant ceremonies."[30] On its face, this isn't an unreasonable interpretation given that all the examples of condemned behavior Paul cites are ceremonial or ritual aspects of the Torah that gave Jews their unique identity.

In Galatians 4:9–10 Paul laments how members of the community were going back to "elemental spirits", which could refer to the angels who originally gave Israel the Mosaic Law. He chides the Galatians for observing "days, and months, and seasons, and years", which correspond to celebrating Jewish holy days and festivals. Paul also mentions circumcision over a dozen times, even going so far as labeling his critics "the circumcision party" (Gal 2:12) and saying he wished they'd take circumcision too far and castrate themselves (Gal 5:12).

N. T. Wright focuses on these ceremonial requirements and says they comprise the curse Paul associates with the Law. He says Paul's complaint is that "the law gets in the way of the promise to Abraham" by creating barriers for Gentile inclusion into the covenant.[31] Dunn says the curse applies to "all who restrict the grace and promise of God

---

[30] John Calvin, *Commentaries on the Epistle of Paul to the Galatians and Ephesians*, trans. Rev. William Pringle, Christian Classics Ethereal Library, commentary on Galatians 2:15, accessed July 15, 2017, https://www.ccel.org/ccel/calvin/calcom41.iii.iv.iii.html.

[31] Wright, *Justification*, 123.

in nationalistic terms, who treat the law as a boundary mark."[32] But against Wright's and Dunn's interpretations, Thomas Schreiner says, "'Works of law' are defined as doing all the things commanded in the law, which shows that a general critique of the law is intended."[33] Other scholars make the same point, saying that Paul was concerned about the Torah as a whole, and not just its ceremonial aspects.

Was Paul condemning obedience to the Torah because it keeps Gentiles from entering the kingdom? Or was Paul condemning obedience to the Torah because obedience to "works of Law" in general cannot justify us before God? The answer is both—in a qualified sense.

Schreiner is correct that Paul is concerned not just with alienation of the Gentiles, but also with belief that obeying the Torah, which for Jews meant obeying *all* of its laws, was necessary for salvation. But Paul was not concerned about obeying the Torah per se. He was concerned about people obeying the laws found in the Torah *because they were found in the Torah*. If someone obeyed the Ten Commandments because that made him "a good Jew" or one of God's chosen people, and he subsequently told other people they had to obey the Ten Commandments for this same reason, then *that* conduct would be under the curse of the Law.

However, just because keeping the Torah is not necessary for salvation, it doesn't follow that every law *in* the Torah is not necessary for salvation. Jimmy Akin provides a good example: just because drinking diet coke isn't necessary for good health (and may even detract from good health), that doesn't mean *water* (the principal ingredient in diet coke) is not necessary for good health.[34] Some Protestants fall into this error when they interpret Galatians 2 and 3 as saying we are not justified by *any* law. Consider this remarkable claim from Geisler and MacKenzie:

> Clearly the message of Galatians is: You are not only justified by faith alone, but you are also being sanctified by faith alone.... Neither

---

[32] James D. G. Dunn, *Jesus, Paul and the Law: Studies in Mark and Galatians* (Great Britain: SPCK, 1990), 229.

[33] Thomas R. Schreiner, *Faith Alone—The Doctrine of Justification* (Grand Rapids, MI: Zondervan, 2015), 229.

[34] Jimmy Akin, *The Drama of Salvation* (San Diego: Catholic Answers Press, 2014), kindle edition.

initial righteousness (justification) nor progressive righteousness (sanctification) is conditioned on meritorious works.... Many Protestants are heretical at this point too, since, at least in practice if not in theory, they too teach that works are a condition for progressive sanctification.[35]

Contra Geisler and MacKenzie, Galatians does not teach that works have nothing to do with either our sanctification or our ongoing justification. As we will see in the next chapter, Paul taught that believers could be separated from Christ for engaging in evil works (Gal 5:4). In addition, believers inherit eternal life, at least in part, because they performed good works. Paul writes, "Do not be deceived; God is not mocked, for whatever a man sows, that he will also reap. For he who sows to his own flesh will from the flesh reap corruption; but he who sows to the Spirit will from the Spirit reap eternal life" (Gal 6:7–8). This passage clearly shows that a believer's actions have a bearing on whether he receives an eternal destiny *with* God or one *apart* from God.

The Protestant apologist Gregg Allison says, "There is no such thing as the Law of the Gospel, for those two are mutually exclusive."[36] But Paul says, "The whole law is fulfilled in one word: 'You shall love your neighbor as yourself'" (Gal 5:14), and he encourages the Galatians to "bear one another's burdens, and so fulfil *the law of Christ* [emphasis added]" (Gal 6:2). This complements James 2:8, which says we do well when we "fulfil the royal law, according to the Scripture, 'You shall love your neighbor as yourself.'"

Paul did not believe that justification came from obeying the Torah *because it is the Torah*, or the means of entering into the New Covenant. Paul even allowed people to retain Jewish customs like feast days (Rom 14:5), provided they did not impose these practices on others (Rom 14:10). He believed that the laws God intended for everyone in the New Covenant to obey were also found in the Torah, such as the Ten Commandments. The Protestant scholar Douglas Moo admits this is true, even if he is hesitant about its implications:

---

[35] Norman L. Geisler and Ralph E. MacKenzie, *Roman Catholics and Evangelicals: Agreements and Differences* (Grand Rapids, MI: Baker Books, 1995), 237.

[36] Gregg Allison, *Roman Catholic Theology and Practice: An Evangelical Assessment* (Wheaton, IL: Crossway, 2014), 429.

Indeed, we can confidently expect that everything within the Mosaic law that reflected God's "eternal moral will" for his people is caught up into and repeated in the "law of Christ." Having recognized the place within "the law of Christ" of specific commandments, however, I want to insist that they must not be given too much prominence.[37]

The key verse that summarizes Paul's view of justification in this letter is Galatians 5:6: "For in Christ Jesus neither circumcision nor uncircumcision is of any avail, but faith working through love." A person will not be justified if he obeys the Torah in order to conform to a Jewish identity that is necessary for salvation. Instead, a person, be he a Jew or Gentile, is justified by faith in Christ. This faith consists not just of belief, but also of faithfulness to Christ and the law of Christ, or the eternal moral principles God requires for members of the New Covenant.

Saint Augustine put it (similar to Pope Benedict XVI) this way: "It can be said that God's commandments pertain to *faith alone*, if it is not dead [faith], but rather understood as that live faith, which works through love."[38]

## Justification in Ephesians

One of the most common verses that is cited in defense of justification by faith alone is Ephesians 2:8–9: "For by grace you have been saved through faith; and this is not your own doing, it is the gift of God— not because of works, lest any man should boast." Ron Rhodes says, "The Roman Catholic position seems to assume that human beings actually *do* things that make them acceptable to God, but such an idea goes against the entire grain of Scripture.... God's grace—God's unmerited favor—is our only chance for salvation (Eph. 2:8–9)."[39]

In Ephesians 2:8–9 Paul is not teaching that the process of salvation involves only faith. Paul is talking about initial salvation because he speaks about being saved as a past, completed reality. Catholics agree

---

[37] Douglas Moo, "The Law, the Gospel, and the Modern Christian", in *Five Views on Law and Gospel*, ed. Willem A. VanGemeren (Grand Rapids, MI: Zondervan, 1996), 370.

[38] St. Augustine, *De Fide et Operibus* 22.40. Cited in Joseph A. Fitzmyer, *Romans* (New York: Doubleday, 1993), 360–61.

[39] Ron Rhodes, *Reasoning from the Scriptures with Catholics* (Eugene, OR: Harvest House Publishing, 2000), 140.

there is no action, including acts of faith, that merits the gift of initial justification, so this verse does not prove justification is by faith alone.[40] In fact, the next verse says, "For we are his workmanship, created in Christ Jesus for good works, which God prepared beforehand, that we should walk in them."

Notice that Paul says we were not saved because of "works" but were created for "good works".[41] This implies that the works in verse 9 that Paul is speaking of are inferior to the *good* works God wants us to do in verse 10. This makes sense if Paul was saying to his audience that salvation "is the gift of God—not because of works of the Law [or works of Torah]". Paul is telling the Gentiles that they don't come into God's covenant through works of the Law like circumcision. Instead, like everyone else they come into the covenant through faith that is a gracious gift from God. That this is Paul's meaning is evident in the fact that verses 11–22 speak of uniting estranged Gentile believers to God through faith in Christ rather than observance of the Torah.

Paul personally addresses the Gentiles (v. 11) and reminds them of both their separation from Christ and their alienation from God's promises (v. 12). He says this separation has been taken away by the blood of Christ (v. 13), and in its place God has given us peace because he "has broken down the dividing wall of hostility, by abolishing in his flesh the law of commandments and ordinances" (v. 14–15). The law is the Torah, and Paul identifies it with the "dividing wall", which some have taken as an allusion to the wall that separated the court of the Gentiles from that of the Jews in the Jerusalem Temple. Now that this boundary marker of the Old Covenant has been abolished, all people can enter into God's covenant by faith in Christ. But this does not mean that works play no role in our salvation *after* this initial entry.

In 1 Corinthians 15:2 Paul speaks of the gospel "by which you are saved, if you hold it fast—unless you believed in vain". The word "saved" (Greek, *sozesthe*) can literally be translated "you are being saved" because it is in the present tense.[42] Just because we have been

---

[40] "We are therefore said to be justified freely, because that none of those things which precede justification—whether faith or works—merit the grace itself of justification." Council of Trent, sixth session, chapter 8.

[41] I owe this insight to Jimmy Akin.

[42] David Garland, *1 Corinthians* (Grand Rapids, MI: Baker, 2008), 683.

saved in the past, as Ephesians 2:8–9 says, that does not mean our salvation was settled once and for all in the past. In Philippians 2:12 Paul implores his audience to "work out your own salvation with fear and trembling." In Romans 13:11 Paul says, "Salvation is nearer to us now than when we first believed." The Protestant biblical scholar Brenda Colijin notes that

> salvation, for Paul, is predominantly future. As we have seen, even his uses of salvation in past and present tense have a forward-looking aspect.... Believers were already saved from their trespasses and sins (Eph. 2:1, 5). In the present, believers are being saved from the power of sin (Phil. 2:13, 2 Cor. 5:15, 17; cf. Eph. 2:1–10). In the last day, believers will be saved from God's wrath (his righteous response to sin) and from death (the result of sin).[43]

In response to this argument, some Protestants say Paul (like James) is only talking about works that automatically flow from an authentic faith. They might cite Philippians 2:13, which says, "For God is at work in you, both to will and to work for his good pleasure." Geisler and MacKenzie conclude, "We do not work in order to get salvation; rather, we work because we have already gotten it. God works salvation *in* us by justification, and by God's grace we work it *out* in sanctification (Phil 2:12–13)."[44]

The point must be repeated because it is so crucial—Catholics do not work in order to receive initial justification, or we don't work to "get salvation". We do, however, perform good works through the grace God has given us, to increase our justification, or righteousness before God. These works don't merely demonstrate we are saved, but they serve to increases our sanctification, or personal holiness, and contribute to our final salvation. Against the view that good works simply "flow" from the fact that we are saved, Dunn asks:

> Can the first half of Philippians 2:12–13 (v. 12: "Work out your own salvation with fear and trembling") be totally absorbed into the second half (v. 13: "for it is God who works in you both to will and to

---

[43] Brenda Colijin, "The Three Tenses of Salvation in Paul's Letters", *Ashland Theological Journal* 22 (1990): 33.
[44] Geisler and MacKenzie, *Roman Catholics and Evangelicals*, 233.

work for his good pleasure")? Paul's talk of "walking by the Spirit" or "being led by the spirit elsewhere" [Rom 8:4, Gal 5:16–18] clearly puts responsibility on the believer to so walk, to be so led.[45]

While Paul places responsibility on the believer to cooperate with God and perform good works, Catholics don't have to perform a certain number of good works in order to be saved. Everything they do in Christ, even mundane, day-to-day tasks, pleases God when done in a spirit of charity. The only thing they "must do" in order to be saved is not remain in a state of unrepentant, mortal sin until the end of their lives. Quoting *Lumen Gentium*, the *Catechism* says, "'All men may attain salvation through faith, Baptism and the observance of the Commandments' (*LG* 24)" (*CCC* 2068). Catholic biblical scholar Michael Barber also provides an excellent summary of how Catholics receive salvation:

> Salvation is first by God's grace and not by works. One receives Christ not because one has performed any good works. However, once one has become united to Christ, one is capable of doing what was previously impossible. In Catholic teaching, works performed by those in union with Christ have meritorious value. They cannot *not* have meritorious value. Why? Because they are the result of Christ's work. The believer says, "It is no longer I who live, but Christ who lives within me" (Gal 2:20).[46]

---

[45] James Dunn, "Response to Wilkin", in *Four Views on the Role of Works at the Final Judgment*, ed. Alan Stanley (Grand Rapids, MI: Zondervan, 2013), 134.

[46] Michael Barber, "A Catholic Perspective: Our Works Are Meritorious at the Final Judgment Because of Our Union with Christ by Grace", in Stanley, *Four Views*, 180.

# 12

# Eternal Security

From 1618 to 1619 the Dutch Reformed Church hosted a synod in the city of Dordrecht, which later came to be known as the Synod of Dort. The synod has a special place in Protestant history because it articulated the five distinctive doctrines of Calvinism: total depravity, unconditional election, limited atonement, irresistible grace, and the perseverance of the saints, which are often summarized in the acronym TULIP.

Dort's fifth head of doctrine specifically refers to the "P" in TULIP when it says believers "do not totally fall from faith and grace, nor continue and perish finally in their backslidings; which, with respect to themselves, is not only possible, but would undoubtedly happen; but with respect to God, it is utterly impossible."[1] In other words, God's grace will make it impossible for any Christian to lose his salvation.

## The Meaning of Perseverance

This doctrine is also called "eternal security" since it claims that nothing the believer does could ever revoke his promise of eternal life with God. Edwin Palmer summarizes the Calvinist conception of the perseverance of the saints this way: "The person who sincerely puts his trust in Christ as his Savior is safe in the arms of Jesus. He

[1] "The Canons of Dort: Fifth Head of Doctrine; Of the Perseverance of the Saints", Article 8, Protestant Reformed Churches in America, last modified January 12, 1997, https://www.prca.org/cd_text4.html.

is secure. No one can hurt him. He will go to heaven. And this is for eternity. He is secure for all time, not just for a little while. He is eternally secure."[2]

Before we critique this doctrine, it's important to define it carefully because Catholics also use the language of perseverance in connection with the saints. For example, the Council of Trent spoke of "that great gift of perseverance" given to those who are destined to spend eternity with God.[3] But Catholics, along with many Protestants, disagree with the idea that every single believer will persevere and receive final salvation.[4]

Some Christians may be given only the gift of initial salvation, or they will be elected by God to become a Christian but not remain a Christian. Saint Augustine notes this distinction by asking, "Of two pious men, why to the one should be given perseverance unto the end, and to the other it should not be given? God's judgments are even more unsearchable."[5] Those who were predestined to initial salvation would be like the person in the Parable of the Sower who, Jesus says, "hears the word and immediately receives it with joy; yet he has no root in himself, but endures for a while, and when tribulation or persecution arises on account of the word, immediately he falls away" (Mt 13:20–21).

One variation of the doctrine of eternal security is called "once saved, always saved" (OSAS). This view is not the same as perseverance of the saints. OSAS advocates believe that a Christian can engage in any sin, or even become an unrepentant apostate, and not lose his salvation. These people, such as Charles Stanley and Robert Wilkin, claim that God justifies sinners solely by faith, and our moral conduct has no bearing on our justification.

---

[2] Edwin Palmer, *The Five Points of Calvinism*, 3rd ed. (Grand Rapids, MI: Baker Books, 2010), 82–83.

[3] "If any one saith, that he will for certain, of an absolute and infallible certainty, have that great gift of perseverance unto the end,—unless he have learned this by special revelation; let him be anathema." Council of Trent, sixth session, On Justification, canon 16, http://www.thecounciloftrent.com/ch6.htm.

[4] Besides the works cited in this chapter regarding the doctrine of eternal security, see also Robert Shank, *Life in the Son* (Bloomington, MN: Bethany House, 1989), and I. Howard Marshall, *Kept by the Power of God: A Study of Perseverance and Falling Away* (Eugene, OR: Wipf and Stock, 2008).

[5] St. Augustine, *On the Gift of Perseverance* 21.

Wilkin says of apostates, "There is no time requirement on saving faith. Even if a person believes only for a while, he still has eternal life."[6] Stanley agrees that not only will apostates be saved, but so will unrepentant believers.[7] He says that a Christian will usually seek forgiveness from God if he commits serious sins, "[but] even if he does not, the fact remains that he is forgiven!"[8] A believer may be punished with a loss of rewards, but he will not suffer a loss of salvation.

Defenders of the Protestant understanding of the perseverance of the saints agree with defenders of OSAS that a true Christian will never lose his salvation. They disagree, however, with the idea that a true Christian could commit a sin like unrepentant apostasy and still be saved. Advocates of perseverance of the saints usually say an unrepentant apostate would be an example of someone who was never saved in the first place, or he was never a "true Christian". When faced with passages that seem to describe the loss of salvation, they usually claim that either these passages are impossible hypotheticals (they describe something that would never actually happen), or they describe the damnation of people who were never saved in the first place.

In our examination of the passages that teach the possibility of losing one's salvation, we will examine replies from both advocates of perseverance of the saints and defenders of OSAS. But before we do that, we should examine some common arguments for these positions that do not cite particular Bible verses.

For example, some people claim that because we did nothing to receive the gift of salvation, we can do nothing to lose it. A quick Internet search reveals dozens of churches whose mission statement includes the phrase "You didn't do anything to earn your salvation, and you can't do anything to lose it." But as anyone who has received presents at Christmas can attest, an unearned gift can be lost or given away. Adam and Eve did nothing to receive their grace with God in the Garden of Eden, but they did something to lose it. If they could fall from grace, then so could we.

Others say salvation makes us children of God, and nothing ever changes the parent/child relationship. But this analogy fails because

[6] Robert Wilkin, *Confident in Christ* (Irving, TX: Grace Evangelical Society, 1999), 29.

[7] "Even those who walk away from the faith have not the slightest chance of slipping from his hand." Charles Stanley, *Eternal Security* (Nashville, TN: Thomas Nelson, 1990), 74.

[8] Ibid., 79.

parents can disown their children and children can leave their parents. Adam was a son of God (Lk 3:38) who fell from God's grace. Likewise, the prodigal son left home, was described as being dead, and then was declared to be alive again after he returned home (Lk 15:24). First John 3:10 says that "whoever does not do right" are "children of the devil", but that does not mean these unbelievers can never become children of God. Since we are God's children by adoption (Rom 8:15), and not by nature in the way Jesus is, this means we can come into a familial relationship with God by the grace of his covenant but still be able to leave that relationship by breaking that same covenant.

Finally, some people say that believers cannot lose their salvation, because they have received "eternal life". If they were ever to be damned, then the life they had received wouldn't truly be "eternal". Those who make this argument often cite 1 John 5:13: "I write this to you who believe in the name of the Son of God, that you may know that you have eternal life." But John says we can know we have eternal life because we can know we are in Christ and, provided we remain in Christ, we will spend eternity with him. Indeed, the First Letter of John is filled with commands to love God and neighbor that, when followed or ignored, confirm if we are in Christ or not (1 Jn 3:10–18). According to the late Baptist scholar Dale Moody,

> [Advocates of perseverance of the saints] work with the false assumption that the adjective "eternal" is an adverb, as if it says the brother eternally has life. It is the life that is eternal, not one's possession of it. Eternal life is the life of God in Christ the Son of God, and this life is lost when one departs from Christ.[9]

## The Evidence from Jesus

Defenders of perseverance of the saints and OSAS cite Jesus' teaching that the will of his Father is that "every one who sees the Son and believes in him should have eternal life; and I will raise him up at the last day" (Jn 6:40). Since Jesus must accomplish the Father's will, this means anyone who comes to believe in Christ will be raised up on

---

[9] Dale Moody, *The Word of Truth: A Summary of Christian Doctrine Based on Biblical Revelation* (Grand Rapids, MI: Wm. B. Eerdmans, 1981), 356.

the last day. Jesus also said that all the Father gives to him will come to him (Jn 6:44), and Jesus will not cast these people out (Jn 6:37). Finally, Jesus promised that "my sheep hear my voice, and I know them, and they follow me; and I give them eternal life, and they shall never perish, and no one shall snatch them out of my hand" (Jn 10:27–28).[10]

While these verses may seem persuasive, the apologist who cites them ignores their respective contexts, none of which teaches the doctrine of perseverance of the saints or OSAS.

For example, John 10:27–28 does not teach that if a person is one of Jesus' sheep, then he will always hear and follow Jesus' voice, and thus have perseverance of the saints. Jesus is actually saying the opposite: those who hear Jesus' voice and follow him are his sheep, and *that* is why they will never perish. Moody says, "Some read the passage as if it says: 'My sheep "heard" my voice, and I "knew" them, and they "followed" me, and I "gave" to them eternal life.'" But, Moody argues, the verbs indicate continuous, ongoing action by the sheep and by the Shepherd, not something that happened at a single moment in the past.[11] Being a sheep does not guarantee one will always be obedient to Christ. Instead, consistently being obedient to Christ is what makes someone his sheep.

Concerning John 6:37, the Greek text of this passage indicates that Jesus is referring to "all" the Father gives him, or the body of believers as a whole.[12] This does not mean that individuals who belong to this body—the Church—do not have to keep spiritually coming to Jesus or that they are unable to turn their backs on Jesus and walk away. Jesus is saying that whoever comes to him in faith will not be arbitrarily denied eternal life. This is, in the words of A. T. Robertson, "[a] definite promise of Jesus to welcome the one who comes".[13]

---

[10] Norm Geisler, "A Moderate Calvinist View", in *Four Views on Eternal Security*, ed. J. Matthew Pinson (Grand Rapids, MI: Zondervan, 2002), 71.

[11] Moody, *Word of Truth*, 357.

[12] "T. W. Manson, 'Entry into Membership of the Early Church.' *JTS* 48, 1947. 25–33, especially 27, suggested that the neuter [noun] was meant collectively (cf. John 6:37) to express the whole body of those begotten of God." I. Howard Marshall, *The Epistles of John* (Grand Rapids, MI: Wm. B. Eerdmans, 1978), 228.

[13] Cited in Shank, *Life in the Son*, 360.

This verse does not mean a person can't choose to stop coming to Jesus. If I say I will not cast out anyone who comes to my book table after a presentation, that doesn't mean he can't leave on his own or that he will be stuck at my table for all eternity. In his study of this passage James White says that "the present tense refers to a continuous, on-going action.... The wonderful promises that are provided by Christ are not for those who do not truly and continuously believe."[14]

In Greek, the present tense often indicates ongoing action, and the emphasis on present-tense verbs also explains the meaning of John 6:40, where Jesus says, "For this is the will of my Father, that every one who sees the Son and believes in him should have eternal life; and I will raise him up at the last day." Jesus is promising that everyone who continues to "see" and continues to believe in him will have eternal life and be raised up on the last day. He is not promising that people can't choose to stop "seeing" or stop believing in him.

In John 6:38–39 Jesus does say it is God's will that no one he has been given would be lost, but it is also God's will that all men be saved (1 Tim 2:4) even though some may be lost.[15] Jesus even refers to the Father giving someone to him who was later lost (i.e., Judas) when he says of the apostles, "While I was with them, I kept them in your name, which you have given me; I have guarded them, and none of them is lost but the son of perdition, that the Scripture might be fulfilled" (Jn 17:12).[16] Saint John Chrysostom cites this very

---

[14] James R. White, *Drawn by the Father* (Lindenhurst, NY: Great Christian Books, 2000), 26.

[15] Calvinists respond to this by saying that 1 Timothy 2:4 only refers to God's desiring that "all kinds of men" be saved rather than every single man or every single human being be saved. Against this view, see I. Howard Marshall, "Universal Grace and Atonement in the Pastoral Epistles", in *The Grace of God and the Will of Man: A Case for Arminianism*, ed. Clark H. Pinnock (Grand Rapids, MI: Zondervan, 1989), 57–63.

[16] One could argue that Judas, or the Son of Perdition, was never a true believer and so his salvation was not lost. But this muddles Jesus' contrast of "losing" Judas in order to fulfill the Scriptures with his faithfulness in not "losing" the other apostles. If Judas were not at one point in a state of grace like the other apostles, then the comparison doesn't make sense. Moreover, in Matthew 19:28 Jesus says to the apostles, "You who have followed me will also sit on twelve thrones, judging the twelve tribes of Israel." According to Arie Zwiep in his monograph on Judas, "It makes no sense to apply the saying to a larger number of followers of Jesus, let alone to all believers. Originally, it was surely addressed to the twelve apostles." Arie W. Zwiep, *Judas and the Choice of Matthias: A Study on Context and Concern of Acts 1:15–26* (Heidelberg: Mohr Siebeck, 2004), 51.

example and says what Jesus meant is, " 'At least *for my part*, I will not lose them' [emphasis added]. So in another place, declaring the matter more clearly, he said, 'I will not reject anyone who comes to me.' "[17] According to Ben Witherington,

> We are not told here that someone God draws, or even Jesus chooses, may not commit apostasy or rebellion.... Even though the Fourth Gospel has a strong view of God's sovereignty, it also recognizes that there are things that happen that are contrary to God's desires and will.[18]

Finally, what about John 6:44? Jesus says, "No one can come to me unless the Father who sent me draws him; and I will raise him up at the last day." Those who believe salvation cannot be lost claim Jesus is teaching that everyone who is drawn by the Father to the Son will be raised up to inherit eternal life.[19] This means every true believer will never lose his salvation. But John 6:44 merely says a person can't come to Jesus unless the Father draws him; it does not say everyone who ever believed in Jesus will be saved.

Whoever comes to Jesus does so because the Father draws him, but the verse does not say that this person must always come to Jesus or that this drawing can't be resisted. In John 12:32 Jesus says, "And I, when I am lifted up from the earth, will draw all men to myself." Jesus uses the same verb here as in John 6:44 (*helkuo*), but he does not mean that no one can resist his drawing of them. John 6:44 does not say that those whom God draws to Jesus are unable either to resist coming to Jesus or that they can't leave Jesus after being drawn.

The perseverance of the saints and OSAS advocates' use of John 6 and 10 is further undermined by passages in John's Gospel that teach about the possible loss of salvation. Jesus says in John 15:6, "If a man does not abide in me, he is cast forth as a branch and withers; and the branches are gathered, thrown into the fire and burned."

It doesn't make sense to say, as some advocates of perseverance of the saints do, that these branches represent false believers since Jesus

---

[17] St. John Chrysostom, *Homilies on the Gospel of John* 81.2. I owe this observation to Jimmy Akin.

[18] Ben Witherington, *John's Wisdom: A Commentary on the Fourth Gospel* (Louisville, KY: Westminster John Knox Press, 1995), 158.

[19] James R. White, *The Potter's Freedom: A Defense of the Reformation and the Rebuttal of Norman Geisler's Chosen but Free* (Amityville, NY: Calvary Press, 2000), 85–86, 160–61.

speaks of the damned as those who don't abide or *remain* in him. Jesus is not talking about true and false believers but believers who produce and don't produce fruit, or good works. That's why he says of the Father, "Every branch of mine that bears no fruit, he takes away, and every branch that does bear fruit he prunes, that it may bear more fruit" (Jn 15:2).

OSAS advocates fare no better, as can be seen in Charles Ryrie's claim that this verse simply refers to the fire of God's judgment and a loss of rewards for the believer rather than a loss of salvation.[20] Throughout the Gospels when Jesus speaks of "the fire", he regularly refers to hell. Protestant scholar Preston Sprinkle says that John 15:6 refers to "the final state of the wicked as burned up chaff, weeds, and branches."[21]

In Matthew 18 Jesus tells the story of the servant who was mercifully forgiven by the king in a large matter but refused to forgive his fellow servant in a much smaller matter. The king threw the servant in jail, and Jesus told his audience, "So also my heavenly Father will do to every one of you, if you do not forgive your brother from your heart" (Mt 18:35). In Matthew 6:15 Jesus makes this teaching even plainer: "But if you do not forgive men their trespasses, neither will your Father forgive your trespasses."

Some perseverance of the saints defenders claim that this is just a parable about the importance of forgiveness and has nothing to do with salvation, but it clearly does. According to Protestant New Testament scholar Mel Shoemaker, "A failure to forgive others may result in the forfeiture and loss of the Father's forgiveness and our salvation."[22] In fact, this parable *directly teaches* the possibility of losing salvation. Note that the servant is *first* forgiven by the king and *then*, when he refuses to forgive his fellow servant, the king *revokes* his forgiveness. Jesus means for us to understand very clearly that we can *be forgiven* by God and *then* become unforgiven, losing our salvation.

Finally, in Matthew 24:47 Jesus says the master, or God, will set the faithful servant "over all his possessions". But the unfaithful or

[20] Charles Ryrie, *So Great Salvation: What It Means to Believe in Jesus Christ* (Chicago: Moody Publishers, 1997), 49–50.

[21] Preston Sprinkle, "Conclusion", in *Four Views on Hell*, ed. Preston Sprinkle, 2nd ed. (Grand Rapids, MI: Zondervan, 2016), 200.

[22] Mel Shoemaker, *The Theology of the Four Gospels* (Bloomington, IN: Thomas Nelson, 2011), 253.

wicked servant who beat his fellow servants will receive a much different fate. Jesus says the master will "put him with the hypocrites; there men will weep and gnash their teeth" (Mt 24:51), a common reference to eternal damnation. Notice the master will "put him" with the hypocrites. According to David Sim in his study on *Apocalyptic Eschatology in the Gospel of Matthew*, "Matthew makes no distinction between the ultimate fate of the wicked inside the ekklesia [or church] and the fate of those outside it."[23]

Robert Wilkin admits that this passage is talking about believers, but he claims that it and others like it are referring to a separate judgment for believers where they will only risk losing their heavenly rewards.[24] However, Scripture never speaks of two separate judgments on the Last Day, and Wilkin's suggestion that Matthew 24:51 only refers to God verbally rebuking Christians who engage in unrepentant, grave sin strains credulity. James Dunn says, "The warning of Matthew 24:48–51 is beyond doubt: that the returning master 'will cut him [the reckless servant] in two and appoint his portion with the hypocrites, where there shall be weeping and gnashing of teeth' (24:51). Can Wilkin really think that this means merely being 'verbally cut up at a future judgment'?"[25]

Throughout the Gospels Jesus links our initial union with him through faith and our final, eternal union with him through continued obedience. A lack of this obedience, as seen in Jesus' parables, can lead to the loss of salvation, or as John 3:36 says, "He who does not obey the Son shall not see life, but the wrath of God rests upon him."

## The Pauline Epistles

Defenders of perseverance of the saints usually appeal to Saint Paul's teaching on predestination and God's active work in finishing our faith to support their case. This includes Paul's promise that "he who began a good work in you will bring it to completion at the day of

---

[23] David Sim, *Apocalyptic Eschatology in the Gospel of Matthew* (Cambridge: Cambridge University Press, 1996), 238.

[24] Robert Wilkin, "Christians Will Be Judged according to Their Works at the *Rewards* Judgment, but Not at the *Final* Judgment", in *Four Views on the Role of Works at the Final Judgment*, ed. Alan Stanley (Grand Rapids, MI: Zondervan, 2013), 35.

[25] James Dunn, "Response to Wilkin", in Stanley, *Four Views*, 61.

Jesus Christ" (Phil 1:6) and the fact that believers are sealed with the Holy Spirit (Eph 1:13; 4:30). God also chose them before the foundation of the world to be holy and blameless in his sight (Eph 1:4). Finally, this sealing is a guarantee or down payment of the heavenly glory we will later inherit (Eph 1:14).[26]

But some of these verses refer to promises only for specific groups of people rather than all believers. In Philippians 1:6 Paul is "sure" or "persuaded" (Greek, *pepoithos*) that God will finish his good work in the Philippians because they supported him during his imprisonment. Even though their love and charity gives Paul confidence that they will persevere, Paul still prays that the Philippians' "love may abound" so they "may be pure and blameless for the day of Christ" (Phil 1:9–10). Even with the evidence of their good works, Paul cautions each of them to "work out your own salvation with fear and trembling" (Phil 2:12). According to the Protestant biblical scholar B.J. Oropeza:

> Paul does not seem to suggest that every individual Philippian believer will necessarily persevere to final salvation regardless of what he or she might believe or practice in the future prior to the Day of Christ. His exhortation for congregants to conduct themselves with a lifestyle befitting the gospel (1:27), his warning against the circumcision party (3:2), and his sorrow over apostates who were once faithful believers like the Philippians (3:18–19) direct us against such a conclusion.[27]

What about Paul's promises of God's predestination and believers being sealed with the Holy Spirit? The defender of perseverance of the saints incorrectly assumes that a seal can't be broken. Even though they are sealed with the Spirit, Paul warns Christians not to grieve that same Spirit (Eph 4:30). The Protestant pastor T. David Beck says that, as a seal, the Holy Spirit "protects Christians from judgment—unless they grieve him, in which case their protection will be removed and God will discipline them, just as he did the Israelites [see Is 63:10]".[28]

---

[26] Geisler, "Moderate Calvinist View", 74–75.

[27] B.J. Oropeza, *Jews, Gentiles, and the Opponents of Paul: Apostasy in the New Testament Communities*, vol. 2, *The Pauline Letters* (Eugene, OR: Wipf and Stock, 2012), 219.

[28] T. David Beck, *The Holy Spirit and the Renewal of All Things: Pneumatology in Paul and Jurgen Moltmann* (Cambridge: James Clarke, 2010), 34.

Later in Ephesians Paul says "immoral or impure" men have no inheritance in Christ (5:5) and applies this warning to his audience, saying, "Let no one deceive you with empty words, for it is because of these things that the wrath of God comes upon the sons of disobedience" (5:6). In his commentary on Ephesians, F. F. Bruce said, "The fact that they still have to be warned against such vices shows how strong, in a pagan environment, was the temptation to indulge in them even after conversion."[29] It also shows that Paul believes Christians need to be warned against these vices lest they commit them and lose their "inheritance in the kingdom of Christ and of God" (5:5).

Concerning Ephesians 1:4, it's true that God chose those elected to final salvation to be "holy and blameless before him", but as Ephesians 2:10 says, he also prepared good works for us to do, and the elect fail to do at least some of them. This means God's election of those who are "in Christ" does not prevent them from sinning, even gravely. Indeed, at the end of Ephesians Paul says Christ will present the Church as a whole to himself "without spot or wrinkle or any such thing, that she might be holy and blameless" (5:27).

Christ will bring the Church to salvation, but whether we remain in a saving union with the Church depends on our cooperation with God's grace given to us on earth. Paul makes this clear in Colossians 1:22–23, where he says that Christ's Crucifixion allows him to present us "holy and blameless and irreproachable before him· *provided that you continue in the faith* [emphasis added], stable and steadfast, not shifting from the hope of the gospel which you heard".

Similar warnings can be found throughout the Pauline corpus. For example, Paul spoke of Alexander and Hymenaeus, who "made shipwreck of their faith" (1 Tim 1:19). He wrote to the Corinthians about the gospel "by which you are saved, *if* [emphasis added] you hold it fast" and warned the Corinthians to "not be deceived" (1 Cor 15:33) about the seriousness of sin. Paul specifically told the Corinthians: "Neither the immoral, nor idolaters, nor adulterers, nor homosexuals, nor thieves, nor the greedy, nor drunkards, nor revilers, nor robbers will inherit the kingdom of God" (1 Cor 6:9–10).

---

[29] F. F. Bruce, *The Epistles to the Colossians, to Philemon, and to the Ephesians* (Grand Rapids, MI: Wm. B. Eerdmans, 1984), 371.

Presbyterian scholar Robert Gagnon says, "Paul was clearly concerned that believers might return to former patterns of sinful practices, including same-sex intercourse, practices that could lead to loss of salvation."[30]

Defenders of perseverance of the saints usually say that this passage does not describe true Christians engaging in these behaviors because Paul says, "And such were some of you. But you were washed, you were sanctified, you were justified in the name of the Lord Jesus Christ and in the Spirit of our God" (1 Cor 6:11). But Paul's reminder that the Corinthian Christians once engaged in gravely sinful behavior does not nullify his warning that they not return to that behavior. Imagine the director of a rehabilitation clinic telling his patients, "No addict will ever be healthy, and such were some of you. But you were treated, you were healed according to this clinic's mission." Just as they could return to their formerly destructive ways of life, so can Christians who reject the grace God gives them.

Paul himself believed he could be one of these Christians since he told the Corinthians, "I pommel my body and subdue it, lest after preaching to others I myself should be disqualified" (1 Cor 9:27). The word often rendered "disqualified" in this verse is *adokimos*, which Paul uses in other contexts to refer to Gentiles whom God gave up to sin (Rom 1:28) and false teachers who opposed the gospel (2 Tim 3:8). Paul considered it a real possibility that he might become an *adokimos* if he was not vigilant about his spiritual life. Regarding this passage, the Protestant biblical scholar C.K. Barrett said that Paul's "conversion, his baptism, his call to apostleship, his service to the Gospel, do not guarantee his eternal salvation".[31]

It was only at the very end of his life that Paul was confident in his salvation. He writes to Timothy, "The time of my departure has come. I have fought the good fight, I have finished the race, I have kept the faith" (2 Tim 4:6–7). This means that it is possible not to fight the good fight, it is possible to abandon the race, and it is possible for a Christian not to keep the faith. Paul makes this clear when

[30] Robert Gagnon, *The Bible and Homosexual Practice: Texts and Hermeneutics* (Nashville, TN: Abingdon Press, 2001), 288.

[31] C.K. Barrett, *First Epistle to the Corinthians*, 2nd ed. (New York: Continuum, 1994), 218.

he warns Timothy, "If we endure, we shall also reign with him; if we deny him, he also will deny us; if we are faithless, he remains faithful—for he cannot deny himself" (2 Tim 2:12–13).

The passage is clearly talking about true Christians since Paul says these same people will reign with Christ if they endure. This parallels Jesus' teaching that "he who endures to the end will be saved" (Mt 10:22) as well as his warning that "whoever denies me before men, I also will deny before my Father who is in heaven" (Mt 10:33). There is nothing in the text to indicate that Paul is talking about a hypothetical denial that could never happen. But doesn't the fact that God will be faithful even if we are faithless prove the OSAS thesis that God will always save us, even if we become unfaithful, unrepentant apostates?

God will never abandon us and God will never deny us, but that doesn't mean we won't do the same to him since we have the capacity to be faithless even though God does not. If God allows us to forsake our salvation, he is still faithful to us because he hasn't broken any of his promises. That's because, contrary to what perseverance of the saints and OSAS advocates claim, God never promises that all Christians are predestined to final salvation or that it is impossible for us to lose our salvation.

Proponents of perseverance of the saints also quote Saint Paul's promise that "neither death, nor life, nor angels, nor principalities, nor things present, nor things to come, nor powers, nor height, nor depth, nor anything else in all creation, will be able to separate us from the love of God in Christ Jesus our Lord" (Rom 8:38–39). They say this passage means that a believer's status as a beloved child of God is eternally secure because nothing in all of creation can separate us from the love of God.[32]

But notice that "sin" is conspicuously absent from this list. God loves everyone, including sinners, but if we sin grievously against God, we can cut ourselves off from his love. Indeed, just three chapters later, Paul describes the Gentiles as branches that were grafted onto the ancient olive tree of Israel. He says the unbelieving Jewish people

---

[32] Robert M. Zins, *Romanism: The Relentless Roman Catholic Assault on the Gospel of Jesus Christ!* (Huntsville, AL: White Horse Publications, 1995), 72.

were broken off because of their unbelief, but you stand fast only through faith. So do not become proud, but stand in awe. For if God did not spare the natural branches, neither will he spare you. Note then the kindness and the severity of God: severity toward those who have fallen, but God's kindness to you, *provided you continue in his kindness; otherwise you too will be cut off* [emphasis added]. (Rom 11:22)

Finally, Paul told the Galatians that if they forsake Christ and return to Judaism through circumcision, then they are "severed from Christ, you who would be justified by the law; you have fallen away from grace" (Gal 5:4). A perseverance of the saints advocate might claim that this only refers to Jews who never chose Christ but trusted in circumcision instead. However, the Greek word translated "severed" (*katargeo*) describes being released or discharged from something. The prominent Bauer-Arndt-Gingrich-Danker (BDAG) Greek lexicon says that just like a woman who is released from the marriage bond upon the death of her spouse (Rom 7:2), "those who aspire to righteousness through the law ... [are] estranged from Christ."[33] Concerning the phrase "fall from grace", Martin Luther said:

> To fall from grace means to lose the atonement, the forgiveness of sins, the righteousness, liberty, and life which Jesus has merited for us by His death and resurrection. To lose the grace of God means to gain the wrath and judgment of God, death, the bondage of the devil, and everlasting condemnation.[34]

## Non-Pauline Letters

Many advocates of perseverance of the saints cite 1 John 2:19 as evidence that apostates were never true believers. In that passage John describes how heretical teachers in his community "went out from us, but they were not of us". However, John is referring to a specific group of heretics, possibly the Docetists, who denied Jesus had a real physical body. He does not say everyone who ever leaves the

---

[33] William Arndt, Frederick W. Danker, and Walter Bauer, *A Greek-English Lexicon of the New Testament and Other Early Christian Literature*, 3rd ed. (Chicago: University of Chicago Press, 2000), 526.

[34] Martin Luther, *Commentary on Galatians*.

faith was not a true Christian. Moreover, he says these apostates were not "of us", not that they were "never of us". They could have been faithful Christians who became heretics and their heresy was exposed when they left the Church. Remember also that John originally recorded Jesus' warning that we must abide in him or we would be gathered and burned like useless, dead branches. In 1 John 2:28 he gives a similar warning: "Now, little children, abide in him, so that when he appears we may have confidence and not shrink away from him in shame at his coming."

Did Saint Peter teach perseverance of the saints or OSAS? Apologists usually appeal to 1 Peter 1:4–5, which speaks of "an inheritance which is imperishable, undefiled, and unfading, kept in heaven for you, who by God's power are guarded through faith for a salvation ready to be revealed in the last time." They might also cite Peter's teaching that believers have been redeemed with the incorruptible blood of Christ and have been born again of the incorruptible word of God (1 Pet 1:23).

These verses teach only that God and his salvation cannot be corrupted, not that believers are incorruptible. Why did Peter say it would be better for Christians to have never "known the way of righteousness than after knowing it to turn back from the holy commandment delivered to them"? (2 Pet 2:21). In commenting on this passage, Martin Luther said, "Through baptism these people threw out unbelief, had their unclean way of life washed away, and entered into a pure life of faith and love. Now they fall away into unbelief and ... soil themselves again in filth."[35]

Finally, perseverance of the saints and OSAS advocates often cite the Letter to the Hebrews where its author says Christ has obtained redemption for us (9:12) through his body being offered once for all (10:10). These apologists claim that salvation cannot be lost, because Christ has perfected for all time those who are being sanctified (10:14). They also say Christ "is able for all time to save those who draw near to God through him, since he always lives to make intercession for them" (7:25). But these passages teach that Christ's sacrifice was the perfect atonement for sin and, unlike older animal sacrifices, it never has to be repeated.

[35] *Luther's Works*, 30:190.

Christ's sacrifice is capable of perfecting us and making us holy, but Hebrews does not teach that Christ's sacrifice will automatically cause every believer to go to heaven. Concerning Hebrews 7:25, this passage could mean that Jesus can save us at all times (unlike the old high priests who eventually died and had to be replaced) or he can save us from any sin. But notice that the salvation Christ provides is only for those who draw near to God through Christ. If we don't, as Hebrews 3:14 says, "hold our first confidence firm to the end," then we will not remain with Christ as partakers of his grace.

The author of Hebrews even says that "if we sin deliberately after receiving the knowledge of the truth, there no longer remains a sacrifice for sins, but a fearful prospect of judgment, and a fury of fire which will consume the adversaries" (10:26–27). He then compares the punishment for lawbreakers in the Old Covenant, which was death, to the worse punishment awaiting lawbreakers in the New Covenant. He then asks, "How much worse punishment do you think will be deserved by the man who has spurned the Son of God, and profaned the blood of the covenant by which he was sanctified, and outraged the Spirit of grace?" (10:29).

If the punishment in the New Covenant is "much worse" than the punishment in the Old Covenant, then it can't be the same punishment, or physical death. It must instead be everlasting spiritual death or separation from God.

This passage can't refer to the fate of false professors, or people who never were "true Christians", because it speaks of those who were previously sanctified and had received knowledge of the truth. Norm Geisler agrees that the author is speaking of true believers, but he denies that these verses refute the doctrine of perseverance of the saints. He claims that the passage refers only to a loss of rewards and not a loss of salvation because the author is "affirming with confidence that believers will not be lost [v. 39]".[36]

But verse 39 is not a promise for all believers. It is an expression of hope that believers would not "shrink back and [be] destroyed" but "have faith and keep their souls". That coheres with the author's other exhortations that his audience keep the possession of their salvation, not throw away their confidence, and maintain their endurance

[36] Geisler, "Moderate Calvinist View", 100.

so they may receive their promised reward. Thomas Schreiner makes the salient point that "the author of Hebrews uses *reward* to describe God's salvation which is of inestimable worth."[37]

If the passage is talking about believers, then it warns about the loss of salvation. Perhaps that's why James White, following the argument set forth by the Puritan theologian John Owen, embraces the incredible interpretation that the "he" in Hebrews 10:29 is not the man who profaned the blood of the covenant that sanctified him (thus earning a divinely decreed punishment). Instead, White says, "The writer is referring to *Christ* [emphasis in original] as the one who is sanctified, set apart, shown to be holy, by His own sacrifice."[38]

While "sanctified" (Greek, *hagiazo*) can mean "set apart", throughout the Letter to the Hebrews it's more commonly associated with making something holy through purification (Heb 9:13; 10:10; 10:14). Jesus uses the word to describe how he set himself apart for the sake of his disciples (Jn 17:19), but nowhere in the New Testament is the blood of Christ said to sanctify Christ himself. In fact, Hebrews 13:12 says, "Jesus also suffered outside the gate in order to sanctify the people through his own blood." Schreiner says of interpretations like White's, "It is awkward and unnatural to see a reference to Jesus in the pronoun instead of believers, for it makes little sense to say Jesus was sanctified by his own blood. Jesus is the one who sanctifies in Hebrews (2:11), not the one who is sanctified."[39] Far from teaching perseverance of the saints, the author of Hebrews says:

> It is impossible to restore again to repentance those who have once been enlightened, who have tasted the heavenly gift, and have become partakers of the Holy Spirit, and have tasted the goodness of the word

[37] Thomas R. Schreiner and Ardel B. Caneday, *The Race Set before Us: A Biblical Theology of Perseverance & Assurance* (Downers Grove, IL: InterVarsity Press, 2001), 92. Schreiner and Caneday claim that those who apostatize only prove, "by their failure to persevere, to be impostors" (ibid., 243). However, the duo fails to derive from Paul's writings any evidence that he believed the apostates he described (Alexander and Hymenaeus) were impostors. They even say Paul is describing their apostasy from the viewpoint of those who assume they are true believers (ibid., 231). This means it is only the authors' theological presuppositions about salvation that support their interpretation, presuppositions we have shown in this chapter to be in error.

[38] White, *Potter's Freedom*, 245.

[39] Thomas Schreiner, *Commentary on Hebrews* (Nashville, TN: B&H Publishing Group, 2015), 327.

of God and the powers of the age to come, if they then commit apostasy, since they crucify the Son of God on their own account and hold him up to contempt. (6:4–6)

Defenders of perseverance of the saints usually admit this is one of the most difficult passages for them to explain. Those who opt for the "false professor" explanation, as Calvin does, claim that it is possible for a person to develop a close, emotional connection to the gospel message, even to the point of tasting heavenly realities, without becoming a true believer.[40] But this doesn't explain how the person once had repentance and the Holy Spirit (both of which only believers possess) and then commits apostasy (which is something only believers can do).[41] As Ben Witherington says, "A more fulsome description of a Christian would be hard to find in the New Testament.... They have partaken of the heavenly gift—this is surely the same thing as saying they are saved."[42]

Others claim that the passage is only speaking of an "impossible hypothetical", or a situation that could never happen to a true Christian. The King James Version opts for this approach by translating the text, "For it is impossible for those who were once enlightened ... *if* [emphasis added] they shall fall away, to renew them again unto repentance." But the word "if" is not in the Greek text. The famous Methodist biblical commentator Adam Clarke said that some early Reformers added this word so that the passage "might not appear to contradict the doctrine of the perseverance of the saints".[43]

---

[40] "I cannot admit that all this is any reason why [God] should not grant the reprobate also some taste of his grace, why he should not irradiate their minds with some sparks of his light, why he should not give them some perception of his goodness, and in some sort engrave his word on their hearts." John Calvin, *Calvin's Commentaries*, vol. 44, *Hebrews*, trans. John King (1847–1850), "Hebrews Chapter 6, Chapter 6:3–6", http://www.sacred-texts.com/chr/calvin/cc44/cc44011.htm.

[41] Craig R. Koester explains how believers can "*become partakers of the Holy Spirit* [emphasis in original]. 'Partakers' share in a heavenly calling and in Christ (3:1, 14). Like the word 'taste' in 6:4b and 6:5a, to become a 'partaker' (*metochos*) means receiving God's Spirit into oneself. Cf. 'partaking' of milk (*metechein*, 5:13)." Craig R. Koester, *Hebrews* (New York: Doubleday, 2001), 314.

[42] Ben Witherington, *Letters and Homilies for Jewish Christians: A Socio-Rhetorical Commentary on Hebrews, James and Jude* (Downers Grove, IL: InterVarsity Press, 2007), 212.

[43] Adam Clarke, *Commentary on the Bible* (1831), "Hebrews Chapter 6, Hebrews 6:6", http://www.sacred-texts.com/bib/cmt/clarke/heb006.htm.

However, does this passage contradict Catholic theology since it claims some sins, such as apostasy, cannot be forgiven? Within the context of Hebrews, it seems most likely that the author is referring to the hard hearts of Jewish Christians who return to Judaism and so "crucify the Son of God on their own account" by defending the validity of the Crucifixion. In this case, the author is using hyperbolic language to describe the difficulty of one of these apostates returning to the faith. Hebrews does not deny that God is willing to forgive any sin a person confesses, including apostasy. It does deny, however, that a believer can never become an apostate or lose his salvation.

## Patristic Evidence

Not only is the Calvinist concept of perseverance of the saints or OSAS unbiblical; these doctrines are also contrary to what Christians in the first fifteen hundred years of Church history believed. In the second century Saint Irenaeus described how "those who do not obey Him, being disinherited by Him, have ceased to be His sons."[44] The doctrine of perseverance of the saints was simply unknown in the Church until the writings of Calvin in the sixteenth century.

OSAS was also unknown before the writings of sixteenth-century antinomians such as Johannes Agricola, who claimed that Christians were not obligated to follow any of the laws of the Old Testament, including the Ten Commandments. Rather than argue for OSAS having a patristic pedigree, Wilkin claims, "The first generation after the Apostles distorted the good news which the Apostles had entrusted to their care." He also says that "the Reformers looked back to Christ and the Apostles rather than the church fathers for their view of salvific repentance and the Gospel."[45]

Some advocates of perseverance of the saints try to trace their doctrine back to Augustine, but he said that if "being already regenerate and justified, [a believer] relapses of his own will into an evil life, assuredly he cannot say, 'I have not received,' because of his own free choice to evil he has lost the grace of God, that he had

---

[44] St. Irenaeus, *Against Heresies* 4.41.3.

[45] Robert Wilkin, "The Doctrine of Repentance in Church History", *Journal of the Grace Evangelical Society* 1, no. 1 (Fall 1988), https://faithalone.org/journal/1988ii/wilkin.html.

received."[46] According to the Calvinist biblical scholar John Jefferson Davis, Augustine believed that "one's justification and baptismal regeneration could be rejected and lost through sin and unbelief."[47]

Finally, some perseverance of the saints and OSAS advocates claim that the denial of their view leads to "works-based salvation" or the futile effort to earn eternal life through one's own merits. But Augustine, as well as the Catholic Church as a whole, has never taught that a person must rely solely on himself to attain salvation. While commenting on 1 Corinthians 10:12 ("let any one who thinks that he stands take heed lest he fall"), Augustine said, "He who falls, falls by his own will, and he who stands, stands by God's will."[48]

This is why the *Catechism* teaches that "to live, grow, and persevere in the faith until the end we must nourish it with the word of God; we must beg the Lord to increase our faith; it must be 'working through charity,' abounding in hope, and rooted in the faith of the Church (Gal 5:6; Rom 15:13; cf. Jas 2:14–26)" (*CCC* 162).

---

[46] St. Augustine, *Treatise on Rebuke and Grace* 9.

[47] John Jefferson Davis, "The Perseverance of the Saints: A History of the Doctrine", *Journal of the Evangelical Theological Society* 34, no. 2 (June 1991): 214.

[48] St. Augustine, *On the Gift of Perseverance* 19.

Part IV

What Is the Body of Christ?

# 13

# Purgatory

At the beginning of the Protestant Reformation the debate over purgatory concerned not its existence, but the Church's authority to remit punishments to be endured there. For example, in his *Ninety-Five Theses* Martin Luther wrote, "The pope does very well when he grants remission to souls in purgatory, not by the power of the keys, which he does not have, but by way of intercession for them."[1] Four years later Luther said, "The existence of a purgatory I have never denied. I still hold that it exists, as I have written and admitted many times though I have found no way of proving it incontrovertibly from Scripture or reason."[2]

But as the Reformation progressed, the vast majority of Protestants came to reject this doctrine. Calvin said, "Since purgatory is constructed out of many blasphemies and is daily propped up with new ones, and since it incites so many grave offenses, it is certainly not to be winked at."[3] For many modern Protestants, purgatory is the paradigmatic example of Catholicism's unbiblical foundation. This attitude is revealed when the first or most popular question Protestants ask Catholics is, where is purgatory in the Bible?

However, in recent years some Protestants have come to see the wisdom of belief in purgatory. For example, after confessing how the desire to pray for the dead comes naturally to him, C. S. Lewis said in his *Letters to Malcolm: Chiefly on Prayer,*

---

[1] Martin Luther, "The 95 Theses", Thesis 26 (KDG Wittenberg, 1997), http://www.luther.de/en/95thesen.html.

[2] Martin Luther, "The Thirty Seventh Article", *Luther's Works*, 32:95.

[3] John Calvin, *Institutes of the Christian Religion* 3.5.6. Cited in *Calvin: Institutes of the Christian Religion*, ed. John T. McNeill, trans. Ford Lewis Battles (Louisville, KY: Westminster John Knox Press, 1960), 676.

Our souls *demand* purgatory, don't they? Would it not break the heart if God said to us, "It is true, my son, that your breath smells and your rags drip with mud and slime, but we are charitable here and no one will upbraid you with these things, nor draw away from you. Enter into the joy"? Should we not reply, "With submission, sir, and if there is no objection, I'd *rather* be cleaned first." "It may hurt, you know"— "Even so, sir." [Emphases in original.][4]

## Purgatory Explained

The Latin word *purgatorius* is an adjective that refers to "cleaning" or "purifying". As we will see when we discuss the history of this doctrine, while the Latin noun *purgatorium* comes from the Middle Ages, the idea that souls undergo *poenae purgatoriae*, or purgatorial punishment, after death can be traced back to the early Church. The *Catechism* explains the Church's current understanding of purgatory in this way:

All who die in God's grace and friendship, but still imperfectly puri-fied, are indeed assured of their eternal salvation; but after death they undergo purification, so as to achieve the holiness necessary to enter the joy of heaven. The Church gives the name *Purgatory* to this final purification of the elect. (*CCC* 1030–31)

This short description clears up two common misconceptions about purgatory. First, purgatory is not an opportunity to accept God's offer of salvation after death. Only those who "die in God's grace and friendship" go to purgatory. Those who die in a state of mortal sin can never have their sins purified after death. Rather, they have put themselves in a "state of definitive self-exclusion from com-munion with God and the blessed", or what is commonly called hell (*CCC* 1033).

Second, purgatory is not an alternative fate to heaven or hell. The Reformed theologian Charles Spurgeon argued that if a person knows he is "saved", or has full assurance of salvation and so he will definitely go to heaven, then he need not worry about purgatory. In one sermon he preached:

[4] C. S. Lewis, *Letters to Malcolm: Chiefly on Prayer* (New York: Harcourt, 1992), 108–9.

If the Roman Catholic could get the full assurance of salvation, surely the Cardinals would hardly find money enough to buy their red hats. For where were purgatory then? Purgatory is an impossibility, if full assurance be possible. If a man knows himself to be saved, then he is not to be troubled with a silly fear about waiting in the intermediate state, to be purified with fire, before he can enter into heaven.[5]

But the *Catechism* says all souls that enter into purgatory are "assured of their eternal salvation", or they will eventually spend eternity with God in heaven (being prepared *for* heaven takes nothing away *from* the hope of spending eternity in heaven).

Remember that Revelation 21:27 says of heaven, "Nothing unclean shall enter it," and James 3:2 reminds us that "we all stumble in many ways" (NIV). Sins that do not separate a person from God's love and friendship, or what are called venial sins, still harm our souls. The *Catechism* says this kind of sin "weakens charity; it manifests a disordered affection for created goods; it impedes the soul's progress in the exercise of the virtues and the practice of the moral good; it merits temporal punishment" (*CCC* 1863).

Prior to entering heaven the believer's soul must be cleansed of the effects of these sins, and this takes place in purgatory. While the imagery of cleansing fire has often been used to describe purgatory, the Church has not defined the nature of this purification or how long it takes. Pope Benedict XVI said that "it is clear that we cannot calculate the 'duration' of this transforming burning in terms of the chronological measurements of this world."[6] In his book *Eschatology* he also said:

Purgatory is not, as Tertullian thought, some kind of supra-worldly concentration camp where one is forced to undergo punishments in a more or less arbitrary fashion. Rather it is the inwardly necessary process of transformation in which a person becomes capable of Christ,

---

[5] Rev. C. H. Spurgeon, "Full Assurance", Sermon no. 384, delivered at the Metropolitan Tabernacle, Newington, April 28, 1861, http://archive.spurgeon.org/sermons/0384.php.

[6] Pope Benedict XVI, encyclical letter *Spe Salvi* (November 30, 2007), no. 47, http://w2.vatican.va/content/benedict-xvi/en/encyclicals/documents/hf_ben-xvi_enc_20071130_spe-salvi.html.

capable of God [i.e., capable of full unity with Christ and God] and thus capable of unity with the whole communion of saints.[7]

## Scripture and the Afterlife

According to the twenty-second article of the Church of England's Thirty-Nine Articles of Religion, "The Romish doctrine of purgatory" is "a fond thing, vainly invented, and grounded upon no warranty of Scripture". Ironically, Protestants who claim that purgatory does not exist because every believer is immediately united with Christ after death are the ones who lack a scriptural warrant for their belief. As the Protestant author William Edward Fudge notes:

> While the Reformers talked about last things, they never did construct an eschatology using the building blocks of scripture.... Luther and Calvin rejected the Roman Catholic doctrine of purgatory, for example, not because they made a thorough study of scriptural eschatology and found it missing, but because purgatory clearly contradicted the doctrine of justification that they had discovered in the Bible.[8]

Protestants usually cite only two passages to prove all believers are immediately united with Christ after death and do not undergo purification: Philippians 1:23 and 2 Corinthians 5:8.[9]

In the first passage, Paul is speaking to the Philippians about his desire to serve Christ on earth and how it conflicts with his desire to be with Christ in heaven. He writes, "My desire is to depart and be with Christ, for that is far better. But to remain in the flesh is more necessary on your account." But Paul never says this union would take place immediately after death or that it would not involve purification.

---

[7] Joseph Cardinal Ratzinger, *Eschatology: Death and Eternal Life*, 2nd ed. (Washington, DC: Catholic University of America Press, 2007), 230. Cited in Jimmy Akin, "How to Explain Purgatory to Protestants", JimmyAkin.com, accessed July 18, 2017, http://jimmyakin.com /how-to-explain-purgatory-to-protestants.

[8] William Edward Fudge, *The Fire That Consumes: A Biblical and Historical Study of the Doctrine of Final Punishment*, 3rd ed. (Eugene, OR: Wipf and Stock, 2011), 13.

[9] "Since Philippians 1:23 and 2 Corinthians 5:8 clearly teach that all believers in Christ go straight to heaven at the moment of death, how do you reconcile this with the Catholic doctrine of purgatory?" Ron Rhodes, *Reasoning from the Scriptures with Catholics* (Eugene, OR: Harvest House Publishing, 2000), 241.

To make a comparison, in 2 Corinthians 5:2 Paul says of our future resurrection bodies that we "long to put on our heavenly dwelling". But Paul describes this taking place at an unspecified time in the future (1 Cor 15:52). Consequently, if there will be an interval after death before our bodies will be perfected, then there is no inconsistency in saying there will be a similar interval after death where our souls will be perfected.

A more egregious error is found in appeals to 2 Corinthians 5:8, which many people paraphrase this way: "To be absent from the body is to be present with the Lord." But that is not what the verse says. Instead, Paul writes:

> So we are always of good courage; we know that while we are at home in the body we are away from the Lord. For we walk by faith, not by sight. We are of good courage, and we would rather be away from the body and at home with the Lord. So whether we are at home or away, we make it our aim to please him. (2 Cor 5:6–9)

If I say, "When I am at work in the office, I am away from my family," that does not mean the moment I leave my office I will be home with my family (I might have to endure a daily commute, for example).[10] Likewise, a desire to be with Christ does not prove there will be no process of purification one must undergo in order to achieve that desire. In fact, 2 Corinthians 5:10 teaches that we can be apart from the body but not at home with the Lord. It says, "We must all appear before the judgment seat of Christ, so that each one may receive good or evil, according to what he has done in the body."

## Purgatory and Ancient Judaism

The *Catechism* says the doctrine of purgatory "is also based on the practice of prayer for the dead, already mentioned in Sacred Scripture" (*CCC* 1032). This is a reference to 2 Maccabees 12:39–45,

---

[10] A very similar example reached independently from this one can be found in Jimmy Akin, *A Daily Defense* (San Diego: Catholic Answers Press, 2016), 41.

which describes how Judas Maccabeus discovered amulets dedicated to pagan idols under the bodies of his fallen comrades. Judas and his fellow soldiers "turned to prayer, begging that the sin which had been committed might be wholly blotted out" (12:42). Judas then collected two thousand drachmas of silver to send as a sin offering to the Temple in Jerusalem. Verse 45 says, "He made atonement for the dead, that they might be delivered from their sin." According to Pope Benedict XVI:

> This early Jewish idea of an intermediate state includes the view that these souls are not simply in a sort of temporary custody but, as the parable of the rich man illustrates [Lk 16:19–31], are already being punished or are experiencing a provisional form of bliss. There is also the idea that this state can involve purification and healing which mature the soul for communion with God. The early Church took up these concepts, and in the Western Church they gradually developed into the doctrine of Purgatory.[11]

Even though Protestants do not regard the deuterocanonical books as Scripture (despite what we've shown), they should at least recognize their role as a *historical* witness to purgatory. Indeed, a careful review of Second Temple and Talmudic literature reveals the belief that Gehenna, or the place for the wicked after death, included a state of purification for less wicked souls prior to their admittance into paradise (the Talmud says this process takes at most twelve months).[12] According to Simcha Paul Raphael, a professor of Jewish studies at Temple University, "Gehenna served as a realm of purgation and purification.... After this experience, the soul is sufficiently purified and able to enter the supernal postmortem realm of Gan Eden, the Garden of Eden."[13]

Some Protestant apologists claim that this passage cannot support the doctrine of purgatory, because the slain soldiers were guilty of

[11] Pope Benedict XVI, *Spe Salvi*, no. 45.

[12] Jacques Le Goff, *The Birth of Purgatory*, trans. Arthur Goldhammer (Chicago: University of Chicago Press, 1986), 40.

[13] Simcha Paul Raphael, *Jewish Views of the Afterlife* (Lanham, MD: Rowan and Littlefield Publishers, 2009), 145.

idolatry, which is a mortal sin that cannot be forgiven after death.[14] But wearing these amulets may represent the less serious sin of superstition and not the graver sin of idolatry (similar to modern people who take horoscopes too literally but don't worship the celestial bodies they are based upon). This objection also anachronistically projects modern Catholic teaching about mortal sin onto Jews who were not sure if idolatry, while a serious offense against God, would condemn someone to everlasting damnation.

But even if these men did commit an objectively grave sin, Judas could not have known that they were damned. The men may have repented of trusting in idols just before dying, or God may have had mercy on them for some other reason. Since Christians pray for the salvation of any person who has died, no matter how sinful he seemed, there would be nothing wrong with Judas making a sacrificial offering on behalf of these men and entrusting their souls to the God whose mercy endures forever (Ps 136).

Finally, Luther said that even if the book of Second Maccabees were inspired, this passage would not support the doctrine of purgatory, because no other passage in Scripture corroborates it. Even if that were true, it represents a double standard since Christians use a Trinitarian baptismal formula even though only one Scripture passage alludes to it (Mt 28:19). But as we will see, the witness of Scripture and Christian tradition supports the doctrine of purgatory.

## The Teaching of Jesus

In Matthew 5:21–22 Jesus concludes a teaching on anger by saying that varying degrees of anger toward a brother will lead to varying degrees of judgment and punishment. He then advises his listeners to reconcile with an "accuser" (v. 25) who makes a charge against them. If they don't befriend their accuser, that person will "hand you over to the judge, and the judge to the guard, and you be put in prison; truly, I say to you, you will never get out till you have

---

[14] See William Webster, *The Church of Rome at the Bar of History* (Carlisle, PA: Banner of Truth Trust, 1995), 112. See also James McCarthy, *The Gospel according to Rome* (Eugene, OR: Harvest House Publishers, 1995), 109.

paid the last penny" (Mt 5:25–26). Saint Cyprian of Carthage used these verses in the third century to compare the immediate reward martyrs receive with the spiritual prison and purification other believers must endure on account of their sins.[15] Calvin even said, "If in this passage the judge signifies God, the accuser the devil, the guard the angel, the prison purgatory, I shall willingly yield to them."[16]

In response, some Protestants (including Calvin) claim that Matthew 5:25–26 contains advice related only to earthly dangers, such as being a victim of Roman law courts, and says nothing about punishment in the afterlife.[17] But this contradicts the eschatological focus of the Sermon on the Mount and its contrast between those who will inherit the kingdom of heaven and those who will suffer in the fires of hell. Moreover, nothing prevents this passage from having a literal meaning about reconciling with earthly debtors as well as a spiritual meaning about reconciling with spiritual accusers.

Note that in Matthew 6:12, according to most translations, Jesus teaches us to ask God to forgive our "debts" (Greek, *opheilema*), whereas Luke 11:4 uses the word "sins" (Greek, *hamartia*), meaning the two concepts are related.[18] Furthermore, the Greek word for prison used in Matthew 5:25 (Greek, *phulake*) is also used to describe the place where souls were kept for Jesus to preach to after his Crucifixion (1 Pet 3:19). Saint Basil said that any saints who have wrestled with sin or demonic powers in this life and were left wounded are

---

[15] "It is one thing, when cast into prison, not to go out thence until one has paid the uttermost farthing; another thing at once to receive the wages of faith and courage." St. Cyprian, *Epistle* 51.20. Tertullian said, "Inasmuch as we understand the prison pointed out in the Gospel to be Hades, Matthew 5:25 and as we also interpret the uttermost farthing to mean the very smallest offense which has to be recompensed there before the resurrection, no one will hesitate to believe that the soul undergoes in Hades some compensatory discipline, without prejudice to the full process of the resurrection." *The Soul* 58.

[16] John Calvin, *Institutes of the Christian Religion* 3.5.7. Cited in McNeill and Battles, *Calvin: Institutes of the Christian Religion*, 677.

[17] See, for example, Wayne Grudem, *Systematic Theology: An Introduction to Biblical Doctrine* (Grand Rapids, MI: Zondervan, 1994), 819.

[18] The second Catholic edition of the RSV translates *opheilema* as "trespasses" to underscore that the debts are our sins or trespasses against God and man. The *Catechism* says, "There is no limit or measure to this essentially divine forgiveness, whether one speaks of 'sins' as in Luke (11:4), 'debts' as in Matthew (6:12). We are always debtors: 'Owe no one anything, except to love one another' " (*CCC* 2845).

"detained" after death while the unwounded are "brought by Christ into their rest".[19]

Some critics say Jesus' declaration to the thief on the cross, "Today you will be with me in Paradise" (Lk 23:43), refutes the doctrine of purgatory. They say the good thief was immediately forgiven of all his sins and did not have to endure any temporal punishment in purgatory. However, it is unwise to take Jesus' treatment of one individual and apply it to believers as a general rule. We are not in a position to know if the thief needed to be purified of sin or how long such purification would take after death (Paul speaks of us being changed at the resurrection of the dead in "the twinkling of an eye" in 1 Cor 15:52). This means Luke 22:43 does not support the view that believers do not require purification prior to admittance into heaven.

## The Teaching of Saint Paul

In the third chapter of his First Letter to the Corinthians, Paul is discussing the role of ministers in the Church who build on the foundation of Jesus Christ (v. 11). He then writes, "Now if any one builds on the foundation with gold, silver, precious stones, wood, hay, straw—each man's work will become manifest; for the Day will disclose it, because it will be revealed with fire, and the fire will test what sort of work each one has done" (vv. 12–13). According to David Garland in his acclaimed commentary on First Corinthians, " 'The day' refers to the end-time judgment.... This fiery day will 'test' each one's work."[20]

Paul continues, "If the work which any man has built on the foundation survives, he will receive a reward. If any man's work is burned up, he will suffer loss, though he himself will be saved, but only as through fire" (vv. 14–15). While Paul initially speaks of ministers, the same principle he articulates here applies to all believers since God has prepared good works for each of us to walk in (Eph 2:10). Therefore, this text is an important witness to how believers in general will be judged after death.

---

[19] St. Basil of Caesarea, *On Psalm* 7.2. Cited in William A. Jurgens, *The Faith of the Early Fathers*, vol. 2 (Collegeville, MN: Liturgical Press, 1979), 21.

[20] David Garland, *1 Corinthians* (Grand Rapids, MI: Baker Academic, 2003), 118.

In his book *Saved through Fire: The Fiery Ordeal in New Testament Eschatology*, Daniel Frayer-Griggs says that while "anti-papal rhetoric" is absent from modern commentaries, "reticence regarding the potentially purifying function of fire persists." He goes on to say, "The prevailing consensus insists that the fire of 1 Cor. 3:13–15 plays no soteriological function in the purification of individuals whatsoever."[21] Frayer-Griggs rejects the idea that the New Testament teaches the doctrine of purgatory, but he accepts that its descriptions of fire often refer to purification in the afterlife, which Joseph Ratzinger called the "root concept" of the Western doctrine of purgatory.[22]

Protestants sometimes argue that the fire in First Corinthians 3:15 tests the builders' work rather than the builders themselves; there is no mention of purification in the passage, and the phrase to be saved "but only as through fire" is a proverbial expression like "to be saved by the skin of one's teeth", which refers to a narrow escape, and not to a cleansing purification after death. This passage, they say, refers to a loss of heavenly rewards only due to lackluster ministerial efforts, not postmortem purification for sins. But Frayer-Griggs shows how each of these claims does not withstand scrutiny.

First, Frayer-Griggs argues that the works to which Paul referred were not activities or deeds, but persons. In 1 Corinthians 9:1 Paul refers to the Corinthians themselves as "my workmanship" (Greek, *Ergon*; also translated "work"), and in chapter 3 he calls them "God's building" (v. 9) and "God's temple" (v. 16). The only other place in Scripture where gold, silver, and precious stones are built on a foundation was Solomon's Temple (1 Kings 5–6). Frayer-Griggs then notes how many of the terms Paul uses concerning precious metals, fire, and temples can be found in the prophet Malachi. He writes:

> These precious metals represent human persons. As fire purifies the sons of Levi in Malachi 3, the fire that attends "the day" in 1 Corinthians 3 will test the converts like silver and gold; what is imperfect will be burned away, and they will be refined and purified.[23]

---

[21] Daniel Frayer-Griggs, *Saved through Fire: The Fiery Ordeal in New Testament Eschatology* (Eugene, OR: Wipf and Stock, 2016), 201.

[22] Ratzinger, *Eschatology*, 224.

[23] Frayer-Griggs, *Saved through Fire*, 208.

Even if the "works" were the builders' deeds and teachings, rather than the people they built up, it makes no sense to say those works are tested without any repercussions for the builders. Works are a reflection of a person's moral character, so inferior works represent inferior moral character. But if the works are persons, then Frayer-Griggs says the fire will reveal the competent builders and purify the incompetent ones. Saint John Chrysostom shares this view, saying the builder must be at fault for the failure of his disciples:

> If, on the contrary, [the builder] was not the cause but the disciples became such through their own perverseness, he is no whit deserving of punishment, no, nor yet of sustaining loss: he, I say, who built so well. In what sense then does he say, "he shall suffer loss?"[24]

One Protestant response is that the builder doesn't receive any heavenly rewards. Merrill Unger describes his situation before God like a man who escapes his burning home and only survives with the clothes on his back. Just as he has no possessions to show anyone, the sinful Christian has no good work to show Christ in order to receive heavenly rewards.[25] But the passage doesn't say he shall "lose rewards" or "not receive his reward"; it says, "If any man's work is burned up, he will suffer loss, though he himself will be saved, but only as through fire."

Frayer-Griggs shows that the phrase "as through fire" is not proverbial, or it is not used as it is in Unger's house fire example. Instead, it is instrumental—the fire, whether literally or metaphorically, is the *means* by which a person is saved and explains why the person suffers a loss at the judgment. This leads Frayer-Griggs to conclude that "the fire of divine judgment on 'the day' appears to be the circumstance through which the builder is purified of his sins and through which Christ saves."[26]

The evidence for this comes from the fact that the phrase "through fire" (*dia puros*) is used in an instrumental sense throughout the Septuagint, including in the intertestamental literature (i.e., the fire is a

[24] St. John Chrysostom, *Homily 9 on First Corinthians*.

[25] Cited in Ron Rhodes, *Heaven: The Undiscovered Country: Exploring the Wonder of the Afterlife* (Eugene, OR: Wipf and Stock, 2003), 139.

[26] Frayer-Griggs, *Saved through Fire*, 216.

means through which something is accomplished and not just part of a proverbial expression). Philo, who was a contemporary of Paul, uses the term primarily in an instrumental sense, and of the two times it is used in the apostolic Fathers it refers to how fire literally judged Sodom and how gold is tested in fire (1 Pet 1:7 speaks of faith being tested by fire in a similar way).[27] Moreover, in the New Testament, as well as the surrounding Greek literature, when the verb "to save" (*sozo*) is combined with the preposition "through" (*dia*) and with a noun in the genitive case, the preposition is almost always used in an instrumental sense.[28] Thus, as E. P. Sanders says:

> Speaking of himself and Apollos, he wrote that the work of a not-very-good apostle would be burned up and that the apostle himself would be saved "only as through fire," that is singed (1 Cor. 3:15).... Paul is discussing people who will be saved, but they will be commended or lightly punished at the judgment, depending on their deeds.[29]

Finally, some apologists claim that First Corinthians 3:15 has no bearing on the doctrine of purgatory because it describes a judgment that will take place on the Last Day, and unpurified believers who die before the end of the world will still go to purgatory.[30] Jimmy Akin provides a helpful reply:

> Paul, at this point in his life, was envisioning the Second Coming as so close that he and other ministers would likely still be alive when it arrived (1 Thess. 4:17). He therefore conflates the end of the world with the end of our lives. However, it would later be made clear that the world would go on for some time, and there is thus an anticipation of the final judgment that occurs with the particular judgment at death. Thus the purifying judgment occurs with death and its results will be reaffirmed at the final judgment.[31]

---

[27] See 3 Macc 2:29; 4 Macc 7:12; *1 Clement* 11:1; *Shepherd of Hermas* 4.3–4; Frayer-Griggs, *Saved through Fire*, 210.

[28] Frayer-Griggs, *Saved through Fire*, 213.

[29] E. P. Sanders, *Judaism: Practice and Belief, 63 BCE–66 CE* (Minneapolis: Fortress Press, 2016), 448.

[30] Norman L. Geisler and Ralph E. MacKenzie, *Roman Catholics and Evangelicals: Agreements and Differences* (Grand Rapids, MI: Baker Books, 1995), 335.

[31] Taken from personal correspondence made during preparation of this manuscript.

## The Historical Evidence

It's not uncommon for Protestants to claim that purgatory was "invented" in the late Middle Ages. For example, the Anglican theologian Gerald Bray calls purgatory "a medieval invention that brought a new sense of order and purpose to previously vague notions of what life after death held in store".[32] Some critics even claim that purgatory was created to enrich the pope through the donations offered for Masses said on behalf of the dead.[33] But placing purgatory this late in Christian history ignores clear references to the doctrine that can be found centuries earlier.

For example, in the *City of God* Saint Augustine writes, "Of those who suffer temporary punishments after death, all are not doomed to those everlasting pains which are to follow that judgment." He also speaks of some who will "not only be saved from eternal punishments, but shall not even suffer purgatorial torments after death".[34]

In these passages Augustine specifically uses the Latin phrases *poenae purgatoriae* (purgatorial punishments) and *poenae temporariae* (temporary punishments), which became widespread in later medieval discussions of the doctrine.[35] Augustine also believed the prayers of people on earth could alleviate these punishments, as is evident in the following prayer for his mother recorded in his *Confessions*: "Forgive her, O Lord, forgive her, I beseech You; 'enter not into judgment' with her. Let Your mercy be exalted above Your justice."[36]

Those who claim that purgatory was "invented" in the Middle Ages often borrow that conclusion from the medievalist scholar Jacques Le

---

[32] Gerald Bray, *God Has Spoken: A History of Christian Theology* (Wheaton, IL: Crossway, 2014), 496.

[33] Consider this excerpt from the Charles Spurgeon sermon we quoted earlier: "The Pope and his priest would have a lean larder if full assurance were well preached. Only conceive my brethren, if the Roman Catholic could get the full assurance of salvation, surely the Cardinals would hardly find money enough to buy their red hats.... [It] becomes what brave old Hugh Latimer used to call it, 'Purgatory Pick-purse,' to the poor sinner, and Purgatory Fill-purse to the vagabond priest." Spurgeon, "Full Assurance". For a response to similar claims, see Karl Keating, *Catholicism and Fundamentalism: The Attack on "Romanism" by "Bible Christians"* (San Francisco: Ignatius Press, 1988), 196.

[34] St. Augustine, *City of God* 21.16.

[35] Jerry Walls, *Purgatory: The Logic of Total Transformation* (New York: Oxford University Press, 2012), 15.

[36] St. Augustine, *Confessions* 9.13.

Goff, who argues in his book *The Birth of Purgatory* that the doctrine came into existence at Notre Dame in the late twelfth century.[37] But Le Goff meant that the idea of purgatory as a *physical place* came into existence in the twelfth century, not the concept of postmortem purification.[38] Le Goff even considers third-century writers such as Clement of Alexandria and Origen to be "inventors" of purgatory. Since the Catholic Church has not defined whether purgatory is also a place along with a process, this development in theological speculation has little bearing on the doctrine's historical pedigree.

William Webster is more conservative in his critique of the historical evidence, saying, "For at least the first two centuries there was no mention of purgatory in the Church."[39] But in the year 167 Abercius, the bishop of Hieropolis, had the phrase "let him [i.e., the reader] pray for Abercius" inscribed on his own epitaph. This would imply that prayer could benefit Abercius after death, which can make sense only if there is a process like purgatory as opposed to simple beatification or damnation.

Some Protestant apologists claim that this could just be a request for an increase in heavenly happiness, but such an explanation is strained. After all, requests for prayer made between living people are usually done in the face of a hardship to be alleviated rather than a blessing to be increased. A state of purification after death better explains these requests for postmortem prayer than a state of heavenly bliss. Although, Webster claims that the intention to seek heavenly blessings for the deceased rather than mercy for sins to be purified can be derived from the meaning of the Latin terms used in these prayers. He writes:

---

[37] "Indeed, preeminent Medievalist French scholar, Jacques Le Goff, in his enlightening book, *The Birth of Purgatory*, validly documents how even the doctrine and the word purgatory did not appear and become a fixed feature of Roman Catholic theology before the late twelfth century. In fact the Latin word for purgatory (purgatorium) did not even appear before then!" Todd Baker, *Exodus from Rome: A Biblical and Historical Critique of Roman Catholicism*, vol. 1 (Bloomington, IN: iUniverse, 2014), kindle edition. First, we have shown that the doctrine of purgatory existed long before the twelfth century, and while the noun *purgatorium* may not have been used, adjectival versions of that word were used in the writings of Augustine. Regardless, the doctrine of purgatory can be known apart from the word "purgatory", just as the Trinity was believed before the word "Trinity" appeared in the Church Fathers.

[38] Le Goff, *Birth of Purgatory*, 158.

[39] Webster, *Church of Rome at the Bar of History*, 114.

As early as Tertullian, in the late second and beginning of the third century, these prayers often use the Latin term *refrigerium* as a request of God on behalf of departed Christians, a term which means "refreshment" or "to refresh" and came to embody the concept of heavenly happiness.[40]

Tertullian mentions the practice of making "offerings for the dead" as being long-held traditions, not theological novelties. He cites the specific example of a widow who "prays for [her husband's] soul, and requests refreshment [*refrigerium*] for him meanwhile, and fellowship (with him) in the first resurrection; and she offers (her sacrifice) on the anniversaries of his falling asleep".[41] But scholars admit that "the meaning of the term is quite vague" and "it is largely unknown in the classical Latin literature."[42] Complicating our understanding of the term is the fact that Tertullian probably used it in a different way than Christians and even non-Christians in other parts of the Empire who were also familiar with that concept.[43]

In her study of purgatory in late antiquity, Isabel Moreira says that this place of refreshment was not heaven but a separate "waiting place" for the soul. She says, "The relationship of purgatory's fire to this waiting place remained unclear even in those later works."[44] What is known is that requests for refreshment or *refrigerium* can be found on dozens of Christian funerary inscriptions during the second and third centuries and that *refrigerium* was about "community in its broadest sense".[45] This may refer to communal meals for the dead in ancient Rome that were designed to provide nourishment and intercession for the dead that some Christians adopted in their own funeral rituals.

What is clear is that early Fathers and ecclesial writers of the Church did not believe that the soul was immediately united to Christ after death. Rather, they believed in an interim period where something

---

[40] Ibid.

[41] Tertullian, *On Monogamy* 10.

[42] Eliezer Gonzalez, *The Fate of the Dead in Early Third Century North African Christianity* (Heidlerberg: Mohr Siebeck, 2014), 139.

[43] Ibid., 140.

[44] Isabel Moreira, *Heaven's Purge: Purgatory in Late Antiquity* (New York: Oxford University Press, 2010), 25.

[45] Gonzalez, *Fate of the Dead*, 152.

important happened to the soul as it was prepared for its heavenly destiny. For example, Moreira says that Tertullian's contemporary Clement of Alexandria "argued that the soul would be purged in the afterlife by two types of fires: the educational fire that corrected the corrigible and the punitive fire that devoured the incorrigible".[46]

This early historical witness, therefore, supports the antiquity of the Catholic doctrine of purgatory rather than the common Protestant position that the soul requires no purification or preparation after death.

## Purgatory and Indulgences

The issue of indulgences is beyond the scope of this chapter, but it should be addressed, at least briefly, due to their relation to the doctrine of purgatory.

Quoting Paul VI's January 1, 1967, apostolic constitution *Indulgentiarum Doctrina*, the *Catechism* defines an indulgence as "'a remission before God of the temporal punishment due to sins whose guilt has already been forgiven' (Norm 1)" (*CCC* 1471). Indulgences do not forgive sins but instead take away the temporal punishment that is due to sin when the sinner makes amends through acts of prayer and charity. Indulgences were never sold, but abuses began to proliferate when the charitable work of almsgiving was attached to certain indulgences; so the Council of Trent prohibited almsgiving from being attached to future indulgences.[47]

Protestants are usually aware of the concept of eternal punishment for sin, but they may be unfamiliar with the concept of temporal, or limited, punishments for sin that remain even after the eternal punishment for sin is remitted. The *Catechism* describes these punishments as follows:

---

[46] Moreira, *Heaven's Purge*, 24.

[47] The Bible teaches that charity covers a multitude of sins (1 Pet 4:8) and describes how God remembered Cornelius' almsgiving (Acts 10:31). Sirach 3:30 even says, "[As] water extinguishes a blazing fire: so almsgiving atones for sin." Unfortunately, because money has an innate tendency to corrupt (1 Tim 6:10), some people treated these indulgences as mere transactions involving their spare funds, and not opportunities to make genuine acts of charity in atonement for sin. The abuses related to money and indulgences was addressed in the twenty-fifth session of the Council of Trent in the Decree concerning Indulgences.

> Grave sin deprives us of communion with God and therefore makes us incapable of eternal life, the privation of which is called the "eternal punishment" of sin. On the other hand every sin, even venial, entails an unhealthy attachment to creatures, which must be purified either here on earth, or after death in the state called Purgatory. This purification frees one from what is called the "temporal punishment" of sin. These two punishments must not be conceived of as a kind of vengeance inflicted by God from without, but as following from the very nature of sin. (CCC 1472)

The fact that believers still suffer the temporal consequences of sin even after God forgives them can be seen in David being punished after God forgave him for committing adultery and murder (2 Sam 12:14). Hebrews 12:10 teaches likewise that God "disciplines us for our good, that we may share his holiness".

Some Protestant commentaries claim that this discipline is not punitive in nature but meant for training in righteousness. However, this misunderstands the nature of parental discipline. Punishment is, by definition, punitive. The word "punitive" means "related to punishment". When a child is punished so that he will learn his lesson, it is by nature a punitive act on the part of the parent. Yet the purpose is to train the child so that he will improve.

The author of Hebrews makes the point that this is the way God disciplines us. He is not saying that every instance of suffering in this life is a direct consequence of sin, but rather that God uses suffering as a way of correcting us so that we can grow in holiness. Even though God has forgiven our sins, we still have unhealthy attachments to sin, so God uses suffering in this life to help us grow and be purged of those attachments.

Apologists who quote Hebrews 10:14 and say purgatory is unnecessary because Christ's sacrifice has "perfected for all time those who are sanctified" forget that sanctification is a process.[48] After all, Paul says of the Resurrection, "Not that I have already obtained this *or am already perfect* [emphasis added]; but I press on to make it my own" (Phil 3:12). Those who fail to receive the perfection Christ has achieved for them before death will, provided they die free from mortal sin, receive it in the next life.

---

[48] Rhodes, *Reasoning from the Scriptures*, 239.

Other objections to purgatory are irrelevant because they misunderstand the doctrine. For example, Calvin asks, "If it is perfectly clear, from what was lately said, that the blood of Christ is the only satisfaction, expiation, and cleansing for the sins of believers, what remains but to hold that purgatory is mere blasphemy, horrid blasphemy against Christ?"[49]

But cooperating with God to have the temporal effects of one's sin remitted (such as by obtaining indulgences) does not refute the necessity of Christ's sacrifice any more than the sinner's initial cooperation with God to have the eternal consequences of one's sin remitted (such as by receiving baptism) refutes the necessity of Christ's sacrifice. Calvin's understanding of the doctrine of purgatory also makes the problematic assumption that something other than Christ is involved in the cleansing of sins in purgatory. But according to Pope Benedict XVI,

> Some recent theologians are of the opinion that the fire which both burns and saves is Christ himself, the Judge and Saviour. The encounter with him is the decisive act of judgement. Before his gaze all falsehood melts away. This encounter with him, as it burns us, transforms and frees us, allowing us to become truly ourselves.[50]

In his *Ninety-Five Theses* Luther did not reject the existence of purgatory or even the concept of indulgences as much as he objected to the authority of the pope to grant indulgences. He asks, "Why does not the pope empty purgatory for the sake of holy love and the dire need of the souls that are there?"[51] Of course, the same objection could be turned against Luther by asking why the Church does not empty hell for the sake of holy love by declaring that Christ, who died for all people, had forgiven the sins of all people, everywhere. The answer in both cases is the same: because God has not given the Church this power.

The apostles and their successors were given the authority to bind and loose "on earth", and God would validate this in heaven

---

[49] John Calvin, *Institutes of the Christian Religion* 3.5.6. Cited in McNeill and Battles, *Calvin: Institutes of the Christian Religion*, 676.

[50] Pope Benedict XVI, *Spe Salvi*, no. 47.

[51] Martin Luther, "The 95 Theses", Thesis 82.

(Mt 16:19; 18:18). However, the key phrase for our purposes is "on earth". They have legitimate authority over members of the Church in this life (1 Thess 5:12; Heb 13:17), but they do not have authority over what happens in the next life. The pope has no power to empty hell or to empty purgatory. Consequently, indulgences can be applied to the dead only by way of prayer—that is, the Church can *pray* that God will apply indulgences so as to help those being purified, but it has no authority to release them from purgatory.

## The Logic of Purgatory

Revelation 21:27 says of the heavenly Jerusalem, "Nothing unclean shall enter it, nor any one who practices abomination or falsehood, but only those who are written in the Lamb's book of life." While the word "unclean" in this passage refers to ceremonial uncleanness, this verse and the context of Revelation as a whole indicate that nothing associated with sin will be in heaven. The Evangelical author Randy Alcorn says of this verse, "Heaven will be completely devoid of evil, with no threat of becoming tainted.... The new nature that'll be ours in Heaven—the righteousness of Christ—is a nature that cannot sin."[52]

Like most Protestants, Alcorn says we receive Christ's righteousness in this life through faith. In another work he writes about Christ's righteousness being imputed to us and how "in regeneration, God grants to the believer a new nature that, as he draws upon God's power, can overcome evil."[53] But this can't be the exact same perfected nature we will have in heaven, because regenerated believers still sin in this life (1 Jn 1:8).

This has led the Protestant scholar Jerry Walls to argue that purgatory makes *logical* sense given that our sanctification is usually not complete at death but will be complete before we enter into heaven. Walls concludes his book with a sentiment that a Catholic can also wholeheartedly stand behind:

---

[52] Randy Alcorn, *Heaven* (Carol Stream, IL: Tyndale House Publishers, 2004), 300.

[53] Randy Alcorn, *The Goodness of God: Assurance of Purpose in the Midst of Suffering* (Colorado Springs, CO: Multnomah Books, 2010), 69.

[God] is good in the moral sense that he hates our evil, and demands our purity, but he is also good in the sense that he loves us and desires our happiness and true flourishing, which can only be complete when we are perfected in holiness. This reminds us one more time that purgatory, properly understood, is not an alternative to grace, but is itself an expression of grace.[54]

---

[54] Walls, *Purgatory*, 181.

# The Intercession and Veneration of the Saints

One of the most important documents of the Lutheran reformation is the Augsburg Confession. Composed in 1530, it summarizes the basic tenets of Lutheran belief and contrasts it with Catholic doctrine. Its twenty-first article states, "Scripture teaches not the invocation of saints or to ask help of saints, since it sets before us the one Christ as the Mediator."

A few years later the Protestant reformer Philip Melanchthon wrote a defense of the Augsburg Confession, where he said, "The bishops, theologians, and monks applaud these monstrous and wicked stories [about the saints] ... because they aid them to their daily bread."[1] While most Protestants wouldn't accuse Catholic hagiography of having such nefarious motives, many still find difficulty with venerating and seeking the intercession of the saints. But when we examine the biblical and patristic evidence, we find compelling reasons to believe in what the Apostles' Creed calls "the communion of saints".[2]

## The Biblical Communion of Saints

Romans 12:4–5 says, "For as in one body we have many members, and all the members do not have the same function, so we, though many, are one body in Christ, and individually *members one of another* [emphasis added]." Similar descriptions of Christ's body can be found in 1 Corinthians 12:27 ("You are the body of Christ and individually

---

[1] Philip Melanchthon, *Defense of the Augsburg Confession* 21.38, BookofConcord.org, accessed July 19, 2017, http://bookofconcord.org/defense_20_saints.php?setSidebar=min.

[2] For a more in-depth treatment of this subject, I recommend Patrick Madrid's book *Any Friend of God's Is a Friend of Mine: A Biblical and Historical Explanation of the Catholic Doctrine of the Communion of Saints* (San Diego: Basilica Press, 1996).

members of it") and Colossians 1:24 ("In my flesh I complete what is lacking in Christ's afflictions for the sake of his body, that is, the Church"). On the road to Damascus the risen Jesus asked Saint Paul, "Why do you persecute me?" (Acts 22:7).

Paul's persecution of the Church was the same as persecuting Christ, which makes sense if the Church is Christ's body. In *The Sacraments in Protestant Faith and Practice*, James F. White (not to be confused with the Protestant apologist James R. White) describes how Lutherans, Episcopalians, and Presbyterians all believe that through baptism one becomes a member of the Church, which is "the body of Christ".[3]

This brings us to the next premise in our argument—Christ has only *one* Body.[4]

Quoting Saint Thomas Aquinas, the *Catechism* says, " 'Since all the faithful form one body, the good of each is communicated to the others. . . . We must therefore believe that there exists a communion of goods in the Church. But the most important member is Christ, since he is the head' (St. Thomas Aquinas, *Symb.*, 10)" (*CCC* 947). This echoes Jesus' description of himself as a vine that unites all the members of the Body into one organic whole (Jn 15:5). Those who belong to the Body of Christ share a connection with one another, just as the individual parts of a physical organism's body share a connection with all the other parts.

Paul says, "There are many parts, yet one body" (1 Cor 12:20), "You are all one in Christ Jesus" (Gal 3:28), and "We, though many, are one body in Christ" (Rom 12:5). Paul explicitly condemned the attitude that one part of Christ's Body would say to the other, "I have no need of you" (1 Cor 12:21; see vv. 22–27). Christ prayed that Christians "may all be one" (Jn 17:21), which includes not just those who heard Jesus' preaching, but all future Christians (Jn 17:20). Dale Martin, professor of New Testament at Yale University, writes,

In the Apostles' Creed, Christians confess to believe in "the communion of saints," referring to all Christians living now or who have

[3] James F. White, *The Sacraments in Protestant Faith and Practice* (Nashville, TN: Abingdon Press, 1999), 64–65.
[4] Madrid, *Any Friend of God's Is a Friend of Mine*, 28.

ever lived. To affirm the doctrine of the communion of saints is to affirm that we accept all Christians as members with us in the body of Christ that has existed throughout all ages and exists now throughout the earth.[5]

Most Protestants agree that all Christians, including those in heaven, belong to the one Body of Christ. After all, Paul taught that death does not separate us from the love of God in Christ Jesus (Rom 8:38), so the saints in heaven must still belong to the Body of Christ. But unlike Catholics, Protestants often imagine Christians in heaven are separated from the other members of the Body of Christ and so they can't intercede for believers on earth.[6] They might even say, "The saints in heaven can't hear our prayers; they're dead!" But we must remember the words of Jesus: "I am the resurrection and the life; he who believes in me, though he die, yet shall he live" (Jn 11:25).

Scripture never describes the dead in Christ as belonging to an amputated or paralyzed part of his Body. On the contrary, it describes these people as being not just alive, but concerned about those who are still on earth. Jesus described how, after death, the rich man pleaded with Abraham to send Lazarus to warn his other wayward brothers (Lk 16:27–28). He also asked the Sadducees, "Have you not read what was said to you by God, 'I am [as opposed to 'I was'] the God of Abraham, and the God of Isaac, and the God of Jacob'? He is not God of the dead, but of the living" (Mt 22:32).

The Protestant theologian Wayne Grudem agrees that the dead are conscious and alive in heaven.[7] In his refutation of soul sleep, or the mistaken view that the dead are unconscious until the final judgment, Grudem says, "Revelation 6:9–11 and 7:9–10 also clearly show how the souls or spirits of those who have died and who have gone to

---

[5] Dale Martin, *Pedagogy of the Bible: An Analysis and Proposal* (Louisville, KY: Westminster John Knox Press, 2008), 44.

[6] They may describe the saints as being like a paralyzed part of the Body that cannot communicate with the other parts. One article on a website that is critical of Catholicism says, "A paralyzed limb is still very much part of the body, yet it does not respond to the body's commands." Joe Mizzi, "Praying to the Saints: An Unbiblical Practice", JustforCatholics.org, accessed July 19, 2017, http://www.justforcatholics.org/a134.htm.

[7] Wayne Grudem, *Systematic Theology: An Introduction to Biblical Doctrine* (Grand Rapids, MI: Zondervan, 1994), 822.

heaven [are] praying and worshipping."[8] But how do we know the saints are aware of what is happening to Christians on earth?

In chapter 11 of the Letter to the Hebrews the author describes heroes of Israel's past like Abraham and Moses whose faith allowed them to perform amazing feats for God and his people (vv. 29–40). In Hebrews 12:1 the author concludes his description with this appeal: "Therefore, since we are surrounded by so great a cloud of witnesses, let us also lay aside every weight, and sin which clings so closely, and let us run with perseverance the race that is set before us."

Some interpretations reduce "the cloud" in Hebrews 12:1 to stories of faith that are witnesses *to us*—examples of how the life of faith should be lived. Other interpretations might see them as witnesses *of God and Christ* by their faith. But these interpretations neglect the race imagery that the author of Hebrews is using. He depicts living Christians as those who are running a race, in imitation of Jesus who also ran it and then sat down in heaven (Heb 12:2).

The Protestant scholar William Barclay says of this passage, "Christians are like runners in some crowded stadium. As they press on, the crowd looks down; and the crowd looking down are those who have already won the crown."[9] Many commentaries describe this passage as incorporating "stadium imagery" that is designed to encourage Christians to finish the race for salvation with perseverance (1 Cor 9:24–27; 2 Tim 4:7).[10] This indicates that those in heaven are witnessing us as we run the race, and thus that they are aware of our situation. But if they are aware of the trials we face, it would only be natural for them to pray for us. Quoting *Lumen Gentium*, the *Catechism* says,

"Being more closely united to Christ, those who dwell in heaven fix the whole Church more firmly in holiness.... They do not cease to intercede with the Father for us, as they proffer the merits which they acquired on earth through the one mediator between God and men,

---

[8] Ibid., 821.

[9] William Barclay, *The Letter to the Hebrews* (Louisville, KY: Westminster John Knox Press, 2002), 202.

[10] See, for example, Ben Witherington, *Letters and Homilies for Jewish Christians: A Socio-Rhetorical Commentary on Hebrews, James and Jude* (Downers Grove, IL: InterVarsity Press, 2007), 325.

Christ Jesus .... So by their fraternal concern is our weakness greatly helped" (*LG* 49). (*CCC* 956)

When he was alive, Saint Paul asked his audience to pray for him (2 Thess 3:1), and he assured them that they were in his prayers as well (Eph 1:16). In 1 Timothy 2:1 Paul urges that "supplications, prayers, intercessions, and thanksgivings be made for all men". He told the Thessalonians, "We always pray for you, that our God may make you worthy of his call" (2 Thess 1:11).

Would Paul cease to pray for those in his care once he was in heaven?

Paul said he imitates Christ (1 Cor 11:1), and Christ is at the right hand of God interceding for us (Rom 8:34), so why wouldn't Paul imitate Christ and do the same? We should recall Saint Jerome, who said, "If Apostles and martyrs while still in the body can pray for others, when they ought still to be anxious for themselves, how much more must they do so when once they have won their crowns, overcome, and triumphed?"[11]

## The Historical Communion of Saints

Jewish evidence from both before and after Christ supports the practice of invoking the intercession of deceased *tzadikim*—righteous or holy ones (saints).

Judas Maccabeus had a dream "worthy of belief" (2 Macc 15:11) that depicted the deceased high priest Onias "praying with outstretched hands for the whole body of the Jews" (2 Macc 15:12), as well as the deceased prophet Jeremiah doing the same (2 Macc 15:13–16). The Talmud also describes the practice of visiting the graves of deceased relatives in order to invoke their prayers and intercession. It says that Caleb went to Hebron so he could utter this prayer at the graves of the patriarchs: "My fathers, pray on my behalf that I may be delivered from the plan of the spies."[12] Even today it is common in Hasidic Judaism, and some other branches of Judaism, to ask for the intercession of departed *tzadikim*.

---

[11] St. Jerome, *Against Vigilantius* 6.

[12] *Bava Metsia* 85. Cited in P. W. van der Horst, *Japheth in the Tents of Shem Studies on Jewish Hellenism in Antiquity* (Leuven, Belgium: Peeters Publishers, 2002), 127.

In regard to early patristic evidence, Clement of Alexandria said in the third century that though a Christian "pray alone, he has the choir of the saints standing with him".[13] Origen likewise spoke of prayers from "the souls of the saints already at rest",[14] and Cyprian reminded his audience, "Let us on both sides [of death] always pray for one another."[15] Coptic Christians in the third century even recited this prayer to Mary, "We take refuge beneath the protection of your compassion, Theotokos. Do not disregard our prayers in troubling times: but deliver us from danger, O only pure and blessed one."[16]

The fourth and fifth centuries include testimony from Cyril of Jerusalem, Gregory of Nyssa, John Chrysostom, Ambrose, Jerome, and Augustine in favor of seeking the intercession of the saints.[17] Augustine says, for example, "At the Lord's table we do not commemorate martyrs in the same way that we do others who rest in peace so as to pray for them, but rather that they may pray for us that we may follow in their footsteps."[18]

Finally, archaeologists have discovered catacomb inscriptions from this period that ask the deceased to pray for the living. The earliest have been found at the tomb of Peter and Paul, one of which says, "Petre et Paule sub/venite Prim[o]/peccatori", or "Peter and Paul: Help Primus, a sinner." According to the Cambridge Manual of Latin Epigraphy, catacomb graffiti served many purposes including "prayers to the saints for intercession".[19]

---

[13] St. Clement of Alexandria, *Stromata* 7.12.

[14] Origen, *On Prayer* 6. Cited in Origen, *On Prayer*, trans. William A. Curtis (London: Aeterna Press, 2015), 20.

[15] St. Cyprian, *Epistle* 56.5.

[16] "The *Sub tuum praesidium* [Beneath your protection] papyrus indicates, then, that least some Christians in Egypt had begun to pray to the Virgin Mary and ask for her intercessions already by the end of the third century." Stephen J. Shoemaker, *Mary in Early Christian Faith and Devotion* (New Haven, CT: Yale University Press, 2016), 69.

[17] St. Gregory of Nyssa, *Sermon on Ephraim the Syrian*; St. John Chrysostom, *Orations* 8.6; St. Ambrose, *The Hexaemeron* 5.25.90 (his six days of creation work); St. Jerome, *Against Vigilantius* 6. Cited in Jimmy Akin, *The Fathers Know Best: Your Essential Guide to the Teachings of the Early Church* (San Diego: Catholic Answers Press, 2010), 358. See also "The Intercession of the Saints", Catholic Answers, accessed July 19, 2017, https://www.catholic.com/tract/the-intercession-of-the-saints.

[18] St. Augustine, *Homilies on John* 84. Cited in Akin, *Fathers Know Best*, 358.

[19] Alison E. Cooley, *Cambridge Manual of Latin Epigraphy* (Cambridge: Cambridge University Press, 2012), 239.

## Objections to Saintly Intercession

Geisler and MacKenzie claim that just as we no longer have a duty to care for a deceased parent physically and just as we can no longer have a friendly conversation with a deceased friend, it follows that "prayer cannot (and should not) occur between the living and the dead."[20] According to them, death changes our relationship with Christians in heaven and thus makes communication with them impossible and inappropriate. But these counterexamples fail to prove the duo's point.

A deceased parent may no longer have a living body to care for, but a child can still care for his deceased parents. He can do this by making sure his parents' bodies are treated with dignity and that their last wishes are carried out. Similarly, if my wife is in a coma, she may be unable to communicate to me, but that wouldn't prevent me from trying to communicate to her in case she hasn't lost that ability. Since we have biblical evidence that the saints are aware of what happens on earth, asking them to pray for us is appropriate and possible because for God "all things are possible" (Mt 19:26).

Geisler and MacKenzie can't simply show that our relationship with loved ones changes after they die; that's obvious. They must show that the saints who are united to Christ are also completely cut off from the living. But as we've seen, Scripture shows that the saints are united to the living through the Body of Christ, and because of this union they can intercede for that part of the Body.

Other Protestant apologists claim that we should not address saints in prayer, because the Bible never records God's people engaging in such behavior. But this assumes that unless the Bible expressly permits a behavior, then the behavior is impermissible, which is a kind of legalism that would invalidate many Christian practices. Consider this version of the "Sinner's Prayer" from the Billy Graham Center:

Dear Lord Jesus, I know I am a sinner, and I ask for your forgiveness. I believe you died for my sins and rose from the dead. I trust and follow you as my Lord and Savior. Guide my life and help me to do your will. In your name, amen.

[20] Norman L. Geisler and Ralph E. MacKenzie, *Roman Catholics and Evangelicals: Agreements and Differences* (Grand Rapids, MI: Baker Books, 1995), 349.

According to Protestant apologists Matt Slick and Tony Miano, "There is not a single verse or passage in Scripture, whether in a narrative account or in prescriptive or descriptive texts, regarding the use of a 'Sinner's Prayer' in evangelism. *Not one*" [emphasis in original].[21] The biblical case for praying to the Holy Spirit fares even worse, or as Slick says, "We never see an instance in the Bible where anyone prays to the Holy Spirit."[22]

Protestants recognize that the absence of these prayers in Scripture does not prove they are illicit, because a fundamental point of law, including moral law, is that people have liberty unless something is expressly or implicitly forbidden. The New Testament describes how Christians have freedom in Christ and they should live as free people provided they don't use their freedom for evil (1 Pet. 2:16; Gal. 5:13). Therefore, to show that we must not pray to the saints, a Protestant must demonstrate that Scripture expressly or implicitly prohibits the practice.

## The "One Mediator" Objection

Most Protestants who put forward biblical evidence against seeking the intercession of the saints cite 1 Timothy 2:5: "For there is one God, and there is one mediator between God and men, the man Christ Jesus." If Christ is our only mediator, then why seek anyone else to mediate our supplications to God? Calvin thought the only reason would be out of fear for Christ. He writes,

> If we appeal to the consciences of all those [who] delight in the intercession of saints, we shall find that this arises solely from the fact that

---

[21] Tony Miano and Matt Slick, "Is the Sinner's Prayer Biblical or Not?", Christian Apologetics and Research Ministry (CARM), accessed July 19, 2017, https://carm.org/sinners-prayer. According to Protestant pastor Timothy Keller, "Only three times after Jesus' ascension—in the rest of the New Testament—is prayer addressed directly to Jesus. In the vast majority of cases, prayer is addressed to the Father. While it is not at all improper to address the Son or the Spirit, ordinarily prayer will be addressed to the Father with gratitude to the Son and dependence on the Spirit". Timothy Keller, *Prayer: Experiencing Awe and Intimacy with God* (New York: Penguin, 2014), 126.

[22] Matt Slick, "To Whom Do We Pray: The Father, the Son, or the Holy Spirit?", Christian Apologetics and Research Ministry (CARM), accessed July 19, 2017, https://carm.org/questions/about-doctrine/who-do-we-pray-father-son-or-holy-spirit.

they are burdened by anxiety, just as if Christ were insufficient or too severe. First, by this perplexity they dishonor Christ, and strip him of the title of sole Mediator, which, as it has been given to him by the Father as a unique privilege, ought not to be transferred to another.[23]

But this argument does not succeed, because if it were taken literally, it would prove too much. If asking a saint in heaven to pray for us contradicts Christ's role as our one mediator, then asking a Christian on earth to pray for us would do the same thing since one could always bring the petition directly to Christ instead. Saint Thomas Aquinas explained Christ's role as our one mediator in this way:

> Christ alone is the perfect Mediator of God and men, inasmuch as, by His death, He reconciled the human race to God.... However, nothing hinders certain others from being called mediators, in some respect, between God and man, forasmuch as they cooperate in uniting men to God, dispositively or ministerially.[24]

The fact that Christ is the one Person who unites men and God in the work of our redemption does not inhibit others from participating in Christ's mediation. For example, the Bible says Christ intercedes for us (Rom 8:34), but so does the Holy Spirit (Rom 8:27). The Father has entrusted all judgment to the Son (Jn 5:22), but Christ said Christians will judge others, including angels (1 Cor 6:3). Believers can participate in Christ's unique roles, including his role as our one mediator, without stripping him of this unique privilege.

Against Calvin's contention that seeking intercession dishonors Christ, the Bible teaches that the prayers of holy people are more efficacious so it is wise to seek that kind of intercession.

God told Job's friends that they should ask Job to pray for them because God would hear his prayers but not theirs (Job 42:8). James 5:16 says, "The prayer of a righteous man has great power in its effects." While this refers to living believers, the principle applies even more to believers in heaven who are more righteous than the

---

[23] John Calvin, *Institutes of the Christian Religion* 3.20.21. Cited in *Calvin: Institutes of the Christian Religion*, ed. John T. McNeill, trans. Ford Lewis Battles (Louisville, KY: Westminster John Knox Press, 1960), 879.

[24] St. Thomas Aquinas, *Summa Theologica* III, q. 26, a. 1.

saints on earth because nothing unclean can enter heaven (Rev 22:11). Scripture even describes how righteous deeds adorn these saints like bright, pure linens (Rev 19:8), and Hebrews 12:23 refers to these saints as "the spirits of just men made perfect".

Finally, it is not out of fear that a Christian would seek the intercession of saints and angels, but out of hope that the holiness Christ has given these people will facilitate the petition they bring to Christ in the heavenly temple. Revelation 5:8 describes how "the twenty-four elders fell down before the Lamb, each holding a harp, and with golden bowls full of incense, which are the prayers of the saints." This is similar to Tobit's description of the "seven holy angels who present the prayers of the saints and enter into the presence of the glory of the Lord" (Tob 12:15).

## The Necromancy and Deification Objections

Lynda Howard-Munro writes in her book *A Rebuttal to Catholic Apologetics*, "The practice of communicating with the dead is referred to as necromancy, a practice that is strictly forbidden by the law (Deut 18:11)."[25] However, the Church also forbids necromancy as is evident in the *Catechism*'s declaration that "all forms of divination are to be rejected: recourse to Satan or demons, conjuring up the dead or other practices falsely supposed to 'unveil' the future" (CCC 2116). But seeking the intercession of the saints is not an act of necromancy. The former involves sharing personal requests with the saints through personal prayer, while the latter involves using magic or the occult to extract information from the dead. According to Jimmy Akin,

> The fact that necromancy was for purposes of gaining information is made clear by the Hebrew terms for "medium" (sho'el'ob, "a spirit inquirer"), "wizard" (yidde'oni, "a spiritist"), and necromancer (doresh, 'el-ha-metim, "an inquirer of the dead"). The focus on gaining information is also made clear by the context in Deuteronomy, which specifies that God will send his people prophets instead of allowing them to use mediums, wizards, and necromancers (Deut 18:15).[26]

²⁵ Lynda Howard-Munro, *A Rebuttal to Catholic Apologetics* (Mustang, OK: Tate Publishing, 2013), 163.

²⁶ Jimmy Akin, *A Daily Defense* (San Diego: Catholic Answers Press, 2016), 150.

Necromancy was condemned in the Old Testament because people were trying to extract information from the dead about earthly or even heavenly matters (which is why God said he would communicate his will through prophets and so necromancers were not needed). For example, when Saul engaged in necromancy, he used the witch of Endor to summon the soul of the deceased prophet Samuel in order to obtain advice about his current military and spiritual troubles (1 Sam 28:3–20). But unlike necromancers, Catholics do not attempt to transmit information from the dead to the living. Instead, the flow is reversed with the living transmitting their requests through personal prayer to the "dead" (who are alive in Christ).

For many Protestants this explanation opens up another objection. Televangelist Jimmy Swaggart asks of the saints in heaven:

> How can finite beings hear the prayers of men who are on this earth? ... The only way they could hear so many thousands of prayers, and discern the heart attitudes of all these people is if they were both omniscient and omnipresent. In other words, each saint would have to be God in order to accomplish this.[27]

Even if a collection of prayers contained a very large amount of information (at least from our perspective), it would still be an infinitesimal sliver of all the truths God knows. Therefore, a saint does not have to be present in all locations or know all truths (i.e., be omnipresent and omniscient) in order to know prayers that are uttered on earth. Svendsen, however, objects to this response by saying, "One may as well argue that omniscience is not needed even by God himself since all things that can be known—no matter how many—are nevertheless limited to a finite number."[28]

Svendsen is mistaken about God's omniscience. God does, in fact, know an infinite number of things. God knows every truth of mathematics, and there are an infinite number of these. He knows what could happen in every possible world he could create, and there are

---

[27] Jimmy Swaggart, *Catholicism and Christianity* (Baton Rouge, LA: Jimmy Swaggart Ministries, 1986). Svendsen makes a similar objection: "In order to hear all those prayers at once she [and other saints in heaven] would have to be *omniscient* ("all-knowing")—an attribute that is the property of God *alone*." Eric Svendsen, *Evangelical Answers: A Critique of Current Roman Catholic Apologetics* (Atlanta: New Testament Restoration Foundation, 2012), 209.

[28] Svendsen, *Evangelical Answers*, 209.

an infinite number of these. It is simply false to say that there are only a finite number of things to know. There is, therefore, an intrinsic difference between the omniscient knowledge of God and the finite knowledge of the saints.

The saints in heaven can answer our prayers even though their knowledge is limited. They don't need to be omniscient to communicate our prayer request to God any more than you or I do. If someone asks us to intercede for a particular request, we can do so without being omniscient. We only need to know that he has something he would like us to pray for. We don't even need to know what it is!

Besides, if God can grant people on earth supernatural knowledge about the future or the afterlife, then there is no reason to think he could not grant angels and saints in heaven knowledge of our prayers. To say God could *not* do this would inhibit his attribute of omnipotence or his being all-powerful. Deuteronomy 29:29 puts it well: "The secret things belong to the LORD our God; but the things that are revealed belong to us and to our children for ever."

## Veneration of the Saints

Many Protestants claim that even if the ability to intercede for us does not deify the saints, other Catholic behavior does. This includes bowing before statues of these individuals and revering relics associated with them such as bones or pieces of their clothes. But in order to answer the charge that Catholics engage in idolatrous "worship" of the saints, we must define the term "worship".

D. A. Carson admits that throughout history the word "worship" did not always have God as its object. For example, the *Old English Prayer Book* instructs a groom to tell his bride on his wedding day, "With my body I thee worship," which Carson agrees does not make her a goddess. He concludes that "in all such usages one is concerned with the 'worthiness' or the 'worthship' (Old English *weorthscipe*) of the person or thing that is reverenced." Carson then proposes a more restricted definition of worship for Christian theology, saying it is, in part, "the proper response of all moral, sentient beings to God, ascribing all honor and worth to their Creator-God".[29]

---

[29] D. A. Carson, "Worship Under the Word", in *Worship by the Book*, ed. D. A. Carson (Grand Rapids, MI: Zondervan, 2002), 26.

Do Catholics worship Mary and the saints? If one adopts the broader, historic definition of giving "worthiness" that is due to someone, then yes, Catholics do worship these people. But in this sense the Bible would also command people to "worship" their father, mother, and even senior citizens (Lev 19:32). Protestants would be guilty of "worshiping" judges whenever they referred to them as "your honor" in a court of law. Since none of these acts of giving honor or veneration to someone constitute idolatrous worship, then acknowledging the appropriate "worthiness" of saints is not idolatrous either.

If one adopts Carson's narrower definition of worship as "one's proper response to God", then the answer is no, Catholics do not worship saints or Mary, because they do not give them the honor and adoration that belongs to God alone. In order to make this clear, the Church uses a threefold distinction to distinguish the honor that is due to the persons of the Trinity from the honor that is due to Mary and the saints. Saint Thomas Aquinas describes it this way:

> "Latria" is due to God alone, it is not due to a creature so far as we venerate a creature for its own sake.... Since, therefore, the Blessed Virgin is a mere rational creature, the worship of "latria" is not due to her, but only that of "dulia": but in a higher degree than to other creatures, inasmuch as she is the Mother of God. For this reason we say that not [just] any kind of "dulia" is due to her, but "hyperdulia."[30]

A concrete example of latria would be sacrifice. Catholics do not offer sacrifices to Mary or the saints, and the Church condemned a fourth-century group of heretics called the Collyridrians for offering cakes to Mary on altars. This parallels Paul and Barnabas' outrage when priests from the temple of Zeus came to offer sacrifices of oxen to them (Acts 14:12–14).

While sacrifices are offered only to God, praise and veneration can be given to God's creatures. This includes offering dulia to creatures like angels and saints as well as hyperdulia to the Blessed Virgin Mary. Mary herself speaks of this veneration when she says, "All generations will call me blessed; for he who is mighty has done great things for me, and holy is his name" (Lk 1:48–49). Just as venerating a work

---

[30] St. Thomas Aquinas, *Summa Theologica* III, q. 25, a. 5.

of art is a way to praise an artist, venerating the saints and especially Mary, the Mother of God, is a way to express praise and gratitude for God's work of salvation within the human family.

Now, let's examine some Catholic devotional practices that Protestants say violate the Ten Commandments by giving worship that is only proper for God to a mere creature instead.

## Prayer

While he opposed seeking intercession from the saints, Melanchthon did believe that "just as, when alive, [the saints] pray for the Church universal in general, so in heaven they pray for the Church in general."[31] Geisler and MacKenzie even admit, "The saints in heaven may be praying for us" (Rev 6:10), but they, like Melanchthon, reject the idea that we should ask the saints to pray for us. They write, "While prayer is not identical to worship, it is a part of it, and worship should always be directed to God."[32]

Unfortunately, Geisler, MacKenzie, and other Protestants who make this objection don't define the terms that are involved. What makes prayer different from worship so that one includes the other but the two are not identical? Like the older definition of the word "worship", the verb "pray" did not always have God as its object. The English word "prayer" comes from the Latin word *precari*, which means "ask, beg, entreat". In Shakespeare's *A Midsummer Night's Dream*, Hermia asks Demetrius concerning her lover Lysander, "I pray thee, tell me then that he is well" (Act III, scene 2). Contemporary translations usually render her request, "Then please tell me he's all right."

Prayer is not always an act of worship, even if it is made to God. An agnostic might pray, "God, if you exist, please give me a sign", but we wouldn't say the agnostic is "worshiping God" through such a prayer. He is instead asking God for help using the medium we call prayer. In the same way, when Catholics ask the saints for help, they pray to the saints but do not worship them as gods.[33] As the

---

[31] Melancthon, *Defense of the Augsburg Confession* 21.8.

[32] Geisler and MacKenzie, *Roman Catholics and Evangelicals*, 349.

[33] This understanding of prayer renders moot Geisler and MacKenzie's objection that it is okay to seek intercession from Christians on earth because "we are not *praying* to them but merely *asking* them to pray for us." Ibid., 352.

Catholic apologist Jimmy Akin observes, "There is something very different happening in my heart, and the heart of every Catholic, when one says, 'Saints Peter and Paul, pray for me' than when one says, 'O Lord God, you are truly supreme, you are the Infinitely-Holy, the All-Powerful, the All-Perfect Father of creation.' "[34]

## Statues

Some Protestants, however, say the Catholic practice of creating and venerating images of saints does constitute idolatry. They quote Exodus 20:4-5, which says, "You shall not make for yourself a graven image, or any likeness of anything that is in heaven above, or that is in the earth beneath, or that is in the water under the earth; you shall not bow down to them or serve them" But God did not forbid the creation of all "graven images", because later in Scripture he commanded they be made. These include angels on the Ark of the Covenant (Ex 25:18) and a bronze serpent the people were told to look at in order to be healed (Num 21:8-9), as well as angels and other earthly objects that were carved into the walls of Solomon's Temple (1 Kings 6).

The fact that God commanded these images to be made does not prove humans cannot create these kinds of images on their own initiative. Since God could never order us to break one of the Ten Commandments, this means the creation of religious images does not break the first of those commandments. Indeed, Protestant Christians often have nativity scenes on their church properties, yet those "graven images" are almost always not thought to be sacrilegious.

What about Catholic veneration of images? R. C. Sproul condemns bowing before statues because he says, "When people are bowing down before statues that is of the essence of worship."[35] But people in Eastern cultures routinely bow when they greet one another, and actors around the world often "take a bow" at the final curtain call of a stage play. The Old Testament records several instances of people

[34]James Akin, "Praying to the Saints", JimmyAkin.com, accessed July 19, 2017, http://jimmyakin.com/praying-to-the-saints.

[35]R. C. Sproul, *Are We Together? A Protestant Analyzes Roman Catholicism* (Stanford, FL: Reformation Trust Publishing, 2012), 115.

bowing in honor to one another (Gen 33:3; 1 Kings 1:16; 2:19), and most Protestants see nothing wrong with choosing to bow or kneel in prayer before a wooden cross.

## Relics

Christians have long venerated the body parts and personal effects of departed saints, and such practice has biblical precedent. The Council of Trent says, "The holy bodies of holy martyrs, and of others now living with Christ ... are to be venerated by the faithful; through which (bodies) many benefits are bestowed by God on men."[36]

In the Old Testament contact with the bones of Elisha brought a dead man back to life (2 Kings 13:21). The sick were brought out in hope that Peter's shadow would fall on them (Acts 5:15), an act Peter never rebukes even though he did rebuke inappropriate kneeling and worship of himself. Finally, according to Acts 19:11–12, "God did extraordinary miracles by the hands of Paul, so that handkerchiefs or aprons were carried away from his body to the sick, and diseases left them and the evil spirits came out of them." Calvin tries to separate this text from the practice of venerating relics in this way:

> It is obtuse of people to twist this to refer to relics, as if Paul sent his handkerchiefs so that people might venerate and kiss them in his honor. On the contrary, he chose worthless things lest any superstition should arise because of their value or splendor. He was fully determined to keep Christ's glory sound and undiminished.[37]

Calvin's exegesis is imaginative given that the text says nothing about Paul choosing rags or aprons as objects to be venerated much less because he wanted to curb superstition. The passage only says, "Handkerchiefs or aprons were carried away from his body to the sick." Paul may have chosen these items because they parallel how

---

[36] Council of Trent, "The Twenty-Fifth Session: On the Invocation, Veneration, and Relics, of Saints, and on Sacred Images", Hanover.edu, accessed July 19, 2017, https://history.hanover.edu/texts/trent/CT25IM.html.

[37] John Calvin, *Acts*, ed. J. I. Packer and Alister McGrath (Wheaton, IL: Crossway, 1995), 323.

Jesus was able to heal people who only came into contact with his clothing (Mk 5:28–30). Or, people may have brought these items to Paul because they were easy to transport and then bring back to sick people who could not come to Paul.

Regardless, Calvin distorts the veneration of relics by turning the practice into something that was created to stoke the saint's egos. Instead, these items have come into possession of the faithful and are venerated because of the tradition, attested to in Scripture, that God often works miracles through objects associated with holy people.

## Bowing

Some apologists appeal to two separate incidents involving the apostles Peter and John in order to justify their claim that bowing before creatures in a religious context is always wrong. Acts 10:25–26 says, "When Peter entered, Cornelius met him and fell down at his feet and worshiped him. But Peter lifted him up, saying, 'Stand up; I too am a man.'" John seemed to commit the same kind of error as Cornelius when he saw an angel in heaven. He says in Revelation 19:10, "I fell down at his feet to worship him, but he said to me, 'You must not do that! I am a fellow servant with you and your brethren who hold the testimony of Jesus. Worship God.'"

In both cases the Greek text says the men were rebuked after "falling down at the feet" and "worshiping" (Greek, *proskuneo*) someone who wasn't God. But this act is not always wrong, because in Revelation 3:9 Jesus promises that, when it comes to opponents of the Church in Philadelphia, "I will make them come and bow down before your feet, and learn that I have loved you" (Rev 3:9).

The Greek text in that verse literally says, "They will come and will worship before the feet of you" (Greek, *hexousin kai proskunesousin enopion tou podon sou*). All three cases involve human beings offering worship (Greek, *proskuneo*) to beings that were not God. John's and Cornelius' offering of divine worship to nondivine beings does not prove it is wrong for Catholics to offer nondivine worship, or dulia, to nondivine beings like Mary or the saints.

In response to this Calvin said, "*Douleia* is servitude; *latreia*, honor. Now no one doubts that it is greater to be enslaved [to someone] than to honor [him]... It would be unequal dealing to assign to the saints what is greater and leave to God what is lesser."[38] White also claims there is no difference between offering someone latria or dulia because, according to him, the Bible condemns the illicit offering of even "dulia" to anyone except God. He cites Galatians 4:9, where Paul asks, "How can you turn back again to the weak and beggarly elemental spirits, whose slaves [douleuein] you want to be once more?" White then asks the reader,

> Are we to assume, then, on the basis of the Roman definitions, that since they only served these idols that they were then free of the charge of idolatry, since they didn't give latria as well? Of course not! Their service of these idols was wrong whether the term latria or dulia is used.[39]

First, this is a strawman argument because it is immoral either to worship (latria) or even venerate (dulia) an idol or a false god. In addition, just because some offerings of dulia are wrong, that does not mean all forms of dulia are wrong. The Bible even refers to a licit form of "dulia" in 1 Timothy 6:2, where Paul tells slaves who have Christian masters, "They must serve [douleuetosan] all the better since those who benefit by their service are believers and beloved."

White grants this point but insists that while "there are examples of people reverencing and honoring other people in Scripture ... the biblical injunction is that in any and all religious contexts this activity is forbidden."[40] But Joshua 5:14 says that, upon meeting the angelic commander of the army of the Lord, "Joshua fell on his face to the earth, and worshiped, and said to him, 'What does my lord bid his servant?'"

Second, this objection doesn't succeed because dulia and latria are Latin theological terms that came to have technical meanings in later centuries that they did not have in the first century. In Scripture, the equivalent Greek terms douleia and latreia both referred to types of honor that could be given to God or to a human being. The terms are not clearly distinguished, and this is why in some passages these

---

[38] John Calvin, Institutes of the Christian Religion 1.12.2. Cited in McNeill and Battles, Calvin: Institutes of the Christian Religion, 119.

[39] James R. White, The Roman Catholic Controversy (Minneapolis: Bethany House, 1996), 211.

[40] Ibid.

terms—and those for related actions (like prostrating oneself, showing homage, worshiping, etc.)—are sometimes used positively and
sometimes used negatively when a human is their object.

It was precisely the need to distinguish between the proper honor
shown to God and the proper honor for a created being that led
theologians to begin restricting dulia to creatures and latria to God.
This shows that Catholic theologians were and still are sensitive to
the need to distinguish between the two forms of honor. But it is a
mistake to expect Scripture to use these terms in the later, technical
senses they acquired. This can even be seen in other theological terms
derived from Scripture.

For example, Hebrews 1:3 says Christ is the exact representation
of God's nature or substance (Greek, *hypostaseos*), but by the fourth
century the word *hypostasis* was no longer the common Greek word
for "nature" or "substance". Among theologians it had been replaced
by the word *ousia* while *hypostasis* came to mean "person" or "individual substance". Hence theologians referred to the Trinity as three
*hypostases* (persons) that share one *ousia* (substance). If we read this
fourth-century understanding of hypostasis back into Hebrews 1:3,
however, then the author would be saying that Christ is the exact
representation of God's *person* rather than his *nature*. Such an error
could lead to the heresy of modalism that claims that the Father, Son,
and Holy Spirit are one person.

Thus, when Thomas Aquinas refers to giving the saints dulia, he
is not using the definition of the word's Greek root that means we
should "enslave" ourselves to the saints, as Calvin claimed. Instead,
he is recommending proper veneration and honor be given to God's
friends in accordance to the honor we see is bestowed on them in
Sacred Scripture.

# 15

# The Blessed Virgin Mary, Mother of God

In his history of the Reformation, the Scottish Reformer John Knox described an incident where a galley ship's chaplain held forth a beautiful, wooden statue of Mary and placed it in the hands of a prisoner on board. The prisoner, who was a Protestant, had already objected to holding the statue, so he angrily threw it overboard, saying, "Let our lady now save herself: she is light enough; let her learn to swim."[1]

Five hundred years later, some Protestant accounts of this incident describe the man being handed an "idol" of the Virgin Mary.[2] While some Protestants refer to Marian devotion as being nothing more than "Mariolatry", there are many who believe their spiritual traditions have, in the words of Southern Baptist A. T. Robertson, treated Mary with an inappropriate "cold neglect".[3] According to Evangelical author Timothy George,

> It is time for evangelicals to recover a fully biblical appreciation of the Blessed Virgin Mary and her role in salvation history.... Evangelicals can and should join the church catholic in celebrating the virgin Mary as the mother of God, the God-bearer, or, as Jaroslav Pelikan suggests that we might better render, Theotokos, "the one who gave birth to the One who is God."[4]

---

[1] John Knox, *The History of the Reformation of Religion in Scotland* (Glasgow: Blackie, Fullarton, 1831), 78.

[2] "The idol was presented to one of the prisoners in chains, and he was required to kiss it." Douglas Wilson, *For Kirk & Covenant: The Stalwart Courage of John Knox* (Nashville, TN: Cumberland House Publishing, 2000), 35.

[3] A. T. Robertson, *The Mother of Jesus: Her Problems and Her Glory* (New York: George H. Doran, 1925), 16.

[4] Timothy George, "The Blessed Virgin Mary in Evangelical Perspective", in *Mary, Mother of God*, ed. Carl E. Braaten and Robert W. Jenson (Grand Rapids, MI: Wm. B. Eerdmans, 2004), 110.

## Evidence for Theotokos

The strongest evidence for the dogma of Mary as the Mother of God (or *theotokos*) is that it logically follows from the Christology that both Protestants and Catholics affirm. The *Catechism* says Jesus is "none other than the Father's eternal Son, the second person of the Holy Trinity. Hence, the Church confesses that Mary is truly 'Mother of God'" (*CCC* 495). In other words, if Jesus is God, and Mary is the Mother of Jesus, it follows that Mary is the Mother of God.

Consider Elizabeth's query to Mary: "Why is this granted me, that the mother of my Lord should come to me?" (Lk 1:43). This is a parallel of 2 Sam 6:9, where David asks, "How can the ark of the LORD come to me?" Second Samuel 6:16 records how David leapt in the presence of the Ark, just as Luke 1:41 describes how John the Baptist leapt in the presence of a pregnant Mary. In addition, the Ark of the Covenant remained in the house of Obed-edom the Gittite for three months, just as Mary stayed with Elizabeth for three months.[5]

If Mary were the Ark of the New Covenant because she contained the incarnate Word, then Elizabeth's "Lord" whose mother came to visit her would be the same "Lord" whose Ark came into the presence of David—namely, the God of Israel. Therefore, Mary is the Mother of the God of Israel.

According to Robert H. Stein, the senior professor of New Testament at Southern Baptist Theological Seminary, "Here 'Lord' is clearly a Christological title and refers to Jesus. The title is used in our account (and in Luke 1–2 in general) both for God (1:46) and Jesus."[6] In his debate about Mary with Father Dwight Longenecker, David Gustafson said, "Mary is the mother of Jesus; Jesus is God; therefore, Mary is the Mother of God—or, as Elizabeth said, 'the Mother of my Lord' (Luke 1:43).... Certainly it was God whom Mary bore, so we gladly affirm that Mary was indeed the 'God–bearer.'"[7]

*Theotokos* was also the accepted title for Mary throughout Church history. Irenaeus said Mary would "carry God" while Cyril of

[5] Tim Staples, *Behold Your Mother: A Biblical and Historical Defense of the Marian Doctrines* (El Cajon, CA: Catholic Answers Press, 2014).

[6] Robert H. Stein, *Luke: An Exegetical and Theological Exposition of Holy Scripture* (Nashville, TN: B&H Publishing Group, 1992), 90.

[7] Dwight Longenecker and David Gustafson, *Mary: A Catholic Evangelical Debate* (Leominster, UK: Gracewing, 2003), 37.

Jerusalem, Ambrose, and Jerome all described Mary as *theotokos*.[8] Protestant Reformers like Zwingli ("I esteem immensely the Mother of God, the ever chaste, immaculate Virgin Mary"[9]) and Luther ("Men have crowded all her glory into a single word, calling her the Mother of God"[10]) also used the title.

Many modern Protestants have also embraced the title as is evident in books like *Mary for Evangelicals*, where Tim Perry writes, "As *Theotokos*, her obedience to the Word of God undid the disobedience of her foremother, and she was honored with a feast day because that same obedience ensured salvation of us all."[11] Even Norm Geisler and Ralph MacKenzie admit, "There are many things Catholics and Protestants hold in common on the doctrine of Mary. These include her being the most blessed among women, her virgin conception of Christ the God-man, and by virtue of that her being in this sense 'the Mother of God'."[12]

## Our Lord and Logic

Some Protestants argue that since Scripture never describes Mary as the "Mother of God", Christians should not refer to Mary by that title. Moisés Pinedo says, "The Bible mentions Mary as the mother of Jesus, but never as the 'Mother of God.'"[13] That's true, but the Bible also never mentions God dying for our sins; it only says Jesus or Christ died for our sins. Since Jesus is God it is appropriate to say that

---

[8] St. Irenaeus, *Against Heresies* 5.19.1; St. Cyril of Jerusalem, *Catechetical Lectures* 10.19; St. Ambrose, *The Virgins* 2.2.7; St. Jerome, *Against Rufinus* 2.10.

[9] Cited in Michael O'Carroll, *Theotokos: A Theological Encyclopedia of the Blessed Virgin Mary* (Eugene, OR: Wipf and Stock, 2000), 378.

[10] "The Magnificat", *Luther's Works*, 21:326.

[11] Tim Perry, *Mary for Evangelicals: Toward an Understanding of the Mother of Our Lord* (Downers Grove, IL: InterVarsity Press, 2006), 148. R. C. Sproul likewise says, "Historically there has been no official Protestant objection to the title 'mother of God.'" R. C. Sproul, *Are We Together? A Protestant Analyzes Roman Catholicism* (Stanford, FL: Reformation Trust Publishing, 2012), 104.

[12] Norman L. Geisler and Ralph E. MacKenzie, *Roman Catholics and Evangelicals: Agreements and Differences* (Grand Rapids, MI: Baker Books, 1995), 299. Geisler and MacKenzie do say in a footnote, however, that the term *theotokos* "was designed to say more about Jesus than to glorify Mary". But as I note in my response to White later in this chapter, the term's original usage praised Mary *and* reinforced orthodox Christology.

[13] Moisés Pinedo, "Is Mary the Mother of God?", Apologetics Press (2009), https://www .apologeticspress.org/apcontent.aspx?category=11&article=2670.

"God died on the Cross for our sins" just as it is appropriate to say, "Mary is the Mother of God," even though both phrases are absent from Scripture.

If our theological vocabulary can contain language found only in Scripture, then Christians could never refer to Jesus as "God the Son" or "The Second Person of the Trinity", because, like "Mother of God", those titles are not found in Scripture. But just as Jesus' inclusion in the Trinity can be deduced from Scripture, Mary's divine motherhood can be deduced from Scripture as well. Pope Saint John Paul II said, "This is a title which does not appear explicitly in the Gospel texts, but in them the 'Mother of Jesus' is mentioned and it is affirmed that Jesus is God (Jn 20:28; cf. 5:18; 10:30, 33)."[14]

Protestants may reply by saying that Jesus can be given nonbiblical titles like "God the Son" because, unlike *theotokos*, they do not lead to contradictions or heresies. In order to prove this, some Protestants take the syllogism used to defend Mary as *theotokos* ("Jesus is God; Mary is the Mother of Jesus; therefore, Mary is the Mother of God") and replace it with something like this:

Jesus is God.
The Trinity is God.
Therefore, Jesus is a Trinity.[15]

Or:

The Trinity is God.
Mary is the Mother of God.
Therefore, Mary is the Mother of the Trinity.[16]

They conclude that if these parallel arguments are absurd, then there is something wrong with the original *theotokos* syllogism. But the problem with these arguments is that, unlike the syllogism that proves Mary is *theotokos*, they commit the fallacy of the undistributed

[14] Pope John Paul II, General Audience (November 27, 1996), https://www.ewtn.com /library/PAPALDOC/JP961127.HTM.

[15] Matt Slick, "There Is a Logical Fallacy in the Argument That Mary Is the Mother of God", Christian Apologetics and Research Ministry (CARM), accessed July 19, 2017, https://carm.org/mary-mother-of-god-logical-fallacy.

[16] Eric Svendsen, *Evangelical Answers: A Critique of Current Roman Catholic Apologetics* (Atlanta: New Testament Restoration Foundation, 2012), 177.

middle. This occurs when the middle term in a syllogism (or the term that appears twice in the premises but nowhere in the conclusion) is not fully distributed in the premises. This means the premises do not contain every instance where the middle term applies and so the other two terms in the argument are not equivalent to one another. Here are two examples of this fallacy:

> Humans are warm-blooded.
> Dolphins are warm-blooded.
> Therefore, all humans are dolphins.

> The Son is God.
> The Father is God.
> Therefore, the Son is the Father.

The second argument is typical of heretical "oneness theology" adherents and is invalid because the middle term, "God", is not fully distributed in the argument's premises. The term "God" refers to entities beyond the Father and Son such as the Holy Spirit and the Trinity, just as the term "warm-blooded" refers to other animals besides humans and dolphins. A Protestant could answer the oneness heretic by saying that the statement "The Son is God" simply means the Son is a divine Person. It does not mean all statements about God apply to Jesus (e.g., God is a Trinity, the Father is God, etc.). Because God is not an individual Person, the Son and the Father can both be God without being identical to one another. The oneness argument only proves that the Father and Son are divine Persons; it does not prove they are the same Person.

This same response also rebuts arguments that claim the *theotokos* syllogism is absurd. Those arguments do not prove that Jesus is the Trinity or that Mary is the Mother of the Trinity, because they contain undistributed middle terms. Arguments for Mary being the *theotokos*, however, do not commit this fallacy, since the middle term, Jesus, is fully distributed in both premises. The *theotokos* syllogism is as valid as this argument most Protestants would accept:

1. Jesus is God.
2. Jesus was born in a manger.
3. Therefore, God was born in a manger.

Or this one:

1. Jesus is a divine Person.
2. Mary is the Mother of Jesus.
3. Therefore, Mary is the Mother of a divine Person.

When Protestant apologists like Matt Slick say, "God has no 'mother.' He is the creator of all things," they misunderstand the doctrine of Mary's divine maternity.[17] The Church does not teach that Mary created the second member of the Trinity or that she gave Christ his divine nature. Motherhood involves the provision of genetic material that results in conception along with nurturing and giving birth to that conceived child.

Mary did not create Jesus' divine nature, but she did contribute genes to him and bear him in her womb. Therefore, she is his mother. The idea that God cannot have a mother because he is eternal is as mistaken as saying God cannot die on the Cross because he is eternal. If God assumes a human nature, he can both be born to redeem humanity and die to atone for its sins. Timothy George even exhorts his fellow Protestants not to treat Mary in a minimalistic way that denies the fullness of her motherhood:

> Mary was not merely the point of Christ's entrance into the world—the channel through which he passed as water flows through a pipe. She was ever the mother who cared for the physical needs of Jesus the boy. She was the one who nursed him at her breast and who nurtured and taught him the ways of the Lord. Doubtless she was the one who taught him to memorize the Psalms and to pray, even as he grew in wisdom and stature and in favor with God and others (Luke 2:52).[18]

## The Return of the Nestorians

The most common objections to the dogma of *theotokos* echo the heresy of Nestorianism. Ironically, this was the heresy that motivated

[17] Matt Slick, "Is Mary, the Mother of God, Theotokos?", Christian Apologetics and Research Ministry (CARM), August 25, 2014, https://carm.org/is-mary-the-mother-of-god.
[18] George, "Blessed Virgin Mary in Evangelical Perspective", 109.

the Council of Ephesus to define Mary as *theotokos* in the first place.[19] Named after the fourth-century bishop Nestorius, this heresy claimed that Jesus existed as two persons, one divine and the other human.[20] Nestorians believed that Mary only gave birth to the human person of Jesus or to Christ's human nature, and not to the divine Son of God. Since Mary did not provide Christ with his divinity, Nestorians claimed, it follows that she is the Christ-bearer (*christotokos*) but not the God-bearer (*theotokos*).

This kind of thinking is evident in Protestant apologists who, in trying to avoid saying that Mary gave birth to God or that she was the Mother of God, instead say, "Mary is the mother of Jesus according to the flesh (Rom 9:5), i.e., Jesus' physical body."[21] A similar sentiment can be found in Jimmy Swaggart, who said, "It was not God that was born of Mary; it was the human child—the Lord Jesus Christ."[22] But these arguments are all exposed as heresies when we ask, "At Jesus' birth, where was the second Person of the Trinity? Where was God the Son when Jesus was born?"

Natures cannot exist apart from beings or persons any more than colors can exist apart from shapes. A woman cannot give birth to a "human nature" apart from a person any more than woman could see the color red apart from a red shape. A woman becomes a mother only the moment a *person* with a human nature is conceived within her womb. But if the "neo-Nestorians" are correct and Mary gave birth only to Christ's human nature, then that would mean the *person* who possessed this human nature (since human natures cannot exist apart from persons) would be a *human person*. If Jesus was a human

---

[19] The first anathema of the council declared, "If anyone does not confess that Emmanuel is God in truth, and therefore that the holy virgin is the mother of God (for she bore in a fleshly way the Word of God become flesh), let him be anathema." Edward R. Hardy, ed., *Christology of the Later Fathers* (Louisville, KY: Westminster John Knox Press, 1954), 353.

[20] Modern scholars have generally concluded that Nestorius did not actually believe the heresy that bears his name, and the controversy in his day was due to a misunderstanding. Nestorius himself claimed that he did not believe the heresy he was charged with, and he died in communion with the Church, not as an excommunicate. Nevertheless, others have held Nestorian views, including modern "neo-Nestorians" who implicitly or explicitly deny that Christ is one divine Person with two inseparable natures.

[21] Pinedo, "Is Mary the Mother of God?"

[22] Jimmy Swaggart, *Catholicism and Christianity* (Baton Rouge, LA: Jimmy Swaggart Ministries, 1986), 101. Cited in Staples, *Behold Your Mother*, 21.

person, then where was the second Person of the Trinity during that fateful night in Bethlehem?

If both the divine Person of God the Son and the human Person of Christ were located within the body of Jesus, then Mary would still be *theotokos*. Of course, this scenario is absurd. Christians reject the idea that Jesus exists as two persons because we have only one Lord (Eph 4:5). As James White says, "When Jesus spoke, He spoke as one Person, not two. One cannot say that, when claiming deity, Jesus' 'deity' spoke, or when He referred to His humanity, it was His 'human nature' that spoke. It can be seen from this that natures don't speak—only Persons do. And, since Jesus is one Person, not two, He speaks as a whole Person."[23] I would add that just as natures do not speak, they also aren't born—only persons are born, and so Mary gave birth to a divine Person, which makes her the Mother of God.

Finally, Protestant apologists often agree with the Christology that is found in the decrees of the Council of Chalcedon and even invoke the council in their arguments. For example, in the previous citation from White he also says, "Modern orthodox Christological formulations have not proceeded beyond the Chalcedonian definition."[24] This has implications for Marian dogmas because Chalcedonian Christology precludes any attempt to downplay Mary's role as Mother of God by saying she gave birth only to the human Jesus or to Christ's humanity. Tim Staples aptly notes, "The council was careful to call Mary 'God-bearer' and not 'man-bearer' precisely because they were defending the truth that Mary gave birth to one divine person."[25]

## An Ignorant Superstition?

Some Protestants object to Mary's divine maternity not on biblical, logical, or historical grounds, but on practical ones. According to them, even if Mary is the Mother of God, Christians should not say she is because that can mislead less educated people. For example, Calvin said, "To call the Virgin Mary the mother of God can only

---

[23] James R. White, "The Trinity, the Definition of Chalcedon, and Oneness Theology", Alpha and Omega Ministries, January 4, 2013, https://www.aomin.org/aoblog/2013/01/04/the-trinity-the-definition-of-chalcedon-and-oneness-theology-vintage/.

[24] Ibid.

[25] Staples, *Behold Your Mother*, kindle edition.

serve to confirm the ignorant in their superstitions."[26] Matt Slick says, "The term, 'mother of God,' runs the risk of suggesting that Mary is somehow divine and part of the Godhead."[27] Gustafson likewise claims it is "creepy" to call Mary the Mother of God because this conjures up images of Mary being God's wife.[28]

This objection is as weak as saying that we should not refer to Jesus as God's Son because that runs the risk of suggesting that God has a wife or that God engaged in sexual relations with Mary. This is not a hypothetical concern, as early Mormons like Brigham Young understood Jesus' identity as "Son of God" to mean Jesus was "begotten of his Father, as we were of our fathers".[29] Many Muslims reject the Incarnation precisely because they think it entails that God physically begot Jesus through Mary. This shows that a doctrine should not be rejected just because it can be misunderstood. If that were the case, our faith would have few or possibly no doctrines at all!

Other Protestants say the term *theotokos* was originally meant to honor Christ, not Mary. White says, "Any use of [*theotokos*] that is not simply saying, 'Jesus is fully God, one divine person with two natures' is using the term anachronistically, and cannot claim the authority of the early church."[30] Gustafson makes the same point but adds the observation that Catholics don't refer to other people related to Christ as being related to God (e.g., John is not called the baptizer of God, Herod is not called the king of God, etc.).[31] Therefore, Catholics give Mary special honor that takes away from Christ when they call her *theotokos*.

---

[26] John Calvin, *Selected Works of John Calvin: Tracts and Letters*, vol. 5, ed. Jules Bonnett (Grand Rapids, MI: Baker, 1983), 362. Michael O'Carroll, however, documents Calvin saying, "The mortal man engendered in the womb of Mary was at the same time the eternal God." O'Carroll, *Theotokos*, 94.

[27] Slick, "Is Mary the Mother of God, Theotokos?" See also Elliot Miller and Kenneth B. Samples, *The Cult of the Virgin: Catholic Mariology and the Apparitions of Mary* (Grand Rapids, MI: Baker Book House, 1992), 22.

[28] Dwight Longenecker and David Gustafson, *Mary: A Catholic Evangelical Debate* (Grand Rapids, MI: Brazos, 2003), 39.

[29] Brigham Young, *Journal of Discourses*, 8:115. "Christ was begotten by an immortal Father in the same way that mortal men are begotten by mortal fathers."

[30] James R. White, *Mary: Another Redeemer?* (Bloomington, MN: Bethany House, 1998), 48.

[31] Longenecker and Gustafson, *Mary: A Catholic Evangelical Debate*, 39.

But it is not true that the title of *theotokos* was originally meant only to honor Christ. Consider an excerpt from this sermon that Cyril of Alexandria preached at the Council of Ephesus: "O Mary Mother of God, venerable treasure of the entire world, inextinguishable lamp, crown of virginity, scepter of orthodoxy, imperishable temple, container of him who cannot be contained."[32] The unending wonder of the Incarnation means there is no shortage of praise both for Jesus and his mother.

Concerning Gustafson's objection, the natural development of Christian devotional language simply hasn't included calling John "the baptizer of God" or Herod "king of God" (a title he is unworthy to have even if it is technically true). Mary herself said that all generations would call her blessed (Lk 1:48), and acknowledging her divine maternity naturally follows from that biblical truth.

Moreover, defining Mary as the Mother of God makes it clear that Jesus was a divine Person from the moment of his conception and refutes the adoptionist claim that Jesus became God only at his baptism. It also affirms the truth that Christ's human and divine natures were inseparably united within one Person, the incarnate Son of God. As Father John Hardon says, "Christology is unintelligible without knowing the role of Christ's mother."[33]

## Evidence for Mary's Perpetual Virginity

According to the *Catechism*, "The deepening of faith in the virginal motherhood led the Church to confess Mary's real and perpetual virginity even in the act of giving birth to the Son of God made man" (*CCC* 499). This can be seen in the writings of people like Origen, Athanasius, Epiphanius, Jerome, and Augustine.[34]

---

[32] St. Cyril of Alexandria, *Fourth Homily at Ephesus Against Nestorius.*

[33] Fr. John Hardon, *The Catholic Catechism: A Contemporary Catechism of the Teachings of the Catholic Church* (New York: Doubleday, 1975), 150.

[34] Origen, *Commentary on Matthew* 10.17; St. Athanasius, *Four Discourses against the Arians* 2.70; St. Jerome, *Perpetual Virginity of Blessed Mary*; St. Augustine, *Holy Virginity* 4.4. Cited in Jimmy Akin, *The Fathers Know Best: Your Essential Guide to the Teachings of the Early Church* (San Diego: Catholic Answers Press, 2010), 350–53. Tertullian may have denied the perpetual virginity of Mary, but he may have done this after he fell into heresy, so his denial is less weighty than that of other figures. In his reply to Helvidius, Jerome said, "Of Tertullian, I say no more than that he did not belong to the Church. But as regards Victorinus, I assert

Augustine claimed that Mary's puzzled response to the angel's dec-laration that she would conceive and bear a son showed that Mary did not plan to engage in sexual relations in marriage. Specifically, Mary says to the angel, "How shall this be, since I know not man? [author's translation]" (Lk 1:34). If Mary was concerned about con-ceiving a child before her marriage to Joseph, she could have said, "How can this be, I know not a man *yet*." Luke 23:53 uses a similar construction when it says Jesus was placed in a tomb, "where no one had ever yet [Greek, *oupo*] been laid." Instead, Mary uses the present tense, which some authors have considered as evidence that Mary took a vow of virginity and was betrothed to Joseph for her protection in society.[35]

Along with historical testimony, the Bible never describes any-one besides Jesus as a son or daughter of Mary. In John 19:26 Jesus entrusted his mother to the apostle John rather than one of his siblings, which is evidence that Jesus had no biological siblings to whom he could entrust her.[36] Zwingli defended the argument that because Jesus is the new Temple (Jn 2:18–22), Ezekiel 44:2 involves a typological description of Mary. Specifically, the passage describes the Temple gate that "shall remain shut" after the God of Israel passes through it. Once God had passed through the body of Mary when he was born, she would be forever sealed in consecration to him.[37] Finally, as we will see in our analysis of the "brethren of the Lord", the makeup of Jesus' kin is best explained by their being his older cousins or step-siblings, and not his younger, biological brothers and sisters.

In response to these arguments, Gustafson claims that the doc-trine of Mary's perpetual virginity "denigrates sex and marriage",

---

what has already been proven from the gospel—that he [Victorinus] spoke of the brethren of the Lord not as being sons of Mary but brethren in the sense I have explained, that is to say, brethren in point of kinship, not by nature." *The Perpetual Virginity of Blessed Mary* 19.

[35] For a more comprehensive defense of this claim, see Staples, *Behold Your Mother*, kindle edition.

[36] Some Protestants respond to this argument by claiming that Jesus' siblings were not believers and so that is why Jesus entrusted his mother to John. But the Bible never says that during Jesus' ministry all of his brethren were unbelievers, and it does say they eventually became believers, so if they were biological siblings, it would have been most appropriate to entrust Mary to their care. For more information, see ibid.

[37] George, "Blessed Virgin Mary in Evangelical Perspective", 109.

but the Church has never taught that sexual relations are intrinsically sinful.[38] However, actions that are permissible in one context can become impermissible in another context. For example, there is nothing intrinsically wrong with touching a box, but when that box contained the word of God (as was the case with the Ark of the Covenant) and thus had become a sacred object, the rules change. According to Numbers 4:15 only the high priest and his family could touch the Ark, which is a lesson Uzzah learned when God struck him down for steadying the Ark when it was being carried on a cart (2 Sam 6:9).

If Mary were the Ark of the New Covenant in virtue of her carrying the Word incarnate in her body, then she would take on an even greater level of holiness than the old ark. Just as a Jewish priest would not have sex in the Temple, nor a pastor and his wife in a church, a righteous man like Joseph would have qualms about engaging in sexual relations with the woman through whom the God of Israel entered into our world.

This also presupposes that Joseph presumed his marriage would include conjugal relations and then changed his mind after Mary's destiny had been revealed to him. If Mary had taken a vow of continence, as we mentioned earlier, then refraining from sexual intimacy would have been an understood part of their marriage. This is especially true if, as we will examine later, Joseph was an elderly widower with children of his own and wed Mary in order to provide for a woman who had dedicated herself to God.

## The Meaning of "Until", and "First Born"

In their book *The Unfinished Reformation*, Gregg Allison and Chris Castaldo make this argument:

> Protestants also disagree with Mary's perpetual virginity because it contradicts scripture. Referring to Joseph, Matthew narrates, "He took his wife, but knew her not until she had given birth to a son" (Matt. 1:24–25). The phrase "until she had given birth" indicates that after Jesus' birth, Joseph engaged in normal sexual intercourse with

---

[38] Longenecker and Gustafson, *Mary: A Catholic Evangelical Debate*, 65.

his wife. Luke's description of Jesus as Mary's "first born" (Luke 2:7) also implies that Jesus had brothers and sisters, as Scripture confirms.[39]

Matt Slick seems to agree with these apologists and says such an interpretation "would seem pretty straightforward". However, the ambiguity of the text eventually compels Slick to say, "Is this conclusion airtight? No, it is not."[40] That's because the Greek word translated "until" in this passage (*heos*) does not always refer to a change in condition. When Jesus quoted Psalm 110 he said, "David himself, inspired by the Holy Spirit, declared, 'The Lord said to my Lord, Sit at my right hand, till [Greek, *Heos*] I put your enemies under your feet'" (Mk 12:36). However, this doesn't mean the Messiah will cease to sit at the Lord's right hand after his enemies have been subdued. Second Samuel 6:23 also cannot imply any reversal in condition given that in the Greek Old Testament it says, "Michal the daughter of Saul had no child to [*heos*] the day of her death."

Since the Protestant apologist is claiming the use of *heos* in Matthew 1:25 refers to a change in Mary's virginity, he carries the burden of proving *heos* has this meaning in this passage. Allison claims the word has this meaning because in every other case in Matthew's Gospel *heos* refers to a change in condition. Therefore, we are justified in saying Matthew 1:25 is not an exception but refers to a similar change in Mary's virginity.[41]

But aside from the fact that authors can use words in unique ways, this argument fails because Matthew 28:20 uses *heos* without implying a change in condition. In that verse Jesus tells the apostles, "Observe all that I have commanded you; and behold, I am with you always, to [*heos*] the close of the age," even though Jesus will be with the apostles even after this present age comes to an end (cf. 1 Thess 4:17). Concerning Matthew 1:25, John Calvin wrote, "No

---

[39] Gregg Allison and Chris Castaldo, *The Unfinished Reformation: What Unites and Divides Catholics and Protestants after 500 Years* (Grand Rapids, MI: Zondervan, 2016), 98. Ron Rhodes likewise says of this passage, "The word 'until' implied that normal sexual relations between Joseph and Mary took place following the birth of Jesus." Ron Rhodes, *Reasoning from the Scriptures with Catholics* (Eugene, OR: Harvest House Publishing, 2000), 58.

[40] Matt Slick, "Mary's Virginity and Matt. 1:25", Christian Apologetics and Research Ministry (CARM), December 3, 2008, https://carm.org/marys-virginity-and-matt-125.

[41] Gregg Allison, *Roman Catholic Theology and Practice: An Evangelical Assessment* (Wheaton, IL: Crossway, 2014), 41.

just and well-grounded inference can be drawn from these words of the Evangelist, as to what took place after the birth of Christ."[42]

In regard to Luke 2:7, it is common for parents to refer to a child as being their "first-born" without asserting anything about a second- or third-born child. Saint Jerome even quipped that this logic would nullify the requirement in Exodus 13:1–2 that parents consecrate their first-born to the Lord. After all, an Israelite parent could say, "I owe nothing to the priest unless the birth of a second should make the one I previously had the first-born." Jerome clarified this absurdity by pointing out that "he is called the first-born who opens the womb and who has been preceded by none, not he whose birth is followed by that of a younger brother."[43]

In his commentary on Luke's Gospel, Robert Stein cites the example of an ancient grave inscription that referred to a woman who died giving birth to her "first-born" son, thus allowing for the term to be used even when other births never took place.[44] The Protestant biblical scholar Victor Hamilton said, "To say that Jesus is Mary's *prototokos* [first-born] is simply to say that Mary had no child before she gave birth to Jesus, without suggesting one way or another whether she had any additional children."[45]

Moreover, if "first-born" always implied the existence of other begotten children, then what should we make of Scripture passages that describe Christ as the first-born of all creation (Col 1:15) or how

---

[42] Svendsen takes another approach and claims that because Matthew used the phrase *heo hou* rather than just *heos*, this means that the verse implies a change in Mary's virginity. But as Tim Staples demonstrates, the Greek conventions used in the Septuagint (Gen 8:5; 2 Sam 6:23; Ps 93:13) as well as writings from the time of the New Testament allowed for *heos* and *heo hou* to be used interchangeably. For example, in Acts 21:25 St. Paul was said to be held in custody (*heous hou*) until Festus could send him to the emperor, but his detainment at the hands of the Romans did not end after he left Festus' custody. Moreover, the apocryphal 4 Maccabees 7:1–3 describes how Eleazar did not turn away from his faith until (*heos hou*) he sailed into the haven of immortal victory. Of course, Eleazar did not commit apostasy after death, and so critics like Svendsen are wrong that the Greek construction requires a change in condition. See Staples, *Behold Your Mother*, kindle edition. See also John Calvin, *Commentary on Harmony of the Evangelist, Matthew, Mark, and Luke*, vol. 1, trans. William Pringle (Edinburgh: Calvin Translation Society, 1845), 107.

[43] St. Jerome, *The Perpetual Virginity of Mary* 12.

[44] Robert H. Stein, *Luke: An Exegetical and Theological Exposition of Holy Scripture* (Nashville, TN: B&H Publishing Group, 1992), 107.

[45] Victor Hamilton, *Exodus: An Exegetical Commentary* (Grand Rapids, MI: Baker Academic, 2011), 204.

God brought his "first-born" into the world (Heb 1:6)? Just as Jesus can be called God's "first-born" without refuting his status as God's only begotten son (Jn 1:18), Jesus can be called Mary's "first-born" without refuting his status as Mary's only begotten child.

## The "Brethren of the Lord"

In their critique of Marian doctrine, Elliot Miller and Kenneth Samples say the strongest evidence that Mary was not a virgin after Christ's birth "is the repeated reference to the 'brothers and sisters' of Jesus, including Matthew 13:55–56 and Mark 6:3, where the brothers are mentioned by name".[46] The former verse describes the incredulous people of Nazareth saying of Jesus, "Are not his brethren James and Joseph and Simon and Judas? And are not all his sisters with us?" The *Catechism* informs us that

> the Church has always understood these passages as not referring to other children of the Virgin Mary. In fact James and Joseph, "brothers of Jesus", are the sons of another Mary, a disciple of Christ, whom St. Matthew significantly calls "the other Mary" (Mt 13:55; 28:1; cf. Mt 27:56). They are close relations of Jesus, according to an Old Testament expression. (*CCC* 500)

Just because the New Testament describes someone being related to Jesus, it does not mean that relationship is biological in nature. Joseph is described as the Father of Jesus (Lk 2:33, 48; Jn 6:42), but Protestants reject the view that Joseph was Jesus' biological father.[47] As I noted earlier, the New Testament never refers to the brethren of the Lord as sons or daughters of Mary. It does use the Greek word for brother and sister (*adelphos* and *adelphé*), but Hebrew and Aramaic lacked many words for extended relatives, so it's possible these "bretheren of the Lord" were related to Jesus in a way that did not include sharing the same mother.

Some Protestants say Matthew and Mark meant that these brothers and sisters were Jesus' biological siblings because even though ancient Hebrew did not have a word for "cousin", ancient Greek

---

[46] Miller and Samples, *Cult of the Virgin*, 26–27.
[47] Staples, *Behold Your Mother*, 292–93.

did (*anepsios*).[48] Ancient Greek also had a generic word for relative (*sungenis*), so, according to these critics, Matthew and Mark's decision not to use either *aenpsios* or *sungenis* to describe these people proves that their use of *adelphoi* and *adelphé* mean they were Jesus' biological brothers and sisters.

But Jews who spoke Greek in the ancient world often used *alephoi* to describe nonsibling relationships. Since in Hebrew and Aramaic, one's relatives were generally spoken of as one's brothers/brethren, it was natural for Greek-speaking Jews to translate the word for "brother" (Hebrew, *akhi*, Aram., *akha*) with its direct Greek equivalent (*adelphos*), even though Greek had other alternatives for particular relationships. They were simply making a literal Greek rendering of the way they normally spoke in their native language. This mode of speech is normal whenever a person speaks in a second language. Thus the Septuagint uses *adelphoi* to describe Abram and his nephew Lot (Gen 14:14) as well as the cousins of Moses and Aaron (Lev 10:4). Tobit 7:2–4 even uses *adelphoi* and *anepsios* interchangeably to describe the relationship between Raguel and his cousin Tobit.

In addition, John 19:25 says that "standing by the cross of Jesus were his mother, and his mother's sister [*adelphé*], Mary the wife of Clopas." Richard Bauckham says that while it is not impossible, "it is certainly unlikely that two full sisters should bear the same name." He goes to say that *adelphé* "need not mean full sister. The two Mary's could be half-sisters, step sisters, sisters in law, or even in some other family relationship for which modern English would not use the word 'sister' at all."[49] Therefore, it seems that the attempt to restrict the New Testament's use of *adelphé* or *adelphoi* is driven more by a desire to refute Mary's perpetual virginity rather than by a desire properly to interpret the sacred texts.

## Cousins or Step-Brothers?

In the fourth century a Roman writer named Helvidius claimed that the Gospel's references to Jesus' brethren were best explained by

---

[48] As well as St. Paul's references in Galatians 1:19 and 1 Corinthians 7.

[49] Richard Bauckham, *Gospel Women: Studies of the Named Women in the Gospels* (Grand Rapids, MI: Wm. B. Eerdmans, 2002), 205.

denying Mary's perpetual virginity (this has come to be known as the
Helvidian view of Mary's virginity). One answer to Helvidius, offered
by Saint Jerome, was that Jesus' brethren were his cousins or other
extended relatives and were not born of either Mary or Joseph.[50]

This explanation is plausible given that two of the brethren, James
and Joseph, are also mentioned in Matthew 27:56. This verse says
that looking at a distance upon the site of the Crucifixion "were
Mary Magdalene, and Mary the mother of James and Joseph, and the
mother of the sons of Zebedee". According to Protestant minister
E. Anne Clements, in her review of the women in the Gospels:

> Some have argued that "Mary the mother of James and Joseph" (Matt
> 27:56) is in fact Mary, the mother of Jesus, because the names James
> and Joseph appear in the list of Jesus' brothers in Matthew 13:55.
> Mary is consistently referred to as Jesus' mother (Matt 1:18, 2:11, 13,
> 20, 21, 13:55). It would seem very strange that at the crucial point of
> Jesus' crucifixion Matthew would name Mary in this way or that she
> would be called "the other Mary" (Matt 27:61, 28:1).[51]

Other scholars agree with Clements' view since it would be strange
for Matthew to introduce an entirely new James and Joseph into his
narrative.[52] It follows, therefore, that these two men were not sons
of Jesus' mother but sons of another Mary. However, on this interpretation, they are still called "brothers of the Lord", which would
be possible if this Mary were related to the mother of Jesus. We
know from John 19:25 that the other Mary at the foot of the Cross
was the wife of Clopas and was probably a relative of Jesus' mother.
This would make James and Joseph cousins or other extended kin of
the Lord.

Finally, Galatians 1:19 describes Paul going to Jerusalem and seeing
none of the apostles, except for Peter and James, the latter of whom

---

[50] This is known as the Heironymian view, named after the Greek translation of Jerome's
name.

[51] E. Anne Clements, *Mothers on the Margin? The Significance of the Women in Matthew's
Genealogy* (Eugene, OR: Wipf and Stock, 2014), 165.

[52] "Matthew, having introduced her as 'Mary the mother of James and Joses' (Matt
27:56), can then call her 'the other Mary' (Matt 27:61, 28:1)." Richard Bauckham, *Jesus and
the Eyewitnesses: The Gospels as Eyewitness Testimony* (Grand Rapids, MI: Wm. B. Eerdmans,
2008), 50.

Paul calls "the Lord's brother". If Paul were referring to the original twelve apostles, then the brother of the Lord would have to be "James the son of Alphaeus" since Acts 12:2 describes "James the brother of John" being martyred in the early 40s, whereas Josephus describes "the brother of Jesus, who was called Christ, whose name was James" being executed in A.D. 62.[53] If Alphaeus and Clopas both referred to the same man (like Saul who was also known as Paul or Simon who was also known as Peter), then we have even more evidence for the existence of "brothers of the Lord" whose mother was not the Blessed Virgin.

The other approach to these references, which was advocated by the Eastern Father Epiphanius (though it was attested from the second century onward, particularly in the East), claims that the brethren were sons and daughters of Joseph from a previous marriage and were therefore Jesus' legal half-siblings or step-siblings. This corresponds to the post-apostolic Infancy Gospel of James that describes Joseph as an old man who had already sired children from a previous marriage. This ancient account says Joseph was chosen by lot to take into his keeping the virgin of the Lord.[54]

The biblical scholar Richard Bauckham, who rejects the idea of Mary's perpetual virginity, does believe there is evidence that, in his words, "may tip the balance of probability slightly in favor of the Epiphanian view".[55] Specifically, it is strange that Jesus is called "the son of Mary" rather than "the son of Joseph". Some might say Jesus was called this because Joseph was deceased, but other scholars have shown that sons of widows were still referred to by their father's names.[56] However, if the people of Galilee knew Jesus was different from his siblings in that he was born from Joseph's second wife Mary, then the description of him as Mary's son rather than Joseph's makes sense. Bauckham explains:

---

[53] Josephus, *Antiquities of the Jews* 20.9.1.

[54] *The Protoevangelium of James* 9.

[55] Richard Bauckham, "The Brothers and Sisters of Jesus: An Epiphanian Response to John P. Meier", *Catholic Biblical Quarterly* 56, no. 4 (October 1994): 687.

[56] Two examples can be found in Tal Ilan, "'Man Born of Woman ...' (Job 14:1): The Phenomenon of Men Bearing Metronymes at the Time of Jesus", *Novum Testamentum* 34, Fasc. 1 (January 1992): 23–45. Other cases where men are referred to as sons of their mother usually involve cases where the mother had a superior lineage to the father, but nothing in the Gospels suggests this of Mary and Joseph.

Whereas outside Nazareth Jesus would have to be identified as "the son of Joseph" [Jn 6:42], in Nazareth, where the family was known, the children of Joseph's two wives would be distinguished by their matronymics. Jesus would be called "the son of Mary" precisely because James, Joses, Judas, and Simon were not sons of Mary.[57]

Bauckham also points out that three second-century Syrian works—the Infancy Gospel of James, the Infancy Gospel of Thomas, and the Gospel of Peter—independently attest to the claim that Jesus' brethren were from Joseph's previous marriage. While he does not consider these works to be completely accurate, he does say,

> The idea that Jesus' brothers and sisters were Joseph's children by a previous marriage is taken entirely for granted in these works as something the readers already know to be the case. It is the only piece of non-biblical information common to these works, the works themselves show no signs of a literary relationship, and so the information can reasonably be considered a tradition which predates both works. These works are, therefore, evidence of a well-established tradition in (probably early) second century Syrian Christianity that Jesus' brothers and sisters were children of Joseph by a previous marriage.[58]

Bauckham's scholarship refutes both the idea that Scripture assumes the Helvidian view of Jesus' brethren and that only a Catholic would argue against such a conclusion. Indeed, many of the Protestant Reformers held to Mary's perpetual virginity including Martin Luther who said, "We should be satisfied simply to hold that she remained a virgin after the birth of Christ because Scripture does not state or indicate that she later lost her virginity. We certainly need not be so terribly afraid that someone will demonstrate, out of his own head apart from Scripture, that she did not remain a virgin."[59]

---

[57] Bauckham, "Brothers and Sisters of Jesus", 700.

[58] Ibid., 696–97.

[59] "That Jesus Christ Was Born of a Jew", *Luther's Works*, 45:206, https://www.uni-due.de/collcart/es/sem/s6/txt09_1.htm.

# 16

## The Immaculate Conception
## and Bodily Assumption

The Immaculate Conception does not refer to Jesus' conception in Mary's womb. Neither does it refer to Christ's virgin birth in Bethlehem. Instead, the dogma of the Immaculate Conception refers to Mary's miraculous conception in the womb of her mother, Saint Anne. Through God's intervention, Mary came into existence free from all stain of original sin. Pope Pius IX infallibly defined this dogma on December 8, 1854, in the apostolic constitution *Ineffabilis Deus*:

> The most Blessed Virgin Mary, in the first instant of her conception, by a singular grace and privilege granted by Almighty God, in view of the merits of Jesus Christ, the Savior of the human race, was preserved free from all stain of original sin, is a doctrine revealed by God and therefore to be believed firmly and constantly by all the faithful.[1]

As it's defined in *Ineffabilis Deus*, the dogma of the Immaculate Conception refers to Mary being free from original sin, or the deprivation of sanctifying grace that man inherited from Adam and Eve. The document also says that Mary was "ever absolutely free of all stain of sin", or she did not violate God's eternal law. In his encyclical *Mystici Corporis Christi*, Pope Pius XII likewise referred to Mary as "the second Eve, who [is], free from all sin, original or personal".[2] The Council of Trent condemned the idea that a person

---

[1] Pope Pius IX, apostolic constitution *Ineffabilis Deus* (December 8, 1854), www.ewtn.com/faith/tachigns/maryel.htm.

[2] Pope Pius XII, encyclical *Mystici Corporis Christi* (June 29, 1943), no. 110, http://w2.vatican.va/content/pius-xii/en/encyclicals/documents/hf_p-xii_enc_29061943_mystici-corporis-christi.html.

can, throughout his whole life, "avoid all sins even venial sins", but it allowed for an exception, "by a special privilege of God, as the Church holds in regard to the Blessed Virgin".[3]

## A Fitting Dogma

Before we examine the evidence for the Immaculate Conception, we must first clarify the dogma in order to answer a common objection to it. Some people ask, "If Jesus could not be conceived in sinful flesh, then how could Mary be conceived in the sinful flesh of her mother? Does that mean her mother, or Saint Anne, was also immaculately conceived?"

The Church does not teach that the Immaculate Conception was *necessary* for God's plan of salvation. Since God is omnipotent, he could have chosen to be conceived in Mary's womb even if she had not been free from original or personal sin (just as he chose to preserve Mary from sin in the womb of her mother, who was a sinner like anyone else). God could have even bypassed the Incarnation and forgiven our sins through a divine decree.[4] Instead, the Church teaches that it was "wholly fitting" that God's mother would be free from the stain of original sin.

Tim Staples gives the analogy of how the pomp and circumstance that follows the president when he visits a small rural town is not *necessary* since he could make the visit without such fanfare. However, it is *fitting* for the president to be celebrated in this way given the dignity of his office. Concerning the Immaculate Conception, Staples writes, "St. Anne did not bear God in her womb, but Mary did; hence, Mary's preparation by God was radically different from St. Anne's, and fittingly so."[5]

Even Martin Luther saw how fitting it would be for Mary to be free from sin in order to bear God. In his earlier writings Luther said of Mary, "God's grace fills her with everything good and makes her

---

[3] Council of Trent, sixth session, canon 23.

[4] St. Thomas Aquinas agreed with this view, saying, "It was possible for God to deliver mankind otherwise than by the Passion of Christ, because 'no word shall be impossible with God' (Luke 1:37)." *Summa Theologica* III, q. 46, a. 2.

[5] Tim Staples, *Behold Your Mother: A Biblical and Historical Defense of the Marian Doctrines* (El Cajon, CA: Catholic Answers Press, 2014), kindle edition.

devoid of all evil."[6] In his later writings Luther seemed to move away from the doctrine that Mary had been conceived without original sin, but he still held in 1540 that at the moment Christ was conceived in Mary's womb, "the flesh and blood of Mary were entirely purged, so that nothing of sin remained."[7]

Also, saying Mary was immaculately conceived and lived a sinless life does not make her equal to God. If Adam and Eve had never disobeyed God, they would not have become deities simply because they were free of original and personal sin. They would still be mere creatures, a point Saint Louis de Monfort also makes about Mary. Even though his writings include many extravagant praises of Mary, he writes:

> I avow with all the Church that Mary, being but a mere [creature] that has come from the hands of the Most High, is in comparison with his infinite majesty, less than an atom, or rather, she is nothing at all, because only He is "he who is" (Exod. 3:14); consequently that grand Lord, always independent and sufficient to himself, never had, and has not now, any absolute need of the holy Virgin for the accomplishment of his will and for the manifestation of his glory. He has but to will in order to do anything.[8]

## "Full of Grace"

One piece of evidence for the Immaculate Conception can be found in Luke 1:28, which contains the angel Gabriel's salutation to Mary. He said, "Hail, full of grace, the Lord is with you!" or as other translations render it, "Hail, favored one." Both make sense given that the Greek verb being translated means "to endue with divine favor or Grace".[9] Since in the Christian context grace is divine favor, the

---

[6] *Luther's Works*, 43:40. Cited in Mark Miravalle, *Meet Your Mother: A Brief Introduction to Mary* (Hopedale, OH: Gabriel Press, 2013), kindle edition.

[7] Martin Luther, *Disputation on the Divinity and Humanity of Christ*, in Luther's Works, 39/2, Internet Christian Library, https://www.iclnet.org/pub/resources/text/wittenberg/luther/luther-divinity.txt.

[8] St. Louis de Montfort, *True Devotion to Mary*, 14. Cited in St. Louis-Marie Grignion de Montfort, *True Devotion to Mary*, trans. Frederick William Faber (Charlotte, NC: TAN Books, 2010), 7.

[9] W. E. Vine, Merrill F. Unger, William White Jr., *Vine's Complete Expository Dictionary of Old and New Testament Words* (Nashville, TN: Thomas Nelson, 1996), 117.

phrase "full of grace" accurately describes the special favor Mary received from the Father for being the mother of his Son.

Matt Slick claims that "full of grace" is an improper translation because that would be *pleres charitos* rather than the Greek word that is found in Luke 1:28, or *kecharitomene*. But a passage does not require the Greek word *pleres* in order for the concept of "fullness" to be in its English translation. For example, the Greek text of Ephesians 6:11 lacks the word *pleres* even though the NIV and NASB render it, "Put on the full armor of God." According to Friedrich Blass and Albert Debrunner in their *Greek Grammar of the New Testament*, "It is permissible, on Greek grammatical and linguistic grounds, to paraphrase *kecharitomene* as completely, perfectly, enduringly endowed with grace."[10] A. T. Robertson said, "The Vulgate *gratia plena* [full of grace] 'is right, if it means 'full of grace which thou hast received.' "[11]

But Geisler and MacKenzie say Luke 1:28 "is only a reference to her state at that moment, not to her entire life".[12] In their book *The Cult of the Virgin*, Elliot Miller and Kenneth Samples claim, "*Charitoo* is used of believers in Ephesians 1:6 without implying sinless perfection."[13]

The verse Miller and Samples reference is "the praise of his glorious grace which he freely bestowed on us in the Beloved". But in Ephesians 1:6 *charitoo* is used in the aorist tense (Greek, *echaritosen*), which is roughly equivalent to the English past tense and indicates past actions without specifying whether they are completed. However, in Luke 1:28 the perfect tense is used, which indicates a past, completed action that continues to have effects into the present. In English, "I loved my wife for twenty years" would be an example of a past action that may or may not be ongoing (a person making this statement might mean that he stopped loving her or that he still

[10] F. Blass and A. Debrunner, *Greek Grammar of the New Testament and Other Early Christian Literature*, trans. Robert W. Funk (Chicago: University of Chicago Press, 1961), 166. Cited in Dave Armstrong, *A Biblical Defense of Catholicism* (Bloomington, IN: Sophia Institute Press, 2003), 178.

[11] A. T. Robertson, *Word Pictures in the New Testament* ([Place of publication not identified] Aeterna Press, 2015), 14. Cited in Armstrong, *Biblical Defense of Catholicism*, 178.

[12] Norman L. Geisler and Ralph E. MacKenzie, *Roman Catholics and Evangelicals: Agreements and Differences* (Grand Rapids, MI: Baker Books, 1995), 310.

[13] Elliot Miller and Kenneth B. Samples, *The Cult of the Virgin: Catholic Mariology and the Apparitions of Mary* (Grand Rapids, MI: Baker Book House, 1992), 34.

loves her). But "I have loved my wife for twenty years" would be an example of the perfect tense, and it indicates that the loving is still ongoing in the present.

According to Greek professor David Alan Black, "The perfect participle, on the other hand, denotes completed action whose results are still felt." Black cites Luke 9:35 ("This is my Son, my Chosen") and says, "Here the perfect passive participle of [*eklego*] ("I choose") emphasizes the Father's permanent choice of the Son".[14] Ephesians 2:8 uses the same kind of construction: "By grace you have been saved [*sesosmenoi*] through faith." According to one commentary on Ephesians, "The perfect passive participle *sesomenoi* (you have been saved) usually indicates a completed action with ongoing effects."[15] Ephesians 2:8–9 refers to salvation taking place in the past that continues to have saving effects in the present, but Luke 1:28 refers to giving grace or divine favor to someone in the past that continues into the present.

Before I continue I should note that, by itself, Luke 1:28 does not *prove* that Mary was immaculately conceived. A masculine equivalent to *kecharitomene* is also used in Sirach 18:17 to refer to "a gracious man" in whom the word and a good gift are found, but obviously that man was not immaculately conceived. However, the word's use in Luke 1:28 becomes evidence for the Immaculate Conception given the context in which it is used.

Unlike in Sirach 18:17, the term "full of grace" is used as an important descriptor of Mary within a personal address.[16] This is similar to how John the Baptist addressed Jesus as "the Lamb of God" (Jn 1:29). Just as that title had significance for the purpose of Jesus' life, so too the title "full of grace" had significance for the purpose of Mary's life. Given this significance, it's no surprise Mary was troubled by this

[14] David Alan Black, *Learn to Read New Testament Greek*, 3rd ed. (Nashville, TN: B&H Publishing Group, 2009), 152.

[15] Stephen Fowl, *Ephesians* (Louisville, KY: Westminster John Knox Press, 2012), 74.

[16] "For the messenger greets Mary as 'full of grace'; he calls her thus as if it were her real name. He does not call her by her proper earthly name: Miryam (= Mary), but by this new name: 'full of grace.' What does this name mean? Why does the archangel address the Virgin of Nazareth in this way?" Pope John Paul II, encyclical letter *Redemptoris Mater* (March 25, 1987), no. 8, http://w2.vatican.va/content/john-paul-ii/en/encyclicals/documents/hf_jp-ii_enc_25031987_redemptoris-mater.html.

greeting (Lk 1:29).[17] According to Craig Keener, "Neither the title ('favored' or 'graced one') nor the promise ('the Lord is with you') was traditional in greetings, even had she been a person of status."[18]

Other contextual clues that support Mary being specially graced include a Spirit-filled Elizabeth exclaiming, "Blessed are you among women" (Lk 1:42), which comes from a Hebrew expression that means "you are more blessed than any other woman."[19] In addition if, as we saw in the last chapter, Mary were the Ark of the New Covenant, then we would expect her to surpass the holiness found in the Ark of the Old Covenant, or an object that people were not even allowed to touch lest they suffer fatal consequences (2 Sam 6:6–7). This provides a suitable backdrop for the words of Saint Gregory the Wonder Worker, who said in his homily on the Annunciation, "For the holy Virgin is in truth an ark, wrought with gold both within and without, that has received the whole treasury of the sanctuary."[20]

## Saviors and All Who've Sinned

Biblical objections to the Immaculate Conception usually take one of two forms. They either claim that Mary was a sinner because all humans except for Jesus Christ are sinners, or they try to produce specific evidence that Mary herself sinned. The latter approach usually cites Mary's sin offering in the Temple (Lk 2:22–24) or her declaration of God being her savior (Lk 1:47). The former approach usually cites Romans 3:10 ("None is righteous, no, not one") and Romans 3:23 ("All have sinned and fall short of the glory of God") in defense of the view that all humans besides Christ have sinned.

In regard to Mary's offering, Luke 2:22–24 describes how Jesus was presented in the Temple in Jerusalem in accordance with the laws of the Old Testament. However, this passage does not prove Mary was a sinner, because the laws in Leviticus 12 governing this

---

[17] Those who say Mary was only troubled at being greeted by an angel neglect the next verse, which says, "She was greatly troubled at *the saying*, and considered in her mind what sort of *greeting* this might be [emphasis added]."

[18] Craig S. Keener, *IVP Bible Background Commentary: New Testament* (Downers Grove, IL: IVP Academic, 1994), 181.

[19] Staples, *Behold Your Mother*, kindle edition.

[20] St. Gregory the Wonder Worker, *Four Homilies*, homily 1.

offering describe a woman being "clean from the flow of her blood" (v. 7) rather than a personal sin. As the *Bible Knowledge Commentary* says, "Having a baby was not a sin but instead was the fulfillment of a divine command (Gen 1:28). Thus the need of a sin offering.... To make atonement was only a matter of ritual purification."[21]

This objection also risks proving too much because Luke describes Mary participating in the redemption of her first-born child (Ex 13:13), even though Jesus is the redeemer, not the redeemed. Likewise, Luke 2:22 refers to *their* purification, which could be attributed to Mary *and* Jesus since newborns were exposed to the same bodily fluids that made their mothers ritually impure.[22] Therefore, if Christ can be ritually purified as an infant and still be free from sin, then so can his mother. The fact that she submitted to this ritual meant that she was obedient rather than sinful in the same way as Jesus agreed to be baptized, not to have his sins washed away, but to fulfill all righteousness (Mt 3:15).

The other alleged biblical evidence against the Immaculate Conception is Mary's declaration, "My soul magnifies the Lord, and my spirit rejoices in God my Savior" (Lk 1:46–47).

God's description as "savior" can refer to saving people from eternal threats like sin, but it can also refer to temporal threats like famine, plague, infertility, and the sword. Mary may be speaking of salvation from temporal threats because in Luke 1:47–48 Mary says, "My spirit rejoices in God my Savior, *for* [emphasis added] he has regarded the low estate of his handmaiden." Mary then describes how God saves people from temporal threats by exalting the lowly (v. 52) and feeding the hungry (v. 53).[23] God is Mary's savior because he has regarded her lowly state that she has been lifted out of by being called to bring the Messiah into the world.

Mary's Magnificat also parallels Hannah's prayer in First Samuel that refers to salvation from similar dangers. Hannah's prayer begins, "My heart exults in the LORD; my strength is exalted in the LORD.

---

[21] F. Duane Lindsey, "Leviticus", in *The Bible Knowledge Commentary: Old Testament*, ed. John F. Walvoord and Roy B. Zuck (Colorado Springs, CO: David C. Cook, 1983), 192.

[22] Robert H. Stein, *Luke: An Exegetical and Theological Exposition of Holy Scripture* (Nashville, TN: B&H Publishing Group, 1992), 113.

[23] Jimmy Akin, *The Drama of Salvation* (San Diego: Catholic Answers Press, 2014), kindle edition.

My mouth derides my enemies, because I rejoice in your salvation"
(1 Sam 2:1). In both prayers the women praise God for casting down
the proud and exalting the weak and humble, and neither mentions
salvation from sin. According to one commentary, "Mary's song, like
Hannah's, declares that security and significance are found in a God
who would care about the broken and poor enough to give himself
to them."[24]

Although, even if Mary were speaking of salvation from sin, that
would not mean she committed any sins herself. She could be prais-
ing God for giving her grace that kept her from sinning just as a man
might say a doctor saved him from a disease through a vaccine that
prevented it rather than a treatment that cured it.[25]

In fact, as we've already seen, the doctrine of the Immaculate Conception holds that Mary was preserved from all stain of original sin "in
view of the merits of Jesus Christ". In other words, the work that Jesus
did on the Cross was applied to her early, as it was to others who were
saved before the time of Christ, in keeping with his role as "the Lamb
that was slain" from "the foundation of the world" (Rev 13:8). What
was different was that it was applied to her in a special and dramatic
fashion to make her a fitting mother for Jesus. Mary, like everyone else,
was redeemed by Jesus' death on the Cross, but that redemption was
applied to her in a special way. The Church thus acknowledges Mary
as "'the most excellent fruit of redemption' (SC 103)" (CCC 508).

What about the Bible's teaching that all have sinned? Some Protestants claim that Mary had to be a sinner because she eventually
died and "the wages of sin is death" (Rom 6:23). But this verse refers
to what we earn from committing sins, not the reason we die. Jesus
died on a cross in spite of the fact that he was free from all sin because
original sin has corrupted human nature and made it mortal. If dying
on a cross does not prove Jesus was a sinner, then the traditional view
that Mary died does not prove she was a sinner either.

Concerning Romans 3:10 ("None is righteous, no, not one") and
Romans 3:23 ("All have sinned and fall short of the glory of God"),

---

[24] Heath Thomas and J.D. Greear, *Exalting Jesus in 1 & 2 Samuel* (Nashville, TN: B&H
Publishing Group, 2016), 45.

[25] The most famous analogy of this sort comes from Duns Scotus, who compared how a
man could be saved from falling in a pit either by being pulled out of it or by being prevented
from falling into it.

these verses describe the universality of personal sin between Jews and non-Jews. Paul is talking about offenses against God that people who belong to both groups have committed. That's why Romans 3:22–24 speaks of there being "no distinction" (v. 22) among those who are justified by grace, and Romans 3:9 says, "All men, both Jews and Greeks, are under the power of sin." Moreover, Romans 3:10 quotes Psalm 14, which describes wickedness among unbelievers. It does not deny that there are any righteous people, because Psalm 14:5 says, "God is with the generation of the righteous."

Personal sins don't apply to every person, because children below a certain age can't commit them. Paul assumes this in Romans 9:11, when he says of Jacob and Esau in Rebecca's womb, "They were not yet born and had done nothing either good or bad." This means children who die in early childhood represent millions of examples of people who never committed a personal sin in their entire lives. Therefore, these verses do not teach that every person, including the Mother of God, has sinned.

## Patristic Evidence

Among the apostolic Fathers, Mary is primarily described in the letters of Ignatius and usually only in relation to the birth of Christ. Critics sometimes object that the absence of Mary being described in these writings as sinless or immaculately conceived shows that this dogma does not have an apostolic origin. But this objection is a double-edged sword, for in both these and many other early Fathers, the subject of original sin is not discussed either. According to William Collinge in his *Historical Dictionary of Catholicism*, "Mary's sinless-ness, in the sense of freedom from personal or actual sin, is affirmed by fourth century writers, but the question of her freedom from original sin could not be raised until the doctrine of original sin had received clear formulation by Augustine."[26]

It's not surprising that in the absence of a theological consensus about original sin, there would be no explicit discussion about anyone being conceived without it. The most we would expect is a

---

[26] William J. Collinge, *Historical Dictionary of Catholicism* (Lanham, MD: Rowman & Little-field, 2012), 209.

recognition of Mary having a form of special holiness, or other signs of not being subject to the penalty of original sin, and that we do find in the early sources. For example, there are early accounts of Mary's birth that describe her as giving birth without physical pain. Since labor pains are multiplied by the fall of man (Gen 3:16), this is indirect evidence that Mary was protected from the effects of Adam and Eve's sin. The first is in an early Christian apocalypse known as the *Ascension of Isaiah*, which likely dates to A.D. 67.[27] The same is indicated in a collection of early Christian hymns known as the *Odes of Solomon*, which dates to around A.D. 125.[28]

Additionally, several apostolic Fathers compared Mary to Eve, an example of which can be found in Irenaeus, who said, "For what the virgin Eve had bound fast through unbelief, this did the virgin Mary set free through faith."[29] Just as the old and new Adam were both created free from sin, yet the latter remained free from sin, it would be fitting that the old Eve and New Eve would parallel one another in the same respect.

It is true that some Church Fathers thought Mary had personal faults like vanity, but many Church Fathers explicitly taught that Mary was free from sin.[30] In the fourth century, Ephraem the Syrian said of Christ, "There is no flaw in thee and no stain in thy Mother."[31] J. N. D. Kelly says Augustine, "Denied the possibility for all other men, but agreed that Mary was the unique exception; she had been kept sinless, however, not by the effort of her own will, but as a result of grace given her in view of the incarnation."[32]

It is important to note that the way doctrine develops in the history of the Church, there is often an initial period in which a doctrine is not clearly formulated, and orthodox authors hold a variety

---

[27] *Ascension of Isaiah* 11.

[28] *Odes of Solomon* 19.

[29] St. Irenaeus, *Against Heresies* 3.22.4.

[30] According to the *Catholic Encyclopedia*, "In regard to the sinlessness of Mary the older Fathers are very cautious: some of them even seem to have been in error on this matter.... But these stray private opinions merely serve to show that theology is a progressive science." Frederick Holweck, "Immaculate Conception", in *The Catholic Encyclopedia*, vol. 7 (New York: Robert Appleton, 1910), http://www.newadvent.org/cathen/07674d.htm.

[31] Ephraem, *Nisibene Hymns* 27.8. Cited in Michael O'Carroll, *Theotokos: A Theological Encyclopedia of the Blessed Virgin Mary* (Eugene, OR: Wipf and Stock, 2000), 132.

[32] J. N. D. Kelly, *Early Christian Doctrines* (New York: HarperCollins, 1978), 497.

of opinions on it. Over time, however, the Spirit guides the Church into recognizing the full truth (Jn 16:13), at which point some of the earlier views are recognized as erroneous or inadequate expressions of the truth.

Thus some early Christian authors do not fully recognize or correctly articulate the divinity of Christ and the Holy Spirit before the doctrine of the Trinity came into sharp focus in the fourth century. The same is true of the doctrine of the Immaculate Conception. Some early authors entertain a variety of opinions while this subject was also being explored. The variance of some early authors does not disprove the latter formulation of the Immaculate Conception any more than the variance of some early authors on how Christ's divinity should be understood invalidates the Trinity.

Kelly points out that Augustine believed Mary was conceived with original sin but was cleansed from it shortly after her conception. But this does not disprove the dogma of the Immaculate Conception, because, as we've seen, all doctrines develop over time. For example, Church Fathers like Irenaus, Origen, and even Augustine described the atonement as being part of a literal ransom God paid to Satan in the form of his Son's death, but that doesn't refute the apostolic origins of later theories of the atonement like the satisfaction theory.[33]

This is important to remember when some Protestant apologists claim that scholastic theologians like Saint Thomas Aquinas "flatly rejected" Mary's Immaculate Conception.[34] Sproul, for example, claims that "Thomas Aquinas repudiated the notion of the sinlessness of Mary in his day."[35] But in the *Summa Theologica* Thomas writes, "She would not have been worthy to be the Mother of God, if she had ever sinned.... The Blessed Virgin committed no actual sin, neither mortal nor venial."[36]

Thomas did not believe Mary had been conceived without original sin, because he held to the mistaken Aristotelian view that an

---

[33] Paul R. Eddy and James Beilby, "The Atonement: An Introduction", in *The Nature of the Atonement: Four Views*, ed. Paul R. Eddy and James Beilby (Downers Grove, IL: InterVarsity Press, 2006), 13.

[34] Geisler and MacKenzie, *Roman Catholics and Evangelicals*, 308.

[35] R. C. Sproul, *Are We Together? A Protestant Analyzes Roman Catholicism* (Sanford, FL: Reformation Trust, 2012), 105.

[36] St. Thomas Aquinas, *Summa Theologica* III, q. 27, a. 4.

unborn child develops through subhuman stages of life before receiving a rational soul after fertilization, before conception was complete. He writes, "Since the rational creature alone can be the subject of sin; before the infusion of the rational soul, the offspring conceived is not liable to sin.... Therefore before the infusion of the rational soul, the Blessed Virgin was not sanctified."[37] But as the moral theologian William May points out:

> St. Thomas, were he alive today and cognizant of the biological evidence known today, would not hesitate in concluding that the body that comes to be when fertilization is completed is indubitably a human body and hence that its organizing and vivifying principle can only be a human soul, an intellectual or spiritual soul.[38]

Thomas believed that Mary was preserved from sin at the moment she began to exist; he was simply mistaken about the first moment of her existence, or when a rational soul that can be subject to sin exists within a human body. Therefore, Thomas' writings cannot support modern Protestant objections to the dogma of the Immaculate Conception.

All doctrines develop over time as new conceptual frameworks and insights allow the Church to understand better God's revelation. Concerning the Immaculate Conception, a trajectory that moves from Mary being declared free from sin to her being immaculately conceived makes more sense than a trajectory that moves from Mary being sinless to her being a "sinner just like us".

The Protestant author David Wright admits that to modern Protestants what is most remarkable about the Reformers was their "almost universal acceptance of Mary's continuing virginity, and their widespread reluctance openly to declare Mary a sinner needing a savior."[39] Luther himself said that at Christ's conception, "God poured out so richly His Holy Spirit into the soul and body of the

---

[37] Ibid., a. 2.

[38] William E. May, *Catholic Bioethics and the Gift of Life*, 3rd ed. (Huntington, IN: Our Sunday Visitor, 2013), 176.

[39] David F. Wright, "Mary in the Reformers", in *Chosen by God: Mary in Evangelical Perspective*, ed. David F. Wright (London: Marshall Pickering, 1989), 180.

Virgin Mary that without any sin she conceived and bore our Lord Jesus."[40]

## The Bodily Assumption

On November 12, 1950, Pope Pius XII solemnly declared and defined that "the Immaculate Mother of God, the ever Virgin Mary, having completed the course of her earthly life, was assumed body and soul into heavenly glory."[41] The phrase "having completed the course of her earthly life" leaves open the possibility that Mary was assumed into heaven after death, or that she was assumed alive into heaven (which is the minority view among theologians). The apostolic constitution *Munificentissimus Deus*, through which it was defined, says this dogma is one which is

> based on the Sacred Writings, which is thoroughly rooted in the minds of the faithful, which has been approved in ecclesiastical worship from the most remote times, which is completely in harmony with the other revealed truths, and which has been expounded and explained magnificently in the work, the science, and the wisdom of the theologians.[42]

Most Protestants refrain from making a biblical case that Mary was *not* assumed into heaven. Some cite John 3:13, which records Jesus saying, "No one has ascended into heaven but he who descended from heaven, the Son of man." But this does not disprove Mary's Assumption, since Mary was taken up into heaven and did not ascend there on her own like her Son. In addition, Jesus is merely proclaiming his authority to teach about heavenly things since he has come down from heaven (Jn 6:38). He is not denying anyone else could go up into heaven since the Bible teaches that Elijah (2 Kings 2:11) and possibly Enoch (Gen 5:24; Heb 11:5) were assumed into heaven.

---

[40] *Luther's Works*, 52:39.

[41] Pope Pius XII, apostolic constitution *Munificentissimus Deus* (November 1, 1950), no. 44, http://w2.vatican.va/content/pius-xii/en/apost_constitutions/documents/hf_p-xii_apc_19501101_munificentissimus-deus.html.

[42] Ibid., no. 41.

Other apologists say Scripture's silence about Mary's Assumption into heaven justifies rejecting this dogma. Besides being another appeal to the false doctrine of *sola scriptura*, this objection assumes that if Mary were assumed into heaven, there would be a description of it in the New Testament.[43] However, the New Testament does not contain accounts of the deaths of Peter, Paul, or John, so there's no reason to suppose it should have included details about the end of Mary's life. Indeed, most or all of the New Testament books may have been written before Mary's Assumption even occurred.

One could object that Scripture should reveal this because the Assumption is a binding dogma of the Church whereas the deaths of the other apostles are just historical details. However, this presupposes the doctrine of *sola scriptura*, which Catholics do not accept. As long as the content of the teaching is found in apostolic Tradition, this is sufficient. And, as we've already seen, the link between the nonexistence of any living apostles and the cessation of public revelation is a truth most Protestants would dogmatically assert even though it is not explicitly taught in Scripture. Therefore, there is no reason Mary's Assumption would need to have been explicitly described in the Bible. However, there is evidence that this event is *reflected* in Scripture, and so it complements the explicit testimony we do have in Sacred Tradition.

## Biblical Evidence for the Assumption

In Revelation 12:1–6 Saint John describes the following vision he had of heaven:

A great sign appeared in heaven, a woman clothed with the sun, with the moon under her feet, and on her head a crown of twelve stars; she was with child and she cried out in her pangs of birth, in anguish for delivery. And another sign appeared in heaven; behold, a great red dragon, with seven heads and ten horns, and seven diadems upon his heads. His tail swept down a third of the stars of heaven, and cast

[43] No one knows exactly when Mary's earthly life ended, but given that she would have been in her midforties when Jesus was crucified, it's probable that took place while the New Testament was being written, provided that process was completed by the late first century. However, if scholars like A. T. Robertson are correct and the New Testament was completed before the destruction of the Temple (A.D. 70), then if Mary had lived into her late seventies or early eighties, her Assumption may have happened after the New Testament was completed.

them to the earth. And the dragon stood before the woman who was about to bear a child, that he might devour her child when she brought it forth; she brought forth a male child, one who is to rule all the nations with a rod of iron, but her child was caught up to God and to his throne, and the woman fled into the wilderness, where she has a place prepared by God, in which to be nourished for one thousand two hundred and sixty days.

The fact that this woman is described as the one who gives birth to the Messiah is a strong clue that she is the mother of Jesus Christ. According to William Barclay, "If the woman is the 'mother' of the Messiah, an obvious suggestion is that she should be identified with Mary but she is so clearly a superhuman figure that she can hardly be identified with any single human being."[44]

It is true that this woman is probably not only Mary, the mother of the Messiah, but that doesn't mean the woman does not represent Mary among many other realities. As the Reformed biblical scholar Gregory Beale notes in his study on Revelation, "Most of Revelation's symbols have multiple associations or meanings and that the interpreter can never be sure that all the multiple meanings of a symbol have been discovered."[45] This means an alternative meaning does not, in itself, refute a Marian meaning for this passage. Ben Witherington makes a similar observation, saying, "This figure is both the literal mother of the male child Jesus and also the female image of the people of God. Again, the text is multivalent!"[46] According to Saint Quodvultdeus, who wrote in A.D. 430:

> The Woman signifies Mary, who, being spotless, brought forth our spotless Head. Who herself also showed forth in herself a figure of holy Church, so that as she in bringing forth a Son remained a Virgin, so the Church also should during the whole time be bringing forth His members, and yet not lose her virgin state.[47]

[44] William Barclay, *The Revelation of John*, vol. 2, 3rd ed. (Louisville, KY: Westminster John Knox Press, 2004), 86.

[45] Gregory K. Beale, *John's Use of the Old Testament in Revelation* (New York: Bloomsbury T&T Clark, 2015), 59.

[46] Ben Witherington, *What Have They Done With Jesus? Beyond Strange Theories and Bad History—Why We Can Trust the Bible* (New York: HarperCollins, 2006), 130.

[47] St. Quodvultdeus, *De Symbolo* 3. Cited in Michael O'Carroll, *Theotokos: A Theological Encyclopedia of the Blessed Virgin Mary* (Eugene, OR: Wipf and Stock, 2000), 375.

Other objections to the Marian interpretation of Revelation 12 note that the dragon "went off to make war on the rest of her off-spring" (Rev 12:17), which they say refers to persecuted believers rather than literal children of the Virgin Mary. In addition, the woman experiences birth pangs (Rev 12:2), which were something Mary never experienced because of her freedom from the effects of original sin. Finally, it is argued, John never even identifies the woman in Revelation 12:1 with the name "Mary".

In response, I would point out that John's calling her "Woman" rather than "Mary" coheres with his own Gospel where he never mentions Mary by name. He does, however, depict Jesus as calling her "Woman" at the beginning and end of his ministry (Jn 2:4; 19:26). Furthermore, when Jesus entrusts Mary to the Beloved Disciple's care, he tells John, "Behold, your mother!" (Jn 19:27), which interpreters have seen as indicating a spiritual relationship between Mary and all of Jesus' disciples (all of whom are beloved of Jesus). According to Raymond Brown:

> In the prophecy of Genesis we hear that God will put enmity between the woman and the serpent and that her seed will crush the serpent [Gen 3:15]. In calling his mother "woman", Jesus may well be identifying her with the new Eve who will be the mother of his disciples as the old Eve was the "mother of all the living."[48]

We thus see another connection between John's Gospel and Revelation, both of which depict Mary as "Woman" and as a spiritual mother of Jesus' disciples. Concerning the woman's pain in labor, just as Israel or the people of God did not experience literal birth pangs but immense suffering while waiting for the Messiah, Mary's trials before the birth of Jesus can be described in the same way (e.g., under suspicion of adultery, the journey to Bethlehem, and fleeing Herod's persecution). It would not be surprising if the text's primary referent was God's people fleeing Egypt during the Exodus or Jerusalem during the First Jewish-Roman War, but that would not exclude the mother of the Messiah also fleeing dangers after she brought him into the world.

---

[48] Raymond Brown, *The Gospel and Epistles of John: A Concise Commentary* (Collegeville, MN: Liturgical Press, 1988), 29.

Other Protestant apologists claim that the absence of Church Fathers who referred to the woman as Mary before the late fourth century counts against the validity of this interpretation. But since these symbols and images in Revelation are multivalent, it is not surprising that the Fathers would identify them in different ways. Second, this argument proves too much because some of the Fathers did not consider the book of Revelation itself to be canonical. In fact, an argument can be made that a Marian interpretation of Revelation 12:1 arose after the book of Revelation as a whole was seen in its full Christian context.

Some scholars have argued that Revelation 12 contains several Jewish sources about the Messiah that were later combined into a Christian story. This is not far-fetched given that the Messiah is not described as defeating the dragon by dying or rising from the dead. George Eldon Ladd's commentary on Revelation is an example of this, for he explicitly denies that Revelation 12:5 refers to the birth of Jesus. Instead, he claims that it refers symbolically to "the hostility of Satan to God's anointed one".[49] But if the Church's understanding of the contexts in parts of Revelation grew over time, then interpretations of the book would progressively reveal their full Christian meaning. In *Mary for Evangelicals* Tim Perry says that when the twelfth chapter of Revelation is set alongside the Gospels,

it is virtually impossible for a Christian reader to perform such a radical act of epoche [i.e., doubt] that all thought of Mary is removed. It is not surprising, therefore, to find that Marian interpretation of Revelation 12 begins in the fifth century, after the New Testament canon is fixed. As part of the New Testament canon, Revelation's depiction of the heavenly woman completes the biblical Marian material.[50]

Finally as we will see, belief in the Assumption of Mary is not primarily based on an interpretation of Revelation 12 but on an early tradition that has been preserved in the life and worship of the Church.

[49] George Eldon Ladd, *A Commentary on the Revelation of John* (Grand Rapids, MI: Wm. B. Eerdmans, 1972), 169.
[50] Tim Perry, *Mary for Evangelicals: Toward an Understanding of the Mother of Our Lord* (Downers Grove, IL: InterVarsity Press, 2006), 113.

## The Patristic Evidence

Protestants who claim that the Assumption was foisted upon the Church in 1950 are simply incorrect. For example, though he expressed less confidence in the doctrine later in his life, in 1539 the Protestant Reformer Heinrich Bullinger wrote, "The pure and immaculate embodiment of the Mother of God, the Virgin Mary, the Temple of the Holy Spirit, that is to say her saintly body, was carried up into heaven by the angels."[51] In 590 Saint Gregory of Tours described Mary's Assumption in this way:

> The Apostles took up her body on a bier and placed it in a tomb; and they guarded it, expecting the Lord to come. And behold, again the Lord stood by them; and the holy body having been received, He commanded that it be taken in a cloud into paradise: where now, rejoined to the soul, she rejoices with the Lord's chosen ones.[52]

This same story can be found in Saint John of Damascus, who, even though he wrote over a century after Gregory, preserves a tradition about how Saint Juvenal, the bishop of Jerusalem, told the same story during the Council of Chalcedon (A.D. 451).[53] The description of Mary's tomb being empty was conveyed to Emperor Marcian and Empress Pulcheria in response to their request for the relics of Mary's body.

Since the second century, Christians routinely collected the bones of martyrs and saints, but no such relics have been associated with the Virgin Mary. Instead, just as the relics associated with Jesus consisted only of what he left behind after his Ascension, like the Shroud of

[51] Heinrich Bullinger, "Die Marienpredigt", in Walter Tappolet, *Das Marienlob Der Reformatoren* (Tubingen: Katzmann, 1962), 327. Cited in Tim Perry, *Mary for Evangelicals: Toward an Understanding of the Mother of Our Lord* (Downers Grove, IL: InterVarsity Press, 2006), 218.

[52] St. Gregory of Tours, *Eight Books of Miracles* 1.4. Cited in William A. Jurgens, *The Faith of the Early Fathers*, vol. 3 (Collegeville, MN: Liturgical Press, 1979), 306.

[53] "St. Juvenal, Bishop of Jerusalem, at the Council of Chalcedon (451), made known to the Emperor Marcian and Pulcheria, who wished to possess the body of the Mother of God, that Mary died in the presence of all the Apostles, but that her tomb, when opened, upon the request of St. Thomas, was found empty; wherefrom the Apostles concluded that the body was taken up to heaven." Frederick Holweck, "The Feast of the Assumption", *The Catholic Encyclopedia*, vol. 2 (New York: Robert Appleton, 1907), http://www.newadvent.org/cathen/02006b.htm.

Turin or the true wood of the Cross, only objects associated with Mary's life rather than her death (like her bones) have been found in the historical record.[54]

But is there evidence that the doctrine of the Assumption predates the fifth century?

At the end of the fourth century Epiphanius wrote about a sect that denied Mary's perpetual virginity. While refuting the charge that Saint Joseph and Mary had carnal relations, Epiphanius says, "Let them search through the scriptures and neither find Mary's death, nor whether or not she died, nor whether or not she was buried.... [I am] not saying that she remained immortal. But neither am I affirming that she died."[55]

Protestant apologists often cite Epiphanius' *Panarion* as evidence against the Assumption because he said, "For her end, no one knows." James White adds the comment, "Since he lived in the general geographic area in which she had lived, surely if there were some tradition associated with her death and burial, he would have known about it."[56] But Epiphanius' agnostic position on the death of Mary does not contradict the dogma of the Assumption since, as we've already seen, the dogma makes no statement on whether Mary died. His comparison between her and the prophet Elijah, however, does count in favor of Epiphanius believing she was assumed into heaven. He writes:

> Like the bodies of the saints, however, she has been held in honor for her character and understanding. And if I should say anything more in her praise, [she is] like Elijah, who was virgin from his mother's womb, always remained so, and was taken up and has not seen death.[57]

The other sources for earlier belief in the Assumption of Mary can be found in early Christian literature that describes the Virgin Mary

[54] Mary Clayton, *The Cult of the Virgin Mary in Anglo-Saxon England* (Cambridge: Cambridge University Press, 1990), 138. See also Stephen J. Shoemaker, *Ancient Traditions of the Virgin Mary's Dormition and Assumption* (Oxford: Oxford University Press, 2004), 67–68.

[55] Epiphanius, *The Panarion of Epiphanius of Salamis, Books II and III. De Fide*, trans. Frank Williams, 2nd ed. (Leiden: Brill, 2013), 609.

[56] James R. White, *Mary: Another Redeemer?* (Bloomington, MN: Bethany House, 1998), 51.

[57] Epiphanius, *On the Collyridians* 5.1. Cited in *Panarion of Epiphanius of Salamis*, 641.

being greeted by an angel who reveals her impending death, the death and her soul being taken into heaven, her body being buried by the apostles, and that same body being taken up into heaven several days later. While the details of these accounts are not to be pressed, they attest to belief in the Assumption of Mary when they were composed. They also attest to previous belief in the doctrine given that these narratives were composed in many different languages over a wide geographical area, which means the belief would had to have been in existence for some time to explain how far it had spread.

According to Stephen Shoemaker, who has probably written the most comprehensive treatment of the traditions surrounding the Assumption of the Virgin Mary, the earliest narrative of Mary's Assumption can be found in the heterodox Book of Mary's Repose, which exists as a single Ethiopic translation with fragments in Syriac that have been dated to the fifth century. Shoemaker notes, however, that

> this Ethiopic version reliably transmits a very early account of Mary's dormition and Assumption that had been composed already by the fourth century and is most likely even earlier than that.... We can locate this text with some confidence to the third century, although the possibility of an even earlier origin, perhaps in the second century, should not be excluded.[58]

Staples notes that the most probable reason we don't find reference to the Assumption in the earliest patristic writings is that the Church's Gnostic opponents agreed with this doctrine. He writes:

> We don't find works from the earliest Fathers on Jesus' celibacy either, but that too was most likely due to the universal agreement on the topic. Much of early Christian literature was apologetic in nature. Just like the New Testament, it mostly dealt with problem areas in the Church that needed to be addressed.[59]

In response to this evidence, White claims that Pope Gelasius I condemned an apocryphal work called "The Assumption of Holy

[58] Stephen Shoemaker, *Mary in Early Christian Faith and Devotion* (New Haven, CT: Yale University Press, 2016), 103.
[59] Tim Staples, "The Assumption of Mary in History", *Catholic Answers Magazine*, April 14, 2015.

Mary".[60] White then finds it ironic that a pope could condemn a dogma in the fifth century but a later pope would declare it a dogma in the twentieth century.

Aside from the fact that the decree White is referring to (or the *Decretum Gelasianum*) was probably a forgery attributed to the pope, it doesn't even condemn the dogma of the Assumption. It only declares certain works to be apocryphal, which does not condemn their entire content—after all, the authors of Scripture quote from apocryphal works (Jude 9, 14), so just because something is apocryphal, that does not mean it is completely inaccurate. That same decree also declares as apocryphal "the book of the nativity of the savior and of Mary or the midwife", but that doesn't mean Pope Gelasius condemned the doctrine of the virgin birth or any of the traditions associated with the nativity.[61]

In closing, let us consider a question Catholic theology professor Matthew Levering asks, "[Given that] Mary's Assumption is a marker of division, would the Church be better off without this doctrine?" He answers, "No more than Christ on earth (or in heaven) would be better off without Mary."[62]

Mary's Assumption along with her Immaculate Conception are not obscure theological truths. Instead, they represent the fulfillment of God's promises as well as a foreshadowing of our future union with Christ that will be free from all sin. Mary is exalted because she uniquely participated in the redemption of humanity, but Mary also represents the Church as a whole, which will experience this same union with Christ when he comes again in glory (1 Thess 4:17–18).

---

[60] White, *Mary: Another Redeemer?*, 54.

[61] White anticipates a reply like this, saying, "Someone might suggest that the Bodily Assumption was orthodox while the rest of the writings in which it was found were not. Yet the fact remains that the first recorded instance of the concept is found in documents condemned as heretical, and there is no reference to Gelasius exempting that doctrine from the condemnation he pronounced upon the literature as a whole." Ibid., 154. But this is an ineffectual argument from silence. There is no record of Pope Gelasius exempting the virgin birth or any of the other orthodox doctrines that would have appeared in these heretical works. Besides if the pope had declared this doctrine to be heretical, then why did saints and Doctors of the Church who lived shortly after him, like St. Gregory of Tours, promote it or acknowledge its allegedly disputed nature?

[62] Matthew Levering, *Mary's Bodily Assumption* (Notre Dame, IN: University of Notre Dame Press, 2015), kindle edition.

# AFTERWORD

The Baptist scholar Timothy George asks, "Why do Evangelicals remember the Reformation critique of Marian excess but not the positive appraisal of Mary's indispensable role in God's salvific work?"[1] He attributes this attitude to the tendency of Evangelicals to define themselves in terms of the theology they opposed. So George says, for example, "To be an evangelical meant *not* to be a Roman Catholic. To worship Jesus meant not to honor Mary, even if such honor were biblically grounded and liturgically chaste. In some quarters of the evangelical world the loss of catholicity was marked by a disdain for creedal Christianity."[2]

George even describes how some Baptist churches in 1742 opposed the Philadelphia Baptist Association's newly published confession of faith by calling it "a new virgin Mary to come between us and God". These Baptists preferred to live instead by the motto "No creed but the Bible." This shows that what lies at the heart of divisions between Catholics and Protestants is not merely Marian dogmas or differing descriptions of Christ's presence in the Eucharist. Instead, the division lies with the subject we first examined: authority.

For example, when John Henry Cardinal Newman preached on Mary's Immaculate Conception and her bodily Assumption, he gave evidence for those teachings, but he also said, "I am not proving these doctrines to you, my brethren; the evidence of them lies in the declaration of the Church. The Church is the oracle of religious truth, and dispenses what the apostles committed to her in every time and place."[3]

We've shown not only that the concept of *sola scriptura* is both unbiblical and unhistorical, but that the Deposit of Faith was handed down to the Church in unwritten forms. Instead of giving her a

---

[1] Timothy George, "Evangelicals and the Mother of God", *First Things*, February 2007.
[2] Ibid.
[3] John Henry Newman, *The Works of Cardinal Newman: Discourses Addressed to Mixed Congregations*, vol. 31 (New York: Longman's, Green, 1899), 356.

book, Christ gave believers an authoritative Church that, through the power of the Holy Spirit, guards and hands on the Deposit of Faith.[4] This is not an admission of "blind obedience" but an acknowledgment of humble submission to God's authority.

The *Catechism* teaches that through baptism all Christians are "put in a certain, although imperfect, communion with the Catholic Church' (*UR* 3)"[5] (*CCC* 838). It is my sincere hope that the biblical and historical evidence in this book can help our Protestant brothers and sisters (as well as nonpracticing Catholics) move closer to a *perfect* communion with Christ's Church. Through this communion every Christian can fulfill Jesus' prayer that all his followers "may be one", just as he and the Father are one (Jn 17:11). They can become one by belonging to the one, holy, catholic, and apostolic Church of Jesus Christ.

[4] See *DV* 10.
[5] "*UR*" is the abbreviation for *Unitatis Redintegratio*, Vatican II's Decree on Ecumenism, promulgated on November 21, 1964.

# INDEX

Abercius, 274

Abraham, 102, 103, 212, 215–18, 228–30

Afanassief, Nicholas, 124, 127

Affair of Sausages, 33

afterlife, 264–65. *See also* purgatory

*Against Heresies* (Irenaeus), 122

Agricola, Johannes, 256

Akiba Ben Joseph, 63

Akin, Jimmy, 204, 214, 232, 272, 290, 295

Albright, W. F., 116–17

Alcorn, Randy, 279

Allen, Ernie, 157

Allert, Craig, 25n37, 26, 88–89

Allison, Gregg, 156, 233, 311–12

Ambrose (saint), 105, 176, 286, 302

Amphilocius, 82

Ananias, 100, 187, 188

Ankerberg, John, 163, 165, 216, 227

Anne (saint), 319, 320

anointing of the sick, 146–47

Apion, 62

*Apocalyptic Eschatology in the Gospel of Matthew* (Sim), 246

apocryphal books, 54, 54n1, 60, 61, 64–66, 69

apostates, 239, 240, 251–52, 254n37, 255–56

Apostles' Creed, 281, 282–83

apostolic succession, 100, 147–52

apostolic tradition, 37–40, 41, 42

Arianism, 131, 132

Ark of the Covenant, 301, 311, 324

Armstrong, John, 47n40, 228

Artaxeres of Persia, 62

Assumption of Mary, 331–39

 Biblical evidence for, 332–35

 dogma of, 331–32

patristic evidence for, 336–39

 time of occurrence, 332n43

Athanasius (saint)

 on baptismal regeneration, 195

 excommunication of, 131

 on Mary (Mother of God), 309

 on New Testament canon, 80, 82

 on Old Testament canon, 71, 72

 on papal primacy, 124

 on Scripture, 29

Athenagoras, 70

Augsburg Confession (1530), 281

Augustine (saint)

 on baptism, 195, 199

 on disinheritance from God, 256–57

 on eternal security, 239

 on Eucharist, 176–77

 on intercession of saints, 286

 on justification, 205–6, 234

 on Mary (Mother of God), 309–10, 328, 329

 on New Testament canon, 83

 on Peter as rock on whom Church is built, 105–6

 on purgatory, 273

 on *sola scriptura*, 31–32, 31n56

 on Zosimus, 132–33

*The Babylonian Captivity of the Church* (Luther), 169

Baker, Todd, 135–37, 154–56

Bamberger, Bernard, 64n34

baptism, 181–200. *See also* baptismal regeneration

 *Catechism* on, 181, 195–96, 342

 Eucharist and, 195

 faith and works as related to, 199–200

 Holy Spirit in, 182, 186–87, 189, 193

343

Council of. *See specific name of council*
covenantal nomism, 220, 220n6
Craig, William Lane, 17
Cullmann, Oscar, 102, 104, 105, 186
*The Cult of the Virgin* (Miller &
  Samples), 322
Cyprian (saint)
  on apostolic succession, 100
  on confession, 147
  on deuterocanonical books, 70
  on Eucharist, 168–69
  on heretics, 129–30
  on infant baptism, 199
  on intercession of saints, 286
  on justification, 205
  on papal primacy, 123–24, 127
  on Peter as rock on whom Church is
    built, 105
  on purgatory, 268
Cyril of Alexandria, 309
Cyril of Jerusalem (saint)
  on baptismal regeneration, 195
  on intercession of saints, 286
  on Mary (Mother of God), 301–2
  on Old Testament canon, 71–72
  on Sacred Tradition, 45, 45n34
  on *sola scriptura*, 30
  on transubstantiation, 176

Dalcour, Edward, 183n6
Damasus I (pope), 82, 124
Damgaard, Finn, 111
Dancy, J.C., 58
Davis, John Jefferson, 257
Dead Sea Scrolls, 60–61
Debrunner, Albert, 322
*Dei Verbum* (Dogmatic Constitution on
  Divine Revelation), 34
Demarest, Bruce, 188
Deposit of Faith, 34–35, 37, 52, 94,
  128–29, 341–42
deSilva, David A., 65, 71, 108–9
deuterocanonical books, 54–74
  alleged errors in, 57–60
  Christian evidence on, 63–68

external attestation arguments for,
  54–55, 60
inspiration of, 55–60, 74
internal composition arguments for,
  55–57
Jewish evidence on, 60–63
manuscript evidence on, 73–74
post-Nicene Church Fathers on,
  71–73
pre-Nicene Church Fathers on,
  68–70
purgatory in, 266
Diatessaron, 79
*Didache* (anonymous), 78, 87, 146,
  166–67, 173, 195
*Did Jesus Teach Salvation by Works?*
  (Stanley), 211
Diet of Worms, 13
divination, 290–91
divine revelation
  inerrant sources of, 26
  *partim-partim* view of, 35–36
  in Sacred Tradition, 35–37
  in Scripture, 24, 25, 28, 35–36
  *totum-totum* view of, 35, 36, 36n9
Docetists, 251
doctrinal development process, 49–50
Dogmatic Constitution on Divine
  Revelation, 34
Duffy, Eamon, 131
dulia, 293, 297–99
Dunn, James, 220–22, 225–26, 231–32,
  236–37, 246
Duns Scotus, 326n25

Eck, Johann, 32, 72
Ehrman, Bart, 223
Eleutherius (pope), 122
Ellingsen, Mark, 31–32
Ellis, Earl, 70
ephebophilia, 157n45
Ephesians, justification teachings in,
  234–37
Ephesus, Council of, 132, 306, 309
Ephraem the Syrian, 328